DERIVATIVES

Financial Management Association Survey and Synthesis Series

The Search for Value: Measuring the Company's Cost of Capital
    Michael C. Ehrhardt

Lease or Buy? Principles for Sound Decision Making
    James S. Schallheim

Derivatives: A Comprehensive Resource for Options, Futures, Interest Rate Swaps, and Mortgage Securities
    Fred D. Arditti

DERIVATIVES

A Comprehensive Resource
for Options, Futures,
Interest Rate Swaps, and
Mortgage Securities

Fred D. Arditti

Harvard Business School Press
Boston, Massachusetts

99 98 97 96   5 4 3 2

Library of Congress Cataloging-in-Publication Data
Arditti, Fred D.
    Derivatives : a comprehensive resource for options, futures,
interest rate swaps, and mortgage securities / Fred D. Arditti.
        p.   cm. — (Financial Management Association survey and
synthesis series)
    Includes bibliographical references and index.
    ISBN 0-87584-560-6
    1. Derivative securities—United States.   I. Title.   II. Series.
HG6024.U6A73   1996
332.64′5—dc20   95-31894
                                                              CIP

Text design by Wilson Graphics & Design (Kenneth J. Wilson)

To my mother and the memory of my father

Contents

Preface xiii

Acknowledgments xix

Part I Options 1

Chapter 1 Stock Option Basics 3

1.1 Definitions, Terminology, and Profit Profiles 3

1.2 Constructing the Return Profiles of More Complicated Positions 10

Chapter 2 The Institutional Environment for Stock Options 19

2.1 The Trade Process on an Exchange 19

2.2 Floor Traders, Order Types, and a Trading Rule 22

2.3 Collateralization of Trade Obligations 26

2.4 Clearing Over-the-Counter (OTC) Option Trades 29

Chapter 3 Stock Option Pricing 31

3.1 Option Pricing Results from Minimum Information 32

3.2 Other Distribution-Free Option Pricing Conditions 37

3.3 The Multiplicative Binomial Option Pricing Model 42

3.4 The Black-Scholes Model as a Limiting Case of the Binomial Model 56

3.5 The Merton Model for a European Call on a Stock Paying Dividends Continuously in Proportion to the Stock Price 58

3.6 Revisions to the Pricing Methodology Necessitated by Recent Empirical Evidence 60

Chapter 4 Risk Management of an Option Portfolio 75

4.1 Determinants of an Option's Value 76

4.2 The Effects of Parameter Changes on an Option's Value 77

4.3 Risk Management of an Option Position 82

4.4 A General Hedging Technique 88

4.5 Calculating the Parameter Sensitivities When the Black-Scholes Model Does Not Hold 91

Chapter 5 **Option Products** 93

   5.1 Portfolio Insurance 93

   5.2 The SCORE: An Option-Like Instrument 98

   5.3 Other Long-Term Option Products 100

Chapter 6 **Exotic Options: Option Innovations to Meet Special Needs** 105

   6.1 The Exchange Option 106

   6.2 Barrier Options 110

   6.3 The Asian Option: An Option on the Average 113

   6.4 Lookback Options 115

   6.5 The Compound Option: An Option on an Option 117

Chapter 7 **Interest Rate Options** 119

   7.1 A Methodology for Pricing Interest Rate Options: The Arbitrage-Free Tree
        Requirement 119

   7.2 Pricing an Interest Rate Option 131

   7.3 Caps, Floors, and Collars 133

   7.4 Estimating the Transition Probabilities 137

   7.5 Instruments with Embedded Interest Rate Options 138

Part II Financial Futures 147

Chapter 8 **Contract Characteristics and the Institutional Environment** 149

   8.1 Futures versus Forward Contracts 149

   8.2 The Futures Exchange 150

   8.3 Issues in Futures Contract Design: The Supply of the Underlying Security or
        Commodity 155

Chapter 9 **Pricing Futures, Forwards, and Options on Futures: General
        Considerations** 161

   9.1 Do Futures and Forward Prices Differ? 161

   9.2 Pricing Forward Contracts 166

   9.3 Options on Futures 169

Chapter 10 **Treasury Bill Futures** 173

   10.1 The Spot Market 173

   10.2 The Three-Month Treasury Bill Futures: Defining Features 177

10.3 Hedging with Three-Month Treasury Bill Futures 178

10.4 Alternative Hedges Using Spot Instruments 183

10.5 Pure Arbitrage Strategies Using T-Bill Futures 189

10.6 Quasi Arbitrage 191

Chapter 11 **Eurodollars** 195

11.1 The Spot Market 195

11.2 Defining Features of the Eurodollar Futures Contract 197

11.3 A Hedging Example 198

11.4 A Pure Arbitrage Example 199

11.5 Forward Rate Agreements (FRAs) 200

11.6 Replicating a Zero-Coupon Instrument with a Eurodollar Strip 202

11.7 A Hedging Subtlety in Using Eurodollar Futures 203

Chapter 12 **U.S. Treasury Bond and Note Futures** 207

12.1 The Spot Market 207

12.2 Clearing and Settling Trades in U.S. Treasury Securities: The Government Securities Clearing Corporation (GSCC) 210

12.3 The Treasury Bond Futures Contract: Defining Features 214

12.4 Futures Pricing, Hedging, and the Optimal Time to Deliver for the Case of Only One Deliverable Bond 216

12.5 Several Deliverable Bonds: Identifying the Cheapest-to-Deliver (CTD) 222

12.6 Hedging a Non-CTD Bond 225

12.7 Options Implicit in the T-Bond Futures Contract 227

Chapter 13 **The Standard & Poor's 500 Stock Price Index Futures Contract** 235

13.1 The S&P 500 Index: The Spot 235

13.2 The S&P 500 Stock Index Futures: Defining Characteristics 236

13.3 Index Arbitrage: Pricing Implications 236

13.4 Hedging with the S&P Futures Contract 241

Part III Interest Rate Swaps 243

Chapter 14 **Basics** 245

14.1 Swaps and Risk Management 245

14.2 An Illustration of the Generic Swap: Fixed-for-Floating 246

14.3 A Comment on Limited Two-Way Payment (LTP) 250

14.4 Real versus Illusory Benefits to the Swap Parties 251

14.5 Some Terminology, Definitions, and Attendant Points 254

Chapter 15 **Swap Pricing and Hedging** 261

15.1 A Relationship between Eurodollar Futures and Swaps 261

15.2 Pricing a Simple Swap: The Case of an International Monetary Market (IMM) Swap 263

15.3 Hedging a Swap 267

15.4 The Convexity Adjustment 269

15.5 Pricing a Swap with Payment Dates That Do Not Coincide with IMM Dates 270

15.6 Valuing an Off-Market Swap 272

15.7 Valuing a Long-Dated Swap 275

15.8 Extending the Hedging Methodology 277

15.9 Trading against a Swap Position: A Futures-Swap Arbitrage 278

Chapter 16 **Nongeneric Swaps** 283

16.1 A General Methodology for Swap Pricing 283

16.2 Other Swap Structures 290

Chapter 17 **Options on Swaps** 297

17.1 Definitions and Terminology 297

17.2 Forming Payment Distributions with Swaptions and with Options Embedded in Swaps 298

17.3 Pricing Swaptions 301

Part IV Mortgage Derivatives 305

Chapter 18 **The Underlying Instruments and Market Characteristics** 307

18.1 Mortgage Types 307

18.2 Mortgage Originators 312

18.3 The Mortgage Pass-Through Certificate (MPT) 313

18.4 Trading and Settlement of Mortgage Pass-Throughs 317

18.5 Clearing and Settlement Facilities 320

Chapter 19 **Valuation and Hedging of Mortgage Pass-Throughs** 327

19.1 Prepayment Rates and Models 327

19.2 Valuation: A Review of Methodology 334

19.3 The Option-Adjusted Spread (OAS): A Relative Valuation Method 336

19.4 Calculating a Mortgage-Backed Security's Price Sensitivity to a Shift in the Yield Curve 339

19.5 The Convexity of the Mortgage-Backed Security 341

Chapter 20 **CMOs, STRIPs, and Other Mortgage Derivative Instruments** 345

20.1 Collateralized Mortgage Obligations (CMOs): Basic Structure 345

20.2 Valuation of a Two-Period CMO: An Example 351

20.3 Planned Amortization Class (PAC) 357

20.4 Targeted Amortization Class (TAC) 360

20.5 Floater and Inverse Floater Classes 362

20.6 Credit Enhancement of a Mortgage Security 364

20.7 Stripped Mortgage-Backed Securities (STRIPs) 366

References and Suggested Reading 375

Index 387

Preface

*T*HE TERM *derivative instrument* is generally accepted to mean a financial instrument with a payoff structure determined by the value of an underlying security, commodity, interest rate, or index. According to some notable surveys,[1] over 80% of private sector corporations consider derivatives to be important in implementing their financial policies. Derivatives have also gained wide acceptance among national and local governments, government-sponsored entities, such as the Student Loan Marketing Association and the Federal Home Loan Mortgage Corporation, and supranationals, such as the World Bank.

Derivatives are used to lower funding costs by borrowers, to efficiently alter the proportions of fixed to floating rate debt, to enhance the yield on assets, to quickly modify the assets' payoff structure to correspond to the firm's market view, to avoid taxes and skirt regulations, and, perhaps most importantly, to transfer market risk (hedge)—where the term *market risk* is used to connote the possibility of losses sustained due to an unforeseen price or volatility change.[2] A firm may execute a derivative transaction to alter its market risk profile by transferring to the trade's counterparty a particular type of risk. The price that the firm must pay for this risk transfer is the acceptance of another type of risk and/or a cash payment to the counterparty.

Objectives

I undertook this project to continue my education in a financial area that occupied a significant portion of my professional life—a part of finance that is at once so practically important and intellectually exciting that it is hard to leave alone. It is an area in which sets

---

1. See *Derivatives: Practices and Principles*, Appendix III: "Survey of Industry Practice." Group of Thirty, March 1994.

2. See, for example, *Derivatives: Practices and Principles*. Washington D.C.: Group of Thirty, July 1993; Allen, F. and D. Gale, *Financial Innovation and Risk Sharing*. Cambridge, Mass.: MIT Press 1994; Miller, M.H., "Financial Innovation: The Last Twenty Years and the Next," *Journal of Financial and Quantitative Analysis*, 21 (December 1986), 459–471; and Van Horne, J.C., "Of Financial Innovations and Excesses," *Journal of Finance*, 40, (July 1985), 621–631.

of instruments are constructed that enable the firm to strip off the distasteful risk component from an asset or liability and retain the palatable parts—and to do so at costs that are small relative to those associated with conventional securities transactions.

Many paths could be taken in writing such a book. Dispensing with a litany of available approaches, here is mine. The book should contain sufficient information to update those who have lost contact with the subject during the past few years, to make the transition more comfortable for those who are about to serve a derivatives apprenticeship, and to enable the reader to enter into derivatives-related discussions without apprehension, though with a modicum of caution. These are the book's goals. The knowledge required to attain these goals is related to the essentials of the valuation models and the rules and conventions that define the markets.

The book reaches for a balance between knowledge of theory and the details of practice. Without a pricing model, hedging programs enter the realm of the surreal and trading programs are best left to those who possess the soul of an artist and the mind of a mathematician (or is it the other way around?). On the other hand, to possess an aesthetically appealing valuation model without knowledge of the market in which the instrument is traded is a fast and often dramatic way to lose one's capital. Be late in delivering a bond that was shorted because your model said it was overpriced, and watch your arbitrage profit evaporate. Enter into a swap without paying attention to how the agreed-upon day count may provide one party with less than one year's stated coupon, and watch the joys of employment become ephemeral. Hedge with a futures contract written on a security in short supply, and behold how you can lose on both the futures and the underlying security. The pricing model identifies a potentially profitable trading opportunity. Knowledge of market practices is invaluable for the successful completion of the trade.[3]

I explain the valuation models and market rules the way I would like them to be explained to me. I don't want the details of an instrument or the market conventions buried in some general statement. I

---

3. In all instances, the valuation methods presented and explained are restricted to those used by professionals. This is consistent with the intent that the book's material have practical import. These models constitute a subset of the pricing models developed by academics and practitioners. The list is not all-inclusive, in the sense that every pricing model used by any professional trader has been discovered and discussed. Rather, the valuation methods presented in the book are some of the more popular ones, so one must assume that they have utility.

might think that I understand the subject, but, upon trying to explain it to someone else, my confidence wanes and the explanation unravels. Anything arcane should be illustrated with a numerical example. The book contains many numerical illustrations that the reader can and should replicate.

Recently, a torrent of criticism has been directed toward the derivative markets. With regard to the alleged abuses, those involved and investigating seem the appropriate parties to comment. All that can be responsibly said by an outside observer is that, given the newspaper stories, it appears that the losses suffered by corporate treasurers, municipalities, fund managers, and banks were the result of particular trading views—for the most part that interest rates would not rise in 1994, and in one highly publicized case, that the Nikkei 225 Stock Average would rise in the beginning of 1995. Extensive trading losses are normally attached to a lack of control. So the association that the financial press draws between the size of the losses and degree of control or lack thereof is to be expected. I have no doubt that a number of books will be forthcoming detailing these events; an examination of these cases is not one of this book's objectives.

The Topics

There are many classes of derivatives. This book focuses on four types: (1) options, (2) futures, (3) interest rate swaps, and (4) mortgage derivatives. While generally separable into categories, the instruments that make up these classes often compete for the risk manager's attention. In a wide range of situations and with varying degrees of effectiveness, an instrument can be found in each of these categories that solves the risk transference problem. For example, a firm that finances its fixed rate assets with floating rate debt is concerned about a near-term rate rise and may choose to transfer that risk through futures, interest rate options, or a swap. A thrift institution with sizable mortgage holdings, concerned that a drop in rates will force the reinvestment of the prepaid balances at unfavorably low rates, can transfer that risk with one of any number of mortgage derivative instruments. Ultimately, the selection of a particular instrument depends upon each instrument's payoff characteristics and its cost (pricing) compared to all other competitive instruments. To make an intelligent selection—that is, to know how much of the desired payoff profile to part with in exchange for a better price—one must understand each instrument, how to use it, and how to price it. This is what the book is about.

Organization

Because of the nature of the material presented, the four parts of the book are interdependent. The options part should be read first. Comprehension of the other three parts, on futures, swaps, and mortgage derivatives, requires an understanding of options. The swaps part relies heavily on the reader's familiarity with the Eurodollar futures and to a lesser extent on the U.S. Treasury bond and note futures contracts. Valuation and hedging of mortgage derivatives demand that one become acquainted first with the standard option and then with the interest rate option.

Each of the book's four parts begins with a description of the institutional arrangements that have come to characterize the markets in which the instruments trade. If the instrument is traded on an exchange, details of the trade process, clearing, settlement, and institutional guarantees are examined. If it is traded over-the-counter, a similar set of descriptive elements is provided. In addition, conventions regarding price quotes (yield quotes on interest rate instruments) are delineated.

Following the institutional discussion, the most basic derivative in each class is examined with respect to its risk transference properties, risk management applications, and pricing. For example, in the options part, the starting point is the standard option on a stock. In the swaps and mortgage parts, the first instruments described and explored are, respectively, the generic swap and the mortgage pass-through security. The futures part also begins with a simple generic contract.

The subsequent chapters in each part follow the evolution of these markets in terms of the new instruments introduced, the factors inspiring their development, and the alterations in pricing technology required by these more complex derivatives. As discussed in the options part, standard puts and calls left risk management gaps. Portfolio insurance and option-like securities, e.g., SCOREs and SuperShares, were developed to fill these gaps. As market participants became more comfortable with these products, they demanded stylized options with complex payoff profiles that addressed more specific needs. Thus the birth of the category of options known as *exotics*. Traders and researchers then noticed that the valuation methodology brought to bear on exotics would provide more precise pricing of standard nonequity options, such as interest rate options. The final chapter of the options part demonstrates the methodology applied to stand-alone interest rate options, such as bond options and caps, and to options embedded in bonds such as callable bonds and bonds with sinking fund requirements. Along the way, numerical examples are presented to clarify the procedures.

The other parts of the book are arranged in parallel form. In the swaps part, the starting point is the institutional environment. A discussion of the generic swap follows. The part then moves on to nongeneric swaps such as constant maturity swaps and index amortizing swaps, and ends with swaptions and options embedded in swaps. The same path is followed in the mortgage derivatives part. It begins with the institutional environment and market conventions, travels through the mortgage pass-through with a discussion of its uses and pricing, then examines the applications and pricing of more complex mortgage derivatives, e.g., CMOs, PACs, TACs, inverse floaters, and STRIPs.

On occasion, maintaining coherence and continuity of subject matter requires that we stray from this path. For example, the *smile* pricing of options is one of the more difficult concepts to absorb. Because of its difficulty it might be more appropriate to present this methodology at the end of the options segment. However, the impetus for the development of the smile methodology arose from discovered weaknesses in the Black-Scholes and multiplicative binomial models in pricing standard equity options. Because standard equity options, the Black-Scholes model, and the multiplicative binomial model are discussed in Chapter 3, the smile methodology is presented there.

By the same token, once the notion of cash settlement of a futures contract in lieu of physical delivery is understood, the S&P 500 futures contract can be explained quite simply. Given its degree of difficulty, it might logically call for placement in an early chapter of the futures segment. However, to do so seems to interfere with the natural presentation of the interest rate contracts, from the T-bill contract—which is fairly straightforward, calling for physical delivery and devoid of embedded options—through the Eurodollar contract, the first cash settlement contract, to the complicated Treasury bond and note contracts.

As the reader proceeds through the book, my hope is that by understanding the instruments and their applications, by becoming familiar with the markets that house these instruments, and by learning the essentials of accepted pricing methodologies, the reader will develop an increased sense of confidence and ease when traversing these markets. I hope the book will also provide the reader with an appreciation of why the instruments and practices that define these markets evolved.

Acknowledgments

$P_{RIOR\ TO}$ this project, I gained some practical experience in the relevant markets and had some academic contact with the subject matter. During this endeavor, a number of individuals furthered my education. None should be blamed for the result. I have benefited from conversations with and comments from all of them. I thank

Mark Adler	Adler Capital Management
Polly Reynolds Allen	University of Connecticut
Terry Belton	Morgan Guaranty
Robert Blower	British Bankers Association
Galen Burghardt	Dean Witter
Randy Clyde	Canadian Imperial Bank of Commerce
Tom Coleman	TMG Financial Products
Georges Courtadon	Canadian Imperial Bank of Commerce
Daniel P. Cunningham	Cravath, Swaine & Moore
Ravi E. Dattatreya	Sumitomo Capital Markets
Emanuel Derman	Goldman Sachs
Jay R. Dietrich	O'Connor & Associates
Robert C. Doebler	O'Connor & Associates
Richard G. DuFour	Chicago Board Options Exchange
Richard Gerrigan	DePaul University
Joanne Hill	Goldman Sachs
Jeffrey Ingber	Government Securities Clearing Corporation
Matthew Jacobs	Lehman Brothers
Carol Jameson	Participants Trust Company
Stanley Jonas	FIMAT Futures
Iraj Kani	Goldman Sachs
Ira Kawaller	Chicago Mercantile Exchange
Sandra Krieger	Federal Reserve Bank of New York

Richard Lewandowski	Chicago Board Options Exchange
Richard McDonald	Chicago Mercantile Exchange
Henry McIntire	Lehman Brothers
Robert C. Merton	Harvard University
Ann-Marie Meulendyke	Federal Reserve Bank of New York
William Michaelcheck	Mariner Investments
George Miller	Public Securities Association
John Olesky	Morgan Stanley
Dennis Paganucci	MBS Clearing Corporation
Brook Payner	Citicorp
James Peaslee	Cleary, Gottlieb, Steen & Hamilton
Leopold Rassnick	Participants Trust Company
George Rose	Government National Mortgage Association
Ramine Rouhani	CDC Investment Management Company
Karen Saperstein	National Securities Clearing Corporation
Paul Schultz	Ohio State University
Elliott Schurgin	Standard & Poor's Corporation
Andrew Sparks	Lehman Brothers
Jeffrey Stehm	Federal Reserve Board of Governors
John F. Tierney	Lehman Brothers
Patricia Trainor	Depository Trust Company
Cliff Viner	Adams Viner & Mosler
Michael Waldman	Salomon Brothers
David Weinberger	O'Connor & Associates
Jack Wing	Chicago Corporation
Phyllis Wise	Sage Clearing
Bruce Wood	Federal Home Loan Mortgage Corporation

I owe particular debts of gratitude to George Constantinides (University of Chicago), William Huth (Bank of America), Ravi Mattu (Lehman Brothers), and Richard Robb (DKB Financial Products) for patiently answering many questions. I also benefited from their comments on sections of the manuscript: George on options and futures, Bill and Richard on swaps, and Ravi on mortgage derivatives. Adam

Gehr (DePaul University), Dick Kazarian (Citicorp), and Chris Piros (Massachusetts Financial) provided a number of valuable comments on large portions of the manuscript. Mark Rubinstein's (University of California at Berkeley) comments and suggestions on some of the options sections were very helpful. I thank Geoffrey Hirt, my department chairman, Michael Long, editor of the Financial Management Association Survey and Synthesis Series, and Marjorie Williams, my Harvard Business School Press editor, for their encouragement and support. Barbara Roth, Managing Editor at the Harvard Business School Press, patiently guided me through the latter stages of the publication process. Suzanne Schafer's editorial work significantly improved the manuscript. I am grateful to DePaul University for providing time and some financial assistance. Typing assistance was provided by Tracey DeForte and Joyce Roeder. Monica Witczak graciously attended to a number of administrative details. Stephanie Berg, a University of Chicago Ph.D. student, and Robert L. Sanders, an M.S. student at DePaul University, carefully read the entire manuscript. Kenneth E. Sherwood efficiently executed most of the diagrams. I was very fortunate to have Daniel Spiegel as my research assistant. Finally, I thank my children, Anne, Beth, and David, for all the usual things, and more—many, many more.

PART *I*

Options

Chapter **1**

Stock Option Basics

$O_{F\ ALL}$ categories of traded financial instruments, options are generally considered to be the most basic, in the sense that they can be used to replicate the return structure of any other security category. Though there are now many types of options that are traded on all sorts of securities and commodities, the general investment community became familiar with options when the Chicago Board Options Exchange was formed in 1973 to trade what might be considered the simplest options on listed stocks—calls and puts. These are now usually referred to as *standard* calls and puts. We begin the options part of this book with the defining characteristics of standard calls and puts, the terminology used in describing and discussing them, their return profiles, and how they are combined, often with the underlying stock, to achieve positions that have some of the more popular return structures.

1.1 Definitions, Terminology, and Profit Profiles

The Call

An option contract grants its owner the right, but not the obligation, to take some action. There are two option types: a call and a put. A call gives its owner (the *long*) the right, but not the obligation, to purchase a specified quantity of the security (named the *underlying* security) at a specific price (termed the *exercise price* or the *strike price*) on or before a given date, at which time the call expires. If the call can (cannot) be exercised prior to its expiration date, then it is referred to as an American (European) call. The buyer of the call pays to the seller or writer of the call (the *short*) the call's price, often referred to as the *call premium*. The five descriptive features of a call have just been mentioned: (1) the identity and quantity of the underlying security that the call owner has the right to purchase, (2) the price at which each unit of the security can be purchased, (3) the call's expiration date, (4) whether it is American or European, and (5) the call's premium.

To illustrate the features and benefits of a call, consider the following example. ABC stock is trading at 45 per share. You purchase a call on one share that expires in six months and has a premium of 5 and an exercise price of 45. Now suppose ABC's price moves to 57 by expiration day. You exercise your right to purchase from the call writer one share of the stock at 45. You sell the share in the market at 57, for a gross profit of 12. The call premium was 5, so the net profit is 7. If instead the share price at the call's expiration date is 41, you do not exercise your right, for to do so would entail buying (calling) the share at 45 and then selling it at the market price of 41; the loss would amount to 4 plus the cost of the call (5), for a net loss of 9. In this latter case, the call owner is said to "walk away" from the call, letting it expire.

What if the stock price at expiration is 46? Is the call worth exercising? Yes. By not exercising and allowing the call to expire, the long's loss is equal to the premium of 5. In contrast, if exercise is selected, the long buys the stock at 45 and sells it at 46, gaining 1. Taking into account the sunk cost of the 5 call premium, the net loss on the call is 4 rather than the 5 obtained by permitting the call to expire.

At this point, the following statements should coincide with one's intuition: A call with a strike of 40 would be more valuable than a call with a strike of 45. The lower the call's strike, the higher the call premium. Conversely, the higher the strike, the lower the call premium. The call premium moves inversely with the strike price. (These statements will be more rigorously addressed in Chapter 3.)

Figure 1.1 shows the long call's net profit on expiration day, π, for each possible stock price on that day, S_T. C and K respectively symbolize the call's premium at initiation and its strike price. It should be emphasized that only on expiration day are linear profit profiles obtained for options.

A glance at Figure 1.1 reveals that a stock price higher than the strike price is favorable to the long call; a stock price lower than the strike price results in a maximum loss equal to the call premium. Some terms have entered the trader's vernacular to describe the state of a call's profitability. Depending upon whether the current stock price, S, exceeds, equals, or is less than the strike price, K, the call is said to be *in-the-money, at-the-money,* or *out-of-the-money.* And there are variations on these terms. If the stock price is considered to be

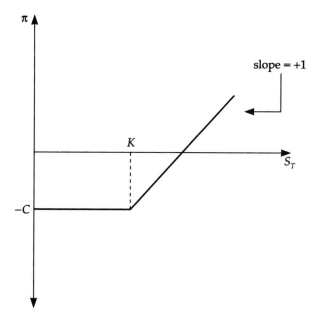

Figure 1.1 Long Call Profit Profile at Expiration

far above the strike, the call is said to be *deep-in-the-money,* and if far below, *deep-out-of-the-money.* Additionally, the call is said to have an *intrinsic value* equal to $S - K$ if this quantity is positive, and equal to zero otherwise. That is, the call's intrinsic value is max$\{0, S - K\}$. A call's *time premium* is defined as the difference between the call premium and the call's intrinsic value.

It will be useful to characterize the long call's profit profile algebraically. Recall that the equation of a straight line in the (S_T, π) plane is given by

$$\pi - \pi^* = m(S_T - S_T^*)$$

where (S_T^*, π^*) represents the horizontal and vertical coordinates of an arbitrary point that lies on the line and m is the symbol for the line's slope, that is, the ratio of the change in profit along the line to the change in the stock price.

In Figure 1.1 there are two lines, one for the region between $S_T = 0$ and $S_T = K$, and another for the region in which S_T lies to the right of K. The line in the first region, $0 \leq S_T \leq K$, has a zero slope,

$m = 0$, and the point $(0, -C)$ lies on this line. Consequently, for this region of S_T, namely $0 \le S_T \le K$, the equation of the profit line is

$$\pi - (-C) = 0(S_T - 0) \quad \text{or} \quad \pi = -C.$$

For $S_T \ge K$ the relevant line has slope equal to $+1$, since for each dollar that the stock price increases above the exercise price, the call profit increases by one dollar. The line passes through the point $(K, -C)$. Therefore the equation is

$$\pi - (-C) = 1(S_T - K) \quad \text{or} \quad \pi = -C + (S_T - K).$$

Bringing these descriptive equations together, we have

$$0 \le S_T \le K \quad \pi = -C$$

$$K \le S_T \quad \pi = -C + (S_T - K)$$

Of course, what the long call (buyer) gains, the short call (writer) loses. Therefore, to obtain an expiration day profit profile for the short call, multiply by -1 the vertical coordinate of the line in Figure 1.1 at each S_T value. Figure 1.2 depicts the result.

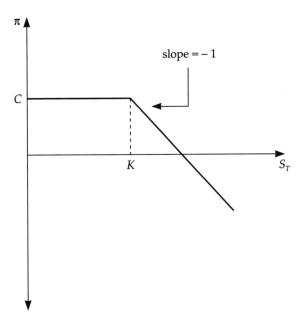

Figure 1.2 Short Call Profit Profile at Expiration

The corresponding linear equations that describe this graph are given by

$$0 \leq S_T \leq K \qquad \pi = +C$$

$$K \leq S_T \qquad \pi = +C - (S_T - K)$$

We will be using this type of algebraic characterization of an option's profit profile to build more complicated profit pictures and, in the process, to obtain a sense of the types of return structures that can be manufactured by combining different option positions with an underlying security position. Before that, we turn to a discussion of the other basic option type, the put.

The Put

A put grants its owner the right, but not the obligation, to sell a specified quantity of the underlying security at the exercise price (strike price) on or before a given date (expiration day). If the put can (cannot) be exercised prior to its expiration date, then it is referred to as an American (European) put. The buyer of the put (the long) pays to the writer or seller of the put (the short) the put price, usually referred to as the put premium. The descriptive features of a put are (1) the identity and quantity of the underlying security that the put buyer has the right to sell to the put writer, (2) the strike price, (3) the expiration date, (4) whether it is American or European, and (5) the put premium.

A numerical example assists in clarifying the put's benefits to the buyer. Consider the purchase of a six-month put on a single share of ABC. The put's strike is 45 and its premium is 4. Suppose that the stock price is 30 at expiration. Then the put owner would exercise his right to sell the stock at 45. The put owner purchases the stock in the market at 30, delivers it to the put writer, and, in turn, receives 45. Accounting for the put premium paid, 4, the net gain would be 11. If, instead, the stock price settled at 50 on expiration day, the put holder would choose not to exercise, but rather to let his put expire. To exercise would mean that the long would buy the stock in the market at 50 and deliver it ("put it") to the writer (the short) at the strike of 45, losing 5 on the exercise in addition to the put premium of 4, for a net loss of 9. Since the put owner has the right to avoid this loss, he does so by not exercising. Clearly, a put with a 60 strike would have provided greater profit opportunities. The higher the strike price, the more valuable the put. A direct relationship exists between the put premium and the strike price.

Denoting by P the put premium paid by the long to the short at the trade's inception, Figure 1.3 graphically portrays the long's net profit versus stock price relation on expiration day. It is clear from Figure 1.3 that a stock price lower than the strike price is favorable to the long put; a stock price higher than the strike price results in a maximum loss equal to the put premium. Depending upon whether the strike price exceeds, equals, or is less than the current stock price, S, the put is said to be *in-the-money, at-the-money,* or *out-of-the-money.* If the strike is considerably above the current stock price, the put is *deep-in-the-money.* If the strike is significantly below the current stock price, the put is *deep-out-of-the-money.* A put's *intrinsic value* is defined as $K - S$ if this difference is positive, and zero otherwise. The mathematical expression for the put's intrinsic value is $\max\{0, K - S\}$. A put's *time premium* is defined as the difference between the put's premium and the put's intrinsic value. The algebraic equations that correspond to the lines in Figure 1.3 are as follows:

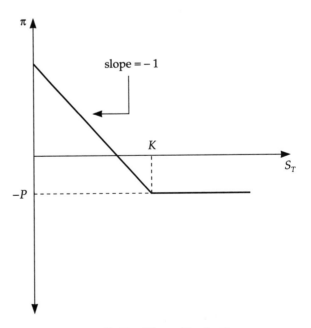

Figure 1.3 Long Put Profit Profile at Expiration

$$0 \leq S_T \leq K \qquad \pi = -P - (S_T - K)$$

$$K \leq S_T \qquad \pi = -P$$

What the put buyer gains, the put seller loses. Therefore, to obtain the short put's profit profile on expiration date, just multiply by -1 the vertical coordinate of the line in Figure 1.3 at each value of S_T. Figure 1.4 depicts the result. The corresponding algebraic equations are

$$0 \leq S_T \leq K \qquad \pi = +P + (S_T - K)$$

$$K \leq S_T \qquad \pi = +P$$

An understanding of call and put payoffs is fundamentally important to security market players because with these basic securities the payoffs of all other security types can be replicated and, perhaps more importantly, new securities can be created with the payoff structures that investors desire—well, almost. Actually, to make this statement true, we need two more building blocks: the long stock

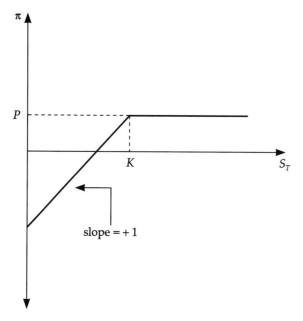

Figure 1.4 Short Put Profit Profile at Expiration

and short stock positions. Recalling that the current stock price is symbolized by S and continuing to use S_T to symbolize the stock price on the date that the options expire, the profit profiles of the long stock and short stock positions are presented in Figures 1.5 and 1.6. The associated algebraic equations are

$$\text{Long stock:} \quad \pi = S_T - S \qquad \text{for all } S_T$$

$$\text{Short stock:} \quad \pi = -(S_T - S) \qquad \text{for all } S_T$$

The stock has no expiration date. But we continue to use S_T and interpret it to mean the stock price on the day an option on that stock expires.

1.2 Constructing the Return Profiles of More Complicated Positions

The Insurance Put

A traditional role for a long put position is to provide a safety net for a long stock position. If the profit coordinate in the long put

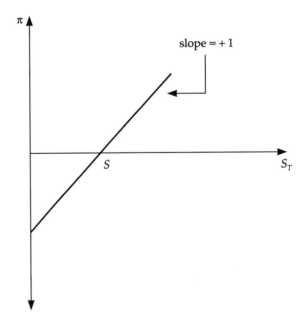

Figure 1.5 Long Stock Profit Profile

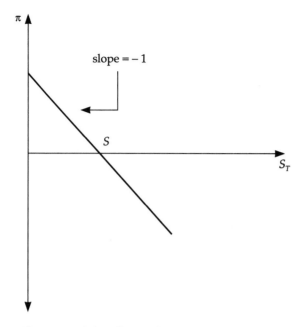

Figure 1.6 Short Stock Profit Profile

(LP) equations is added to the profit coordinate of the long stock (LS) equation at each S_T value, we arrive at a set of equations for the composite position that describes the insurance put (IP). Assuming that the put was initially at-the-money, $S = K$, we obtain

$$0 \le S_T \le K \qquad \pi_{IP} = \pi_{LP} + \pi_{LS} = -P - (S_T - K) + (S_T - K) = -P$$

$$K \le S_T \qquad \pi_{IP} = \pi_{LP} + \pi_{LS} = -P + (S_T - K)$$

These are the line equations that describe the profit profile of the insurance put on expiration day. These lines can be plotted by finding two points on each line and then connecting them. For the $0 \le S_T \le K$ region, this is trivial, for no matter what the value of S_T, $\pi_{IP} = -P$. So for the $0 \le S_T \le K$ region, the insurance put's profit profile consists of a horizontal line set at a height equal to $-P$. To plot the insurance put's line in the $K \le S_T$ region, we need two points. Choose $S_T = K$ and substitute into the equation to obtain a π_{IP} coordinate of $-P$, producing a point with coordinates $(K, -P)$. Choose $S_T = K + P$, substitute into the equation, and obtain $\pi_{IP} = 0$, producing a point with coordinates $(K + P, 0)$. Plot and connect these two points to complete the insurance put graph (see Figure 1.7).

Notice that the insurance put has the same dollar profit profile as the long call (Figure 1.1), except that the premium paid for this *synthetic* long call is P instead of C. There is a bit more to replicating a long call than simply bringing together a long put and a long stock position. It will be shown that some leverage is needed. Nevertheless, you can see how other return distributions can be replicated through the appropriate choice and combination of the six basic building blocks.

The Covered Call

A common yield-enhancing strategy used by account executives for retail customers and by mutual fund managers is to sell a call on a stock position that is already owned, or one that is purchased at the same time the call is sold. This short call–long stock position is known as a *covered call*. It is often thought to be a relatively conservative trading strategy. If the stock fails to rise, the investor earns the

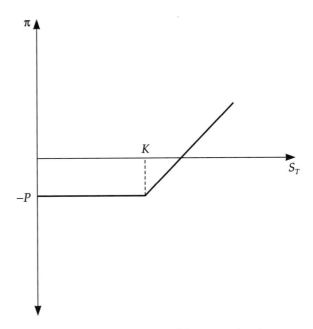

Figure 1.7 Insurance Put Profit Profile at Expiration

call premium, because the call expires out-of-the-money. If the stock moves higher and is called away by the call owner, the stock is simply delivered out of the portfolio, and the investor is not exposed to the risk of having to enter the market to purchase the stock at a higher price.

To draw the profit profile for the covered call, use the same methodology discussed for constructing the insurance put diagram. Add the vertical (profit) coordinates of the short call (assume it to be at-the-money) and long stock positions at each S_T value. After obtaining the covered call's equations, plot them to obtain Figure 1.8.

Compare Figure 1.8 with Figure 1.4. The covered call has essentially the same profit profile as the short put—sometimes referred to as a *naked put*. The only difference is that the call premium, C, plays the role of the standard put premium, P. So, in fact, the covered call can be considered a somewhat risky strategy. This makes sense, for the investor who writes the call on his long stock position gives away all of the stock's upside potential in exchange for the call premium and retains all of the risk of a stock price drop. In fact, in the early

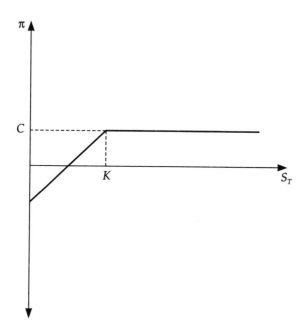

Figure 1.8 Covered Call Profit Profile at Expiration

days of option trading, the Securities Exchange Commission deemed this strategy safe enough for mutual funds to use while not permitting these same funds to write puts—the latter positions were judged to be too risky.

Apart from this observation, we again see that by using two of the building blocks, we have constructed the return structure of a third, the short put. As we shall see, the covered call is not precisely equal to a short put, for some borrowing must be done in order to replicate a short put with a short call and long stock position.

Combining Options to Form Other Return Distributions

From the discussion so far, it may appear that a trader would use options to place bets on a stock's direction. Rather, the primary use of options by the trader is to place bets on the stock's price volatility. For example, suppose a trader purchases a call and a put, both with the same strike K and the same expiration date. The position, named a *long straddle*, has the profit profile presented in Figure 1.9.

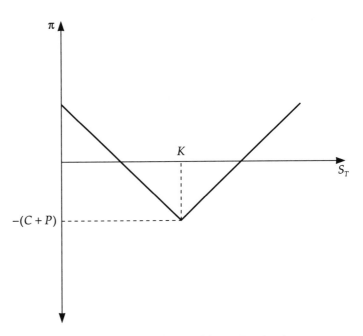

Figure 1.9 Long Straddle Profit Profile at Expiration

As is evident, the holder of the straddle gains if there is a significant stock price move in either direction. The position loses when the stock price change is small. In what circumstances would a long straddle be employed? If an earnings announcement is imminent, but all you know is that it will either be highly favorable or unfavorable, purchasing a long straddle with K at or near the current stock price, S, is a sensible trading alternative. The trader who takes a long straddle is said to be "buying volatility." Conversely, if the trader thinks that the forthcoming earnings announcement will have a negligible effect on the stock price, then he "sells volatility" by going short the straddle, i.e., selling both a call and a put. If the stock price stays at its current level, the seller of the straddle keeps $C + P$. Any move away from S ($= K$) results in a decline in profits. See Figure 1.10.

Another type of volatility play is to take long positions in an out-of-the-money put and an out-of-the-money call. With K_C and K_P respectively denoting the call and put strikes, then $K_P < S < K_C$. *This call and put combination is referred to as an out-of-the-money strangle* (See Figure 1.11).

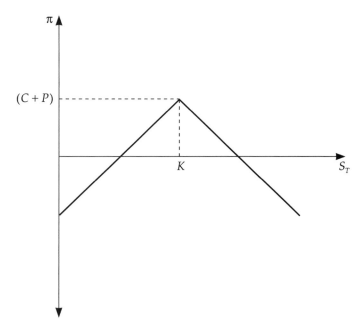

Figure 1.10   Short Straddle Profit Profile at Expiration

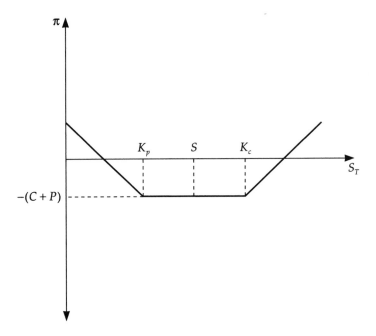

Figure 1.11 Long Out-of-the-Money Strangle Profit Profile at Expiration

Why choose this strangle over the straddle? Because if large stock price variations do not materialize, the total premium loss for the strangle will be less than that for the straddle—out-of-the-money premiums are less than at-the-money premiums. Of course the trader gives up something in exchange for this gain in loss protection: the break-even points and subsequent profitable areas are farther away from the current stock price and therefore are less likely to be reached.

A short out-of-the-money strangle is drawn in Figure 1.12. This position is taken by a trader who believes the market has overestimated the stock's price volatility. As the diagram shows, the trader is afforded a wider margin of loss protection than that provided by the short straddle, for the break-even points are farther away from the current stock price. Of course, the trade-off is lower profit potential, since the sum of the strangle's premiums is less than that of the straddle's.

Among the many other return distributions that can be formed by combining the equations of the six building blocks, there is a

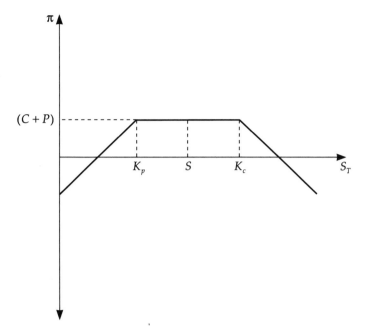

Figure 1.12   Short Out-of-the-Money Strangle Profit Profile at Expiration

category that traders frequently use: spreads. A spread is a position consisting of only calls or only puts where a call (put) at a particular strike and/or expiration is purchased and the call (put) at a different strike and/or expiration is sold. If the spread results in a net cash outflow (inflow) at initiation, the spread is called a debit (credit) spread.

One spread is particularly interesting—not because it is an obvious play on volatility, although many may say it is. It is interesting because the more sophisticated option traders use this spread, called a *butterfly*, to build more complicated positions, while academics view butterflies as a means of forming securities that pay off at only one stock price level and at no other level. See Breeden and Litzenberger 1978.

A long butterfly is formed by using three different calls (or puts). They have different strikes but the same expiration date. Specifically, given calls with identical expiration dates and strikes $K_1 < K_2 < K_3$

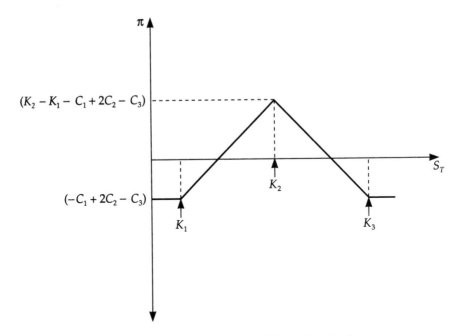

Figure 1.13   Long Butterfly Profit Profile at Expiration

and chosen such that $K_2 = (K_1 + K_3)/2$, one each of the K_1 and K_3 strikes are purchased and two of the K_2 strikes are sold. The profit profile of a butterfly is presented in Figure 1.13.

An exact pricing model, such as that presented in Chapter 3, will verify that $(-C_1 + 2C_2 - C_3) < 0$. However, one immediately sees that this must be true, for if $(-C_1 + 2C_2 - C_3) \geq 0$, then the long butterfly position would offer the promise of possible gains and no losses, a situation that is not descriptive of market equilibrium.

Chapter 2

The Institutional Environment for Stock Options

*O*PTIONS *ARE* either exchange traded or off-exchange traded in the over-the-counter (OTC) market. On exchanges they are identified by *class*, either a put or a call, and by *series*, the identifying features of which are strike and expiration date. The stock option contracts traded on an exchange are standardized with respect to the quantity of shares on which the option is written, generally 100 shares per option contract, and with respect to the strikes and expiration dates that may be traded. Since the only dimension negotiated on the floor is the premium, standardization results in faster trading, which in turn translates into greater liquidity.

The structures of the various exchanges on which stock options are traded are virtually identical. The Chicago Board Options Exchange (CBOE) was the first to be formed, remains the largest, and is the one whose specific structure is discussed here. We begin with a description of the entities that interact to initiate and complete a trade on the CBOE. The discussion then turns to the credit protection that counterparties to a trade require in order to ensure that trade obligations will be satisfied. In the process, we touch upon various collateralization rules. The chapter ends with the essentials of clearing an OTC option trade.

2.1 The Trade Process on an Exchange

An options exchange is a membership organization. Only an individual who holds a membership (a seat), through purchase or lease, may trade on the floor. A corporation may own a seat but must designate an individual who is authorized to use that seat to trade. Ownership of a seat does not in itself permit a member to trade on the floor. The member must first obtain a financial guarantee from a clearing firm (clearing member).

The clearing firm pledges to satisfy any financial obligations incurred by that trader—such as the payment for or delivery of the underlying stock on an exercised option—if the trader cannot meet them. A clearing firm is required to own at least one seat or to have a member assign (pledge) a seat to the corporation. The clearing firm must maintain a capital level that is no less than the minimum set by the Options Clearing Corporation (OCC). Every trade is submitted by a clearing firm to the exchange in the name of the individual trader. The clearing firm charges the floor trader a fee for guaranteeing and processing the trade. Processing involves recording trade information and transferring it to the exchange.

The exchange verifies if the trade is "good," that is, if the trade is recognized by the exchange as a financial contract between the two parties to the trade. To do this, the exchange compares the information submitted by the buying trader's clearing firm and by the selling trader's clearing firm to see if the reported information is consistent. Each clearing firm submits a record of the trade containing the following information: (1) buy or sell, (2) put or call, (3) quantity of option contracts traded, (4) underlying security, (5) expiration, (6) strike price, (7) trade price, (8) the trader's identification, (9) the opposite trader's identification, (10) the trader's clearing firm, (11) the opposite trader's clearing firm, and (12) if the trade opens a new position or offsets an existing position in that option series. If the trade records received from both firms identified in (10) and (11) match in all of the above categories, then the trade is accepted by the exchange and is said to *match* or *clear*. If a trade clears, then the OCC receives a report of the trade and issues an option position to each clearing firm, collects the premium from the buying clearing firm and passes it to the selling clearing firm, collects margin (good faith collateral) from the selling clearing firm, marks this margin to market as the option's premium changes, guarantees the trade to both clearing firms—becoming seller to the buying clearing firm and buyer to the selling clearing firm—and oversees the delivery of stock for cash when an option is exercised.

Trades that remain unmatched are called *out-trades*. They are resolved between clearing firms (really by the opposite traders represented by those clearing firms) prior to the next day's opening and then submitted as *as of* trades with the original trade date recorded.

For example, suppose all categories on the seller's and buyer's records match except price. The seller wrote that he sold 10 at 5, and the buyer recorded that he paid 4¾ for 10. In this case, the traders would most likely split the difference and submit the trade at 4⅞. But if an out-trade cannot be quickly resolved between opposite traders, then both traders should step back onto the floor at the next morning's opening and redo the trade with other parties. This action limits their losses. After both traders achieve the positions they need through the next morning's transactions, they can proceed to take their dispute to arbitration.

Illustration: Dealing with an Out-Trade

The ABC clearing firm has a broker who has sold 1,000 IBM Jan 50 calls[1] at 5 for a customer. That night ABC is informed by the exchange that no buy has been reported corresponding to any part of that sale. Since there is no apparent buy side at another clearing firm, the broker is, in effect, long 1,000 of those calls at 5. This follows because the customer to whom the trade was reported expects to receive any gain from a drop in the call premium, and the broker is responsible for making good the customer's gain. But if the broker does not have the capital to make good this assurance, then the broker's clearing firm, ABC, must make good. So if the Jan 50 call immediately dropped to 3, ABC would be liable for $200,000 (net profit of $2 × 100 shares per option contract × 1,000 contracts). ABC, which views itself as equivalently long 1,000 IBM Jan 50 calls, must offset this position as quickly as possible by selling 1,000 of these calls on the opening. If they are sold at 4¾, then ABC's liability and the broker's loss is limited to $25,000 ($0.25 × 100 × 1,000). Waiting any longer to even out the position exposes ABC to a higher probability of a greater drop in the premium.

The Exercise Process

The exercise process proceeds as follows. The long option holder notifies his clearing firm that he wishes to exercise. The clearing firm informs the OCC, which then randomly assigns the exercise to an outstanding short position in that option. The clearing firm's customer (public customer or individual member) gives securities, in the case

---

1. The calls expire on the Saturday following the third Friday of January and have a strike price of 50.

of a short call or long put, or cash, in the case of a long call or short put, to the firm. The securities or cash are then transferred to the OCC, which sends them to the appropriate clearing firm. The clearing firm then redelivers the securities or cash to its customer.

2.2 Floor Traders, Order Types, and a Trading Rule

The Market Maker

In a particular option series on a given day, a floor trader can be either a broker, trading for others, or a market maker, trading for his own account. The market maker is required to provide a continuous bid and offer on ten puts and ten calls, referred to as "ten up," in each option series that he selects to trade. His bid is the price at which he is willing to immediately buy an option contract; his offer is the price at which he is willing to immediately sell an option contract. In fact, the CBOE computes theoretical bids and offers, where the market makers decide on the model's parameters. The computed bids and offers are posted by the CBOE, and anyone may buy or sell at those posted prices. The CBOE calls the system Autoquote. If a public customer wishes to buy ten or fewer options at the posted offer, he may do so. The sale is sequentially assigned to one of the market makers trading that option series. Of course, a market maker is permitted to enter a better quote than the Autoquote calculation.

A public customer who wishes to trade options need not work off of the market maker's quote. He can instruct his brokerage firm to enter his own bid or offer through its floor broker. If the order is for a lot size of ten or less, then the brokerage firm can enter the order directly into the CBOE's computerized Retail Automatic Execution System (RAES). Once entered into the system, the order is executed by the CBOE's computer, which assigns the executed trade to a market maker who has logged into RAES. The first day's assignment is made randomly. Subsequent assignments are made to those members whose names alphabetically follow the name of the member who received the first assignment.

As we have noted, a market maker trades for his own account. Within this definition, there are several operating forms. He may sell one call (put) series and buy another call (put) series. This would classify him as a spreader. He may simply take long or short positions in various options and keep them overnight. This classifies him as a position trader. Obviously, the market maker will gravitate toward that type of trading in which he has an edge.

The form of trading practiced by the largest proportion of market makers is scalping. A scalper is there to provide liquidity. When a public customer wishes to execute immediately and there is no other public customer order to take the other side, the scalper does so. Since he is buying (selling) when there are no other available buyers (sellers), he is often performing this task as the market is falling (rising). He will often acquire his long (short) inventory, as prices are moving, from his viewpoint, in an unfavorable direction. To limit his risk of loss, he will attempt to rid himself of this inventory as quickly as possible by selling at the offer, the lowest price at which the option is currently being "offered" for sale, and buying at the bid, the highest price that is currently bid for the purchase of the option. For his business to be profitable, what he earns on the bid-offer spread must outweigh the capital losses that occur due to the nature of the market environment in which he gathers his inventory.

Because the scalper's goal is to obtain the opportunity to be on the other side of the public customer's market orders—orders that are to be immediately filled at the best possible price—he will do what he can to gain the broker's attention. For example, knowing that the broker would like to consummate the entire customer order with one trader to lessen the chance of an out-trade, the scalper will take the entire order, even though it is large by his risk standards. To mitigate the risk of loss from entering this larger-than-normal trade, he will immediately sell (buy) part of that order to another market maker. Thus part of the position that was obtained in the trade done with the broker is "scratched"—bought and sold at the bid or sold and bought at the offer. No profit is made on the scratched part of the trade. Another way of gaining a broker's interest is to stand ready to make a market in the more illiquid option series favored by the broker's customers. Still another ploy is to allow the broker to search about for a better price and yet provide him with the opportunity to buy (sell) at your original offer (bid) should his search prove unsuccessful.

The previous paragraphs describe scalping as a small business enterprise, managed and staffed by a single individual. But scalping is often done by large securities firms as one of their many business lines. The operational principles are almost the same, except for the division of labor and the sophistication required to manage the option inventory's risk. In large operations, the scalper's tasks are divided among two groups: those whose responsibilities are restricted to selling at the offer and buying at the bid, and those who manage the risk of the portfolio formed by these transactions. The scalping operation may take on an even more sophisticated form. The first group might be responsible for selling any overpriced and buying any underpriced options—the valuation information being supplied by a computer model—and as soon as each transaction is completed, immediately executing a hedge, that is, a risk-reducing transaction. This first group has been given several epithets, but the most descriptive might be "hunter-gatherers." They find and take the positions and take a first swipe at a hedge. The second group handles the hedging of the complete portfolio of options at a more sophisticated level.

Order Types

Market Order   The market order is to be filled at the best possible price, immediately upon receipt by the floor trader acting as broker. There is no price specified on the order form, because it is to be filled "at the market."

Limit Order   The limit order instructs the floor broker to fill the order at the specified price or better. For example, "Buy 10 IBM Jan 50 calls at 5" means that the broker must not pay more than 5 for each call. A limit order poses some risks for the broker who holds it in his deck of orders. Say the call is currently trading at 5½, so the order cannot be executed. The broker's attention wanders, during which time the call's price breaks 5½, trades down to 4¾, and then jumps to 6 before the broker is aware of what is occurring. The broker owes the customer a fill of all ten contracts (calls on 1,000 shares) at 5, because if he had been alert his 5 bid would have been filled prior to any sales occurring at 4¾. Therefore, he must buy the ten contracts at 6 and give them to his customer at 5. Strictly speaking, he is supposed to give them to his customer at 6 and present the customer with a check for 1,000 ($1 \times 10 \times 100$). To protect himself against the price breaking a limit, causing the kind of loss just described, the broker may leave the limit order with the CBOE's Designated Primary Market Maker (DPM). Unlike the market maker, the DPM may act as broker and market maker on the same day in the options assigned to him. In effect, the DPM plays the role of a New York Stock Exchange specialist.

Stop Loss Order   The stop loss order takes two forms. A sell stop is used to limit losses (protect gains) on a long position and is activated at a price below the current market price. It becomes a market order when the option trades or is offered at the stop level. For example, "Sell 10 IBM Jan 50 calls, 4½ stop"; if this call trades at or is offered at 4½, then the broker must sell 10 of these calls on behalf of his customer at the going bid, which could be significantly less than 4½. A buy stop is used to limit losses (protect gains) on a short position and is activated at a price above the current market price. It becomes a market order when the option trades or is bid at the stop price.

No Dual Trading

As stated earlier, a member may not trade for his own account and act as a market maker on the same day, with the exception of the DPM. This rule, which is known as *no dual trading*, is intended to protect the public customer's order.

Here is an example of an abuse that the rule is intended to prevent. Suppose a member is permitted to trade for his own account and for the customer on the same day. He is short ten calls for his own account at 7, and he holds a customer sell stop for ten of the same calls at 5. The call price breaks to 5. The broker is delighted, for he is ahead by 20 [(7 − 5) × 10]. He does not execute his customer order; he should, but he does not. The call price jumps to 8. If the broker now attempts to cover his short position by purchasing ten calls, he will lose 10 [(7 − 8) × 10]. Instead he executes his customer's sell stop, buying ten calls from his customer at 5, and reports the trade as having occurred at the earlier time when the call was trading at 5. The customer has sold ten calls at 5, and the broker has made 20 [(7 − 5) × 10] instead of losing 10 [(7 − 8) × 10].

Is this fair to the customer? After all, the broker did sell ten calls at the stop price of 5. Absolutely not. The broker sold those ten calls at 5 when the call was trading at 8. Obviously, if the customer had been aware of this, he would not have sold at 5 when he could have obtained 8. Furthermore, if the call price had kept dropping past 5 rather than reversing and rising to 8, the broker, feeling more comfortable with his short position, would finally have activated the customer sell stop at a price below 5. This behavior by the broker, termed *leaning on a customer order*, takes the upside away from the customer and leaves him with the downside. The no dual trading rule is an attempt to suppress such behavior.

Unfortunately, outlawing dual trading cannot stop execution abuses. Consider another situation. The last recorded trade of the IBM calls occurred at 6. The market for these calls is presently 6¼–6½. A broker receives a market order to sell ten calls. Before he does so, he tells a friend, who is acting as a market maker that day, to sell ten of the calls. His friend sells ten at the 6¼ bid for his own account. The broker then executes his customer order by selling ten calls to his friend at 6, which he knows is the price of the last recorded trade. The market-making friend is even, having sold and bought ten calls; his profit is ¼ per call on ten calls. This can be shared with the broker. The trade at 6 is reported before the trade at 6¼—although they were prearranged and therefore took place simultaneously.

What is the common feature of these types of trading abuses? It is the leeway to report a trade at a price that is different from the current market price, and to report that trade as if it had occurred at an earlier time. If every trade were time stamped at the moment the trade occurred, such practices would be eliminated. The open question is whether the costs of preventing such trading infractions outweigh the benefits.

2.3 Collateralization of Trade Obligations

The clearing firm, which guarantees the completion of trade obligations by its customers and market makers, must minimize the incentive that these parties might have to walk away from a losing position. If a party to a trade should walk away, the clearing firm must possess the resources to meet the financial obligations that the defaulting party assumed when the trade was made. To this end, the clearing firm requires collateral for any trade positions that it guarantees. Because the OCC guarantees the financial performance of the clearing firm, the OCC requires that each clearing firm deposit sufficient collateral with the OCC in order for the OCC to have the necessary funds to meet the financial obligations of the clearing firm should it fail. The basic precept behind all required capital formulas is that there be sufficient collateral at day's end such that the guaranteeing party can convert the collateral to cash and have sufficient funds to close out the position at tomorrow's prices.

Collateral Required for a Public Customer (Non-Market-Maker) Position

For each type of position composed solely of options and for a position composed of both options and the underlying security, the Federal Reserve Board ("the Fed") has granted the CBOE and the other option exchanges the authority to stipulate the amount of collateral (margin) that a customer must keep on deposit with his clearing firm.

These margin rules, though devised by the exchange, are referred to as *Reg T margin requirements* in reference to the Fed's Regulation T, which addresses the amount of margin required on the stock positions of public customers.

Example: Margin Required on a Naked Call Position

A short call on a stock has a margin requirement equal to the maximum of *the call premium collected on the sale plus 20% of the underlying stock's value at the day's close, less the amount that the call is out-of-the-money* or *the call premium collected on the sale plus 10% of the underlying stock's value at the day's close.* The amount of collateral that this formula dictates be posted at day's end is referred to as *initial margin.* For example, if a call with a 50 strike is sold when the underlying stock price is 49 and a premium of 3 is collected, then the public customer must post collateral with his clearing firm equal to

$$\max\{[3 + 0.2(49) - 1], [3 + 0.1(49)]\} = 11.8$$

If the call is written on a broadly based index, such as Standard & Poor's 500 Stock Price Index (S&P Index), then the 20% figure in the margin formula is reduced to 15%.

After the trade date, the position must continue to be collateralized at a level that the clearing firm considers sufficient to meet the financial obligations it might have to assume. This post-trade date collateral is called *maintenance margin.* The same formula used to calculate initial margin is applied to the calculation of maintenance margin, except that the premium value at the end of the current trade date is substituted for the initial premium collected on the trade date. The calculation of maintenance margin is often referred to as *marking-to-market* or simply *marking.* To continue the example, if the call premium rose to 6 and the stock price to 55 on the day after the trade day, the collateral required (maintenance margin) would change to

$$\max\{[6 + 0.2(55)], [6 + 0.1(55)]\} = 17$$

The same margin formulas apply to naked puts. Positions composed of two or more option series or of two option classes usually have less onerous margin requirements.

Collateral Required for Market Maker Positions

A market maker's positions are not generally subject to the Reg T margin requirement, but he does have a nonnegative equity require-

Table 2.1   Account Composition, Market Values, and Haircuts

Position	Market Value	Haircut*
Cash	$10,000	0%
Long Stock	$ 5,000	15%
Long Calls with 50 Strike	$ 1,500	50%
Short Calls with 55 Strike	$ 1,200	75%
Short Puts	$ 2,000	75%

*The haircuts for short and long option positions, irrespective of strike or expiration date, are 75% and 50%, respectively.

ment, where equity is measured as the difference between the market values of his assets (long positions) and liabilities (short positions). This requirement for a market maker is detailed in section 15c3-1, paragraph (c)(2)(x)F of the amended 1934 Securities Exchange Act. Under 15c3-1, paragraph (c)(2)(x)G, if the market maker's equity is negative, he is not permitted to trade, and all his existing positions must be liquidated.[2]

There is another computation that the clearing firm must make with regard to its market makers. Percentages, known as *haircuts*, are applied to the market maker's asset and liability values. This calculation provides dollar amounts to be deducted from the equity figure to arrive at a final equity figure or *haircut equity*. The size of an asset or liability haircut is meant to reflect the risk of the position. The option and underlying security haircuts are listed in paragraphs (c)(2)(x) and (c)(2)(vi)J, respectively, of 15c3-1. If the market maker's haircut equity is negative, then the clearing firm that guarantees the market maker must reduce its net capital by the amount of the short-fall.[3] The computation of haircut equity for a simple account is illustrated in Table 2.1.

Example of the Equity Calculation for a Market Maker

Equity = $10,000 + $5,000 + $1,500 − $1,200 − $2,000 = $13,300

$$\text{Haircut Equity} = \$13,300 - 0(\$10,000) - 0.15(\$5,000) - 0.5(\$1,500) \\ - 0.75(\$1,200) - 0.75(\$2,000) = \$9,400$$

---

2. The clearing firm will usually impose a more stringent equity requirement.

3. Regardless of market maker equity, the sum of all dollar haircuts across all market maker accounts may not exceed the clearing firm's net capital.

Collateralization of the Clearing Firm's Position

The clearing firm posts collateral for its positions with the OCC. The amount of collateral that must be deposited with the OCC, called *margin* for a clearing firm, is arrived at by calculating the change in the market value of each position for a hypothesized daily percentage change in the respective underlying security. Using a pricing model, such as that discussed in the next chapter, this calculation is performed for a variety of percentage changes. The position's margin is equal to the maximum loss in the position's value across all hypothesized percent changes in the underlying asset. Adding these figures across all positions produces the clearing firm's total margin requirement. The system by which the OCC arrives at these clearing firm margin requirements is called TIMS (Theoretical Intermarket Margin System).[4] Because a customer or a market maker may fail to provide the clearing firm with the collateral that it must post with the OCC to margin a new or old position, the clearing firm must meet a minimum capital requirement, which is set by the SEC.

2.4 Clearing Over-the-Counter (OTC) Option Trades

The matching process for OTC trades is similar to that of exchange traded options. After the trade occurs, the firm's back office, its paper processing center, confirms the details of the trade with the counterparty's back office. The items compared are (1) who bought and who sold, (2) put or call, (3) strike price, (4) exercise date, (5) quantity of options, (6) underlying security, (7) identification of traders and firms, (8) the timing of the premium payment, and (9) if, upon exercise, the long is to receive a cash payment, determined by the difference between the security's price and the strike price, in lieu of the securities, what security price should be used—the opening or the close? If the two firms have a master option agreement covering all such option trades, then (8) need not be confirmed between back offices, for this information is specified in the master agreement. If all information fields match, the back offices of the respective firms agree that the

---

4. Under a pilot program with the SEC, the TIMS is being extended to market maker accounts. A theoretical maximum loss is computed by applying the TIMS to the market maker's positions. This figure becomes the dollar haircut to be deducted from the account's equity to arrive at haircut equity. If the pilot program is deemed successful, the percentage haircuts presently listed in 15c3-1 paragraph (c)(2)(x), such as 75 percent on a short option position, will be discarded.

trade is good, and each sends a paper confirmation to the other. Since an OTC trade does not take place under the auspices of an exchange, there is no third party to guarantee the financial performance of the counterparties to the trade. This requires that each party to the trade have some knowledge of the creditworthiness of the opposite party. The party whose credit is stronger will usually require collateral from the opposite party to the trade. The SEC has set the corresponding capital to be maintained for the life of the trade; it is given in 15c3-1.

Chapter 3

Stock Option Pricing

*T*HIS CHAPTER begins with a presentation and discussion of several propositions that relate to option prices or that provide information on the question of option exercise. These propositions either furnish some guidance as to the relative pricing of a call and a put, provide upper and lower bounds on call and put prices, or indicate the circumstances under which an option should not be exercised. In proving these propositions, the only principle that need be invoked about investor behavior is that an individual prefers more wealth to less. Besides the standard academic assumptions with regard to taxes, transaction costs, and differences between lending and borrowing rates, namely that there are none, the only market condition that must be met in proving these propositions is that there be no-riskless arbitrage opportunities. A riskless arbitrage is any trading strategy that is characterized by a nonnegative cash flow now and positive cash flows later, or a positive cash flow now and nonnegative cash flows later. The no-riskless-arbitrage condition is a necessary condition for market equilibrium. Because of the relatively weak conditions assumed in arriving at these propositions, they are sometimes referred to as *pricing results from minimum information.*

The main part of the chapter is directed toward the derivation, discussion, and illustration of a formula that gives an exact price for an option: the binomial model for option pricing. A European option price obtained from the binomial model will converge to the Black-Scholes option price if trading is assumed to be continuous. The remaining sections explain some revisions to this pricing theory that are necessitated by recent empirical evidence.

3.1 Option Pricing Results from Minimum Information

Put-Call Parity: A Relative Pricing Relation between a European Put and a European Call

Let C, P, i, S, K, T, and D, respectively, symbolize the call and put premiums, the annual interest rate (in decimal form), the current stock price, the options' common strike and time to expiration (measured in years), and the present value of the stock's cash dividends through expiration day. In the derivation of this relationship, the dividends paid through expiration day are assumed to be perfectly predictable.

Today, at $t = 0$, you buy the call, sell the put, short the stock, and lend at rate i the present value of the strike, $K/(1 + i)^T$, plus the present value of the dividends, D. The net cash flow from this set of transactions is $-C + P + S - K(1 + i)^{-T} - D$. The symbol t has been introduced to index time; $t = 0$ marks the current date and $t = T$ the options' expiration date.[1]

Because these are European options, we are not concerned with the cash flow consequences of a possible early exercise of the short put, so we can focus on the portfolio's value at expiration day. Table 3.1 sets out the cash flows of the portfolio's components at $t = T$ for the two possible occurrences, $S_T \leq K$ and $S_T > K$.

Table 3.1   Portfolio's Component and Total Cash Flows on Expiration Day $(t = T)$

Stock Price at Expiration	$S_T \leq K$	$S_T > K$
Position		
Long Call	0	$S_T - K$
Short Put	$-(K - S_T)$	0
Short Stock	$-S_T$	$-S_T$
Loan of $K/(1 + i)^T$	K*	K
Loan of D**	0	0
Total	0	0
*$[K/(1 + i)^T][1 + i]^T = K$		
**Cash flows from this loan are used to pay the dividends owed on the short stock.		

---

1. Interest can be compounded discretely or continuously. The expression $(1 + i)^T$ represents discrete compounding. In subsequent sections, you will see the expression e^{iT}, which represents continuous compounding.

Since the cash flows of this portfolio on expiration day sum to zero in all situations, the sum of the current cash flows generated through construction of this portfolio must be zero; otherwise a riskless arbitrage would be available.[2] Therefore,

$$-C + P + S - K/(1 + i)^T - D = 0$$

or

$$C = P + S - K(1 + i)^{-T} - D$$

This is the *put-call parity* relationship. By the way, the relationship could have been derived by effecting the opposite set of transactions at $t = 0$: sell the call, buy the put, buy the stock, borrow $K/(1 + i)^T + D$.

The put-call parity relation teaches us something about the characteristics of a call. First, if dividends are increased, then D, the present value of these dividends, increases. Other things equal, this lowers the call's value. Intuitively, a higher dividend lowers the stock's value, which, all other things equal, leads to a fall in the call's value. Second, set $D = 0$ and look at the altered put-call parity relation:

$$C = P + S - K(1 + i)^{-T}$$

The right-hand side of this equation contains a long stock position, protected against a decline by a long put—the insurance put case from Chapter 1. In addition, the term $K(1 + i)^{-T}$ appears on the right-hand side, representing the amount that must be borrowed in order to make the investment in the stock plus put equal to the investment in the call. So buying a call can be interpreted as equivalent to buying a stock, levering that position, and buying a put to provide insurance. The long is willing to pay, in addition to the call's intrinsic value, the time premium, because the call gives the long something he cannot

---

2. If the portfolio generated a positive cash flow at $t = 0$, then arbitragers would attempt to undertake this set of transactions, knowing that they would receive a positive current cash flow and pay nothing at $t = T$. As they attempted to undertake these transactions, prices would quickly change until the arbitrage opportunity disappeared. On the other hand, if the transactions at $t = 0$ generated a negative cash flow, arbitragers would simply undertake the reverse transactions, generating a positive cash flow at $t = 0$ and nothing at $t = T$. As this is attempted, prices adjust, removing the arbitrage opportunity.

obtain through the straight stock purchase: insurance and leverage. With an exact pricing model for options, it can be seen that as these two attributes, leverage and insurance, decrease, so does the time premium. This occurs as the option goes deep-in-the-money. As the call's premium is driven up by the increase of intrinsic value, the long's investment in the call increases and, commensurately, his leverage decreases. In addition, the more invested in the call, the more can be lost if the stock suffers a severe fall in price, and the less valuable is the insurance characteristic of the call.

Similar statements may be made about a put with respect to dividends and the factors determining the put's time premium. Simply use the put-call parity relation to isolate the put and study the other side of the equation. A long put can be viewed as short a stock with an insurance call plus lending. Higher dividends raise the put's value.

The Trader's View of Put-Call Parity

A trader uses the put-call parity relation to arbitrage, but he sees it in a way that is somewhat different than the form the proof took in the previous section. To illustrate, assume the call is overpriced. The trader believes that if he can effect a set of transactions at current prices in the call, the put, and the stock, then he can earn a riskless profit. The trader reasons that if he sells a call and buys a put, both European with the same strike and time to expiration, he is effectively agreeing to sell the underlying stock on expiration at the strike price, K. His logic is that if the stock price finishes above the strike price, then the call that he is short is exercised by the holder, and upon delivering the stock, he receives payment equal to the strike; his long put expires worthless. Conversely, if the stock price finishes below the strike, the trader exercises his long put, and upon delivering the stock, he receives payment equal to the strike; the short call expires worthless. No matter where the stock price ends up, the short call–long put position locks in a sale price of K for delivery at $t = T$. The trader recognizes, however, that this commitment to sell the stock at K on expiration is risky, for if the stock to be delivered should rise, then a loss occurs. To avert this risk, he buys the stock at the same time as he sells the call and buys the put. At this point, his total *cost* is $S + P - C$. If the stock pays dividends, he borrows the present value of the dividends and lets the future dividend flow retire the loan. After borrowing the present value of the dividend stream to expiration, his cost is $S + P - C - D$. He borrows this amount from his clearing firm or bank. On expiration day, the balance due on the loan will be $(S + P - C - D)(1 + i)^T$. Since he will be delivering the stock at K, he will profit if $K - (S + P - C - D)(1 + i)^T > 0$. This arbitrage transaction is known as a *conversion*. It is *unprofitable to undertake a conversion if* $K - (S + P - C - D)(1 + i)^T \leq 0$.

If, instead, the call is relatively underpriced, then the trader buys the call and sells the put. The purchase of the call and the simultaneous sale of the put lock him into the purchase of the stock at K on expiration day. If the stock price finishes above the strike price, then he exercises the call, receiving the stock and paying K; the short put expires worthless. If the stock price finishes below the strike price, then the put that he is short is exercised by the holder, and upon receiving the stock, the trader pays K; his call is allowed to expire. Therefore, whatever the level of the stock price on expiration day, the long call–short put position commits the trader to the purchase of the stock at a price of K. He understands that this commitment to purchase the stock at K is risky, for if the stock price should fall, then a loss is possible. To avert this possibility of loss, he shorts the stock at the same time that he buys the call and sells the put. At this point, his total *revenue* is $S + P - C$—the amount received on the short sale of the stock and the sale of the put exceeds the cost of the call. If the stock pays dividends, the trader lends the present value of the dividends and uses the loan's future cash flows to pay the dividends on the short stock position as they come due. After lending the present value of the dividend stream to expiration, his revenue is $S + P - C - D$. He lends this amount to his clearing firm or bank. On expiration day, his deposit has grown to $(S + P - C - D)(1 + i)^T$. On that same day, $t = T$, he will receive the stock, paying K, and use it to cover his short stock position. He will profit if $(S + P - C - D)(1 + i)^T - K > 0$. This arbitrage transaction is known as a *reverse conversion*. *It is unprofitable to undertake a reverse conversion if* $(S + P - C - D)$ $\times (1 + i)^T - K \leq 0$.

If it is unprofitable to undertake a conversion, then

$$K - (S + P - C - D)(1 + i)^T \leq 0 \qquad (3.1)$$

or

$$C \leq P + S - K(1 + i)^{-T} - D$$

If it is unprofitable to undertake a reverse conversion, then

$$(S + P - C - D)(1 + i)^T - K \leq 0$$

or

$$C \geq P + S - K(1 + i)^{-T} - D \tag{3.2}$$

For there to be no possibility of a riskless arbitrage from the *relative* mispricing that characterizes conversions and reverse conversions, conditions (3.1) and (3.2) must simultaneously hold. The only way for that to be possible is for the equality to hold in both (3.1) and (3.2). That is,

$$C = P + S - K(1 + i)^{-T} - D$$

But this is the put-call parity relation.[3]

The Box: A Parity Pricing Relation for Pairs of European Puts and European Calls

Given two calls and two puts having the same time to expiration, T, but with strikes K_2 and K_1 ($K_2 > K_1$) and premiums of C_1, C_2, P_1, and P_2, where the subscripts indicate the strike, a no-arbitrage equality exists between these option premiums and the difference in strikes. Floor traders continuously calculate $C_1 - C_2 + P_2 - P_1$ and compare this amount to the present value of $K_2 - K_1$. If the former amount is less (greater) than the latter, the trader buys (sells) the K_1 call and K_2 put and sells (buys) the K_2 call and K_1 put. The former set of transactions is known as *buying the box*; the opposite set is referred to as *selling the box*. Either set of transactions may lead to a riskless arbitrage. The no-arbitrage environment is characterized by an equality relation between these pairs of option prices and the difference in strikes. Specifically, the no-arbitrage condition is

$$C_1 - C_2 + P_2 - P_1 = (1 + i)^{-T}[K_2 - K_1]$$

---

3. As a practical matter, the arbitrager cannot ignore taxes, transaction costs, and differences between lending and borrowing rates. They become side calculations to the arbitrager, who must decide whether the basic proposition has been sufficiently violated to warrant undertaking the necessary set of arbitrage transactions.

Table 3.2 Cash Flows at Expiration from Buying the Box

Stock Price at Expiration	$S_T < K_1$	$K_1 \leq S_T \leq K_2$	$K_2 < S_T$
Position			
Long K_1 Call	0	$+ (S_T - K_1)$	$+ (S_T - K_1)$
Short K_2 Call	0	0	$- (S_T - K_2)$
Long K_2 Put	$+ (K_2 - S_T)$	$+ (K_2 - S_T)$	0
Short K_1 Put	$- (K_1 - S_T)$	0	0
Total	$+ (K_2 - K_1)$	$+ (K_2 - K_1)$	$+ (K_2 - K_1)$

To see why, assume the trader buys the box. The payoffs at $t = T$ are delineated in Table 3.2.

For any stock price level on expiration day, the payoff is $+ (K_2 - K_1)$. Therefore, if the cost of buying the box and financing its cost is less than the difference in strikes, a riskless arbitrage exists. Thus

$$(C_1 - C_2 + P_2 - P_1)(1 + i)^T < [K_2 - K_1]$$

cannot describe a no-arbitrage environment. Analogously,

$$(C_1 - C_2 + P_2 - P_1)(1 + i)^T > [K_2 - K_1]$$

cannot be descriptive of a no-arbitrage environment, because traders could sell the box and lend the money until T, more than covering the certain outflow of $(K_2 - K_1)$ at $t = T$. If neither of the above inequalities describes a no-arbitrage state, then the equality must.

3.2 Other Distribution-Free Option Pricing Conditions

The put-call parity formula and the box relationship that was just derived are known as distribution-free restrictions on option prices. Such results are classified under that title because they were derived without making any assumptions about the probability distribution of the stock price.

Some of the other distribution-free restrictions for American calls and puts, derived by Merton (1973), are as follows:

$$S \geq C \geq \max\left\{0,\ S - K,\ S - K(1 + i)^{-T} - D\right\}$$

$$C(S,K_1,T) \geq C(S,K_2,T) \qquad \text{where} \qquad K_2 > K_1$$

$$C(S,K_1,T) - C(S,K_2,T) \leq K_2 - K_1 \qquad \text{where} \qquad K_2 > K_1$$

$$C(S,K_2,T) \leq \left(\frac{K_3 - K_2}{K_3 - K_1}\right)C(S,K_1,T) + \left(\frac{K_2 - K_1}{K_3 - K_1}\right)C(S,K_3,T) \qquad \text{where} \qquad K_3 > K_2 > K_1$$

$$C(S,K,T_2) \geq C(S,K,T_1) \qquad \text{where} \qquad T_2 > T_1$$

where $C(S,K,T)$ symbolizes the premium of an American call with strike K and time to expiration T written on an underlying stock with current price S. For each of the above propositions and those that will follow, the same manner of proof is employed. Start by assuming that the proposition is false and that the contrary proposition is true. Then show that this contrary assumption leads to a riskless arbitrage. This means that the contrary proposition cannot describe a no-arbitrage situation and therefore that the original proposition must be true.

We demonstrate the method of proof by using it to obtain the third of the above propositions, $C(S,K_1,T) - C(S,K_2,T) \leq K_2 - K_1$ for $K_2 > K_1$.

PROOF.

1. Assume the contrary of the proposition to be proved is true. The contrary is $C(S,K_1,T) - C(S,K_2,T) > K_2 - K_1$. Rewrite it as $C(S,K_1,T) - C(S,K_2,T) - (K_2 - K_1) > 0$.

2. Now look for transactions that will generate the identical cash flow sum that appears on the left-hand side of the inequality. To obtain a positive cash flow (an inflow) equal to $C(S,K_1,T)$, sell the K_1 call; to obtain a negative cash flow (an outflow) equal to $-C(S,K_2,T)$, buy the K_2 call; and, finally, to generate a negative cash flow equal to $-(K_2 - K_1)$, lend $(K_2 - K_1)$ dollars. The net current cash flow from this set of transactions is $C(S,K_1,T) - C(S,K_2,T) - (K_2 - K_1)$, which we know to be positive by the assumption of the contrary and the equivalent inequality expression found in step 1. So we have a set of transactions that generates a positive current cash flow.

3. Check to see if this set of transactions results in nonnegative future cash flows. Since you are short the K_1 call, the owner of that call is in control as to the date when you are forced to unwind all

Table 3.3 Future Cash Flows

Situation	K_1 *Call Exercised* ($S' > K_1$)	K_1 *Call Not Exercised* ($S_T \leq K_1$)
Position		
Short K_1 Call	$-(S' - K_1)$	0
Long K_2 Call	$+(S' - K_2)$	0
Loan of $(K_2 - K_1)$	$(K_2 - K_1)$ + interest	$+(K_2 - K_1)$ + interest
Total Cash Flow	interest > 0	$+(K_2 - K_1)$ + interest > 0

parts of this arbitrage position. If and when the K_1 call is exercised, you must simultaneously rid yourself of all parts of the position; if part of the position was allowed to remain, then your arbitrage has turned into a speculative position. To check to see if this transaction set provides nonnegative future cash flows, consider two market cases: (i) The owner of the K_1 call exercises when the underlying stock price is S'; and (ii) the owner of the K_1 call lets it expire, at which point the underlying stock price is S_T. Table 3.3 lists the cash flows attached to each position and the total flows for cases (i) and (ii).

In both cases, the future cash flows are positive. So the contrary assumption leads to a riskless arbitrage and must be rejected. The original proposition is accepted. Notice that in case (i) of this step, it was assumed that the K_2 call is exercised rather than sold when the K_1 call is exercised. This is obviously the worst-case assumption from the arbitrager's point of view, because, if $S' - K_2 < 0$, he will not exercise, but instead will either sell the K_2 call or walk away from it. Nevertheless, under the most severe of profitability assumptions, future cash flows are nonnegative.[4]

---

4. For the $C \geq S - K$ part of the first of these propositions, the method of proof just described will not work. To see this, assume the contrary, $C < S - K$, and rearrange to $-C + S - K > 0$. This instructs us to buy the call, short the stock, and lend K, resulting in a positive cash flow today. However, suppose at some future time—say, expiration day—$S_T > K$, then the call is exercised. Then at this same time, the short is covered and the loan matures, providing cash flows, including those relating to the exercise of the call, of $+(S_T - K) - S_T -$ (dividends on short stock) $+ K +$ (interest on the loan) $= +$ (interest on the loan) $-$ (dividends of the short stock). If the dividends paid on the short stock position exceed the interest received on the loan of K, then the cash flows at $t = T$ are negative. In this instance, this form of proof fails. Instead, to prove the proposition $C \geq S - K$, a different tack must be employed. Again assume the contrary, $C < S - K$. But now simply buy the call, short the stock, and immediately exercise, paying K dollars to the call writer. Use the stock certificate received from the call's exercise to cover the short stock position. All obligations are now satisfied. The current net cash flow is $-C + S - K > 0$, by assumption of the contrary. Future cash flows are zero, since there are no outstanding financial positions. Positive cash flows today and zero future cash flows conform to the definition of a riskless arbitrage. Therefore, the contrary is rejected, and the proposition $C \geq S - K$ is accepted.

The following distribution-free restrictions are proved in the same manner:

1. If the present value of the dividends to be paid on the stock over the remaining life of the call is less than the present value of the interest that can be earned on an amount of money equal to the call's strike, do not exercise the call. Be careful. This is a proposition that provides the holder of the call a condition for *no exercise*. So, if the present value of the dividends is 2 and the present value of the interest on the strike, K, is 3, do not exercise. However, nothing can be gleaned from this proposition with regard to exercise if the present value of the dividends is 3 and the present value of the interest on the strike is 2.

2. A call should never be exercised at any time other than just prior to an ex-dividend day or expiration day. The proof of this proposition is particularly interesting because it requires an understanding that one does not exercise a call if its premium, C, exceeds its intrinsic value, $S - K$. This principle will be referred to often to illustrate the exact pricing of American options in later sections. For this reason and for the benefits that accrue from repeating a methodology, the proof that a call should not be exercised between ex-dividend dates is presented here.

PROOF.   The objective is to demonstrate that, on a day that is not an ex-dividend date, $C > S - K$. This means that the call can be sold for an amount that exceeds the proceeds received from exercise, the in-the-money amount. Recall the proposition

$$S \geq C \geq \max \{0, S - K, S - K(1 + i)^{-T} - D\}$$

Part of this restriction on the call's price is that $C \geq S - K$. So one of the following must hold: (i) $C > S - K$, or (ii) $C = S - K$. Suppose (ii) holds on a day between ex-dividend dates. Then we will show that a riskless arbitrage opportunity exists. Consequently, this case, $C = S - K$, must be rejected as descriptive of a no-arbitrage environment and $C > S - K$ accepted.

If $C = S - K$, then immediately undertake the following transactions: buy the call, paying C; borrow the stock certificate and sell it, receiving S; and deposit K in an interest-bearing account. The cash flows are $-C + S - K$, which sum to zero, since, by assumption,

$C = S - K$. Just prior to the ex-dividend date, unwind the position. Close the bank account, withdrawing K plus interest; exercise the call, paying K and receiving the stock certificate to cover the short position. All obligations are satisfied, and the net cash flow is K + interest $- K =$ interest > 0. Zero cash flow at the onset and a single future cash flow that is positive qualify this trading strategy as a riskless arbitrage. Therefore, $C \neq S - K$, and we reject case (ii), accepting by default case (i), $C > S - K$. This completes the proof.

It is important to note that if the arbitrager does not close out his position prior to the ex-dividend date, he could end up losing money. Come the ex-dividend day, the arbitrager becomes responsible for payment of the cash dividend on the short stock position, and this amount might exceed the interest earned on the deposit of K. Furthermore, since it is only economically sensible to exercise a call just prior to an ex-dividend date or on an expiration day, a call on a stock that pays no dividends will not be exercised prior to expiration day. (Of course, it might be sold.) Therefore, holding an American call on a non-dividend-paying stock is identical to holding a European call on that stock.

Whereas a deep-in-the-money American call on a non-dividend-paying stock will not be exercised prior to expiration, a deep-in-the-money American put might be exercised prior to expiration. Here is a numerical illustration—the numbers chosen are somewhat extreme—of a situation where the long put holder would exercise early. You are long a put with a strike of 100 and one year to expiration; the current stock price is one dollar and the one-year interest rate is 20%. Holding on to the put and not exercising, your maximum potential income would be one, if the stock price were to fall to zero. In contrast, if the put is immediately exercised, the cash flow of 99 can be invested at 20% for one year, providing income equal to 19.80. Clearly, the optimal strategy in this case is to "kill" the put by exercising. (Of course, you could sell it for 99, and the buyer could, in turn, sell it, but some buyer must exercise prior to expiration; otherwise the sure 19.80 would be lost for the potential of a one-dollar profit).

Why is a put, as opposed to a call, on a non-dividend-paying stock likely to be exercised? By not exercising a put, you are losing the interest on the strike. In contrast, once the call is exercised, money must be paid equal to the strike, resulting in an opportunity loss equal to the interest you could have earned by keeping those funds in the bank.

Concerning puts, the following distribution-free restrictions apply:[5]

$$K \geq P \geq \max \{0, K - S, K(1 + i)^{-T} + D - S\}$$

$$P(S,K_2,T) \geq P(S,K_1,T) \qquad \text{where} \qquad K_2 > K_1$$

$$P(S,K_2,T) - P(S,K_1,T) \leq K_2 - K_1 \qquad \text{where} \qquad K_2 > K_1$$

$$P(S,K_2,T) \leq \left(\frac{K_3 - K_2}{K_3 - K_1}\right)P(S,K_1,T) + \left(\frac{K_2 - K_1}{K_3 - K_1}\right)P(S,K_3,T) \qquad \text{where} \qquad K_3 > K_2 > K_1$$

$$P(S,K,T_2) \geq P(S,K,T_1) \qquad \text{where} \qquad T_2 > T_1$$

If the present value of the dividends to be paid on the stock over the remaining life of the put exceeds the present value of the interest on an amount of money equal to the strike, K, do not exercise. Again, this proposition provides a guide as to when *not* to exercise. It is not to be used in deciding when to exercise.

There is a put-call parity relation for American options. It is stated as two inequalities:

$$C(S,K,T) - S + K(1 + i)^{-T} \leq P(S,K,T) \leq C(S,K,T) - S + K + D$$

The proof of this last proposition is identical in form to that used in each of the preceding propositions.

3.3 The Multiplicative Binomial Option Pricing Model

The term *stochastic process* is used to describe the development of some observable variable through time in accordance with a probabi-

---

5. For the $P \geq K - S$ part of the first of these put propositions, the method of proof must be altered. If the method described earlier in the text is followed, you would find that the sign of the future cash flows from the arbitrage position formed by borrowing K and buying both the stock and the put is dependent on the relative size of the interest and dividend payments. If the dividend payments received outweigh the interest paid on K, future flows will be positive. But this may not be so—as in the case of a non-dividend-paying stock. So this arbitrage position is not riskless, and the proposition, $P \geq K - S$, would not be proved. Instead we must adopt the form of proof used in the earlier validation of the $C \geq S - K$ proposition (see footnote 4). In particular, buy the put and the stock, and immediately exercise the put upon purchase, delivering the stock. The current cash flow is $K - S - P$, which, by assumption of the contrary, is positive. Future cash flows are zero, so the proposition is proved.

listic law. Let us assume that the relevant variable is the stock price and that the probabilistic law controlling its evolution through time can be described as follows: If the current stock price is S, the probability that the stock price will rise and earn a rate of return r_u is q, and the probability that it will fall and earn a rate of return r_d is $(1 - q)$, where $r_u > r_d$. These are the only two possibilities; every other outcome has probability zero of occurring. The one-period stock price realizations (sample paths) and associated probabilities are depicted in Figure 3.1, where the constant multipliers, u and d, are defined as $u \equiv 1 + r_u$ and $d \equiv 1 + r_d$.

Whatever the outcome at $t = 1$—that is, whether the stock price is uS or dS—the probability that the stock price at $t = 2$ will be u times whatever it was at $t = 1$ is q; the probability that it will be d times whatever it was at $t = 1$ is $(1 - q)$. The two-period realizations are depicted in Figure 3.2. The points where the branches of this treelike structure connect are called *nodes*. The statistical summary of this probabilistic law is: (1) At each trial (period) there are two possible outcomes, a constant u times the preceding outcome's value or a constant d times the preceding outcome's value; (2) the probabilities of these outcomes at each trial (period) are q and $(1 - q)$, respectively; and (3) any trial's outcome is independent of the preceding trial's outcome. Such a stochastic process is called a *multiplicative binomial*. The option pricing model based on this stochastic process was developed by Cox, Ross, and Rubinstein (1979) based upon an idea provided by William Sharpe (1978).

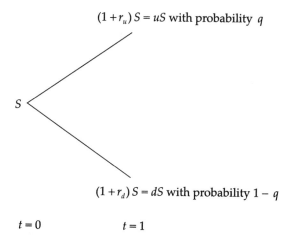

$$(1 + r_u)S = uS \text{ with probability } q$$

$$S$$

$$(1 + r_d)S = dS \text{ with probability } 1 - q$$

$t = 0 \qquad\qquad t = 1$

Figure 3.1 One-Period Stock Price Realizations

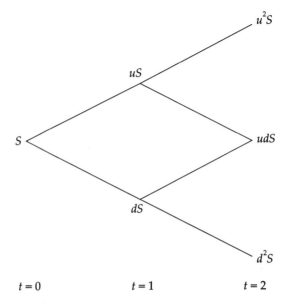

Figure 3.2 Two-Period Stock Price Realizations

There are other stochastic processes that could have been used to describe the evolution of the stock price. The choice of this particular one may at first appear rather arbitrary and the process somewhat coarse. After all, in any period the stock price may move to an infinite number of new levels. But if we make the period length very small, then this multiplicative binomial price distribution looks very much like the lognormal distribution of relative stock prices. Real stock price changes seem to adhere closely to this lognormal distribution. So the choice of the binomial can be defended, because in-the-limit i.e., as the measured period between price changes shrinks toward zero, the multiplicative binomial approaches the lognormal. Moreover, as the interval of time between stock price observations becomes smaller, the multiplicative binomial option pricing formula will converge to the Black-Scholes option pricing formula, a model that has found wide acceptance. See Black and Scholes 1973.

Pricing a One-Period Call on a Non-Dividend-Paying Stock

We use the notation introduced in the previous sections, except that for $(1 + i)$ the symbol r is substituted. From the information in

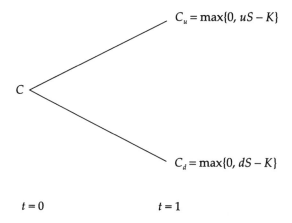

$$C_u = \max\{0,\, uS - K\}$$

$$C_d = \max\{0,\, dS - K\}$$

$t = 0 \qquad\qquad t = 1$

Figure 3.3 One-Period Call Payments

Figure 3.1, we construct the corresponding binomial tree for the call, where C denotes the unknown, current call premium, and C_u and C_d, respectively, denote the call's possible values at $t = 1$ if the stock price moves up to uS or down to dS. Since $t = 1$ is expiration day, C_u and C_d must equal the call's exercise values, max $\{0,\, uS - K\}$ in the stock's up state and max $\{0,\, dS - K\}$ in the down state. See Figure 3.3.

We now show that a portfolio comprised of n_s shares of the underlying stock and B dollars of riskless debt, paying interest of $i = r - 1$, can be formed that will exactly replicate the payoffs of the call at $t = 1$. If the stock price rises, then the replicating portfolio must be worth $n_s uS + Br$, but if the stock falls, the portfolio's value is $n_s dS + Br$. The terms $n_s uS$ and $n_s dS$, respectively, represent the value of the n_s shares in the up and down states. The Br term consists of the principal amount of the debt plus interest. Our objective is to select n_s and B so that the two portfolio values, respectively, equal the call's up state and down state values, C_u and C_d. This reasoning translates into the following algebraic statements:

$$n_s uS + Br = C_u$$

$$n_s dS + Br = C_d$$

Solving for n_s gives

$$n_s = \frac{C_u - C_d}{S(u - d)}$$

Using this result in either of the above equations provides the solution for *B*.

$$B = \frac{1}{r}\left[\frac{uC_d - dC_u}{u - d}\right]$$

If *B* is positive, we are lending; if *B* is negative, we are borrowing.

These expressions uniquely identify the replicating portfolio of stock and bonds (debt). Because there is no chance that the call will be exercised early (at $t = 0$)—recall that the stock will not pay a dividend at $t = 0$—then the call will be held to expiration. But its expiration values are exactly matched by the replicating portfolio's value at expiration. Consequently, at $t = 0$, the call's current value must equal the replicating portfolio's value; otherwise, a riskless arbitrage would be available. This gives

$$C = n_s S + B$$

Substituting the expressions we have found for n_s and *B*, we have

$$C = \frac{C_u - C_d}{u - d} + \frac{1}{r}\left[\frac{uC_d - dC_u}{u - d}\right]$$

Rearranging terms, this expression for *C* can be written as

$$C = \frac{1}{r}\left\{\left[\frac{r - d}{u - d}\right]C_u + \left[\frac{u - r}{u - d}\right]C_d\right\}$$

This is the equation that defines the one-period call's value.

There is something of interest to note about this equation. First, the terms inside the brackets that multiply C_u and C_d add to 1. Furthermore, it can be shown that *r* must lie between *u* and *d*. To prove this, follow the form of the proofs used to obtain the distribution-free results. Assume the contrary situations and show that they lead to riskless arbitrages.

PROOF.

Case 1: $u > d \geq r$: At $t = 0$, borrow *S* dollars for one period at the riskless rate and purchase a share of the stock. The net cash flow from these transactions is zero at $t = 0$ ($+S$ from borrowing and $-S$ due to the stock purchase). At $t = 1$, if the up state occurs, sell the stock at uS and repay rS, netting a positive amount equal to $(u - r)S$. If the down state occurs, again sell the stock and repay the borrowing. Since $d \geq r$, the net profit, $(d - r)S$, cannot be less than zero. As long as there is a positive probability that the up state will occur, this is a riskless arbitrage.[6] Therefore, the contrary, $u > d \geq r$, must be rejected.

Case 2: $r \geq u > d$:   At $t = 0$, short the stock, receiving S dollars, and deposit the funds in an interest-paying instrument. The net cash flow is zero. At $t = 1$, you receive rS upon the debt instrument's maturity and use that to pay either the uS or dS owed on the short stock position. If d obtains, the net is $(r - d)S > 0$. If u occurs, then the net is $(r - u)S \geq 0$. Again, as long as the probability that d will occur is positive, the arbitrage will be undertaken and prices will be altered. Thus, the contrary, $r \geq u > d$, must be rejected.

Since r lies between u and d, then $(r - d)/(u - d)$ and $(u - r)/(u - d)$ are both positive, and because the sum of these two terms is one, they have the properties of probabilities. So define

$$p \equiv \frac{r - d}{u - d} \qquad (1 - p) \equiv \frac{u - r}{u - d}$$

as the *pseudo*probabilities of the call's having value C_u or C_d, respectively. Recall that the real probabilities are q and $(1 - q)$. Now, using these definitions of p and $(1 - p)$, the call value equation may be rewritten as

$$C = \frac{1}{r}[pC_u + (1 - p)C_d] \qquad\qquad (3.3)$$

It is this valuation expression that will be used for the pricing of one-period calls and also iteratively used for the pricing of calls that expire many periods into the future. What is particularly interesting is that nowhere in this call price equation does q appear. This implies that traders can differ on the probability of a stock price rise and yet agree upon the call price. Additionally, nowhere in the expression is there

6. If there was zero probability that the up state could occur, then either the stock would dominate the riskless asset or be identical to it; both are uninteresting cases.

a parameter that can be identified as describing the risk tolerances of market participants. So individuals with quite different risk preferences can agree upon this formula for the call's current value.

This last point means that a risk neutral individual should arrive at this same call valuation formula. A risk neutral individual does not require a higher rate of return to be induced to accept a more risky investment. In a world with only risk neutral investors, the expected rate of return on any asset equals the riskless rate, i. With regard to the rate of return on the underlying asset, this means that

$$q(u - 1) + (1 - q)(d - 1) = (r - 1) = i$$

which implies that

$$q = \frac{r - d}{u - d} = p \quad (1 - q) = \frac{u - r}{u - d} = (1 - p)$$

The risk neutral investor values an asset by first calculating the expected value of its payoffs and then discounting by the riskless rate. Applying this valuation methodology to the call gives

$$\frac{1}{(1 + i)}[qC_u + (1 - q)C_d] = \frac{1}{r}[pC_u + (1 - p)C_d]$$

Remember that q equals p in a risk neutral world. The risk neutral individual arrives at the binomial call pricing formula (3.3) by simply discounting the call's expected value by the riskless rate. This insight, provided by Cox and Ross (1976), gives us a simple and direct method for valuing European options: act as a risk neutral investor with q set to $(r - d)/(u - d) \equiv p$.

Pricing a Call on a Dividend-Paying Stock

If the stock's ex-dividend date occurred at $t = 0$, then early exercise is a possibility. Now the call owner must decide whether to retain the call, "keep it alive," until $t = 1$, and receive whatever value obtains or to exercise the call, "killing it," at $t = 0$. He will choose the action that returns him the greatest addition to wealth. The last expression of the preceding section provides the current value of those future

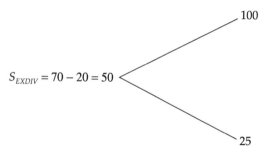

$S_{EXDIV} = 70 - 20 = 50$

100

25

Figure 3.4 Stock Prices: A Numerical Illustration

call values, C_u and C_d. The value of exercising the call today is $S - K$. The call holder will exercise if

$$S - K > \frac{1}{r}[pC_u + (1 - p)C_d]$$

If rational pricing behavior is the rule, then the call price at $t = 0$ will be bid up to the maximum of the values provided by these expressions. That is, the American call's value is

$$C = \max \left\{ S - K, \frac{1}{r}[pC_u + (1 - p)C_d] \right\} \qquad (3.4)$$

Numerical Illustration   Let $S = 70$, $K = 40$, $r = 1.1$, $u = 2$, $d = 0.5$, and the dividend paid today, $t = 0$, be 20 per share. Calculate C. The stock's binomial tree appears in Figure 3.4.

Notice that the new prices at $t = 1$ are computed from the ex-dividend stock price at $t = 0$. The call's tree appears in Figure 3.5. The call should be immediately exercised.

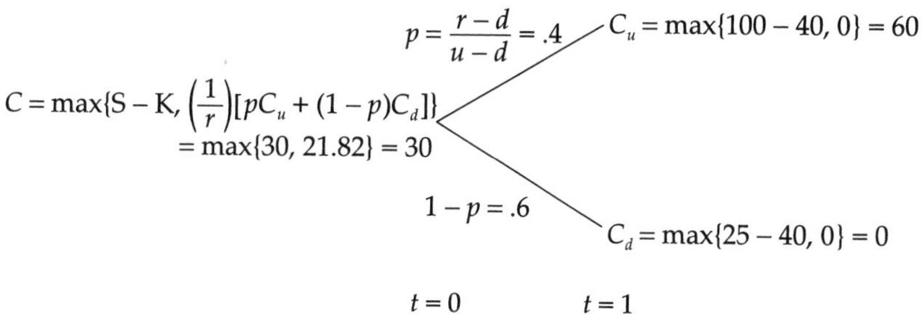

$$p = \frac{r - d}{u - d} = .4 \qquad C_u = \max\{100 - 40, 0\} = 60$$

$$C = \max\{S - K, \left(\frac{1}{r}\right)[pC_u + (1 - p)C_d]\}$$
$$= \max\{30, 21.82\} = 30$$

$$1 - p = .6$$

$$C_d = \max\{25 - 40, 0\} = 0$$

$$t = 0 \qquad t = 1$$

Figure 3.5 A Numerical Illustration of Call Payouts

Pricing a One-Period Put

If the put is European, then, following the same reasoning used in the case of the call, we would arrive at the following valuation equation for the put:

$$P = \frac{1}{r}[pP_u + (1 - p)P_d] \tag{3.5}$$

where P_u and P_d, respectively, symbolize the put's value in the stock's up state, max $\{0, K - uS\}$, and in its down state, max $\{0, K - dS\}$. For an American put, early exercise may be more valuable than retaining the put until expiration day. Therefore, at each moment, the put holder must compare the put's value if exercised, $K - S$, to its unexercised value, given by equation (3.5). If $K - S$ exceeds the unexercised value, then exercise commences. Rational pricing behavior dictates that the put premium will be bid up to the maximum of the values given by these two expressions. Thus the American put's value is

$$P = \max\left\{K - S, \frac{1}{r}[pP_u + (1 - p)P_d]\right\} \tag{3.6}$$

Numerical Illustration Let S, the ex-dividend price at $t = 0$, be 50, with $K = 50$, $r = 1.1$, $u = 2$, and $d = 0.5$. Then

$$P = \max\left\{50 - 50, \frac{1}{1.1}[.4\max\{0, 50 - 100\} + .6\max\{0, 50 - 25\}]\right\}$$
$$= 13.63$$

A Pricing Formula for a Two-Period Call on a Non-Dividend-Paying Stock

Figure 3.6 contains a tree of the possible call values at $t = 0$, $t = 1$, and $t = 2$. Look back to Figure 3.2, which is a diagram of possible stock values for the two-period case. The call's values at $t = 2$ are $C_{uu} = \max\{0, u^2S - K\}$, $C_{ud} = \max\{0, udS - K\}$, and $C_{dd} = \max\{0, d^2S - K\}$. The manner in which we proceed to solve for C is to start at $t = 2$, the expiration date, and work our way back to $t = 0$, backing up one period at a time.

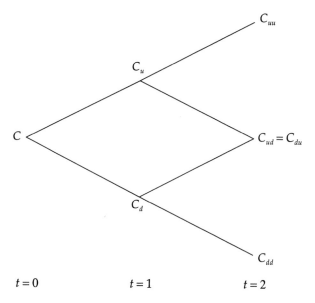

C_{uu}

C_u

C

$C_{ud} = C_{du}$

C_d

C_{dd}

$t = 0$ $\qquad\qquad$ $t = 1$ $\qquad\qquad$ $t = 2$

Figure 3.6 A Two-Period Call Value Tree

Begin by stepping back to the C_u node or to the C_d node and look ahead to $t = 2$. If the C_u node is chosen, then, looking ahead to $t = 2$, we see that the problem of solving for C_u is a one-period problem. Applying (3.3), the solution in terms of C_{uu} and C_{ud} is given by

$$C_u = \frac{1}{r}[pC_{uu} + (1 - p)C_{ud}] \qquad\qquad (3.7)$$

Similar reasoning gives

$$C_d = \frac{1}{r}[pC_{ud} + (1 - p)C_{dd}] \qquad\qquad (3.8)$$

Now back up to the $t = 0$ node. Looking ahead to $t = 1$, we again see a one-period problem, to which we again apply (3.3), obtaining

$$C = \frac{1}{r}[pC_u + (1 - p)C_d] \qquad\qquad (3.9)$$

Substituting for C_u and C_d from (3.7) and (3.8) into (3.9) gives the formula for the value of a two-period call on a non-dividend-paying stock.

$$C = \frac{1}{r^2}[p^2 C_{uu} + 2p(1 - p)C_{ud} + (1 - p)^2 C_{dd}] \qquad (3.10)$$

or, equivalently,

$$C = \frac{1}{r^2}[p^2 \max \{0, u^2 S - K\} + 2p(1 - p) \max \{0, udS - K\} \qquad (3.11)$$
$$+ (1 - p)^2 \max \{0, d^2 S - K\}]$$

We could apply this iterative technique to an n-period call and arrive at

$$C = \frac{1}{r^n}\sum_{j=0}^{n}\frac{n!}{j!(n - j)!}p^j(1 - p)^{n - j} \max \{0, u^j d^{n - j}S - K\} \qquad (3.12)$$

Reference will be made to this valuation expression for an *n*-period call on a non-dividend-paying stock—effectively a European call—when we discuss the Black-Scholes price expression for a European call.

Observe that since *p* equals the risk neutral probability, the valuation expressions for the two-period and *n*-period calls alternatively could have been obtained by multiplying each path's terminal payoff by the risk neutral probability of that path's occurring, adding the products and discounting the sum back to the present, using the riskless rate. This method will not work for American options, since at each node there is an early exercise choice. It is only after one makes that choice that one knows the value that must be multiplied by that path's probability.

Numerical Valuation of a Two-Period American Call and a Two-Period American Put by Iteration

Suppose $S = 50$, $K = 40$, $u = 2$, $d = 0.5$, $r = 1.1$, and the underlying stock pays a dividend of 10 at $t = 1$. The stock and call value trees appear in Figure 3.7. At $t = 1$, two numbers appear at each node of the stock price tree; the lower number represents the ex-dividend stock price. Exercise of a call occurs prior to the time that the stock goes ex-dividend, while the put is exercised after the stock goes ex-dividend. This means that the exercise value of the call is calculated as the difference between the stock price prior to the ex-dividend moment and the strike price. However, the relevant stock price to use in computing the next period's stock prices is this period's ex-dividend stock price.

Notice that in this case of a dollar dividend, $C_{ud} \neq C_{du}$. If, on the other hand, the dividend paid is proportional to the stock price, then $C_{ud} = C_{du}$. Continuing with the case at hand, we see that $p = 0.4$ and

$$C_u = \max\left\{100 - 40, \frac{1}{1.1}[.4(140) + .6(5)]\right\} = 60$$

$$C_d = \max\left\{25 - 40, \frac{1}{1.1}[.4(0) + .6(0)]\right\} = 0$$

Then

$$C = \max\left\{50 - 40, \frac{1}{1.1}[.4(60) + .6(0)]\right\} = 21.82$$

Note that the upper node at $t = 1$ of the call tree in Figure 3.7 is marked "ex." This is done so that, as time evolves, we know to exercise should we reach that node.

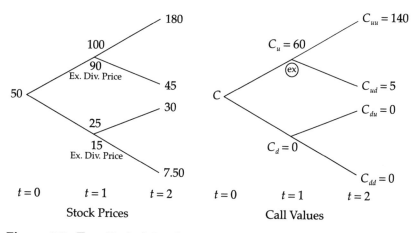

Figure 3.7 Two-Period Stock and Call Values

The American put value is computed in an identical manner. Consider an at-the-money put with $S = 50$, $K = 50$, $u = 2$, $d = 0.5$, $r = 1.1$, and a dividend of 10 to be paid at $t = 1$. The stock price tree is the same as in the previous example. The put's values at the corresponding nodes appear in Figure 3.8. Notice that the lower node is marked "ex."

The above examples illustrate how the value of any American equity option can be calculated. If the problem is to calculate the value of a nine-month option on a dividend-paying stock, begin by dividing the nine months into n periods—9 months, 39 weeks, days, hours, etc. Of course, u, d, and r must be adjusted to be compatible with the length of the period chosen. For example, if the period of subdivision is one day, then u and d represent the one-day stock price multipliers and r represents one plus the daily interest rate. The finer the subdivision of the time to expiration—that is, the more periods—the more accurate the option value calculated using the iterative technique on the binomial lattice. The problem remains of how to obtain numbers for u, d, and r.

Estimating u, d, and r

Earlier we said that as the measured period between stock price changes shrinks toward zero, the multiplicative binomial converges

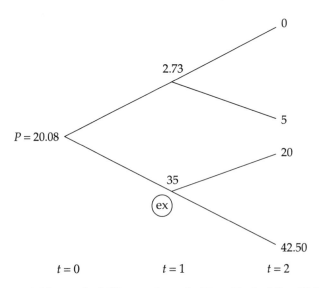

Figure 3.8   A Numerical Illustration of a Two-Period Put Value Tree

to a normal in the variable $\ln(S_T/S)$, the natural logarithm of the ratio of the expiration day stock price to the current day stock price, with mean μ_T and variance σ_T^2. These symbols are statistically defined as

$$\mu_T = E\left[\ln\left(\frac{S_T}{S}\right)\right]$$

and

$$\sigma_T^2 = E\left[\left(\ln\left(\frac{S_T}{S}\right) - \mu\right)^2\right]$$

where E is the expectation operator and T is measured in years or fractions of a year. This convergence to the normal distribution in $\ln(S_T/S)$, or, equivalently, the lognormal distribution in (S_T/S), is what one would hope for, since empirical studies find that this variable, which can be thought of as a continuously compounded rate of return over the period T, tends to be normally distributed.[7]

If the binomial is to converge to the lognormal distribution of stock price returns with mean μ_T and variance σ_T^2, then the u, d, and q parameters of the n-period binomial model must be chosen so that the mean and variance of the binomial model converge to μ_T and σ_T^2, respectively. One way to accomplish this is to select

$$u = e^{\sigma\sqrt{T/n}} \qquad d = 1/u \qquad q = \frac{1}{2} + \frac{1}{2}\left(\frac{\mu}{\sigma}\right)\sqrt{\frac{T}{n}}$$

where μ and σ are the mean and the standard deviation of the *annualized* rate of return of the stock. They represent the expected value and volatility of $\ln(S_T/S)$, if S_T is observed one year after S is observed. Estimates for μ and σ would be obtained from stock price data. (If risk neutral probabilities are desired, substitute the riskless rate i for μ.)

Example: Estimating u and d Given σ   The binomial pricing model does not require an estimate of q. All that is required is an

---

7. Let g be the continuously compounded rate of return applied to S to obtain S_T. Then g is defined by $S_T = Se^g$ or $g = \ln(S_T/S)$. Of course, g is a random variable, since S_T is a random variable.

estimate of σ, the standard deviation of the annual rate of return. The usual procedure is to estimate the standard deviation of the daily rate of return. That is for $T = 1$, compute the standard deviation of $\ln(S_1/S)$. Label it σ_1. Assuming that daily rates of return are independent of each other, that is, the observed rate of return on any single day does not provide probabilistic information about any future rate of return, then the relation between the standard deviation of the annual return, σ, and the standard deviation of the daily return, σ_1, is $\sigma = \sigma_1 \sqrt{250}$—assuming 250 trading days in the year.[8] Say $\sigma_1 = 0.01264911$; then $\sigma = 0.2$. Suppose T is one year, and you wish to divide that year into weeks for binomial pricing purposes; then $T = 1$ and $n = 52$. The corresponding u and d values are

$$u = e^{0.2\sqrt{(1/52)}} = 1.028123 \qquad d = 1/1.028123 = 0.972646$$

We close out this section by reminding you that if you are given an annual interest rate and you have a three-month option to be priced using weekly subdivisions, then you need a weekly interest rate. The relation between the interest rate applicable to each of the n periods and the annual interest rate is

$$period\ interest\ rate = (1 + annual\ interest\ rate)^{1/n} - 1$$

If the annual interest is 10%, then the weekly rate is 0.183%.

3.4 The Black-Scholes Model as a Limiting Case of the Binomial Model

As the trading interval (the time between stock price observations) shrinks, the binomial formula (3.12) for the value of a European call on a non-dividend-paying stock will converge to the Black-Scholes formula:

$$C = SN(d_1) - e^{-iT}KN(d_2)$$

where i is the annual interest rate and $N(d_1)$ represents the probability of a normally distributed variable having a value less than d_1. Graphi-

---

8. This follows from the property that the variance of a sum of independent variables equals the sum of the variances of these variables.

cally, $N(d_1)$ is the area under the standard normal density function to the left of d_1 (see Figure 3.9). The arguments d_1 and d_2 are given here:

$$d_1 = \frac{\ln\left(\frac{S}{K}\right) + \left(i + \frac{\sigma^2}{2}\right)T}{\sigma\sqrt{T}}$$

$$d_2 = d_1 - \sigma\sqrt{T}$$

All other symbols have been previously defined.

The variance of the T-year return is $T\sigma^2$ when the variance of the one-year return is σ^2. The corresponding standard deviation of the rate of return for that T-year period is $\sigma\sqrt{T}$. So the $\sigma\sqrt{T}$ term in the denominator of the d_1 expression is the standard deviation of the underlying stock's continuous rate of return for the time interval T, the call's time to expiration.

Given a pricing formula for a European call, an expression for a European put with the same strike price and time to expiration as the call and written on the same underlying stock can be obtained through application of the put-call parity formula. Rewriting that formula for the continuous case and recalling that the stock does not pay dividends, we have

$$C = P + S - Ke^{-iT}$$

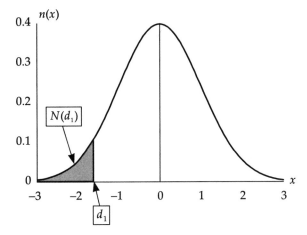

Figure 3.9 The Normal Density Function

Substituting the expression for C and solving for P yields

$$P = -S[1 - N(d_1)] + e^{-iT}K[1 - N(d_2)]$$

A Numerical Illustration Using the Black-Scholes Model

We calculate the premium of a one-month European call on a non-dividend-paying stock, where $S = 40$, $K = 40$, $\sigma = 0.20$, $i = 0.05$, and $T = 0.0833$, as follows:

$$d_1 = \frac{\ln\left(\frac{40}{40}\right) + (0.05 + 0.020)0.0833}{0.20\sqrt{0.0833}} = 0.1010$$

$$d_2 = 0.1010 - 0.20\sqrt{0.0833} = 0.0433$$

Using the standard cumulative normal table, $N(0.1010) = 0.5402$ and $N(0.0433) = 0.5173$. The call's value is

$$C = 40(0.5402) - (0.9958)40(0.5173) = 1.0029$$

Employing the put-call parity formula, the corresponding put's value is

$$P = 1.0029 - 40 + 40(0.9958) = 0.8349$$

These numbers illustrate a point. Because the put holder cannot exercise until expiration day, he must forgo the interest on the strike until expiration day. The European call holder is earning interest on the strike by not exercising until expiration day. This factor explains why the European call premium exceeds the European put premium.

3.5 The Merton Model for a European Call on a Stock Paying Dividends Continuously in Proportion to the Stock Price

Among his numerous contributions to the option pricing literature, Robert Merton (1973) derived the following modification to the Black-Scholes formula for a European call on a stock paying a dividend at every instant of time in proportion to the stock price at that time.

The dividend paid at time t is δS_t, where δ is a proportionality constant that represents the annual dividend yield, and S_t is the stock price at time t. The Black-Scholes model must be modified because, as we know, dividends reduce the call's price. In addition, be aware that a pricing formula cannot be obtained unless the option is European; early exercise would require a numerical solution for the option price through application of the binomial model or some other numerical method.

With the introduction of the proportional dividend concept into the analytic framework, the European call formula becomes

$$C = e^{-\delta T} SN(d_1) - e^{-iT} KN(d_2)$$

where the expression for d_1 is now altered to

$$d_1 = \frac{\ln\left(\dfrac{S}{K}\right) + \left(i - \delta + \dfrac{\sigma^2}{2}\right)T}{\sigma\sqrt{T}}$$

and the expression for d_2 remains

$$d_2 = d_1 - \sigma\sqrt{T}$$

The European Put Expression When the Underlying Stock Pays a Proportional Dividend

For the continuous time case, the put-call parity formula, from which the corresponding put value is obtained, must be altered. Proceed as follows. Divide one year into n periods. Each period is of length $1/n$, and the corresponding dividend yield for each period is δ/n. The dividend paid in the period beginning at t is $(\delta/n)S_t$. Consequently, beginning at $t = 0$ with one share and reinvesting the dividend received during this first period at price S_1 results in a total number of shares equal to $1 + (\delta/n)(S_1)/S_1 = 1 + \delta/n$. Repeating this reasoning for n periods, the expression obtained for the number of shares after one year is $[1 + (\delta/n)]^n$. For a holding period of T years, one share grows into $[1 + (\delta/n)]^{nT}$. If we shrink the length of the periods to zero by indefinitely increasing their number, we obtain

$$\lim_{n\to\infty}\left[1 + \left(\frac{\delta}{n}\right)\right]^{nT} = \left[\lim_{n\to\infty}\left(1 + \frac{\delta}{n}\right)^n\right]^T = e^{\delta T}$$

Table 3.4 Cash Flows for the Put-Call Parity Proof in the Continuous Case

Stock Price at Expiration	$S_T \leq K$	$S_T > K$
Position		
Long Put	$K - S_T$	0
Long $e^{-\delta T}$ Shares	S_T	S_T
Borrowed $e^{-iT}K$ Dollars	$-K$	$-K$
Short Call	0	$-(S_T - K)$
Total Cash Flow	0	0

So, beginning with one share at $t = 0$ and reinvesting all subsequent dividends, we end up with $e^{\delta T}$ shares on the day the option expires.

Because the put-call parity proof will require only one share at $t = T$, we must calculate how many shares to buy at $t = 0$. Symbolize this share number by x. In order to have one share at $t = T$, x must satisfy $xe^{\delta T} = 1$. Therefore, $x = e^{-\delta T}$ is the number of shares to buy at $t = 0$ in order to have one share at $t = T$. We proceed with the put-call parity proof for the continuous case.

The result is

$$C = P + e^{-\delta T}S - e^{-iT}K$$

Here is the proof. At $t = 0$, buy a put, buy $e^{-\delta T}$ shares of stock, borrow $e^{-iT}K$ dollars, and short the call. The cash flow from this set of transactions at $t = 0$ is $-P - e^{-\delta T}S + e^{-iT}K + C$. Now consider the cash flows at $t = T$. The two possible cases at expiration are presented in Table 3.4.

Since the portfolio's cash flows are zero at $t = T$ for all S_T, then to avoid a riskless arbitrage possibility, its current cash flows must sum to zero. Thus $-P - e^{-\delta T}S + e^{-iT}K + C = 0$, and the proof is complete.

Substitution of the call expression into the put-call parity expression gives the corresponding put expression:

$$P = -e^{-\delta T}S[1 - N(d_1)] + e^{-iT}K[1 - N(d_2)]$$

3.6 Revisions to the Pricing Methodology Necessitated by Recent Empirical Evidence

Some option prices seem to be substantially different from those predicted by the Black-Scholes model. In particular, the CBOE European options on the S&P 500 trade at prices that contradict an underlying assumption of the Black-Scholes model. This violation has been discovered through study of the estimates of the underlying security's volatility, in this case the S&P 500's, applying the concept of implied volatility. Obviously, if the Black-Scholes model's assumptions are invalid, then a new pricing methodology must be employed. This section begins with a discussion of the implied volatility concept and progresses to a discussion and illustration of an alternate pricing methodology.

Implied Volatility

Except for the underlying stock's volatility, all of the parameters of the Black-Scholes pricing equation can be observed. The stock's volatility can be estimated by computing the standard deviation of a recent series of the stock's continuous rates of return. Another approach used to arrive at the market's estimate of the stock's volatility is to infer it from an option's current price. This entails substituting the option's trade price and the values for the observable parameters, S, K, i, δ, and T of the Black-Scholes model into the formula and solving for the volatility parameter, σ. The resulting σ estimate is called the stock's *implied volatility*. It is implied by the option's market price. Suppose a European call on a non-dividend-paying stock has parameter values of $S = 40$, $K = 40$, $i = 0.05$, and $T = 0.0833$ and is observed to trade at a price of 1.0029. Then the Black-Scholes equation can be solved through an iterative technique, such as the Newton-Raphson procedure (see Hadley 1964), to arrive at a σ value of 0.20. The observed call price of 1.0029 implies a stock volatility of 0.20.

An assumption of the Black-Scholes model is that the stock's return volatility, σ, is a constant. Therefore it should not be influenced by an option's time to expiration, the underlying stock price, or the strike price of the option. It has been observed that European options trading on the S&P 500 Index, having the same expiration date but different strikes, provide different implied volatility estimates for the S&P 500 Index. Some observed patterns of implied volatilities across strikes appear in Figures 3.10a and 3.10b. The pattern in 3.10a is known as the *smile*; the pattern in 3.10b is often referred to as the volatility skew or the *sloppy smile*. Clearly these findings are inconsistent with the constant volatility assumption of the Black-Scholes model. It appears that in pricing European options on the S&P 500, the market is not using the Black-Scholes model.

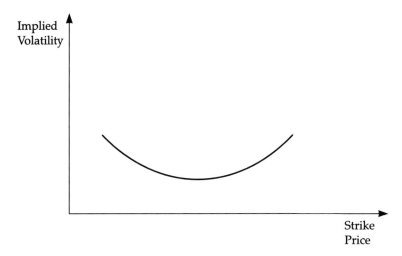

Figure 3.10a Smile Pattern of Implied Volatilities vs. Strikes

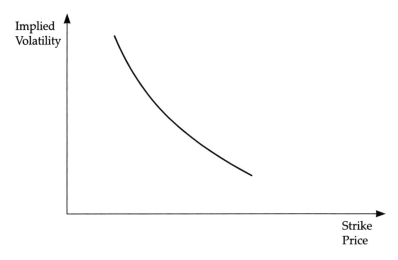

Figure 3.10b Volatility Skew Pattern

Pricing with a Smile

We know that if the option's payoffs can be replicated with a portfolio of stock and debt, then the option can be priced as if the investor is risk neutral. (See equation (3.12) and the paragraph that follows it.) It has been shown that a replicating portfolio can be constructed if the volatility of the underlying stock's rate of return depends only on the stock's price, or time, or both. Consequently, if this condition holds and if the risk neutral probability distribution can be inferred from the current structure of implied volatilities, then a theoretical European option price can be determined by calculating the option's terminal value as expected by a risk neutral individual and discounting that number by the riskless rate, i. For a call with a strike of K and time to expiration T, this statement translates into the formula

$$C = e^{-iT}E[\max(0, S_T - K)] = e^{-iT}\sum_{j=0}^{n} f(S_{j,T})[\max(0, S_{j,T} - K)] \qquad (3.13)$$

where $f(S_{j,T})$ denotes the risk neutral probability of the stock price $S_{j,T}$, $j = 0,1, \ldots, n$, occurring at $t = T$, and e^{-iT} is the continuous time discount factor applied to the expectation of the call's intrinsic value at expiration. Our immediate objective is to obtain the risk neutral density function, $f(S_{j,T})$.

Inferring the Risk Neutral Probability Density Function

Mark Rubinstein (1994) has devised a numerical procedure for obtaining the risk neutral density function $f(S_{j,T})$. Given the implied volatilities of m calls with different strikes, first establish a prior estimate of the $f(S_{j,T})$ probabilities. Symbolize these prior probabilities by $f^*(S_{j,T})$. Do this by averaging the implied volatilities of the two nearest at-the-money strike calls. Label this average volatility σ_A. The stock's continuous rate of return, $\ln(S_T/S)$, is *initially* assumed to be normally distributed. It follows that this rate of return can be written in terms of the standardized normal variate, z, which has zero mean and standard deviation equal to 1. In particular, $z = (\ln(S_T/S) - \mu T)/(\sigma_A\sqrt{T})$. The mean parameter $\mu = i - \sigma^2_A/2$. Choose a specific S_T value; call it $S_{j,T}$. Substitute it into the z equation. A numerical value for z is obtained. From the standard normal density function, find the corresponding value of the normal density, $n(z)$, at the calculated z value. Do this for each $S_{j,T}$ price. Sum all such $n(z)$ values. Divide each $n(z)$ value by this sum to obtain the corresponding $f^*(S_{j,T})$ value. This produces the initial or prior probabilities of terminal stock prices, the $f^*(S_{j,T})$s.

Next, think of the final stock price $S_{j,T}$ as the result of traversing an n-period binomial tree. Again use r to denote one plus the one-period interest rate. There are m calls, each with a different strike but all having the same time to expiration. The symbol K_i represents the *i*th strike, where $i = 1, \ldots, m$. Let S^b and S^a be the current bid and asked prices for the underlying stock. C_i^b and C_i^a denote the same prices for a European call with strike K_i expiring at T. S^{TH} and C_i^{TH}, respectively, denote the current theoretical stock price and the current theoretical price for the *i*th call, calculated by using the risk neutral probabilities to arrive at the expected value of the security at $t = T$ and then discounting this quantity by the riskless rate for *n* periods. The number of periods that make up the tree, *n*, must be significantly larger than the number of options, *m*. (In Rubinstein's example, $m = 16$ and $n = 200$.)

The numerical values for the $f(S_{j,T})$s, the posterior probabilities, are obtained from the minimization of the squared differences between $f(S_{j,T})$, the posterior probability, and $f^*(S_{j,T})$, the prior probability, subject to a number of constraints. The formal statement of the problem follows.[9]

$$\min_{f(S_{j,T})} \sum_{j=0}^{n} [f(S_{j,T}) - f^*(S_{j,T})]^2$$

subject to

$$\sum_{j=0}^{n} f(S_{j,T}) = 1 \quad \text{and} \quad f(S_{j,T}) \geq 0 \quad \text{for} \quad j = 0, \ldots, n$$

$$S^b \leq S^{TH} \leq S^a \quad \text{where} \quad S^{TH} = \frac{1}{r^n}\left[\sum_{j=0}^{n} f(S_{j,T})S_{j,T}\right]$$

$$C_i^b \leq C_i^{TH} \leq C_i^a \quad \text{where}$$

$$C_i^{TH} = \frac{1}{r^n} \sum_{j=0}^{n} f(S_{j,T}) \max[0, f(S_{j,T}) - K_i]$$

$$\text{for} \quad i = 1, \ldots, m$$

Notice that the information contained in all of the implied volatilities is not discarded. Although, initially, only the two nearest at-the-money implied volatilities were used to obtain the prior probabilities, $f^*(S_{j,T})$,

---

9. To simplify the explanation, the stock is assumed not to pay dividends from the current date to the options' expiration date. If dividends are paid, then the terminal stock prices must be grossed up by the shares that could have been purchased with the dividends. See section 3.5 on put-call parity with dividends in continuous time. However, the call's intrinsic value at expiration is still calculated using the value of one share at expiration.

the requirement that the theoretical call values lie between the observed bid and asked prices incorporates all of the information in the implied volatility structure, since there is a one-to-one relationship between the call price and the volatility parameter.

Rubinstein finds that the resulting $f(S_{j,T})$ produces a density function that is markedly different from the normal density. The inferred continuous rate of return distribution has a higher mode (the mode is the highest probability coordinate of the density function) and exhibits some skewness (the density function is asymmetric). Thus the Black-Scholes formula, which assumes the normality of continuous returns, is inappropriate for pricing options on the S&P 500 Index. However, having derived the risk neutral probabilities, we can insert them into equation (3.13) to calculate directly a theoretical price for any European call with the same expiration date on the S&P 500. The insertion of these probabilities into the put valuation equation, which is analogous to (3.13), provides the means for calculating theoretical put prices on the S&P 500.

Generating a Binomial Tree Consistent with the Risk Neutral Terminal Probabilities

We are aware that the methodology used for pricing a European option is generally inappropriate for pricing an American option. To price an American option, the early exercise decision must be taken into account, for it affects the option's current value. In fact, we know that to value an American option, we must proceed node-by-node backward through the binomial tree, comparing the exercised and unexercised option values at each node. Consequently, from the estimated risk neutral terminal probabilities, $f(S_{j,T})$, a binomial tree consistent with the terminal probabilities must be constructed. The technique is demonstrated for a two-period tree. The stock price multipliers and single-period transition probabilities are no longer constants, but are now node dependent.

At the initial node, $t = 0$, the parameters to be deduced are the up and down multipliers, u and d, respectively, and the one-period risk neutral probability of an up move, p. At $t = 1$, numbers for the parameters $\{u(u), d(u), p(u)\}$ and $\{u(d), d(d), p(d)\}$ must be obtained. The symbols that make up the first triplet denote the up and down multipliers and up probability at $t = 1$, after an up move from $t = 0$. The second triplet contains symbols that have similar meanings, except that they refer to the multipliers and up probability at $t = 1$

subsequent to a down move from $t = 0$. The current ($t = 0$) stock price is assumed to be equal to one.

Figure 3.11 contains a two-period stock price tree with the parameters to be determined laid out along the branches or on the nodes. It is assumed that the risk neutral probabilities of the stock's terminal values, the $S_{j,2}$, have been determined. These terminal stock prices, along with their corresponding probabilities, are attached to the $t = 2$ nodes. Note that the tree is assumed to be recombining in the sense that $ud(u) = du(d)$. This means that if two paths have the same number of up and down moves, then they must provide the same stock price on expiration day.

Reviewing the tree, we see that we must determine values for u, d, $u(u)$, $d(u)$, $u(d)$, $d(d)$, p, $p(u)$, $p(d)$, and of course r, which is assumed to be a constant across all nodes. (This last assumption could be relaxed.) With ten unknowns, we need ten independent equations. Four equations come from the fact that the product of the one-period returns along a path must equal the path's return at expiration. Thus

$$uu(u) = 1.625 \tag{3.14a}$$

$$ud(u) = 1.08 \tag{3.14b}$$

$$du(d) = 1.08 \tag{3.14c}$$

$$dd(d) = 0.70 \tag{3.14d}$$

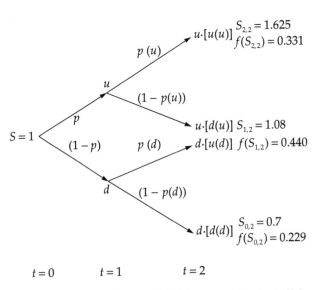

Figure 3.11 **A Tree Consistent with Terminal Probabilities and Terminal Stock Prices**

Equations (3.14b) and (3.14c) reflect the recombining assumption. The terminal probabilities must satisfy

$$pp(u) = 0.331 \tag{3.15a}$$

$$p[1 - p(u)] + [1 - p]p(d) = 0.440 \tag{3.15b}$$

$$[1 - p][1 - p(d)] = 0.229 \tag{3.15c}$$

And because the single-period transition probabilities p, $p(u)$, and $p(d)$ are those of an individual whose expected rate equals the riskless rate, they must satisfy

$$pu + [1 - p]d = r \tag{3.16a}$$

$$p(u)[u(u)] + [1 - p(u)]d(u) = r \tag{3.16b}$$

$$p(d)[u(d)] + [1 - p(d)][d(d)] = r \tag{3.16c}$$

We have ten equations. But 3.15a–c are linearly dependent. Just choose probabilities that satisfy (3.15a) and (3.15c), and you will see that those same probabilities automatically satisfy (3.15b). For example, if $f(1.625) = 0.25, f(1.08) = 0.50$, and $f(0.70) = 0.25$, then selecting $p = 0.5, p(u) = 0.5$, and $p(d) = 0.5$ to satisfy (3.15a) and (3.15c) means that (3.15b) is satisfied, for $(0.5)(1 - 0.5) + (1 - 0.5)0.5 = 0.5$. So we really have nine independent equations in ten unknowns.

We need another equation. Rubinstein obtains it by assuming that all paths to the same expiration day node have equal probability of occurring.[10] Thus the two paths that end at the 1.08 node at $t = 2$, which has terminal probability 0.44 of occurring, are assumed to have the same probability of occurring, namely 0.22. This means that two equations are added to the set of equations in (3.15) when (3.15b) is deleted. Specifically,

$$p[1 - p(u)] = 0.22 \tag{3.15d}$$

$$[1 - p]p(d) = 0.22 \tag{3.15e}$$

Now it seems that we have eleven equations and only ten unknowns. But since the terminal probabilities sum to one, one of the equations

---

10. This assumption that all paths leading to the same final node have equal probability can be discarded if the transition probabilities can be obtained from other data sets, such as prices of options that mature at dates prior to the termination date—at $t = 1$ in our example.

in the set (3.15a), (3.15c), (3.15d), and (3.15e) is linearly dependent on the other three. We do end up with ten linearly independent equations in ten unknowns.

Generating the Tree's Parameters by Recursively Working Backward

It is difficult to solve ten equations with ten unknowns. The problem can be simplified by a solution technique that involves recursively working backward through the tree, one step at a time. Start at $t = 2$. If the node has more than one path leading to it, then divide the probability of arriving at that node—the terminal probability of the stock price attached to that node—by the number of paths to that node. In this example, 0.44 is divided by 2. Now examine the one-period trees that lead from each of the $t = 1$ nodes to the nodes at $t = 2$ (see Figure 3.11). Numerical values must be attached to the transition probabilities, $p(u)$ and $p(d)$, to the multipliers, $u(u)$, $d(u)$, $u(d)$, and $d(d)$, and to r. The calculation of the r value is straightforward. The risk neutral individual expects the stock's value at $t = 2$ to equal r^2. Thus r must satisfy

$$r^2 = 0.331(1.625) + 0.44(1.08) + 0.229(0.70) = 1.173375$$

So $r = 1.0832$. In addition to the aforementioned parameters, in order to apply the backward recursive technique at the next stage, we need the stock value and the probability of that stock value at each of the $t = 1$ nodes. Designate these $t = 1$ stock values by S_u and S_d and their corresponding probabilities by f_u and f_d.

The following sets of equations must be satisfied at each of the $t = 1$ nodes. For the u node at $t = 1$, we have

$$f_u = f_2 + f_1/2 = 0.551$$

$$f_u p(u) = f_2 \Rightarrow p(u) = 0.331/0.551 = 0.601$$

$$S_u = \frac{1}{r}\{p(u)S_{2,2} + [1 - p(u)]S_{1,2}\}$$

$$= \frac{1}{1.0832}[0.601\,(1.625) + 0.399\,(1.08)] = 1.299$$

$$[u(u)]S_u = S_{2,2} = 1.625 \Rightarrow u(u) = 1.251$$

$$[d(u)]S_u = S_{1,2} = 1.08 \Rightarrow d(u) = 0.831$$

The first of these equations might seem unfamiliar. It simply says that the probability of reaching the u node at $t = 1$ equals the sum of the joint events involving the u node that occur subsequent to $t = 1$. This type of calculation is demonstrated in a first statistics course: the probability of a particular event equals the sum of the probabilities of joint events that involve that particular event. And for the d node at $t = 1$, we have

$$f_d = f_1/2 + f_0 = 0.449$$

$$f_d p(d) = f_1/2 \Rightarrow p(d) = \frac{0.220}{0.449} = 0.490$$

$$S_d = \frac{1}{r} \{p(d)S_{1,2} + [1 - p(d)]S_{0,2}\}$$

$$= \frac{1}{1.0832} [0.490 \, (1.08) + 0.510 \, (0.70)] = 0.818$$

$$[u(d)]S_d = S_{1,2} = 1.08 \Rightarrow u(d) = 1.320$$

$$[d(d)]S_d = S_{0,2} = 0.70 \Rightarrow d(d) = 0.856$$

Finally, stepping back to the $t = 0$ node, we have the following set of equations.

$$p = f_u \Rightarrow 0.551$$

$$u \cdot 1 = S_u = 1.299$$

$$d \cdot 1 = S_d = 0.818$$

The tree is complete. To obtain current option prices, the tree is used in the manner that was demonstrated in the earlier examples of this chapter.

The Derman-Kani Model

Derman and Kani (1994) provide another approach to filling in the binomial tree's nodes when implied volatilities exhibit a smile pattern. First, for each time demarcation on the tree an implied volatility curve across strikes is obtained. Thus, if the nodes are to be spaced at one-month intervals, then the implied volatilities would be calculated for options expiring in one month, in two months, etc. A curve is then fitted to the one-month volatilities, another to the two-month volatilities, and so on. As you will see, the curves are used to associate volatilities with option strikes that are not being traded, but for which current prices are needed to complete the binomial tree. Such prices for nontraded options are labeled *inferred prices*. Second, the one-period riskless rates for the present and future periods are estimated from the yield curve. So in the Derman-Kani model, the riskless rates are exogenously determined. With these volatility curves, the one-period rate estimates, and the current stock price, Derman and Kani start at $t = 0$ and roll forward through the tree, calculating the risk neutral transition probabilities and the stock price of each node. Again the methodology is explained here using a two-period example that delineates the required inputs, the necessary equations, and the nodal calculations.

Let $r = 1.07$ for both periods. The stock pays no dividends, its current price is 1.00, and the implied volatility for a one-period call with a strike of 1.00 is 22.31%. To derive an implied price for this call, use the Cox, Ross, and Rubinstein formulas for u and d of the standard binomial tree:

$$u = e^{\sigma\sqrt{T/n}} \qquad d = 1/u$$

Recall that in these equations, T and n, respectively, symbolize the option's time to expiration and the number of subdivisions of T. In this case, $T = 1$ and $n = 1$. Consequently, $u = 1.25$ and $d = 0.8$. Then the one-period, at-the-money call has an inferred price of 0.14019. This follows from

$$C(S,K,T) = C(1,1,1) = (1/1.07)[p(\max\{0, 1.25 - 1.00\})$$
$$+ (1 - p)(\max\{0, 0.80 - 1.00\})]$$
$$= (1/1.07)0.6(0.25) = 0.14019$$

where $p = (r - d)/(u - d) = 0.60$.

With this information, $r = 1.07$, $S = 1.00$, and $C(1,1,1) = 0.14019$, we can solve for the smile tree's transition probabilities at $t = 0$ and the subsequent stock prices at the $t = 1$ nodes. Since the individual is assumed to be risk neutral, the discounted expected stock price at $t = 1$ must equal the current stock of 1.00 at $t = 0$. That is,

$$\frac{1}{1.07}[p_u S_u + (1 - p_u)S_d] = 1.00 \qquad (3.17)$$

where p_u, S_u, and S_d, respectively, denote the probability of an up move at $t = 0$ and the up state and the down state stock prices at $t = 1$. In addition, the current call price must satisfy

$$\frac{1}{1.07}\{p_u \max (0, S_u - 1) + (1 - p_u) \max (0, S_d - 1)\} = 0.14019$$

Since the current stock price, $S = 1$, lies between S_u and S_d, then max $\{0, S_d - 1\} = 0$. Therefore the above equation reduces to

$$\frac{1}{1.07}p_u(S_u - 1) = 0.14019 \qquad (3.18)$$

With three unknowns, p_u, S_u, and S_d, and two equations, one more equation is needed. Derman and Kani choose a tree-centering constraint of $S_u S_d = S^2$, which is in the spirit of selecting $d = 1/u$. Thus the third equation is

$$S_u S_d = (1.00)^2 \qquad (3.19)$$

Solving (3.17), (3.18), and (3.19) gives $p_u = 0.6$, $S_u = 1.25$, and $S_d = 0.80$. The smile tree starts out just like the standard binomial tree.

Now move to the up node at $t = 1$, where $S_u = 1.25$. Suppose the implied volatility for a two-period call with a strike of 1.25 is 25.348%. Then using the Cox, Ross, and Rubinstein transformation gives u and d values for the standard binomial tree of

$$u = e^{0.25348\sqrt{\frac{2}{2}}} = 1.2885 \qquad d = \frac{1}{u} = 0.7761$$

For the standard tree, the implied probability of an up move is

$$p = (r - d)/(u - d) = \frac{(1.07 - .7761)}{(1.2885 - .7761)} = .5736$$

Then, using the standard tree, the inferred price of a two-period call with a strike of 1.25, given a current stock price of 1.00, is $C(1, 1.25, 2) = (1/1.07)^2(.5736)^2$ max $\{0, (1.2885)^2(1.00) - 1.25\} = 0.1179$. See Figure 3.12.

The following equations must be satisfied by the smile tree's parameters:

$$\frac{1}{1.07}[p_{uu}S_{uu} + (1 - p_{uu})S_{ud}] = 1.25 \tag{3.20}$$

$$\left(\frac{1}{1.07}\right)^2 \begin{bmatrix} p_u p_{uu} \text{ max } (0, S_{uu} - 1.25) \\ + \ p_u p_{ud} \text{ max } (0, S_{ud} - 1.25) \\ + \ (1 - p_u)p_{du} \text{ max } (0, S_{du} - 1.25) \\ + \ (1 - p_u)p_{dd} \text{ max } (0, S_{dd} - 1.25) \end{bmatrix} = 0.1179 \tag{3.21}$$

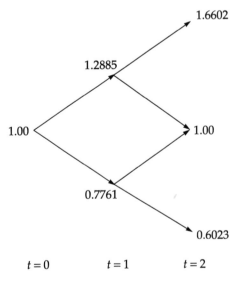

$t = 0$ \qquad\qquad $t = 1$ \qquad\qquad $t = 2$

Figure 3.12 Standard Stock Price Tree for 25.348% Volatility

The parameter p_u has already been discovered to be 0.6. This leaves the unknowns p_{uu}, p_{ud}, p_{du}, p_{dd}, S_{uu}, S_{ud}, S_{du}, and S_{dd}. Derman and Kani add the tree-centering constraint:

$$S_{ud} = S_{du} = S = 1.00 \tag{3.22}$$

This tree-centering constraint means that the last three terms inside the brackets of equation (3.21) are zero. With $p_u = 0.6$, (3.20) and (3.21) can be written as

$$\frac{1}{1.07}[p_{uu}S_{uu} + (1 - p_{uu})1.00] = 1.25 \tag{3.23}$$

$$\left(\frac{1}{1.07}\right)^2 [(0.6)p_{uu} \max (0, S_{uu} - 1.25)] = 0.1179 \tag{3.24}$$

Their solution is $p_{uu} = 0.45$ and $S_{uu} = 1.75$ with $S_{ud} = 1.00$.

Finally, move down to the $t = 1$, $S_d = 0.8$ node. Now an implied price for a two-period put with a strike of 0.80 must be inferred from the two-period implied volatility curve, following the same steps used in obtaining the implied two-period call price. Suppose this put's inferred price is 0.02516. Then the smile tree's parameters must satisfy

$$\frac{1}{1.07}[p_{du}S_{du} + (1 - p_{du})S_{dd}] = 0.8 \tag{3.25}$$

$$\left(\frac{1}{1.07}\right)^2 \left[\begin{array}{l} (p_u)p_{uu} \max (0, 0.8 - S_{uu}) \\ + p_u p_{ud} \max (0, 0.8 - S_{ud}) \\ + (1 - p_u)p_{du} \max (0, 0.8 - S_{du}) \\ + (1 - p_u)p_{dd} \max (0, 0.8 - S_{dd}) \end{array} \right] = 0.02516 \tag{3.26}$$

The centering constraint requires that $S_{ud} = S_{du} = S = 1.00$. This implies that the first three terms in the brackets of equation (3.26) are zero. Given $p_u = 0.6$, $p_{dd} = 1 - p_{du}$, and the centering constraint of $S_{du} = 1.00$, these equations reduce to

$$\frac{1}{1.07}[p_{du}1.00 + (1 - p_{du})S_{dd}] = 0.8 \tag{3.27}$$

$$\left(\frac{1}{1.07}\right)^2 (1 - 0.6)[(1 - p_{du}) \max (0, 0.8 - S_{dd})] = 0.02516 \tag{3.28}$$

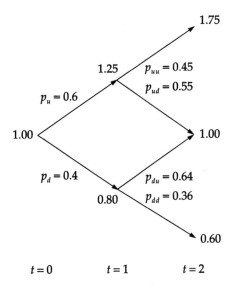

Figure 3.13   Smile Stock Price Tree

The solution is $p_{du} = 0.64$ and $S_{dd} = 0.60$ with $S_{du} = 1.00$. See Figure 3.13 for the completed tree.

Chapter **4**

Risk Management of an Option Portfolio

*C*HAPTER 2 DESCRIBED a general operational approach by which a securities firm trades its own money and mentioned the firm's concern for managing the risk of its position. Using a pricing model, such as the Merton version of the Black-Scholes model, the firm might identify options that are mispriced and have its traders sell (buy) the overpriced (underpriced) options. The executing trader is often asked to make a first pass at hedging each trade by immediately effecting an opposite position in a fairly priced option or in the underlying security, so that the position composed of the initial and hedge trades is insensitive to a small price change in the underlying security. This type of hedge has been labeled with the Greek letter *delta* (Δ) and has come to be known as a delta neutral hedge. The firm's risk management group then takes over. Its job is to step beyond this first, somewhat rough, hedge and make the portfolio of its positions insensitive to larger price changes in the underlying security and to changes in all of the other pricing model's parameters. These other sensitivities have also been given Greek letter names: *gamma* (Γ) for the sensitivity of Δ to a small price change in the underlying security; *kappa* (κ), or sometimes the name *vega*, for the sensitivity of the option price to a small change in the volatility of the underlying security; *theta* (θ) for the change in the option's price with respect to time to expiration; and *rho* (ρ) for the option's price sensitivity with respect to a small change in the short-term, riskless interest rate.

This chapter begins by discussing the effects of changes in the parameter values of an option pricing model. Using Merton's dividend variation of the Black-Scholes model, the chapter continues by providing formulas that quantify the option's price sensitivities to the determining parameters. A discussion follows of the technique employed to make the portfolio simultaneously insensitive, or *neutral*, with respect to small (local) parameter changes. Because this risk management technique, by its very nature, is vulnerable to large changes in the underlying security price, another (global) hedging technique is presented and discussed. While this global technique might be superior in some respects to the Δ-Γ-κ-θ-ρ neutral hedge, it has its flaws. In particular, it does not explicitly attempt to hedge the portfolio's value to changes in the riskless rate, the security's rate of return volatility, and the option's time to expiration.

4.1 Determinants of an Option's Value

From the option pricing models presented in Chapter 3, we see that the determinants of the option's premium are the S, K, T, σ, i, and δ parameters. The effects of changes in these parameter values on the premium level are often apparent. An increase in S and a decrease in K serve to increase a call's premium and decrease a put's premium. Similarly, an increase in the dividend yield will decrease a stock's price, which, in turn, will cause the call's premium to fall and the put's premium to rise.

The greater the length of time until the call's expiration, the greater the call's premium. This makes sense, for as the length of time increases, so does the probability that the stock price will be greater than the strike. The higher the interest rate, the greater the call's premium. Understanding this effect is not as intuitive as understanding the effects of the previously mentioned factors. Nevertheless, the reason becomes apparent when one recalls that the call holder is able to participate in any of the stock's future price increases without having to invest the full stock price. It is as if the call holder has bought the stock with a loan. He does, in effect, pay interest on the loan, in the form of a higher call premium. The higher the interest rate, the more valuable the loan embedded in the call.

On the other hand, one cannot say that the European put premium will increase with time to expiration.[1] As time to expiration increases, the possibility that the stock price will be below the strike increases, but a further delay in the opportunity to exercise increases the forgone interest on the strike. So an unambiguous statement cannot be made about the relationship between time to expiration and the European put's premium. While higher interest rates are favorable to the call's

---

1. For an American put, one can say that its premium increases with time to expiration.

premium, they have the opposite effect on the European put's premium. Again it is the forgone interest to be earned on the strike that accounts for this—the European put cannot be exercised until expiration day.

Finally, the higher the stock's return volatility, the greater the chance of a large stock price change. Since the call (put) holder can take advantage of a higher (lower) stock price through exercise and need not exercise if the price falls below (rises above) the strike price, higher return volatility increases the option premium.

4.2 The Effects of Parameter Changes on an Option's Value

The effect of a change in a parameter value on the European call and put premiums can be quantified by simply calculating the change in the option premium with respect to a unit change in the parameter value, while holding all other parameter values constant. In other words, one calculates the partial derivatives of the option premium with respect to each parameter to obtain these price sensitivities. These partial derivatives (price sensitivities) have been named with Greek letters. We obtain them from the Merton pricing model; they are listed below. Figures 4.1–4.8 depict the variation in their values with respect to the level of the underlying security. The parameter

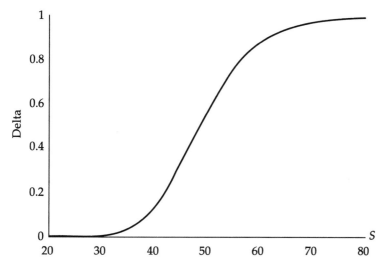

Figure 4.1   Call's Delta vs. S

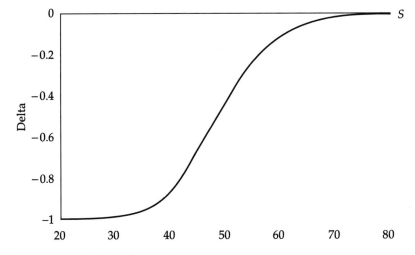

Figure 4.2 Put's Delta vs. *S*

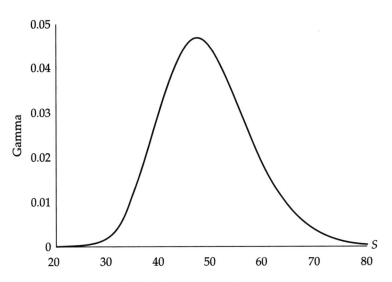

Figure 4.3 Call's and Put's Gamma vs. *S*

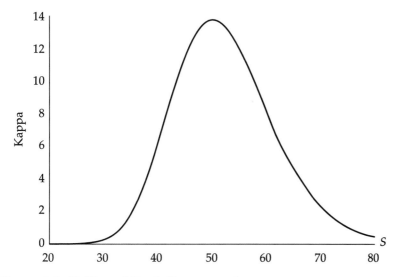

Figure 4.4　Call's and Put's Kappa vs. *S*

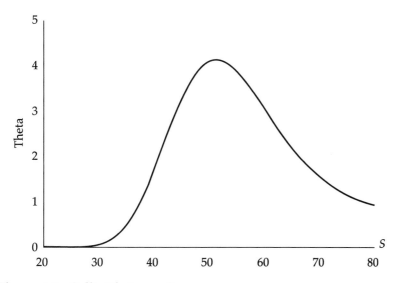

Figure 4.5　Call's Theta vs. *S*

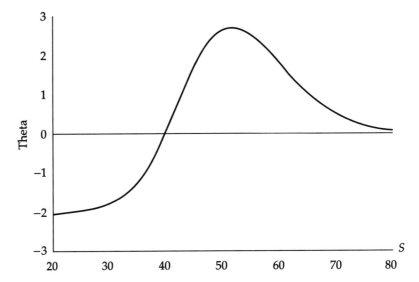

Figure 4.6 Put's Theta vs. *S*

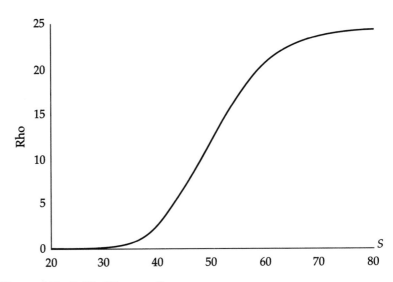

Figure 4.7 Call's Rho vs. *S*

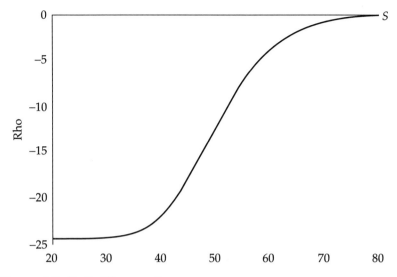

Figure 4.8 Put's Rho vs. S

values assumed for these plots are $K = 50$, $T = 0.5$, $i = 0.05$, $\delta = 0.02$, and $\sigma = 0.25$.

1. *Delta* (Δ): The change in the option premium for a small change in the current stock price.

$$\Delta_{call} = e^{-\delta T}N(d_1) > 0$$
$$\Delta_{put} = \Delta_{call} - e^{-\delta T} < 0$$

2. *Gamma* (Γ): The change in the option's delta for a small change in the current stock price.

$$\Gamma_{call} = \Gamma_{put} = \frac{e^{-\delta T}n(d_1)}{S\sigma\sqrt{T}} > 0$$

Here $n(d_1)$ gives the height of the standard normal density function at the horizontal coordinate d_1. See Figure 3.9.

3. *Kappa* (κ): Measures the change in the option premium for a small change in the rate of return volatility (σ).

$$\kappa_{call} = \kappa_{put} = e^{-\delta T}S\sqrt{T}n(d_1) > 0$$

4. *Theta* (θ): Measures the change in the option's premium for a small change in the time to expiration.

$$\theta_{call} = \frac{e^{-\delta T} S \sigma n(d_1)}{2\sqrt{T}} - \delta e^{-\delta T} SN(d_1) + ie^{-iT} KN(d_2) > 0$$

$$\theta_{put} = \theta_{call} + \delta Se^{-\delta T} - ie^{-iT} K \lessgtr 0$$

5. *Rho* (ρ): Measures the change in the option's premium for a small change in the interest rate.

$$\rho_{call} = e^{-iT} KT\, N(d_2) > 0$$

$$\rho_{put} = \rho_{call} - Te^{-iT} K < 0$$

4.3 Risk Management of an Option Position

During a day, an option trader will sell options that he believes are overpriced and buy underpriced options. His method for deciding whether an option is over- or underpriced might involve application of a mathematical model such as the binomial, or, on the other end of the spectrum, intuition. These options rarely become fairly priced by day's end, which would enable the trader to unwind his positions. Most likely, the trader is looking at an end-of-day position that exposes him to risk of loss from an unforeseen overnight event. He may be content to take on this risk, but more often he will try to neutralize the various types of portfolio risks. After all, he may have been correct in identifying calls that were underpriced and proceeded to buy them. However, if an overnight news event is quite bearish, the stocks on which these calls are written will decline in value by more than the underpricing advantage. So even if these options adjust to correct prices by the next morning, the trader loses money. It would have been prudent to hedge this call exposure. We have already identified these risks with regard to a single option: delta, gamma, kappa, theta, and rho. These same types of risk measures, price sensitivities to parameter changes, apply to a portfolio of options. The conservative options trader will attempt to "zero out" these risks—at least for the period during which the market is closed. To use the vernacular of the business, the trader will try to leave the office with a delta neutral, gamma neutral, kappa neutral, theta neutral, and rho neutral portfolio. This means that for moderate changes in S, σ, T, and i, the option's portfolio value should not be affected.

A Delta Neutral Hedge

To obtain the delta of a complex position—one made of several puts and calls on the same underlying stock—multiply the delta of each jth option by the number of options held, n_j, where $n_j < 0$ if the options have been sold, and then add across all N option positions:

$$\Delta_{options\ portfolio} = \sum_{j=1}^{N} n_j \Delta_j$$

Numerical Illustration

Portfolio composition:

Long 5 March 100 (strike) calls, $\Delta = 0.7$

Long 7 June 120 calls, $\Delta = 0.2$

Short 6 March 100 puts, $\Delta = -0.3$

$$\Delta_{options\ portfolio} = 5(0.7) + 7(0.2) + (-6)(-0.3) = 6.70$$

So, for each one-point increase (decrease) in the value of the underlying stock, the value of the option portfolio will increase (decrease) by 6.70. In order to calculate a portfolio's loss exposure to moves in several underlying stock prices, what was done in the above example for the options on one underlying stock must be repeated for the options on each different stock.[2]

Now suppose that you do not know in which direction a particular stock will move—a reasonable assumption. You have evaluated that the March 40 (M40) calls are overpriced and the March 45 (M45) calls are underpriced. An obvious strategy is to sell the 40 calls and buy the 45 calls, and to choose the ratio of options sold to options bought so that you will be indifferent to the direction of stock price movements. If you can insulate your overall position value from the underlying stock's price moves, you can simply wait until the option prices come back into line. You achieve this objective by selecting the amount to sell and buy of each option so that the total option position has a zero delta value. Knowing that you should sell the 40s and buy the 45s, calculate the ratio of the number of M40s, n_{40}, in the position to

---

2. We could also use a position in the underlying stock to achieve delta neutrality. By definition, the stock's delta is 1.

the number of M45s, n_{45}, by setting n_{40} equal to -1 and solving for the n_{45} value that gives a position delta of zero. That is,

$$-1(\Delta_{M40}) + n_{M45}\Delta_{M45} = 0$$

Thus $n_{M45} = \Delta_{M40}/\Delta_{M45} > 0$, which is the number of 45 calls you should buy for each 40 call sold short.

Notice from the mathematical statement of delta that delta is a function of $N(d_1)$, which is itself a function of the stock price. In fact, since d_1 increases with S and $N(d_1)$ increases with d_1, the delta of a call will increase and the delta of a put will decrease in absolute value as S increases (see Figures 4.1 and 4.2). The point is that the delta of an option position changes with the level of the underlying stock price. A delta neutral position is insulated only against the first tick of a stock price change, for as the stock price changes, the deltas change. In light of this, the position must be rebalanced to maintain delta neutrality. Rebalancing is most frequent when the stock price is near the strike price. In this region, the option's gamma is greatest (see Figure 4.3), resulting in the most dramatic delta changes. In this sense, a delta neutral hedge is said to be locally insulated but not globally insulated from the stock's price changes. To protect, in a larger sense, against unfavorable stock price moves that may harm the arbitrage position, the trader must take further steps to insulate against changes in the position's overall delta.

Since we wish to protect the position against both local stock price changes and delta changes, the objective now is to sell the M40 calls and buy the M45 calls in a ratio that will achieve both delta and gamma neutrality of the overall position. This objective cannot be achieved by using only the M40 and M45 calls. This is apparent if we set up the equations that must be satisfied.

$$n_{M40}\Delta_{M40} + n_{M45}\Delta_{M45} = 0$$

$$n_{M40}\Gamma_{M40} + n_{M45}\Gamma_{M45} = 0$$

The only solution to these equations is the trivial one, $n_{M40} = n_{M45} = 0$.

To obtain a nontrivial solution, another option series must be introduced into the portfolio. Of course, we remain under the constraint that $n_{M40} < 0$ and $n_{M45} > 0$. Proceed by choosing two fairly priced options, say the M50s and the M55s. You do not care if you buy or sell them. Then n_{M50} and n_{M55} must be selected to satisfy the following equations:

$$(-1)\Delta_{M40} + (+1)\Delta_{M45} + n_{M50}\Delta_{M50} + n_{M55}\Delta_{M55} = 0$$

$$(-1)\Gamma_{M40} + (+1)\Gamma_{M45} + n_{M50}\Gamma_{M50} + n_{M55}\Gamma_{M55} = 0$$

Notice that to meet our purchase and sale requirements, n_{M40} and n_{M45} are set equal to -1 and $+1$, respectively.[3] The n_{M50} and n_{M55} values that satisfy these equations provide a delta neutral and gamma neutral portfolio.

To neutralize the portfolio's risk exposure in all dimensions, the portfolio's kappa, theta, and rho measures must be set to zero. To satisfy these constraints, we must proceed along the same path followed in arriving at a delta-gamma neutral portfolio. Suppose we wish to extend our risk protection to the insulation of the portfolio's value from moderate interest rate changes. We find another fairly priced option on the same underlying stock, say the March 60 calls—a fairly priced put could also be used. The preceding set of equations is altered to the following set:

$$(-1)\Delta_{M40} + (+1)\Delta_{M45} + n_{M50}\Delta_{M50} + n_{M55}\Delta_{M55} + n_{M60}\Delta_{M60} = 0$$

$$(-1)\Gamma_{M40} + (+1)\Gamma_{M45} + n_{M50}\Gamma_{M50} + n_{M55}\Gamma_{M55} + n_{M60}\Gamma_{M60} = 0$$

$$(-1)\rho_{M40} + (+1)\rho_{M45} + n_{M50}\rho_{M50} + n_{M55}\rho_{M55} + n_{M60}\rho_{M60} = 0$$

Solving for the n_{M50}, n_{M55}, and n_{M60} values that satisfy the equations, gives a Δ-Γ-ρ neutral portfolio.

The next step in this progression might be to make the portfolio insensitive to changes in the stock's return volatility, σ. To do this, add another fairly priced call to the set and solve for the option mix that makes the portfolio Δ-Γ-ρ-κ neutral. But do not choose another option with the same expiration date. Go to another expiration month and choose a fairly priced option expiring in that month, e.g., the

---

3. If n_{M40} were set to -1 but n_{M45} were allowed to be determined by the equations with only one other option series needed for a solution, say the M50s, then there would be no guarantee that the solution would give $n_{M45} > 0$. The choice of -1 and $+1$ is arbitrary. What is important is to ensure that the positions in the M40 and M45 calls have the correct signs.

June 45 calls. The reason for taking this precaution becomes apparent upon studying the Γ and κ formulas:

$$\Gamma = \frac{e^{-\delta T}n(d_1)}{S\sigma\sqrt{T}} \qquad \kappa = e^{-\delta T}S\sqrt{T}n(d_1)$$

For given S, σ, T, and δ, the terms multiplying $n(d_1)$ in the Γ and κ expressions can be grouped and called B_Γ and B_κ, respectively. In the equations we use to solve for the neutralizing n_j's, B_Γ and B_κ do not vary as we move from one March strike to another. So B_Γ and B_κ are essentially constants for the purpose that the Γ and κ expressions are being used—attempting to achieve a portfolio that is insensitive to parameter changes.

Using the Γ equation, we can write $n(d_1) = \Gamma/B_\Gamma$. Substituting this for $n(d_1)$ in the κ expression, we arrive at

$$\kappa = \left(\frac{B_\kappa}{B_\Gamma}\right)\Gamma$$

What we see is that the kappa of a call is simply a constant times the gamma of that call. Understanding this, suppose we introduce another fairly priced call, say the March 65s, into the set and add a kappa-neutralizing constraint to an already existing gamma-neutralizing constraint. The equation set looks like this.

$$(-1)\Delta_{M40} + (+1)\Delta_{M45} + n_{M50}\Delta_{M50} + n_{M55}\Delta_{M55}$$
$$+ n_{M60}\Delta_{M60} + n_{M65}\Delta_{M65} = 0$$
$$(-1)\Gamma_{M40} + (+1)\Gamma_{M45} + n_{M50}\Gamma_{M50} + n_{M55}\Gamma_{M55}$$
$$+ n_{M60}\Gamma_{M60} + n_{M65}\Gamma_{M65} = 0$$
$$(-1)\rho_{M40} + (+1)\rho_{M45} + n_{M50}\rho_{M50} + n_{M55}\rho_{M55}$$
$$+ n_{M60}\rho_{M60} + n_{M65}\rho_{M65} = 0$$
$$(-1)\kappa_{M40} + (+1)\kappa_{M45} + n_{M50}\kappa_{M50} + n_{M55}\kappa_{M55}$$
$$+ n_{M60}\kappa_{M60} + n_{M65}\kappa_{M65} = 0$$

Now use the above $\kappa = (B_\kappa/B_\Gamma)\Gamma = b\Gamma$ expression, where b is the constant B_κ/B_Γ, to substitute for the kappas in the last equation. We obtain

$$(-1)b\Gamma_{M40} + (+1)b\Gamma_{M45} + n_{M50}b\Gamma_{M50} + n_{M55}b\Gamma_{M55}$$

$$+ \; n_{M60}b\Gamma_{M60} + n_{M65}b\Gamma_{M65} = 0$$

Notice that this equation is a linear multiple of the gamma equation, the multiplier being b. Since this gives us two linearly dependent equations in our four-equation set, a unique solution to the four-equation set cannot be obtained. Moreover, dividing the above equation through by b shows that if all of the portfolio's options have the same expiration date, then κ neutrality implies Γ neutrality and vice versa.

However, if the portfolio contains options with different expiration dates, then this result is no longer true, and the four-equation set can and must be solved to achieve Δ-Γ-ρ-κ neutrality. To see this, simply choose at least one option in the set from a different expiration month, say June. Now, for the March strikes, we have the following relations:

$$\Gamma_{March} = \frac{e^{-\delta T_{March}}n(d_1)}{S\sigma\sqrt{T_{March}}} \qquad \kappa_{March} = e^{-\delta T_{March}}S\sqrt{T_{March}}n(d_1)$$

And for the June strikes,

$$\Gamma_{June} = \frac{e^{-\delta T_{June}}n(d_1)}{S\sigma\sqrt{T_{June}}} \qquad \kappa_{June} = e^{-\delta T_{June}}S\sqrt{T_{June}}n(d_1)$$

We may again define constants for these sets of expressions such that

$$\kappa_{March} = \left(\frac{B_{\kappa March}}{B_{\Gamma March}}\right)\Gamma_{March} \qquad \kappa_{June} = \left(\frac{B_{\kappa June}}{B_{\Gamma June}}\right)\Gamma_{June}$$

Or, equivalently,

$$\kappa_{March} = b_{March}\Gamma_{March} \qquad \kappa_{June} = b_{June}\Gamma_{June}$$

Notice that the constants, $b_{March} = S^2\sigma T_{March}$ and $b_{June} = S^2\sigma T_{June}$, for these two expressions are different because $T_{March} \neq T_{June}$. Now substitute the κ_{March} expression for all the kappas but the last, the June 65s, in the kappa-neutralizing constraint. Then substitute the κ_{June} expression for the kappa of the last call in the constraint, the June 65s. The resulting kappa equation is written beneath the companion gamma equation.

$$(-1)\Gamma_{M40} + (+1)\Gamma_{M45} + n_{M50}\Gamma_{M50} + n_{M55}\Gamma_{M55}$$

$$+ n_{M60}\Gamma_{M60} + n_{J65}\Gamma_{J65} = 0$$

$$(-1)b_M\Gamma_{M40} + (+1)b_M\Gamma_{M45} + n_{M50}b_M\Gamma_{M50} + n_{M55}b_M\Gamma_{M55}$$

$$+ n_{M60}b_M\Gamma_{M60} + n_{J65}b_J\Gamma_{J65} = 0$$

The subscripts M and J denote March and June. A single b constant is no longer common to all terms in the kappa equation (the second equation), and therefore cannot be factored out of the kappa equation to make it appear equal to a constant times the gamma equation. Consequently, the two equations are no longer linearly dependent.

Finally, we consider the completion of this risk-neutralizing process by focusing on the position's theta. Before proceeding, it is worthwhile to study the composition of the θ_{call} expression. Using the expressions for Δ, Γ, and ρ, the θ_{call} expression can be rewritten as

$$\theta_{call} = \frac{S^2\sigma^2\Gamma}{2} - \delta S\Delta + \frac{i\rho}{T}$$

The exact same expression holds for the θ of a put in terms of its Γ, Δ, and ρ values. Therefore, since the Γ, Δ, and ρ values for a portfolio of options are linear combinations of the Γ, Δ, and ρ of the individual options that form the portfolio, the above expression also holds for the θ of the option portfolio, if all options in the portfolio have the same expiration date. Consequently, if the portfolio, composed of options that expire on the same date, is Δ, Γ, and ρ neutral, then it is also θ neutral. And we are finished. However, if there are options in the portfolio with different expiration dates, then a θ neutral constraint must be added to those for Δ, Γ, κ, and ρ.

4.4 A General Hedging Technique

Recall that the option parameter price sensitivities, Δ, Γ, κ, θ, and ρ, are obtained by calculating the partial derivatives of the Merton version of the Black-Scholes formula. As such, they can provide an accurate measure of the option premium change only for small perturbations in the parameter values—technically, infinitesimal parameter value changes. Consequently, using these formulas to insulate the option portfolio against unforeseen stock price changes, among other parameter changes, should not be expected to perform well unless the hedge ratios are continuously adjusted. This may entail significant transaction costs. In addition, noncontinuous changes in any of the parameter values will result in underperformance. Given such shortcomings, other techniques have been developed to reduce the risk exposure of the option portfolio.

Suppose that one has formed a position in mispriced options. Call this the object portfolio. The manager's aim is to hedge an underlying stock price move of any size. To this end, the manager selects a portfolio of fairly priced options that best mimics the value of the object portfolio over a wide range of stock prices. This replicating portfolio would then be shorted to effect the hedge of the object portfolio.

One approach is to write the theoretical value of the object portfolio as a function of the *known amounts of each of its options* at each possible stock price. $P(S_i)$ symbolizes the calculated value of the object portfolio at the ith stock price, where $i = 1, \ldots, N$. The Merton version of the Black-Scholes option pricing model might be used. Then write the theoretical value of the portfolio of fairly priced options as a function of the *unknown amounts of each fairly priced option*. The same option pricing model is normally used. Find the composition of this portfolio of fairly priced options, the replicating portfolio, that minimizes the expected value of the sum of squared differences between the object portfolio's value and the replicating portfolio's value at every possible stock price that may be reached during the hedge period. Using n_j, S_i, $f(S_i)$, and $O_j(S_i)$, respectively, to denote the number of the jth type of option in the replicating portfolio, $j = 1, \ldots, M$, the ith level of the underlying stock price, $i = 1, \ldots, N$, the probability that S_i will occur,[4] and the theoretical value of the jth option in the replicating portfolio at stock price, S_i, the mathematical statement of the problem is

$$\min_{\{n_j\}} \left\{ \sum_{i=1}^{N} f(S_i) \left[\left(\sum_{j=1}^{M} n_j O_j(S_i) \right) - P(S_i) \right]^2 \right\}$$

The first-order conditions for a minimum are found by taking the partial derivatives of the expression inside the braces with respect to

---

4. Stock prices are usually assumed to be lognormally distributed.

each n_j and setting the result equal to zero. This gives M equations in M unknowns.

$$2\sum_{i=1}^{N} f(S_i)\left[\left(\sum_{j=1}^{M} n_j O_j(S_i)\right) - P(S_i)\right]O_k(S_i) = 0 \qquad \text{for} \qquad k = 1, \ldots, M$$

or

$$\sum_{j=1}^{M} n_j \sum_{i=1}^{N} f(S_i)O_j(S_i)O_k(S_i) = \sum_{i=1}^{N} f(S_i)O_k(S_i)P(S_i) \qquad \text{for} \qquad k = 1, \ldots, M$$

This set of linear equations can be solved directly for the n values that make up the replicating portfolio. Equivalently, a solution may be found by running the following multiple linear regression:

$$\sqrt{f(S_i)}P(S_i) = n_1\left(\sqrt{f(S_i)}O_1(S_i)\right) + n_2\left(\sqrt{f(S_i)}O_2(S_i)\right) + \ldots$$

$$+ n_M\left(\sqrt{f(S_i)}O_M(S_i)\right) + u_i$$

where u_i is the error term. The values of the regression coefficients, n_1, $n_2, \ldots, n_m$, are the amounts of the various options in the replicating portfolio. A plot of both $P(S_i)$, the object portfolio's value, and $\sum_{j=1}^{M} n_j O_j(S_i)$, the replicating portfolio's value, versus S_i will provide an idea of the potential effectiveness of the hedge. See Figure 4.9.

A global hedging method, such as the one just described, has some decided advantages over the local delta-gamma neutral hedge. The former approach does not require continuous adjustments over the hedge horizon and is expected to perform better in the face of discontinuous stock price changes. Given that the replicating portfolio consists of options, its value should be responsive to changes in the levels of volatility and the interest rate. Although it is extremely unlikely that the extent of the replicating portfolio's value changes in response to perturbations in volatility and/or the interest rate will match that of the object portfolio. In contrast, the local hedge, formed by setting $\Delta = \Gamma = \kappa = \rho = \theta = 0$, provides, by design, a better hedge against small movements in all of the parameters.

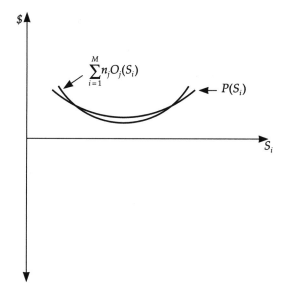

Figure 4.9 Replicating and Object Portfolio Values

4.5 Calculating the Parameter Sensitivities When the Black-Scholes Model Does Not Hold

Suppose the pattern of implied volatilities across strikes is not constant. This possibility was discussed in Chapter 3. It would be inappropriate to use the formulas for delta, gamma, etc., listed at the beginning of this chapter, since they were derived from the Merton version of the Black-Scholes model. How do we calculate the parameter sensitivities? Recall the case of the volatility smile. Look at the two-period binomial tree that was constructed to illustrate a valuation methodology for that case. At the $t = 0$ node, look ahead to the call values at the two $t = 1$ nodes. Then

$$\Delta = \frac{(C_u - C_d)}{(S_u - S_d)}$$

From the $t = 1$ nodes, label the nodes u and d, look ahead one period to $t = 2$, and calculate $\Delta(u)$ and $\Delta(d)$. Then

$$\Gamma = \frac{(\Delta(u) - \Delta(d))}{(S_u - S_d)}$$

where S_u and S_d are the respective stock prices at the u and d nodes at $t = 1$.

The sensitivity of the call price to an interest change, ρ, can be determined by perturbing r and then recalculating the risk neutral probabilities. Then generate a new tree with a corresponding new call price. The difference in call prices, the new price minus the old price, divided by the change in r is a measure of ρ.

To calculate the sensitivity of the call price in response to a change in volatility, κ, you might shift the entire implied volatility curve by 1% or any other percentage that might be of interest. Then, using the Black-Scholes model, invert these new implied volatilities into call prices. Add the observed bid-ask spread to obtain initial C_i^b and C_i^a values. Substitute these into the Rubinstein constraint and recalculate the new terminal probabilities and a corresponding binomial tree. Use the new tree to compute a new call price. The change in call prices divided by the percentage change in volatility provides a measure of κ.

Calculation of a θ value is somewhat problematic. One must be able to compute the change in the option value between two nodes adjacent in time while keeping the stock price constant. But the tree may not have two nodes at adjacent time periods with the same stock price. Rubinstein advocates the use of a discrete form of the partial differential equation that relates the option price to the price of the underlying security. In particular, it can be demonstrated that, as long as σ is a function of S and t, the following equation, which relates θ to Δ and Γ, must hold:

$$\theta = \frac{[-(\ln(r))C + (\ln(r))S\Delta + 0.5\sigma^2 S^2 \Gamma]}{h}$$

where h is the elapsed time interval, the horizontal distance between nodes.[5] Given estimates of Δ and Γ, and of course r and σ, a θ estimate can be obtained.

---

5. Recall that θ is the partial derivative of the option price with respect to time to expiration, T, and not with respect to time, t.

Chapter 5

Option Products

*T*HIS CHAPTER looks at two areas: portfolio insurance and the introduction of some securities, whose intent was to fill strike and expiration date gaps in the listed options. Portfolio insurance was developed in the early 1980s to allow investment managers to synthetically replicate a European put on a portfolio of securities with a strike and expiration date designated by the manager. The objective of this synthetically created put was to provide downside protection for the stock portfolio, much in the same way as the insurance put described in Chapter 1. Though the portfolio insurance product was enormously popular, some thought their goals would be more effectively served by exchange traded, long-dated options. Consequently, securities such as SCOREs and SuperShares were introduced, along with a number of others.

5.1 Portfolio Insurance

Portfolio insurance is a concept that gained wide acceptance in the mid-1980s as a number of mutual funds and pension fund managers were attracted by a strategy that promised to protect the capital gains of the previous few years without conceding the opportunity for future capital gains. Perhaps the intent of portfolio insurance is best explained through an example. Suppose a manager of a 110 million fund is offered the following opportunity by a security firm: If the market is higher at year end, keep the stock; if the market is lower, sell us the entire portfolio for 110 million. This strategy has some obvious attractions for the portfolio manager, for if the portfolio's value rises, the fund gains, but should it fall, the fund's principal is preserved. The portfolio is insured against loss of principal.

The manner in which this goal can be achieved is to have the portfolio retain 100 million in stock and use the remaining 10 million to purchase a one-year European put on the entire portfolio with a strike of 110 million. If at year end the portfolio's value exceeds 110 million, the stocks are retained. However, if after one year the portfolio's value is less than 110 million, the put is exercised and 110 million is received by the fund. There were some hurdles to be stepped over before this strategy could be implemented. Primarily, there were no exchange traded one-year European puts on specific stock portfolios that also had the exact strike price necessary to protect the fund's capital. In fact, it wasn't until some time later that exchange traded one-year European options on stock indices became available. So the one-year European put with the correct strike price for the particular portfolio had to be synthesized.

Operationally, the manner in which the synthesis is achieved is seen by studying the value formula for a long stock–long put position, $S + P$. For purposes of this illustration, the Black-Scholes formula for a European put on a non-dividend-paying stock is used.

$$S + P = S - S(1 - N(d_1)) + e^{-iT}K(1 - N(d_2))$$

$$= SN(d_1) + e^{-iT}K(1 - N(d_2))$$

Look at the right-hand side of this equation. It is composed of a number, $N(d_1)$, times the current share price, S, plus another number, $(1 - N(d_2))$, times the discounted value of K, $e^{-iT}K$, where $B(T) \equiv e^{-iT}K$ can be interpreted as the current value of a U.S. Treasury bill with a life of T years and a maturity value (face value) of K. Therefore, a put-protected stock position, i.e., portfolio insurance, is equivalent to an investment in $N(d_1)$ shares of stock plus the purchase of $(1 - N(d_2))$ T-bills, each with face value K. Consequently, even if a one-year European put does not exist on a particular stock portfolio, it can be manufactured by distributing the portfolio's funds among the requisite number of shares and T-bills.

Of course, as the left-hand side, $S + P$, changes in response to a stock price change, the right-hand side must be rebalanced. If the stock price rises, then $N(d_1)$ increases and $(1 - N(d_2))$ decreases, so the funds must be reapportioned from T-bills to stock. On the other hand, if the stock price falls, then $N(d_1)$ decreases and $(1 - N(d_2))$ increases; stocks must be sold and the receipts used to purchase additional T-bills. Theoretically, this method of portfolio insurance means that one must continuously adjust the proportion of stock to T-bills.

A couple of other technical points should be addressed. First, how does one know that a put with the necessary attributes can be synthesized? To answer this question, consider the following problem. A client of a securities firm wishes to purchase a particular stock valued at S and, in addition, wants portfolio insurance for T years. How much money (call it K^*) must he provide to the securities firm? The amount, K^*, must be sufficient to purchase a share of stock and a European put, which must have a strike of K^* and a time to expiration of T. That is, K^* must satisfy

$$S + P(S, K^*) = K^*$$

where P is explicitly shown to be a function of S and the strike of K^*. Rewrite this equation as

$$S + P(S, K^*) - K^* = 0$$

Is there a K^* value that satisfies this equation? Define

$$g(K) \equiv S + P(S, K) - K$$

and plot it against K. At $K = 0$, the put has zero value, so $g(0) = S > 0$. Furthermore, it is easy, but somewhat tedious, to show that the derivative of $g(K)$ with respect to K—call it $g'(K)$—is

$$g'(K) = e^{-iT}[1 - N(d_2)] - 1 < 0$$

This derivative is negative for all K because the first term on the right-hand side of the equal sign is less than 1. Given that $g(0) > 0$ and $g'(K) < 0$, a plot of $g(k)$ is presented in Figure 5.1.

The value at which the $g(K)$ curve intersects the horizontal axis is the K^* value. We see from Figure 5.1 that the K^* value does exist, so the desired put can be formed.

The other technical point to be considered is how to rebalance. Since K^* satisfies $S + P = K^*$, then initially, at $t = 0$, there is enough capital to form the synthesizing portfolio. But what happens when the stock price changes from S to S_1 and the portfolio value changes from $V = K^*$ to $V_1 \neq K^*$? We know that the ratio of shares to T-bills

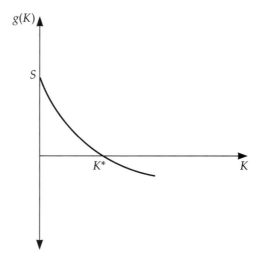

Figure 5.1 $S + P - K$ vs. K

must continue to be $N(d_1)/[1 - N(d_2)]$, where d_1 and d_2 are evaluated at the new stock price. But now

$$S_1 N(d_1) + [1 - N(d_2)]e^{-iT}K \neq V_1$$

where V_1 is the amount of capital now available for redistribution among shares and T-bills. To deal with this problem, define a scale factor z, whose value is selected such that

$$z([N(d_1)]S_1 + [1 - N(d_2)]e^{-iT}K) = V_1$$

and solve for z. The number of shares in the revised portfolio is now $zN(d_1)$, and the number of T-bills is $z[1 - N(d_2)]$. Practically, we do not want to rebalance the proportions if the stock price change is very small, because transaction costs will absorb too much of the portfolio's capital. So we test. If the new ratio of stock to T-bills is not significantly different from the old ratio, we do not rebalance.

How can the return of principal be guaranteed if the market drops? After all, isn't there a cost to synthesizing the put, and doesn't that eat into the initial capital, K^*? The answer lies in the fact that since only K^* is promised to be returned if the market falls, the portfolio insurance manager uses the interest on the capital held to implicitly pay for the cost of the put.

A somewhat intuitive explanation supplements the mathematics of rebalancing. Recall from the insurance put diagram of Chapter 1, Figure 1.7, or the put-call parity relation, that the put plus stock position is equivalent to owning a call—without the leverage that the standard call carries. The delta of a call on a non-dividend-paying stock is $N(d_1)$ (see Chapter 4). As the stock price rises, $N(d_1)$ increases; consequently the equivalent call's delta increases toward one, making the call look more and more like the underlying stock. But, for the portfolio insurance program's position to match that same delta, more money must be shifted to the stock position. Conversely, as the stock price falls, the stock plus put—the equivalent call—goes out-of-the-money, and its delta, still given by $N(d_1)$, decreases toward zero. To emulate the decreasing delta of the equivalent call, the insurance program must shift money from stock into T-bills.

In the operational aspects of this rebalancing, we must be aware of an important point. With each downtick in the value of the underlying portfolio, the manager must ask: If I sell all of the remaining stock held and place all funds into T-bills, will I have enough money at year end to be able to pay no less than the initial principal received, K^*? Because stock price changes, in reality, are discontinuous, there is the real danger that the next price drop will take the insured portfolio's market value below the critical dollar amount necessary to ensure that K^* can be returned at year end. Consequently, the portfolio insurance manager will normally sell out the stock position and place all funds into Treasury bills before the portfolio insurance equation dictates that it should be done.

Unfortunately, this seemingly prudent behavior may have dire consequences. Suppose that the stock position's value continues to fall and prior to the point where the balancing equation dictates the switch to T-bills, the manager, playing it safe, moves completely out of stock. After this switch, the stock market turns around and heads straight up. At year end, the stock portfolio, had it been retained, would have a value in excess of the initial capital amount, K^*. The client, for whom the portfolio insurance program is being run, expects substantially more than K^* but receives only K^*. This type of scenario underlines the fact that the performance of this portfolio insurance technique is path dependent, i.e., it depends on the way that the year-end portfolio value is reached.

In contrast to owning a standard put—if one could be obtained on a particular stock portfolio—there are some other drawbacks to this operational technique for portfolio insurance. At year end, if the portfolio value is below K^*, the fund has been successfully protected against principal loss. However, the fund must now incur the costs of moving a 100% cash position back into the desired stock portfolio. In addition, there are what might be significant transaction costs due to a larger-than-expected number of rebalancings; this is path dependent. Finally, recall that a standard put's value increases as the market perceives volatility to increase. But, since a position composed solely of stock and T-bills will not increase in value with a perceived increase in volatility, the synthesized put's value will not increase.

To provide portfolio insurance without the above deficiencies, attempts have been made to use short-term, exchange traded options to replicate a long-term put. For example, the global hedging technique discussed in Chapter 4 would advocate the use of short-term options to construct a portfolio whose value replicates the value of the desired long-term put. Since short-term options inherently perform the required rebalancing as the underlying security price changes, this technique should entail smaller transaction costs. Furthermore, the short-term option portfolio's value will increase if the underlying security's perceived volatility increases—although not by as much as the value of the long-term option that one is attempting to replicate.

5.2 The SCORE: An Option-Like Instrument

The section on portfolio insurance pointed out some difficulties in replicating an insurance put through continuous rebalancing. As one would suspect, these difficulties extend to the replication of a European call. In light of these less-than-perfect attempts at long-term option replication, it is worthwhile to explore an event in the securities market in which long-term European calls on a number of blue chip stocks were manufactured and strongly demanded.

Beginning in 1983, some of the larger financial institutions were asked by investment banking firms to deposit the shares they held of a selected blue chip company in a unit investment trust.[1] For each

---

1. A trust indenture and a corporate charter represent two different paths to organizing a company. Among the more important contrasting features are (1) whereas a corporation may issue redeemable or nonredeemable shares, the trust may issue only redeemable shares; (2) subsequent to the initial investment of capital, the trust, except in unusual circumstances (such as defaults or refinancings) may not alter the asset mix; (3) the trust has a limited life; (4) the trustees, who supervise the trust, appoint their successors.

share received, a unit of the trust would be exchanged. The life of the trust would be five years, at which time the trust's units would be reexchanged for the common shares held. Each unit of the trust would contain two securities:

1. The PRIME (Prescribed Fix Right to Income and Maximum Equity) had allocated to it all of the underlying stock's dividend income minus a five-cents-per-year management fee, plus any capital appreciation up to a level set above the initial stock price. This level, named the Termination Claim, was set about 20%–25% above the share price at the initiation of the trust.

2. The SCORE (Special Claim on the Residual Equity) received all of the stock's price appreciation above the Termination Claim by the Termination Date, which coincided with the trust's dissolution date—five years after inception.

When a share was submitted to a trust, a unit was issued. The unit's two parts, the PRIME and the SCORE, were traded separately on the American Stock Exchange (ASE), along with the underlying stock. If a PRIME and a SCORE were presented to the trust, the underlying share of the stock was returned.

Approximately thirty of these trusts were formed before a federal tax ruling made the formation of other trusts uneconomical. Tax legislation of 1986 classified any new trusts as corporations that would have to pay the corporate tax rate on any income received by the trust. So a PRIME owner would see the dividend income taxed at the trust level and then suffer the additional personal tax on income. After each existing trust reached its Termination Date, a new trust on those shares was not formed. The last of the trusts, that holding American Express shares, closed in August 1992.

Why did financial institutions agree to exchange shares for PRIMEs and SCOREs? The most frequently cited reason is that the Termination Claim was set at a level such that the financial institution considered the odds long of the stock price exceeding that level. So a share was converted into a PRIME and a SCORE, and the part of the stock's return distribution above the Termination Claim was sold as a SCORE.

The sum of the PRIME and SCORE prices exceeded the price of the underlying stock. Why did the value of the parts exceed the whole? The favored explanation is that since the SCORE is a five-year European call on the underlying stock, and such calls are difficult to replicate, those who wished to include them in their portfolios were willing to pay up for them.

Why is it difficult to replicate a five-year European call? Think back to the discussion of the portfolio insurance technique that required continuous rebalancing between stocks and bonds. A glance at the Black-Scholes formula for a European call reveals that, theoretically, it can be considered equivalent to a long position in $N(d_1)$ shares of the stock and a short position in $N(d_2)$ T-bills, each with a face value of K. A continuous rebalancing of these proportions should synthesize the desired call. But, as has been pointed out, the attendant costs are path dependent and may be significant. So one would willingly pay more for a standard five-year call rather than accept the expected cost of replicating it.

If the sum of the parts exceeded the whole, why wasn't there an arbitrage to force convergence? Theoretically, there was. You could have bought the stock, converted to a PRIME and a SCORE, and then sold the PRIME and the SCORE. Or, if the trust had reached the maximum number of shares of a corporation that it was permitted to hold—making further conversions impossible—you could have shorted the PRIME and the SCORE, bought the stock trading on the ASE, and pocketed the difference in values. The position would have been held until the Termination Date, when the PRIME plus SCORE values had to converge to the stock price. The trade would then have been unwound. However, the price discrepancies could not be arbitraged. The reason is that the transaction costs, including the bid-ask spread, commissions, the maintenance of the trading operation, and the below-market interest rate received on the proceeds from the short sale, were too high. Consequently, the value discrepancy was caused by the development of an instrument that produced a cost saving, and it remained because of the transaction costs that made arbitrage unprofitable.

5.3 Other Long-Term Option Products

LEAPs

Partly in response to the success of SCOREs in the 1980s, the Chicago Board Options Exchange (CBOE) offered longer-term options dubbed LEAPs (Long-Term Equity Participation Product) on 40 of the most widely held stocks. LEAPs are American puts and calls listed with an original maturity of 39 months. Every 6 months, a new series of LEAPs is listed.

LEAPs provide an example of a security being introduced not just to imitate but to improve. Clearly, there was demand for exchange traded options that exceeded the nine-month maximum traded on the CBOE. The success of SCOREs was evidence of that. In addition, traders were having difficulty in shorting SCOREs; they couldn't borrow them to short. Consequently, it was difficult to sell a long-dated call on the blue chip companies. Since positions in LEAPs are like other CBOE options, meaning short sales are merely book entries, one could readily enter into a short position in LEAPs.

FLEX Options

With the increasing growth in the OTC options market, the CBOE decided that it must defend—and, ideally, expand—its market share. In 1993, FLEX options (FLEXible exchange traded options) were introduced for institutional-size trades. For a minimum transaction size of $10 million, two parties to a trade in an option on either the Standard & Poor's 100 Index, the Standard & Poor's 500 Index, or the Russell 2000 Index can set whatever expiration date is desired. In addition, these parties are permitted to set the strike price, choose whether the option is to be American or European, and decide whether, on exercise/expiration day, the final index level for profit calculation purposes should be set to that day's close, the average of that day's high and low, or the next day's opening level. For in-the-money options, a cash payment equal to the difference between the final level and the strike is made by short to long. This venture is aimed at providing institutional traders with the flexibility of the OTC market, as opposed to the more rigid standardization of contract terms set by the exchange, while permitting the traders to receive the credit guarantee of the Options Clearing Corporation (OCC) and the greater liquidity normally associated with a central marketplace.

Performance Equity Redemption Cumulative Stock (PERCS)

A PERCS is a composite security consisting of a long share of common stock and a short call, written with a strike that is frequently 30% to 60% higher than the stock price on issue date. The life of a PERCS is finite; its expiration date is usually set three to four years from the issue date and is known at the issue date. The PERCS issuer normally pays for the embedded call through the dividend stream of the PERCS. Consequently, the current value of that dividend stream exceeds the current value of the common stock's dividend stream by the cost of the call. Because the call is paid for through the dividend stream, the PERCS is initially offered at a price equal to the then-current common stock price.

The issuing corporation has the right to exercise the embedded call at any time during the life of the PERCS. However, since the corporation has promised to continue to pay the dividend to the PERCS holder until the PERCS's expiration date, the call is rarely exercised prior to expiration day. If on expiration day the common stock price is below the strike price of the PERCS, then each PERCS is exchanged for one share of common stock. If the common stock price is above the strike price on expiration day, then the PERCS is exchanged for a fractional share of common stock, where the fraction is equal to the ratio of the strike price to the common stock price on expiration day. This serves to cap the possible gains to the PERCS's holder at the strike price. For example, suppose the strike is set at 150. If the expiration day common stock price is 200, then each PERCS is exchanged for $150/200 = 0.75$ shares of common. The value of that fractional share is $0.75(200) = 150$.

Various reasons have been offered for the introduction of the PERCS. One that is typically cited is that the PERCS provided a vehicle for raising new equity when some firms could not do so through conventional common stock offerings. The investor who had a limited view of the stock's upside potential and desired an exceptional dividend found the PERCS attractive. Some of the issuing firms found the PERCS attractive because they believed that the market would underprice the PERCS's embedded call and therefore overprice the PERCS.

SuperShares

To assist both large and small investors in purchasing and trading stock options on the S&P 500 index, SuperShares were listed for trading in November 1992. These option-like instruments are created by splitting the payoffs from two underlying securities, the Index Trust SuperUnit, a share in a portfolio that mimics the S&P 500, and the Money Market Trust SuperUnit, a share in a short-term portfolio composed of U.S. Treasury securities and loans collateralized by U.S. Treasury securities. Both types of SuperUnits are issued at their net asset values, are traded on the American Stock Exchange, and expire on November 5, 1995—hereafter referred to as expiration day. Each may be redeemed on or before that date at its net asset value.[2]

Each type of SuperUnit can be divided into two types of SuperShares, each of which expires on the date that the underlying SuperUnit expires and trades on the CBOE. The Index SuperUnit can be divided into

1. An Appreciation SuperShare, which receives all of the Index SuperUnit's value above $125 on expiration day. It is equivalent to owning an out-of-the-money call on an Index SuperUnit with a 125 strike.

2. A Priority SuperShare, which receives all dividends paid to the Index SuperUnit and that part of the Index SuperUnit's value not paid to the Appreciation SuperShare. It is equivalent to owning one Index SuperUnit and being short an out-of-the-money call with a 125 strike.

The Money Market SuperUnit can be divided into

1. A Protection SuperShare, which receives, on expiration day, the difference between $100 and the price of the Index SuperUnit if that difference is positive, and zero otherwise. The possible gain is capped at $30. Thus the Protection SuperShare is equivalent to a put spread in which the holder is long the 100 strike and short the 70 strike. Protection SuperShares can be purchased to provide downside protection of up to 30% for an S&P portfolio, i.e., portfolio insurance of up to 30%.

2. An Income and Residual SuperShare, which receives the interest earned by the Money Market SuperUnit plus any remaining value of the Money Market SuperUnit not paid out to the Protection SuperShare on expiration day. The security can be characterized as the ownership of a Money Market SuperUnit plus short a 100 put and long a 70 put.

---

2. At the time of this writing, it was uncertain whether SuperUnits would be issued after November 5, 1995.

Chapter *6*

Exotic Options: Option Innovations to Meet Special Needs

*A*S SECURITY market participants became knowledgeable and, in turn, confident in their dealings with standard options, they began to devise options with more intricate payoff structures that would better fit their needs. These options became subsumed under the name *exotic options*. Securities firms either began to provide such options directly or found other investors to write them, since they are not available as listed options.

In this chapter, five types of exotics are discussed: the exchange option, the up-and-out put (a form of a barrier option), the Asian option, the lookback option, and the compound option. The exchange and compound options apparently attracted academic interest well in advance of serious market interest. Perhaps the reason for the academic interest was that exchange options already existed as part of other financial instruments (Margrabe 1978), and certain existing security classes could be interpreted as compound options (Geske 1979). The lookback option had not been traded heavily in the OTC market, but a key academic article (Goldman, Sosin, and Gatto 1979) seemed to increase interest in this option type. Of late, Asian and barrier type options have attracted a great deal of attention; the Asian mostly as a hedging tool for entities involved in managing currency risk and commodity positions, and the barrier as a low-cost speculative instrument on equity indices, interest rates, and foreign exchange rates. While some of these exotics have been more popular in the currency area and others in the equity markets, this chapter describes each one's characteristics and discusses its pricing, assuming that the underlying security is a stock.

6.1 The Exchange Option

When the Treasury bond futures contract is discussed in Chapter 12, we shall see that the seller of the futures may choose any one of a number of Treasury bonds to deliver. The seller will choose the worst from the perspective of the long. If two bonds are deliverable with values B_1 and B_2, respectively, the one with the lower value will be selected for delivery. Consequently, if bond 1 is currently cheaper than bond 2, the long futures position may be viewed as the ownership of bond 1 with payment deferred until delivery and an option that was sold to the short. This option that the short futures holder possesses grants the right to call bond 1 away from the long in exchange for bond 2. Therefore, in valuing a Treasury bond futures contract, it is useful to view it as the value of bond 1, perhaps adjusted for the financing interest saved because payment is deferred, less the value of an option to exchange bond 2 for bond 1. It is this option to exchange one asset for another that is named the exchange option. There are other instances in which it is useful to understand how to analyze an exchange option. One is that in which the owner of a bond is permitted to accept payment in either currency A or currency B.

Here we apply the binomial methodology to the exchange option valuation problem (Rubinstein 1992b). The methodology is applied only for a one-period option. However, this is all that is needed, for we know that we can apply the one-period formula iteratively to arrive at the option's current value. Start at the expiration date nodes and work backward through the tree, obtaining values at each node until a value is found at the current day node.

Consider the option to obtain asset A in exchange for asset B. Let $S_0^A, S_0^B, S_u^A, S_d^A, S_u^B, S_d^B, u(>1)$, and $d(<1)$, respectively, represent the current $(t = 0)$ prices of the non-dividend-paying stocks A and B, their prices one period later $(t = 1)$, and the multipliers of the ratio S_0^A/S_0^B to obtain S_u^A/S_u^B and S_d^A/S_d^B.[1] The expiration day up state payoff of a call to obtain asset A in exchange for asset B is

$$C_u = \max (0, S_u^A - S_u^B)$$

In the down state the payoff is

$$C_d = \max (0, S_d^A - S_d^B)$$

---

1. Modeling the change in the ratio of asset prices in this manner will lead to a lognormal distribution of the ratio as the time interval between price changes becomes smaller.

From these payoff expressions, one sees that the exchange option can be viewed as either a call on A with a strike price equal to the price of B or a put on B with a strike price equal to the price of A. These payouts can be expressed as

$$C_u = S_u^B \max\left(0, \frac{S_u^A}{S_u^B} - 1\right)$$

$$C_d = S_d^B \max\left(0, \frac{S_d^A}{S_d^B} - 1\right)$$

Recall that u and d multiply S_0^A / S_0^B to obtain the new stock price ratios at $t = 1$. That is,

$$\frac{S_u^A}{S_u^B} = u\left(\frac{S_0^A}{S_0^B}\right) \tag{6.1}$$

$$\frac{S_d^A}{S_d^B} = d\left(\frac{S_0^A}{S_0^B}\right) \tag{6.2}$$

Using these last two expressions, the expiration day payoffs, C_u and C_d, may be rewritten as

$$C_u = S_u^B \max\left[0, u\left(\frac{S_0^A}{S_0^B}\right) - 1\right] = S_u^B X_u$$

$$C_d = S_d^B \max\left[0, d\left(\frac{S_0^A}{S_0^B}\right) - 1\right] = S_d^B X_d$$

where X_u and X_d denote $\max[0, u(S_0^A / S_0^B) - 1]$ and $\max[0, d(S_0^A / S_0^B) - 1]$. The one-period binomial stock and call trees appear in Figure 6.1.

Now, just as before, set up the call's replicating portfolio, but in the case of the exchange option, the portfolio is composed of the stocks A and B rather than one risky asset and a riskless asset. To replicate, the portfolio's values at $t = 1$ must match the call's values

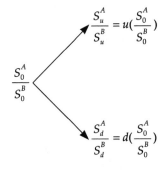

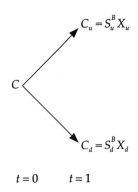

$$t = 0 \qquad t = 1$$

Figure 6.1 Stock and Exchange Option Payoff Trees

at $t = 1$. Using n_A and n_B to denote the shares of A and B in the portfolio, this condition translates into

$$n_A S_u^A + n_B S_u^B = C_u = S_u^B X_u$$

$$n_A S_d^A + n_B S_d^B = C_d = S_d^B X_d$$

Using (6.1) and (6.2), we can substitute for S_u^A and S_d^A to obtain

$$n_A u S_u^B \left(\frac{S_0^A}{S_0^B} \right) + n_B S_u^B = C_u = S_u^B X_u$$

$$n_A d S_d^B \left(\frac{S_0^A}{S_0^B} \right) + n_B S_d^B = C_d = S_d^B X_d$$

Noting that the random variable S_u^B cancels in the first equation and S_d^A cancels in the second equation, we solve for n_A and n_B:

$$n_A = \frac{X_u - X_d}{(u - d)\left(\dfrac{S_0^A}{S_0^B}\right)}$$

$$n_B = \frac{uX_d - dX_u}{(u - d)}$$

The value of the European exchange call can now be written as

$$C = \left[\frac{(X_u - X_d)}{(u - d)(S_0^A/S_0^B)}\right] S_0^A + \left[\frac{(uX_d - dX_u)}{(u - d)}\right] S_0^B$$

$$= S_0^B \left[\frac{(X_u - X_d)}{(u - d)} + \frac{(uX_d - dX_u)}{(u - d)}\right]$$

$$= S_0^B \left[\frac{(1 - d)}{(u - d)} X_u + \frac{(u - 1)}{(u - d)} X_d\right]$$

To prevent arbitrage, an American call's value must satisfy

$$C = \max\left\{S_0^A - S_0^B,\ S_0^B \left[\frac{(1 - d)}{(u - d)} X_u + \frac{(u - 1)}{(u - d)} X_d\right]\right\}$$

An Example of an American Exchange Call

Given $u = 2$, $d = 0.5$, $S_0^A = 100$, and $S_0^B = 125$, then

$$X_u = \max\left[0,\ 2\left(\frac{100}{125}\right) - 1\right] = 0.6$$

$$X_d = \max\left[0,\ 0.5\left(\frac{100}{125}\right) - 1\right] = 0.0$$

$$C = \max\left\{-25,\ 125\left[\left(\frac{0.5}{1.5}\right)0.6 + \left(\frac{1.0}{1.5}\right)0.0\right]\right\}$$

$$= \max(-25, 25) = 25$$

The exchange option can be the building block for many other payoff structures. For example, once the value of an exchange option has been ascertained, it is easy to see how one can obtain the price of an option on the maximum value of two assets. The payoff at expiration of this type of option in our one-period world is the max (S_1^A, S_1^B), where the subscript 1 indicates the stock's value at expiration $(t = 1)$. This can be written as

$$\max (S_1^A, S_1^B) = S_1^B + \max (S_1^A - S_1^B, 0) \qquad (6.3)$$

This follows because if $S_1^A > S_1^B$, then $\max (S_1^A - S_1^B, 0) = S_1^A - S_1^B$; this implies that $S_1^B + \max (S_1^A - S_1^B, 0) = S_1^B + S_1^A - S_1^B = S_1^A$. Conversely, if $S_1^A < S_1^B$, then $\max (S_1^A - S_1^B, 0) = 0$; this implies that $S_1^B + \max (S_1^A - S_1^B, 0) = S_1^B$. By equation (6.3), the current value of max (S_1^A, S_1^B) must equal the present value of the right-hand side of (6.3). Assuming no dividends, the present value of S_1^B is the current stock price, S_0^B, for this is what you would have to pay today to be entitled to receive stock B's value at $t = 1$. The present value of the second term on the right-hand side of equation (6.3) is the current value of the exchange option, which was previously derived. Consequently, the current price of a call on the maximum of the values of two stocks is equal to the sum of the current price of stock B plus the current price of an option to obtain stock A in exchange for stock B.

6.2 Barrier Options

The term *barrier option* is applied to any option that is extinguished or comes to life if the underlying security price crosses a prespecified level, the barrier, during the option's life. For a barrier option to pay off, a joint event must occur: the barrier must (or must not) be crossed prior to expiration, and the option must finish in-the-money. There are two general categories of barrier options: *in-barriers*, popularly called *knock-in options*, and *out-barriers*, usually referred to as *knock-out options*. Since the barrier may be set above or below the current underlying security price, knock-out options can be further sorted into *up-and-out* and *down-and-out* options, and knock-in options can be sorted into *up-and-in* and *down-and-in* options. Table 6.1 classifies the types of knock-out and knock-in calls and puts according to the location of the underlying security price (hereafter referred to as the

Table 6.1 Types of Barrier Options

Barrier Option	Barrier Location Relative to Stock Price When Option is Written	Effect of Barrier Crossing on Option Payoff	
		Crossed	Not Crossed
down-and-out call	below	rebate	standard call
down-and-in call	below	standard call	rebate
up-and-out call	above	rebate	standard call
up-and-in call	above	standard call	rebate
down-and-out put	below	rebate	standard put
down-and-in put	below	standard put	rebate
up-and-out put	above	rebate	standard put
up-and-in put	above	standard put	rebate

stock price) relative to the barrier and the effect of crossing the barrier on the option's payoff value.[2]

The Up-and-Out Put: A Discussion of the Payoff and Pricing of a Type of Barrier Option

An up-and-out stock put—simply referred to as a knock-out put in this section—is a standard European put unless the stock rises above a boundary, called the knock-out boundary, at which time the put is canceled and the put holder receives either a small rebate or nothing. For example, suppose an at-the-money knock-out put is purchased with current stock and strike prices both equal to 50 and the knock-out boundary (H) equal to 55. If, during the put's life, the stock price never rises above 55, then the knock-out put's payoff at expiration is identical to that of a European put, $\max(0, 50 - S_T)$. On the other hand, if the stock price does rise above 55, then the put is canceled, and the put buyer receives the rebate R, independent of the stock's value on expiration day.

One can see that depending on the choice of H and R, these types of instruments may find a receptive market. To continue with the above example, if $R = 0$, then the knock-out put resembles a short sale of the stock at 50 with a buy stop at 55, absent the concern of being able to cover the short at the stop price of 55; the maximum

---

2. This type of classification and description, along with a significant amount of information on barrier options, appears in Derman and Kani 1993.

potential loss is fixed at the knock-out put's premium. Additionally, the knock-out put provision will carry a lower put premium than that of a standard European put. This might induce its purchase by speculators who would like to take a put position in the stock but find standard European puts too expensive.

Let us consider the valuation of a two-period knock-out put. Draw a two-period stock price tree using the following set of parameter values: $S = K = 50$, $H = 55$, and u, d, and r have respective values of 1.5, 0.5, and 1.1. See Figure 6.2. The knock-out put's terminal values appear in Figure 6.3. Notice that for a terminal stock price of 37.5, the knock-out put's value is not uniquely defined, but rather depends upon the path taken by the stock price. If the stock price rises to 75 at $t = 1$, then the knock-out put is canceled and its value at $t = 2$ will be zero. On the other hand, if the stock price arrives at 37.5 without having risen above 55 at $t = 1$, then the put's value at $t = 2$ is 12.5. Because of this property the knock-out put is classified as a path-dependent option. In contrast, the standard European put's terminal value depends only on the final stock price and is independent of the path taken to arrive there.

We price this option as a risk neutral individual would. Multiply each terminal payoff that appears at the end of each path by the risk neutral probability of that path's occurring, and add all products.

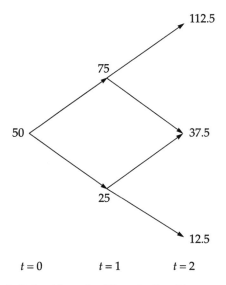

Figure 6.2 Stock Price Tree for Knock-Out Put

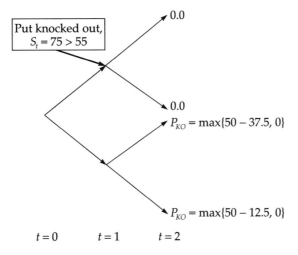

$t = 0 \qquad t = 1 \qquad t = 2$

Figure 6.3 Knock-Out Put's Terminal Values

Discount by the risk-free rate. Calculating the put's value as the discounted expected payoff and symbolizing the probability of a stock price event over the put's life by $pr(\cdot)$, we have

$$P_{KO} = \frac{1}{(1.1)^2} \left[\begin{array}{l} (0)pr(S_1 > 55) + (12.5)pr(S_2 = 37.5 \text{ and } S_1 \leq 55) \\ \qquad + (37.5)pr(S_2 = 12.5 \text{ and } S_1 \leq 55) \end{array} \right]$$

Since the risk neutral probabilities of up and down moves are respectively $(r - d)/(u - d) = 0.6$ and $(u - r)/(u - d) = 0.4$, then $pr(S_1 > 55) = 0.6$, $pr(S_2 = 37.5$ and $S_1 \leq 55) = (.4)(.6) = 0.24$, and $pr(S_2 = 12.5$ and $S_1 \leq 55) = (0.4)^2 = 0.16$. Consequently, $P_{KO} = 7.44$.

Although working along a binomial tree's paths and calculating the expected value of the put's terminal payoffs from a risk neutral point of view is theoretically acceptable, it is not practical. Instead, the preferred approach is to take the view of the risk neutral individual but to assume that the probability of the stock's continuous returns is normally distributed. The expected value of terminal payoffs is calculated by integration and then discounted back at the riskless rate. The result is an exact solution to the pricing problem, analogous to the formula obtained in the standard Black-Scholes case.

6.3 The Asian Option: An Option on the Average

Asian options may have received their impetus from the advent of commodity-linked bonds in which the bond holder is entitled to choose the larger of the average value of the underlying commodity, calculated over a given time period, or the face value of the bond. Especially in illiquid markets, traders liked the fact that the Asian option's final payoff is dependent on an average of prices[3] rather than the price on termination. After all, there has always been the possibility in a thinly traded market for the underlying asset that an in-the-money call could be pushed out-of-the-money by driving down the underlying asset's price. The average price is not so easily manipulated.

Whatever the reason for their initial growth, Asian options are now quite popular. Average options are offered on commodities such as silver, gold, and oil. They are used by corporate treasurers to cover the exposure of a series of transactions in a foreign currency or in an interest rate instrument. They can be employed by a dealer who makes a continuous market in a particular stock. Whereas standard options are appropriate for reducing the risk of a particular position whose size is known or of a cash flow to be made or received on a specific date, the Asian option is suitable for reducing the risk of one's average asset position or that of a stream of continuous cash flows whose size and timing cannot be easily predicted.

The Asian option is path dependent. For the same underlying asset price on expiration day, two different averages may be obtained. Therefore, in obtaining a price for the option, we must move forward through the tree to expiration day. Using the parameter values presented in the knock-out put section, we can demonstrate the pricing of an Asian call with a strike of 50. There are four stock price paths. The paths, their averages, and the risk neutral probabilities of their occurrence are presented in Table 6.2.

Table 6.2 Stock Price Paths and Probabilities for the Asian Option

Path	Price Sequence	Average Price	Path Probability
1	50 → 75 → 112.5	79.17	0.36
2	50 → 75 → 37.5	54.17	0.24
3	50 → 25 → 37.5	37.50	0.24
4	50 → 25 → 12.5	29.17	0.16

---

3. The averaging may be done on daily prices, weekly prices, or whatever price observation interval the two parties to the trade find agreeable.

Only at the end of paths 1 and 2 is the Asian option in-the-money, respectively paying $79.17 - 50 = 29.17$ and $54.17 - 50 = 4.17$. The discounted expected value of the call's payoffs are

$$C_{Asian} = \frac{1}{(1.1)^2}[.36(29.17) + .24(4.17) + .40(0.0)] = 9.51$$

By the way, the standard European call's value would be

$$C_{European} = \frac{1}{(1.1)^2}[.36(112.50 - 50) + .64(0)] = 18.60$$

The reason for the higher European premium is that the stock price has higher volatility than the average of the stock prices.

It is impractical to do this forward type of calculation through a tree with many divisions. For n periods, there are 2^n paths. If $n = 40$, there are over a trillion paths. The problem is often described as dealing with an "exploding tree." A pragmatic approach is to randomly generate a large number of price paths—perhaps 2,000—from a lognormal return distribution. The average price of each path is calculated, the corresponding option value at the end of each path is computed, their expected value is calculated, and this number is discounted back to the current date to obtain the Asian option's value.

6.4 Lookback Options

At expiration, a lookback call (put) has its strike set to the minimum (maximum) stock price attained during the life of the option. Suppose that you held a three-month lookback call on 100 shares of IBM. Then, on expiration day, you would exercise your call and take delivery of 100 shares of IBM at the lowest price that prevailed during the preceding three-month period. Your per-share profit would equal the stock price at expiration less the lowest stock price during the preceding three months. Notice that since the exercise price for a call (put) can never be higher (lower) than the expiration day stock price, the call (put) will always be exercised. Practically, transaction costs associated with exercise may prevent exercise of the call (put). This will occur if the final stock price is very close to the minimum (maximum) stock price of the period.

Clearly, the value of a lookback option is path dependent. What the option holder receives depends upon where the stock price has been. We apply the risk neutral valuation methodology to obtain the lookback option's current price. Denoting the minimum and maximum stock prices for the period up to and including the expiration date by S_{min} and S_{max}, respectively, then the current prices of the lookback call and put, C_{LB} and P_{LB}, are given by

$$C_{LB} = r^{-T}E\,[\max\,(0,\,S_T - S_{min})]$$

$$P_{LB} = r^{-T}E\,[\max\,(0,\,S_{max} - S_T)]$$

where E symbolizes that we are taking the expectation of the term in the brackets.

Since we have already reasoned that $S_T - S_{min} \geq 0$ and $S_{max} - S_T \geq 0$, the above formulas can be reduced to

$$C_{LB} = r^{-T}E(S_T - S_{min}) = r^{-T}E(S_T) - r^{-T}E(S_{min})$$

$$P_{LB} = r^{-T}E(S_{max} - S_T) = r^{-T}E(S_{max}) - r^{-T}E(S_T)$$

For simplicity of exposition, we assume that the stock pays no dividend over the lives of the lookback options. Then, for our risk neutral investor, the present value of the stock's expiration day value is the current stock price. The price equations become

$$C_{LB} = S - r^{-T}E(S_{min})$$

$$P_{LB} = r^{-T}E(S_{max}) - S$$

For lognormally distributed stock returns, this computation has been done.[4] To become more comfortable with the valuation technique, try computing P_{LB} for a two-period lookback put, where the binomial model's parameters are $u = 2$, $d = 0.5$, $r = 1.1$, and $S = 100$. Develop the stock price tree. Pick out the maximum stock price of each path, and note the risk neutral probability of that path. Weight each maximum price by the path's probability and add to obtain $E(S_{max}) = 0.16(400) + 0.24(200) + 0.6(100) = 172$. Then $P_{LB} = [1/(1.1)^2](172) - 100 = 42.15$.

---

4. See Goldman, Sosin, and Gatto 1979 and Garman 1992.

6.5 The Compound Option: An Option on an Option

Consider an option that permits the holder to purchase yet another option on a stock. In this case, the compound option is a compound call with a two-period life. The stock price tree is presented in Figure 6.4 and evolves according to the parameter values $S = 100$, $u = 1.5$, $d = 0.5$, and $r = 1.1$.

Assume that this compound call requires that the holder must decide at $t = 1$ whether to exercise the first call by paying 30 for a one-period call on the stock. If exercise is selected at $t = 1$, then a one-period call with a strike of 100 is received that can, in turn, be exercised at $t = 2$. Clearly, the first call will be exercised at $t = 1$ if the one-period call to be received on the stock at $t = 1$ has a value in excess of 30.

Employing the risk neutral approach, the value at $t = 1$ of the one-period call on the stock, given a stock price of 150, equals

$$C_{150} = \frac{1}{1.1}[(0.6)\max(0, 225 - 100) + (0.4)\max(0, 75 - 100)]$$

$$= 68.18$$

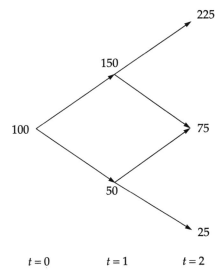

| $t = 0$ | $t = 1$ | $t = 2$ |

Figure 6.4 Stock Price Tree for the Compound Call

Given a stock price of 50 at $t = 1$, then the one-period call on the stock is worth

$$C_{50} = \frac{1}{1.1}[(0.6)\max(0, 75 - 100) + (0.4)\max(0, 25 - 100)] = 0.0$$

These calculations tell us that if the stock price is 150 at $t = 1$, the holder should exercise the first call, because the payoff from exercise is $\max(0, 68.18 - 30) = 38.18$. In contrast, it would not be worthwhile to exercise the first call to obtain the second call if the stock price is 50 at $t = 1$. So the two intrinsic values of the compound call at $t = 1$, when the first exercise decision must be made, are 38.18 at the higher node and 0 at the lower node. Understanding that the first call derives its value from the second call's values at $t = 1$, we again apply the risk neutral methodology to the value of the complete compound call:

$$C_{compound} = \frac{1}{1.1}[(0.6)38.18 + (0.4)0] = 20.83$$

The classic use of a compound option is in tendering. A U.S. corporation bids for a British firm in sterling. The venture has two uncertainties: (1) whether or not the bid will be accepted, and, if so, (2) what will be the dollar cost of sterling at that future date. To mitigate the associated financial risk, the U.S. firm buys a European call on another European call, a compound call. The second call in the sequence is written on a stipulated amount of sterling at an agreed-upon strike price. Should the tender not be accepted, the firm lets the call die. If the bid is accepted, the firm pays the first call's strike, in dollars, and accepts in return another call on the British pound with a strike price that was set in $/£. This second call, whose expiration date is most likely set to the date that the pounds are to be delivered to complete the purchase, will be exercised at termination if the British pound's dollar price exceeds its strike price.

Chapter **7**

Interest Rate Options

LIKE A STOCK option, an interest rate option grants the buyer the right to an asymmetrical payoff, for which the buyer pays an option premium. However, for a variety of reasons, the multiplicative binomial and the Black-Scholes models are inappropriate for pricing interest rate options. Among the reasons are that (1) the volatility of the underlying instrument cannot be assumed to remain constant (for example, a bond's return volatility is compressed as maturity nears, since its price cannot stray far from its redemption value); and that (2) the yield tends to revert to a long-run level. The chapter begins by demonstrating, through a numerical illustration, why the multiplicative binomial might fail. Another model must be used. The essence of this alternative model is the arbitrage-free, one-period interest rate tree. Most of the chapter is devoted to explaining the construction of this tree. The remainder of the chapter demonstrates how the arbitrage-free tree is applied to the pricing of interest rate options, such as an option on a bond, a cap, and options that are embedded in other interest rate instruments, e.g., callable bonds and bonds with sinking fund features.

7.1 A Methodology for Pricing Interest Rate Options: The Arbitrage-Free Tree Requirement

It would seem natural to extend the multiplicative binomial model that we applied to equity options to the valuation of interest rate options. In that regard, we might generate an interest rate tree by multiplying the interest rates of various maturities by a constant u in order to ascribe up state values to these rates or a constant d to provide down state values. Unfortunately, this procedure will often lead to an interest rate tree that is useless in attempting to find arbitrage-free values for interest rate options or any other interest rate instruments.

Suppose that you are managing a U.S. Treasury bond portfolio. Among your concerns are the valuation and rate sensitivity of the maturities that you hold. You set out to generate an interest rate tree for future periods. Your objective is to obtain for each future period a probability distribution of default-free term structures. Therefore, to each node of the tree, a yield to maturity for each bond must be attached. Since your concern is valuation, the yield curve that you focus on is the U.S. Treasury spot yield curve, that is, the yields that zero-coupon U.S. Treasury bonds would carry as a function of their maturities.

Let us look at the beginning of a tree generated using the multiplicative methodology. We focus our attention on three of the many maturities. At $t = 0$, the one-, nine-, and ten-year bonds have yields to maturity of 6%, 9%, and 10%, respectively; the ten-year bond becomes a nine-year bond at $t = 1$. Assume the u multiplier is 1.05 and d is $1/1.05$. At $t = 1$, the new yields for the then-current one-, nine-, and ten-year bonds are depicted in Figure 7.1, where the subscripted r_T variable in the diagram symbolizes the yield for a zero-coupon, one-dollar face value bond maturing in T years.

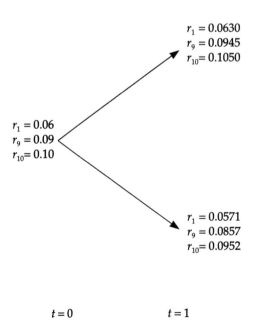

Figure 7.1 An Interest Rate Tree

A comparison of the rate of return of the one-year bond, which earns 6% over the initial period, with the rate of return of the ten-year bond, reveals that no one would wish to hold the one-year bond. The ten-year bond has a first-period percentage price change of 15.08% ($[1/(1.0945)^9 \div 1/(1.1)^{10}] - 1$) if the up state occurs and 23.75% ($[1/(1.0857)^9 \div 1/(1.1)^{10}] - 1$) should the down state occur. The one-year bond is dominated by the ten-year bond, given this interest rate evolution. Clearly this cannot persist. Since everyone would prefer the ten-year bond to the one-year bond at $t = 0$, yields would have to change. A riskless arbitrage at $t = 0$ is to short a one-year bond and use the receipts from the short sale to purchase 2.447 ten-year bonds. This results in a zero net investment at $t = 0$. If at $t = 1$ the up state occurs, the net proceeds from selling the now nine-year bonds and repaying the money owed on the one-year bond amounts to 0.0857 ($2.447 \cdot [1/(1.1)^{10}] \cdot 1.1508 - 1.00$). Should the down state occur, the net proceeds would be 0.1675 ($2.447 \cdot [1/(1.1)^{10}] \cdot 1.2375 - 1.00$). The generated structure cannot represent equilibrium.

To eliminate arbitrage possibilities when generating a tree, the following condition must be satisfied by bond prices at adjacent nodes:

$$P_i^t(T) = P_i^t(1)[\theta P_{i+1}^{t+1}(T - 1) + (1 - \theta)P_i^{t+1}(T - 1)] \qquad (7.1)$$

where $0 \le \theta \le 1$ and $P_i^t(T)$ symbolizes the price at time t of a bond with one dollar of face value and T periods to maturity at a node reached by an interest rate path that had i up moves. Since interest rates and prices are inversely related, $P_1^t(T - 1) < P_0^t(T - 1)$. The one-period tree at the $t = 0$ node appears in Figure 7.2.

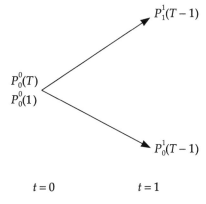

Figure 7.2 The Price Tree between Two Dates

The equation says that the price today of a bond with T periods remaining to maturity must equal the discounted value of the weighted average of prices of the bond one period later, when the bond has $T - 1$ periods remaining to maturity. $P_i^t(1)$, which equals $1/[1 + r_i^t(1)]$, does the discounting, where $r_i^t(1)$ is the one-period rate at the node identified by t and i. The weights are θ and $1 - \theta$. The θ and $1 - \theta$ parameters may be considered to represent the probabilities of an up move and a down move in interest rates. Observe that if θ is set equal to the risk neutral probability, then equation (7.1) gives the precise methodology by which the risk neutral individual would arrive at a value for $P_i^t(1)$. The individual would calculate the expected value of the bond's price one period later and discount that back by the one-period risk-free rate. We can quickly calculate an implied θ value for the interest rate tree depicted in Figure 7.1—the tree with arbitrage possibilities—to show that the θ for that tree falls outside of the [0, 1] interval. Solve

$$\frac{1}{(1.1)^{10}} = \frac{1}{1.06}\left[\theta\left(\frac{1}{(1.0945)^9}\right) + (1 - \theta)\left(\frac{1}{(1.0857)^9}\right)\right]$$

to obtain $\theta = 2.05$.

Academic Terminology Describing the No-Arbitrage Condition

The academic literature has a particular way of looking at and talking about equation (7.1). Since $P_i^t(1) = 1/(1 + r_i^t(1))$, the right-hand side of the equation can be thought of as the expectation of a relative value variable. This variable, R, can be viewed as the long-term bond's value one period later divided by what one dollar would accumulate to if invested at the riskless one-period rate. So the relative value of the bond at $t + 1$ will be either

$$R_{i+1}^{t+1}(T - 1) = P_{i+1}^{t+1}(T - 1)/[1 + r_i^t(1)] \text{ or}$$

$$R_i^{t+1}(T - 1) = P_i^{t+1}(T - 1)/[1 + r_i^t(1)]$$

Then the right-hand side of equation (7.1) can be written as $\theta R_{i+1}^{t+1}(T - 1) + (1 - \theta)R_i^{t+1}(T - 1)$. The left-hand side of equation (7.1) can be interpreted, trivially, as the ratio of the bond's current price to the current value of a one-period, one-dollar investment at the riskless rate, i.e., $R_i^t(T) = P_i^t(T)/1$. Employing these definitions, equation (7.1) can be rewritten as

$$R_i^t(T) = \theta R_{i+1}^{t+1}(T-1) + (1-\theta)R_i^{t+1}(T-1)$$

This equation says that the expectation of the random variable R is equal to the current value of that variable. Stochastic variables that have this property are called *martingales.* Consequently, a statement that the tree is arbitrage-free is equivalent to the statement that there exist probabilities, θ and $(1 - \theta)$, such that the relative value R is a martingale, i.e., its expected value equals its current value.

Generating an Arbitrage-Free Term Structure

As long as we are generating an arbitrage-free term structure, it might as well be realistic, in the sense that the term structure generated is consistent with the observed U.S. Treasury spot yield curve. After all, if we generate a tree that is inconsistent with the observed term structure, then we will be unable to price the bonds correctly. If we cannot correctly price an underlying instrument, we will almost surely misprice the option written on that bond. This methodology is demonstrated in the simplest of cases, where changes in the term structure are driven by changes in the one-period interest rate. This is often referred to as a one-factor model of the term structure. In a one-factor model, one random variable drives the entire term structure. A multifactor model has more than one random variable driving changes in the term structure.

Consider the scenario where the one-period rate, $r_i^t(1)$, changes according to the following probability law:

$$r_{i+1}^{t+1}(1) = r_i^t(1) + \alpha(t) + 0.01 \qquad \text{with probability} \qquad \tfrac{1}{2}$$

$$r_i^{t+1}(1) = r_i^t(1) + \alpha(t) - 0.01 \qquad \text{with probability} \qquad \tfrac{1}{2}$$

The $\alpha(t)$ parameter measures the drift over time in the one-period rate. It is this parameter, which may vary with time, that will be assigned numerical values so that the one-period generated rates provide an arbitrage-free tree that is consistent with the current term structure. The other feature of the stochastic process that is worth discussing is that the volatility of the one-period rate is encompassed in the ± 0.01 parameter. This volatility magnitude has been arbitrarily assigned to the process. Later, it will be shown how this parameter can be deduced from the interest rate data and then incorporated into the tree-generating methodology. Figure 7.3 contains the current term structure and the layout of the variables for which numerical values are sought. As the diagram indicates, our interest is in demonstrating how to obtain the one- and two-period bond rates at $t = 1$ and the one-period rates at $t = 2$.

Imposition of the no-arbitrage condition that the current price of the two-period bond must equal its discounted expected value gives

$$P_0^0(2) = P_0^0(1)[0.5P_1^1(1) + 0.5P_0^1(1)]$$

Inserting the stochastic expression for the one-period rate with the assumed interest rate levels at $t = 0$, we obtain

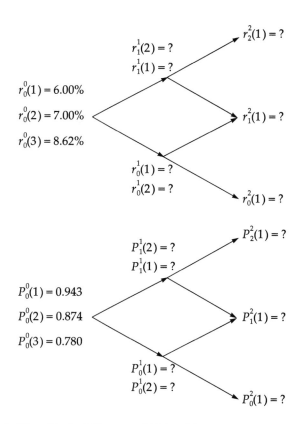

Figure 7.3 Two-Period Rate and Price Trees

$$\frac{1}{(1.07)^2} = \frac{1}{1.06} \left(\begin{array}{l} 0.5 \left\{ \dfrac{1}{1 + [0.06 + \alpha(0) + 0.01]} \right\} \\ + 0.5 \left\{ \dfrac{1}{1 + [0.06 + \alpha(0) - 0.01]} \right\} \end{array} \right)$$

Solving this equation for $\alpha(0)$ gives $\alpha(0) = 0.02$. Upon substitution of this α value into the stochastic process, we obtain $r_1^1(1) = 0.09$ and $r_0^1(1) = 0.07$.

We use the same technique to obtain the rates on a two-period zero-coupon bond in the up and down states at $t = 1$. The arbitrage-free condition applied to a three-period zero-coupon bond at $t = 0$ provides the following relation.

$$P_0^0(3) = P_0^0(1) \, [0.5P_1^0(2) + 0.5P_0^0(2)]$$

This equation says that the current three-period bond price is equal to the discounted value of the expectation of the two-period bond prices at $t = 1$. Before we begin the substitution of numbers, let us further reduce the right side of the above equation into an expression in one-period rates.

Applying the no-arbitrage condition to the two-period bond prices at $t = 1$ and then substituting the stochastic expression for the one-period rate, we have

$$P_1^1(2) = P_1^1(1) \, [0.5 \, P_2^2(1) + 0.5P_1^2(1)]$$

$$= P_1^1(1) \left(\begin{array}{l} 0.5 \left\{ \dfrac{1}{1 + [r_1^1(1) + \alpha(1) + 0.01]} \right\} \\ + 0.5 \left\{ \dfrac{1}{1 + [r_1^1(1) + \alpha(1) - 0.01]} \right\} \end{array} \right)$$

and

$$P_0^1(2) = P_0^1(1) \, [0.5P_1^2(1) + 0.5P_0^2(1)]$$

$$= P_0^1(1) \left(\begin{array}{l} 0.5 \left\{ \dfrac{1}{1 + [r_0^1(1) + \alpha(1) + 0.01]} \right\} \\ + 0.5 \left\{ \dfrac{1}{1 + [r_0^1(1) + \alpha(1) - 0.01]} \right\} \end{array} \right)$$

Now substitute these expressions for $P_1^1(2)$ and $P_0^1(2)$ into that for $P_0^0(3)$. Then

$$P_0^0(3) = P_0^0(1) \left\{ \begin{array}{l} 0.5 \left[P_1^1(1) \left(\begin{array}{l} 0.5 \left\{ \dfrac{1}{1 + [r_1^1(1) + \alpha(1) + 0.01]} \right\} \\ + 0.5 \left\{ \dfrac{1}{1 + [r_1^1(1) + \alpha(1) - 0.01]} \right\} \end{array} \right) \right] \\ + 0.5 \left[P_0^1(1) \left(\begin{array}{l} 0.5 \left\{ \dfrac{1}{1 + [r_0^1(1) + \alpha(1) + 0.01]} \right\} \\ + 0.5 \left\{ \dfrac{1}{1 + [r_0^1(1) + \alpha(1) - 0.01]} \right\} \end{array} \right) \right] \end{array} \right\}$$

In the previous stage, we obtained $r_1^1(1) = 0.09$, $r_0^1(1) = 0.07$. Inserting these numbers into the above equation and remembering that $P_0^0(3) = 1/(1.0862)^3$, $P_0^0(1) = 1/(1.06)$, $P_1^1(1) = 1/(1.09)$, and $P_0^1(1) = 1/(1.07)$, we obtain an equation in $\alpha(1)$. The solution is $\alpha(1) = 0.04$. Insertion of this $\alpha(1)$ value into the stochastic equation provides the remaining one-period rates: $r_2^2(1) = 0.14$, $r_1^2(1) = 0.12$, and $r_0^2(1) = 0.10$.

We now have the necessary data to obtain $P_1^1(2)$ and $P_0^1(2)$, the two-period bond prices at $t = 1$. From these prices, the corresponding two-period yields are obtained, $r_1^1(2)$ and $r_0^1(2)$. The no-arbitrage condition tells us that

$$P_1^1(2) = \frac{1}{1.09} \left[0.5 \left(\frac{1}{1.14} \right) + 0.5 \left(\frac{1}{1.12} \right) \right] = 0.8120 = \frac{1}{(1.1098)^2}$$

and

$$P_0^1(2) = \frac{1}{1.07} \left[0.5 \left(\frac{1}{1.12} \right) + 0.5 \left(\frac{1}{1.10} \right) \right] = 0.8420 = \frac{1}{(1.0898)^2}$$

The equations imply that $r_1^1(2) = 0.1098$ and $r_0^1(2) = 0.0898$. The question marks in the interest rate tree can now be filled out. See Figure 7.4.

Using the current prices of four-, five-, and six-period bonds, etc., we can generate the full interest rate tree with a term structure at each node.

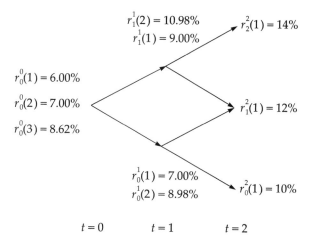

$r_1^1(2) = 10.98\%$ $r_2^2(1) = 14\%$
$r_1^1(1) = 9.00\%$

$r_0^0(1) = 6.00\%$

$r_0^0(2) = 7.00\%$ $r_1^2(1) = 12\%$

$r_0^0(3) = 8.62\%$

$r_0^1(1) = 7.00\%$
$r_0^1(2) = 8.98\%$ $r_0^2(1) = 10\%$

$t = 0$ $t = 1$ $t = 2$

Figure 7.4 The Completed Two-Period Interest Rate Tree

An Arbitrage-Free Interest Rate Tree Consistent with Market Yields and Volatilities

In the previous section, a technique for generating an arbitrage-free interest rate tree consistent with the existing term structure was demonstrated. The technique assumed a specific stochastic process for the evolution of one-period rates, specifically that the next one-period rate would be equal to this period's rate and a drift term plus or minus 1%—each with probability 0.5. We then searched for the drift term value at each time t that would not only force the evolving one-period rates to be arbitrage-free but also would obtain a one-period rate configuration that would be consistent with the current term structure. While we allowed the drift term values to be determined by the characteristics of the term structure and the arbitrage-free condition, we arbitrarily assigned values to the one-period rate's volatility parameter, in particular $+.01$ and $-.01$. A more general procedure would allow the volatility parameter estimate to be derived from the interest rate data, while of course adhering to the no-arbitrage principle. The following method was developed by Black, Derman, and Toy (1990).

One-period rates evolve along a binomial tree with probability of an up move 0.5 and that of a down move 0.5. The generated one-period rates must again be consistent with the current yield curve and, in addition, must be consistent with the volatility structure. The

Table 7.1 Term Structure and Volatility Data

Period	Yield to Maturity	Estimated One-Period Rate Volatility
1	10.00%	—
2	10.48%	18.39%
3	10.72%	15.92%

latter is defined as the relationship between the volatility of one-period rates and time. The volatilities in this structure are estimates of the volatility of the one-period rate, one period from today; the one-period rate two periods from today, and so on. Table 7.1 presents a sample of such term structure data.

The tree to which we wish to attach one-period rates and the symbols denoting these rates are depicted in Figure 7.5.

Before starting our search for the appropriate $r_i^j(1)$ values, we need some information on the volatility calculation. Assume that the natural logarithm of the ratio of next period's rate to this period's rate obeys the following probability distribution.

$$p(\ln [r_1^1(1)/r_0^0(1)]) = 0.5 \quad \text{and} \quad p(\ln [r_0^1(1)/r_0^0(1)]) = 0.5$$

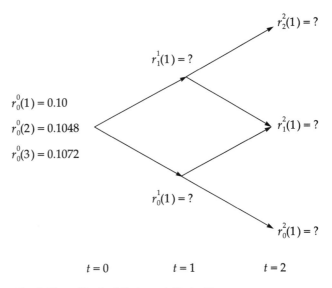

Figure 7.5 A Two-Period Interest Rate Tree

where p(·) symbolizes the probability density function. The expected value, μ, of this ln ratio is

$$\mu = 0.5 \ln [r_1^1(1)/r_0^0(1)] + 0.5 \ln [r_0^1(1)/r_0^0(1)]$$

and the corresponding variance, σ^2, is

$$\sigma^2 = 0.5 (\ln [r_1^1(1)/r_0^0(1)] - \mu)^2 + 0.5 (\ln [r_0^1(1)/r_0^0(1)] - \mu)^2$$

Substituting the expression for μ and simplifying gives

$$\sigma^2 = (0.5 \ln [r_1^1(1)/r_0^1(1)])^2$$

The standard deviation, taken as the measure of the one-period rate's volatility, is

$$\sigma = 0.5 \ln [r_1^1(1)/r_0^1(1)]$$

Employing the one- and two-period zero-coupon yields at $t = 0$, 0.10, and 0.1048, and the volatility estimate for the one-period rate at $t = 1$, values for $r_1^1(1)$ and $r_0^1(1)$ can be obtained. The no-arbitrage condition requires that $r_1^1(1)$ and $r_0^1(1)$ satisfy

$$\frac{1}{(1.1048)^2} = \frac{1}{1.1} \left[0.5 \left(\frac{1}{1 + r_1^1(1)} \right) + 0.5 \left(\frac{1}{1 + r_0^1(1)} \right) \right]$$

And these rates must also be consistent with the expected volatility level, so

$$0.1839 = 0.5 \left\{ \ln \left[\frac{r_1^1(1)}{r_0^1(1)} \right] \right\}$$

The two equations in two unknowns are solved to obtain $r_1^1(1) = 0.13$ and $r_0^1(1) = 0.09$.

Following the same path, values for $r_2^2(1)$, $r_1^2(1)$ and $r_0^2(1)$ can be produced. But now three equations are needed. The third equation comes from the additional assumption that the one-period rate volatility at $t = 2$ is constant across nodes. This translates into the mathematical condition that

$$0.5 \ln \left[\frac{r_2^2(1)}{r_1^2(1)}\right] = 0.5 \ln \left[\frac{r_1^2(1)}{r_0^2(1)}\right]$$

or, equivalently,

$$\frac{r_2^2(1)}{r_1^2(1)} = \frac{r_1^2(1)}{r_0^2(1)}$$

The three equations to be solved are

$$\frac{1}{(1.1072)^3} = \frac{1}{1.1}\left[\begin{array}{l} 0.5\left(\frac{1}{1.13}\left\{0.5\left[\frac{1}{1+r_2^2(1)}\right] + 0.5\left[\frac{1}{1+r_1^2(1)}\right]\right\}\right) \\ + 0.5\left(\frac{1}{1.09}\left\{0.5\left[\frac{1}{1+r_1^2(1)}\right] + 0.5\left[\frac{1}{1+r_0^2(1)}\right]\right\}\right) \end{array}\right]$$

$$0.1592 = 0.5 \ln \left[\frac{r_2^2(1)}{r_1^2(1)}\right]$$

$$0.1592 = 0.5 \ln \left[\frac{r_1^2(1)}{r_0^2(1)}\right]$$

The equations' solution is $r_2^2(1) = 0.15125$, $r_1^2(1) = 0.11$, and $r_0^2(1) = 0.08$. The two-period tree with its rates filled in appears in Figure 7.6.

With more data, we could continue to fill out the interest rate tree for subsequent future periods. Remember that in order to obtain that extra equation for that extra unknown, as we step one more period into the future, we assume that interest rate volatility may vary across time but must be constant across nodes at any particular time. There is a limit on how far out we may generate one-period rates. Given current yields on one-, two-, and three-period bonds, we were able to generate one-period rates through $t = 2$. Correspondingly, with a yield structure whose longest bond is a T-period bond, we can produce one-year rates only up through period $T - 1$.

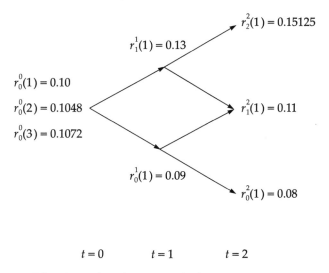

$r_2^2(1) = 0.15125$

$r_1^1(1) = 0.13$

$r_0^0(1) = 0.10$

$r_0^0(2) = 0.1048$

$r_1^2(1) = 0.11$

$r_0^0(3) = 0.1072$

$r_0^1(1) = 0.09$

$r_0^2(1) = 0.08$

| $t = 0$ | $t = 1$ | $t = 2$ |

Figure 7.6 The Completed Two-Period Interest Rate Tree

Apart from providing us with a methodology to incorporate volatility estimates into the rate structure, the Black, Derman, and Toy
model has another attractive attribute. If interest rates are *mean
reverting*, then that information is included in the one-period rates
generated by the model. An interest rate is said to be mean reverting
if it tends to be drawn back to a long-run level. Suppose that the
long-run level is 11%, then if the current one-period rate is 14%, it is
likely to be lower in the next period. Conversely, if the one-period
rate is presently 9%, then it is likely to be higher in the next period.
Interest rates appear to exhibit this property. In addition, mean rever-
sion implies that the volatility of short-term rates exceeds the volatility
of long-term rates. Rates seem to possess this property. Since it is
desired that the one-period rates to be generated have properties
consistent with those of the actual term structure, any methodology
that is used to generate the rate tree should allow for the inclusion
of the mean-reverting property.

7.2 Pricing an Interest Rate Option

In order to price a bond option, one must first find the bond price
at each node of the tree. This requires that you start at the next-to-
last nodes and work your way back to the current node, applying
the no-arbitrage principle at each stage. Suppose your objective is to

price a three-period, zero-coupon bond that has a 100 face value. The transition probabilities for an up move and a down move are equal. The set of one-period rates is presented in Figure 7.7. To price the bond at a particular node, simply calculate its expected value one period later and discount back at the one-period rate. This is the no-arbitrage condition. Start at $t = 2$, calculate the value at each of the three nodes in this manner, and then move back to $t = 1$. Repeat the procedure for the two nodes at $t = 1$. Move back to $t = 0$ and complete. The computed bond prices are placed at the appropriate nodes of the tree. See Figure 7.7.

The calculation for the $t = 2$, 18% node is $[0.5(100) + 0.5(100)]/1.18 = 84.75$, and that for the $t = 1$, 13% node is $[0.5(84.75) + 0.5(89.29)]/1.13 = 77.01$. The bond's price at any node could also have been computed by looking forward. For example, the bond's price at $t = 0$ could have been obtained by calculating the present value of each path, in this case 100 divided by the product of the three relevant one-period rates, and weighting by the probability of the path 0.125.

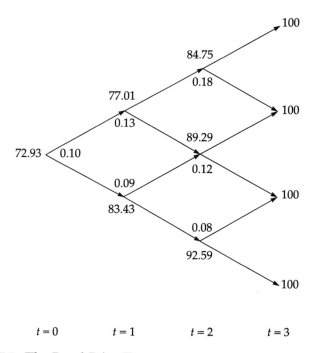

$$t = 0 \qquad t = 1 \qquad t = 2 \qquad t = 3$$

Figure 7.7 The Bond Price Tree

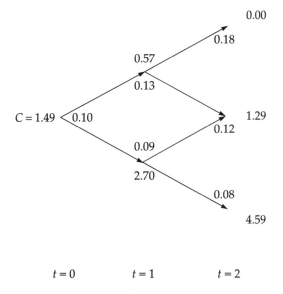

0.00

0.18

0.57

0.13

$C = 1.49$ 0.10

1.29

0.12

0.09

2.70

0.08

4.59

$t = 0$ $t = 1$ $t = 2$

Figure 7.8 The Tree of Call Values

To price a two-period American call (expiring at $t = 2$) with a strike of 88 on this three-period bond, draw a two-period tree, write in the call's values at expiration, and work backward, applying the no-arbitrage principle at each node. Remember to compare each computed value with the exercise value of the call; the call's price at a node will equal the greater of these two values. Figure 7.8 contains a tree with the call's value presented at each node.

7.3 Caps, Floors, and Collars

A cap, as its name is meant to imply, is used to limit the interest cost of a floating rate loan. The cap's life, the length of time from initiation date (usually two days after the trade date and called the *effective date*) to expiration date is divided into a number of payment periods, each of which ends with a payment day. Two business days prior to the beginning of each payment period, known as the *reset date*, the cap's reference rate level is determined. If the cap's reference rate exceeds a previously agreed upon figure, termed the *cap rate* or *strike rate*, the seller of the cap makes a cash payment equal to the difference between the reference rate and the cap rate, multiplied by the principal amount on which the cap is written. The principal amount is used only for calculation purposes. It is often referred to as the cap's *notional amount.* Though the cash payment by the seller is determined at the beginning of a payment period, the actual payment occurs at the end of the period. In essence, the purchase of a cap ensures that the floating rate borrower will pay the lesser of the reference rate and the cap rate. For the benefits conferred by cap ownership, the buyer pays the seller an amount termed the *cap premium.*

Consider an example. A two-year cap is purchased on a 100 million notional amount. The reference rate is on six-month loans, and the cap rate is 6% (annualized). The reference rate's level for payment calculation purposes is determined two days prior to the beginning of each six-month payment period—the reset date—and payment, if any, is made six months after the period's beginning date. Since the rate for the first of these four six-month periods is known on the trade date, the parties to the trade agree that no payment is necessary at the end of this first six-month period. Therefore, there are only three payment dates in this cap agreement. If, at the end of the first six-month period, the reference rate is 10%, then the payment that the seller must make six months later to the buyer amounts to $(0.10/2 - 0.06/2) \times 100,000,000 = 2,000,000$. (To deannualize, the rates in this example are divided by 2.) If, after a year, the reference rate is 5%, no payment will be made six months later. And so on for the final six-month period.

What one immediately sees is that the purchase of a two-year cap is, in effect, the purchase of three consecutive European six-month calls on the reference rate.[1] This three-call sequence is termed a "strip" of three calls. Consequently, to value a cap, decompose it into a strip of calls, value each call, and sum.

A floor is purchased to set the minimum rate that would be earned on a floating rate loan. This is ensured for the life of the floor. If the reference rate is below the *floor rate* (strike rate) on a reset date, the seller makes a payment to the buyer at period's end equal to the difference between the floor rate and the reference rate levels times the notional principal. Just as a cap can be viewed as a strip of European calls on the reference rate, a floor can be viewed as a strip of European puts on the reference rate. The price paid for the floor is named the *floor premium.*

---

1. There is a subtle difference. A standard European call has seller paying buyer on the call's expiration day, while the cap payment occurs six months later. This difference must be accounted for in the valuation process.

If a cap is purchased and a floor is sold, perhaps to defray the cost of the cap, the position formed is called a *collar*. Whereas the cap rate is normally set at the reference rate prevailing on the cap's trade date, the floor rate is set below the current reference rate level. In a collar, the floor is out-of-the-money when initiated. The payoff diagram for a collar is provided by Figure 7.9, where π, R, C, F, R_C, and R_F, respectively, symbolize profits, the reference rate, the cap premium, the floor premium, the cap rate, and the floor rate.

At reference rate levels below the floor rate, the short floor loses money and the long cap is out-of-the-money. Any gain realized from paying a lower borrowing rate is offset by the payment made on the short floor. Additionally, the difference in premiums is lost. If the reference rate falls between the floor and cap rates, both options finish out-of-the-money. There is a loss on the collar equal to the difference in premiums. At reference rates above the cap rate, the cap is in-the-money and the floor is out-of-the-money. Payoffs from the long cap serve to offset the higher costs of borrowing. In short, a collar is a trade-off of the lower cost of insuring against higher rates in exchange for parting with the reduced borrowing costs to be realized if rates are lower.

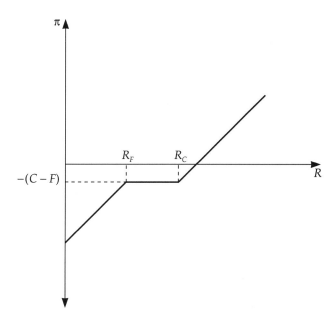

Figure 7.9 Payoff to a Collar

A *corridor* is another option position that trades off some possible gains from a higher interest rate for a lower insurance premium. A corridor is formed by purchasing a cap with a low cap rate and selling another cap with a high cap rate. The corridor's payoff diagram on payment day appears in Figure 7.10, where C_1, C_2, R_1, and R_2 denote the respective cap premiums and cap rates with $R_1 < R_2$.

Pricing an Interest Rate Cap

Consider a three-period cap, traded at $t = 0$, on a notional principal of 100. The cap rate is 10%, and the reference rate levels are the one-period rates of Figure 7.8. No payment is made at $t = 1$, since the rate for that payment date was known with certainty at $t = 0$, the trade date—it is 10%. Consequently, this cap can be viewed as two European calls on the one-period rate. The first expires at $t = 1$ and pays at $t = 2$; the second expires at $t = 2$ and pays at $t = 3$. Both have the same strike, 10%, and notional principal of 100.

The two-period call pays off if the rate at $t = 2$ is either 18% or 12%, paying 8 and 2, respectively, at $t = 3$. If the $t = 2$ rate is 8%, the payoff is zero at $t = 3$. Since these amounts are paid one period in arrears, they are valued at $t = 2$ as $8/(1.18)$, $2/(1.12)$, and $0/(1.08)$. Apply the no-arbitrage principle to the values computed at $t = 2$ and

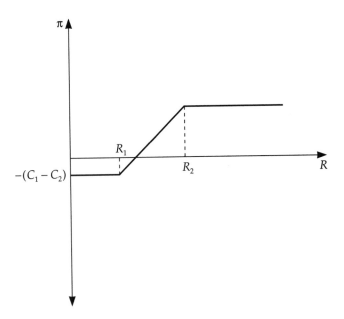

Figure 7.10 Payoff to a Corridor

work backward toward $t = 0$ to obtain the current value of the two-period call, C_2:

$$C_2 = \frac{1}{1.1}\left(0.5\left\{\frac{1}{1.13}\left[0.5\left(\frac{8}{1.18}\right) + 0.5\left(\frac{2}{1.12}\right)\right]\right\}\right.$$

$$\left. + 0.5\left\{\frac{1}{1.09}\left[0.5\left(\frac{2}{1.12}\right) + 0.5\left(\frac{0}{1.08}\right)\right]\right\}\right) = 2.095$$

The one-period call pays 3 at $t = 2$, if the rate is 13% at $t = 1$. Nothing is paid at $t = 2$, if the rate at $t = 1$ is 9%. Its value at $t = 0$ is

$$C_1 = \frac{1}{1.1}\left[0.5\left(\frac{3}{1.13}\right) + 0.5\left(\frac{0}{1.09}\right)\right] = 1.207$$

The cap's value is the sum of the two calls' values, 3.302—normally quoted as 330 basis points (dollar value/notional principal).

7.4 Estimating the Transition Probabilities

In the previous examples, it was assumed that the probability of an up move equaled that of a down move. Of course, this need not be so. How does one estimate the risk adjusted or risk neutral probability parameter, θ? To demonstrate the methodology, we return to the one-period rate stochastic process, in which values were assigned to the one-period rate's volatility parameter and only the drift term, $\alpha(t)$, remained to be estimated (see Figure 7.3). Now suppose that, in addition, the transition probability, θ, is unknown. The stochastic process would be written as

$$r_{i+1}^{t+1}(1) = r_i^t(1) + \alpha(t) + 0.01 \quad \text{with probability} \quad \theta$$

$$r_i^{t+1}(1) = r_i^t(1) + \alpha(t) - 0.01 \quad \text{with probability} \quad 1 - \theta$$

At $t = 0$, the no-arbitrage condition imposed on the price of the two-period bond must be satisfied by the $\alpha(t)$ and θ parameters. This gives us the following equation:

$$\frac{1}{(1.07)^2} = \frac{1}{1.06}\left(\theta\left\{\frac{1}{1 + [0.06 + \alpha(0) + 0.01]}\right\}\right.$$

$$\left. + (1 - \theta)\left\{\frac{1}{1 + [0.06 + \alpha(0) - 0.01]}\right\}\right)$$

We have one equation in two unknowns. Another equation is needed. Suppose there is a one-period call, expiring at $t = 1$, with a strike of 0.92 on this two-period bond. The call's current, $t = 0$, premium is observed to be 0.006877. Then, if the market has accurately valued the call, its premium must satisfy the no-arbitrage condition at $t = 0$. Namely,

$$0.006877 = \frac{1}{1.06}\left[\theta \max\left(0, \left\{\frac{1}{1 + [0.06 + \alpha(0) + 0.01]}\right\} - 0.92\right)\right.$$
$$\left. + (1 - \theta) \max\left(0, \left\{\frac{1}{1 + [0.06 + \alpha(0) - 0.01]}\right\} - 0.92\right)\right]$$

The solution to this pair of equations is $\alpha(0) = 0.02$ and $\theta = 0.5$. This θ value is then used to generate the interest rate tree, which in turn is used to price other securities.

Notice that an implicit assumption of the estimation technique is that one can identify fairly priced instruments, e.g., the one-period call. Few possess the confidence to identify several correctly priced instruments. At any single time, all instruments may be mispriced to some degree. In these situations, an alternative mathematical procedure has been advocated to discover the unknown parameter values. Take a group of actively traded instruments. Presumably, if any are mispriced, the mispricing is faint. Write the theoretical price for each instrument in terms of the parameters. Then find the parameter values that minimize the sum of squared differences between the theoretical and actual prices.

7.5 Instruments with Embedded Interest Rate Options

Callable Bonds

Many corporate bonds have a provision written into the bond indenture that allows the corporation to repurchase the bonds at a price, referred to as the *call price (strike price)*, that is set above the bond's face value. If rates fall, the issuer has the option of repurchasing the bonds at the call price and financing the purchase with a new issue of lower coupon bonds. Alternatively, the firm could finance the call by issuing bonds with the old, higher-than-current coupon rate and collect an amount above the "call price." The amount that is in excess of the "call price" is the value upon exercise of the bond's call provision.

From this brief description, one sees that the purchase of a callable bond is equivalent to the purchase of a noncallable bond and the simultaneous sale of a call on the noncallable bond. The equivalent mathematical statement is

Price of a callable bond = Price of a noncallable bond
− Price of a call on the noncallable bond

The valuation of a callable bond involves the valuation of a call.

Study the equation for a moment. As rates fall, the noncallable bond's price increases, but so does the value of the call, as the noncallable bond value moves up through the "call price." Consequently, as interest rates drop, the callable bond's price rise is attenuated by the increase in the value of the short call. A typical plot of a callable bond's price–interest rate relationship appears in Figure 7.11.

At rates above r^*, the curve is convex.[2] At rates below r^*, the price action of the short call subtracts from the noncallable bond's price increase, causing the curve to become concave. Adopting the vernacu-

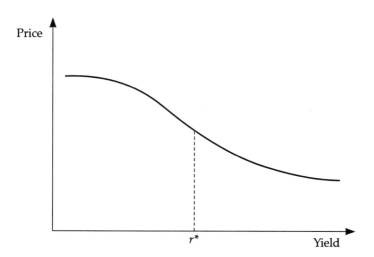

Figure 7.11 Callable Bond Price vs. Noncallable Bond Yield

2. A curve is said to be convex (concave) if a line drawn between any two points on the curve lies above (below) the curve.

lar of the trade, the concave portion is described as being *negative convex.*

The binomial tree structure coupled with the no-arbitrage principle can be used to address a variety of questions regarding the pricing of callable bonds. One of these is, What coupon rate must a callable bond carry in order to be priced at par? If the bond has two years to maturity and will be called at 101 if rates fall below 10%,[3] then, employing the interest rate tree of Figure 7.8, the par coupon (label it C_P) must satisfy

$$1 = \frac{1}{1.1}\left(0.5\left\{C_P + \frac{1}{1.13}[0.5(C_P + 1) + 0.5(C_P + 1)]\right\} + 0.5[C_P + 1.01]\right)$$

The solution is $C_P = 10.57\%$. In contrast, a bond of identical maturity but that is noncallable must carry a coupon of 10.46% to be priced at par. The market's added charge for callability is 0.11%.

Sinking Funds

A sinking fund is a requirement that the bond issuer repay a number, M, of the outstanding bonds, U, at face value, 100, on each of a sequence of scheduled dates (redemption dates). The sinking fund may grant the issuer a set of options with respect to the number of bonds that can be retired on a redemption date. Clearly, such options will serve to lower a bond's market value. These embedded options assume various forms:

---

3. Criteria suggested for the callable bond's exercise are complex. One simple and compelling principle should be part of any criterion: the timing of the callable bond's exercise should be selected so as to maximize shareholder wealth. Abstracting from refunding costs, this leads to the interesting prescription that as soon as the callable bond's price reaches the "call price," the holder should exercise. Why? Because, as the argument goes, if the corporate treasurer delays, there will be an increase in the market's confidence that the bond will be allowed to live a bit longer and pay the higher coupon a while longer. The callable bond's price would be bid up further to capture the added time on which the higher-than-market rate would continue to be paid. But, assuming that the firm's total value is strictly a function of its asset's income stream, then as the callable debt's value rises, shareholder equity falls. To avert this occurrence, the bond should be called at the "call price" and not be permitted to rise above it. (The effect of refunding costs is to allow the callable bond to trade above the "call price.")

1. *Purchase Substitution:* The issuer purchases a number of bonds, P, of the U outstanding bonds and substitutes the purchased bonds for all or part of the required purchase of the M bonds.

2. *Voluntary Redemption:* On a redemption date, the bond issuer chooses to retire the mandatory number, M, plus a voluntary number, V, for a total of $M + V$ bonds redeemed. If $V = M$, then $2M$ are retired; this has been named the *doubling up* option.

3. *Leftover Substitution:* The issuer chooses to substitute L number of bonds that were voluntarily retired at an earlier redemption date for some or all of the M bonds required to be retired at the current redemption date.

Employing a binomial valuation methodology originated by Jamshidian and Russell (1990) to the sinking fund analysis, we illustrate how the availability of the purchase substitution and voluntary redemption options are employed to reduce the value of the outstanding bonds. It should be remembered that any action that serves to reduce the market value of the firm's debt will increase the market value of the firm's equity.

The key to the analysis is the definition of two market values on the same redemption date, B^- and B^+. B^- represents a bond's value prior to a cash flow emanating from a redemption, while B^+ symbolizes the bond's value subsequent to the redemption cash flow. It is important to understand that these values for all intents and purposes are assumed to occur so closely together that no discounting factor intermediates between them. Both B^- and B^+ are gross prices in the sense that they include accrued interest. In the succeeding examples, accrued interest will be of no concern. Since the coupon payment date and redemption date are assumed to be the same, accrued interest on a redemption date is zero. If none of the options are selected and the required number, M, of the U outstanding bonds are retired at 100, then B^- and B^+ are related by

$$B^- = \left(\frac{M}{U}\right)100 + \left(1 - \frac{M}{U}\right)B^+$$

where the equation implicitly assumes that a fraction (M/U) of the bond's face value is paid in cash and the remaining portion of the bond issue is permitted to live and trade at B^+. Thus B^- equals the immediate redemption cash flow plus the value of that portion of the bond issue that survives redemption.

Example: The Doubling Up Option   Voluntary redemption will be exercised if it can reduce the bond's market value, B^-. Consequently, the corporate treasurer will compare the cost of exercising, that is, retiring an additional number, V, at 100, to that of simply retiring the mandatory number, M. In particular, he will choose the option that provides

$$B^- = \min\left(\left\{\left[\frac{M}{U}\right]100 + \left[1 - \left(\frac{M}{U}\right)\right]B^+\right\}, \left\{\left(\frac{M + V}{U}\right)100\right.\right. \tag{7.2}$$

$$\left.\left. + \left[1 - \left(\frac{M + V}{U}\right)\right]B^+\right\}\right)$$

If $B^+ > 100$, that is, the bond's after cash flow value exceeds 100, then the voluntary option will be exercised. The firm will be able to retire liabilities valued in excess of 100 for 100. How do Jamshidian and Russell get the B^+ value necessary to implement the above decision rule? By working backward from the bond's maturity date. On maturity day, there is no option; whatever bonds remain outstanding must be retired. So this date, on which the bond's value is known to be coupon plus face value, is the starting point for the analysis.

Assume a two-period tree with the structure of Figure 7.8. At $t = 0$, two bonds are outstanding, $U = 2$, each with a face value of 100, a coupon of 10% and a two-period maturity. The mandatory redemption at $t = 1$ is one bond, i.e., $M = 1.00$. However, the issuer may choose to retire an additional bond at $t = 1$, i.e., $V = 1.00$. Absent the voluntary redemption option, the bond issue's value would be

$$2 \cdot \frac{1}{1.1}\left[0.5\left(10 + 50 + \frac{55}{1.13}\right) + 0.5\left(10 + 50 + \frac{55}{1.09}\right)\right] = 199.21$$

The numbers in the parentheses represent the coupon, 10, at $t = 1$, the cash flows due to the mandatory redemption per bond (0.5(100)), plus the discounted value of the flows at $t = 2$ from the fraction of each bond that remains. After the mandatory redemption of 0.5 per bond at $t = 1$, 0.5 of each bond survives to $t = 2$ and pays the 10% coupon on the principal of 50 plus the principal of 50.

The voluntary redemption option reduces the bond price. Subscript the B^- and B^+ prices with the one-period interest rate of the node to which the values correspond. Application of equation (7.2) at the $t = 1$ nodes, where the one-period rate is either 13% or 9%, gives

$$B_{13}^- = \min\,[0.5(100) + 0.5B_{13}^+, 100] \qquad (7.3)$$

$$B_9^- = \min\,[0.5(100) + 0.5B_9^+, 100]$$

The term preceding the comma in the braces represents a bond's value from the mandatory redemption at $t = 1$. The 100 term in the braces is the value if the voluntary option is exercised and both bonds are retired. To evaluate these expressions, values for B_{13}^+ and B_9^+ are required. The figures needed are the present values of a whole bond's cash flows at $t = 2$. Therefore, $B_{13}^+ = 110/1.13 = 97.35$ and $B_9^+ = 110/1.09 = 100.92$. The expressions in (7.3) can now be evaluated.

$$B_{13}^- = \min\,[0.5(100) + 0.5(97.35), 100]$$

$$= \min\,(98.68, 100) = 98.68$$

$$B_9^- = \min\,[0.5(100) + 0.5(100.92), 100]$$

$$= \min(100.46, 100) = 100.00$$

So at the 9% node, "double up" by retiring both bonds. At the 13% node, where the bond trades below par, retire the mandatory one bond. With these numbers in hand, we step back to $t = 0$ and compute the bond issue's value as

$$2 \cdot \frac{1}{1.1}\,[0.5(10 + 98.68) + 0.5(10 + 100)] = 198.80$$

where the $t = 1$ coupon interest of 10 and the bond's values, B_{13}^- and B_9^-, are inserted into the no-arbitrage condition to arrive at the issue's value at $t = 0$. Multiplication by two is necessary to account for the two bonds that make up the issue. Access to the voluntary redemption option reduces the issue's value from 199.21 to 198.80.

But also note that if at $t = 1$ the one-period rate is 13%, then the issue's payment at the $t = 2$, 12% node is 110, since there is one bond outstanding. If at $t = 1$ the one-period rate is 9%, then the issue's payment at that same ($t = 2$, 12%) node is zero. The issue's balance could either be 110 or 0, depending upon which path was taken to arrive at that node. The voluntary redemption option introduces path dependency.

Example: The Purchase Substitution Option   Recall that the presence of this option enables the issuer to purchase bonds in the open market and substitute them for all or part of the mandatory number. Assume the same bond issue and interest rate tree as in the prior illustration. With the availability of the purchase substitution option, the issuer's action will be consistent with the minimization of B^-. That is,

$$B^- = \min\left(\left\{\left[\frac{M}{u}\right]100 + \left[1 - \left(\frac{M}{u}\right)\right]B^+\right\}, \atop \left\{\left[\frac{M}{u}\right]B^- + \left[1 - \left(\frac{M}{u}\right)\right]B^+\right\}\right) \qquad (7.4)$$

The second part of the minimization expression represents B^- if the purchase substitution option is exercised. We assume, if exercised, it will be exercised to its full extent—enough bonds are purchased at B^- to satisfy the mandatory requirement, i.e., $P = M$.

To be able to use this minimization expression to arrive at a decision, the B^- term on the right-hand side must be eliminated. Notice that if the purchase substitution option is worth exercising, then (7.4) says

$$B^- = \left(\frac{M}{u}\right)B^- + \left(1 - \left(\frac{M}{u}\right)\right)B^+$$

The equation tells us that $B^- = B^+$. And this makes intuitive sense, for in a purchase substitution there are no redemption cash flows to the bond holder separating B⁻ from B⁺. Expression (7.4) may be rewritten as

$$B^- = \min\left(\left\{\left[\frac{M}{u}\right]100 + \left[1 - \left(\frac{M}{u}\right)\right]B^+\right\}, \atop \left\{\left[\frac{M}{u}\right]B^+ + \left[1 - \left(\frac{M}{u}\right)\right]B^+\right\}\right) \qquad (7.5)$$

$$= \min\left(\left\{\left[\frac{M}{u}\right]100 + \left[1 - \left(\frac{M}{u}\right)\right]B^+\right\}, B^+\right)$$

If B⁺ < 100, the purchase substitution option should be exercised.

At $t = 1$, $B_{13}^{+} = 110/1.13 = 97.35 < 100$, so the option should be exercised. If the rate is 9% at $t = 1$, then $B_{9}^{+} = 110/1.09 = 100.92 > 100$; the option should not be exercised. Since $B_{13}^{-} = B_{13}^{+} = 97.35$, then at the $t = 1$, 13% node, each bond receives the coupon of 10 plus a cash payment from the purchase of half the bond equal to 0.5×97.35; the outstanding half bond is worth 0.5×97.35. Therefore, the total value of cash plus the half of a bond outstanding at the $t = 1$, 13% node is $10 + 97.35$. At the $t = 1$, 9% node, each bond receives the coupon of 10 plus the mandatory payment required to retire half of a bond, 0.5×100; the outstanding half of a bond is worth 0.5×100.92. Therefore, the total value of cash plus the half bond outstanding at the $t = 1$, 9% node is $10 + 100.46$. Applying the no-arbitrage condition, the issue's value at $t = 0$ is

$$2 \cdot \frac{1}{1.1} [0.5(10 + 97.35) + 0.5(10 + 100.46)] = 198.01$$

The purchase substitution option serves to reduce the issue's value from 199.21 to 198.01.

PART II

Financial Futures

Chapter 8

Contract Characteristics and the Institutional Environment

IN GENERAL, financial futures and forward contracts both represent a commitment by one party to make delivery of the underlying security or commodity to the contract's counterparty for a cash payment. Since the subject of this part is financial futures, the subsequent discussions assume that contracts are written on securities, unless otherwise stated. Whereas futures and forwards are similar to each other, there remain significant differences in design that make one or the other the choice of hedgers and/or speculators at any particular time. This chapter begins with a description of those differences. A discussion of the structure of a futures exchange and how it differs from that of an options exchange follows. A section is devoted to an explanation of the initial and subsequent daily cash flows between parties to a futures trade. The chapter concludes with some issues involved in the design of futures contracts and the concept of settling such contracts at expiration by a final cash payment as opposed to the physical delivery of the underlying security.

8.1 Futures versus Forward Contracts

A forward contract specifies the delivery of a security at some future date. The delivery or forward price is determined at the time the contract is entered into, and it is set at a level so that the contract has no initial monetary value—that is, no money changes hands. The parties to a forward contract, the buyer (the long) and the seller (the short), retain the flexibility to designate the grade (quality) and the quantity of the goods to be delivered, as well as the time and place of delivery. A futures contract has essentially the same characteristics as a forward contract but differs in four aspects that affect the ease with which it is traded relative to a forward contract.

First, a futures contract is highly standardized. The exchange on which it trades, and not the parties to the trade, sets the date on which the contract terminates, the delivery location, and the exact quality and quantity of the goods to be delivered per contract. This means that the pit trader wastes no time negotiating quality, quantity, or delivery date. This standardization enhances the liquidity of the market. (A market is said to be more liquid than another market if, for a transaction of any size, the price in the first market moves by less than that in the second market.) Consequently, the direct cost of trading will be less in the more liquid market. In particular, the difference between the bid price and the asked price for a given quantity will be smaller.

Second, the exchange guarantees the performance of both clearing firms involved in the trade. Each clearing firm, in turn, guarantees the performance of the traders for whom it processes trades. This means that one party to a trade need not be overly concerned with the creditworthiness of the opposite party. This increases liquidity as well.

Third, to exit a long (short) futures position, that is, to rid yourself of a contract that has been purchased (sold), you simply sell (buy) an identical contract. The exchange will then cancel the long (short) position against the short (long) position, so that your net position is zero. You need not make or take delivery, as is usual on a forward contract.

Fourth, at the end of each day, the gain or loss on a futures position is computed. If the position has made money, the exchange pays cash to the clearing firm that guarantees the position for the trader; conversely, if the position has sustained a loss, the guaranteeing clearing firm pays the exchange that day's loss in cash. These daily cash payments are referred to as *settlement variation*—marking-to-market through cash payments.

Apart from forward and futures transactions, reference will be made to spot transactions. A spot transaction calls for immediate delivery or delivery "on the spot." Such transactions occur at the *spot price*.

8.2 The Futures Exchange

Because the Chicago Board Options Exchange was founded by the members of the Chicago Board of Trade (CBOT), a futures exchange, the structural essentials of a futures exchange are the same as those described in the chapters on options. However, there are a few important differences:

1. The functions of trade matching, guaranteeing, collecting margin, etc., are all performed by the futures exchange's clearing house and are not split between two entities, i.e., the CBOE and the Options Clearing Corporation (OCC).

2. On the floor of a futures exchange, dual trading is generally permitted.

3. After each day's trading, the losses on a futures position must be paid in cash by the clearing firm carrying the loser's position to the clearing house, which in turn passes that cash payment to the clearing firm carrying the winner's position. Settlement variation has no counterpart on the CBOE or any other options exchange. Figure 8.1 provides a diagram of the trade and clearing process on a futures exchange.

Settlement Variation and Margin

With respect to all trades that have matched—i.e., that are *cleared*—the clearing house notifies each clearing firm of the settlement variation to be paid to or collected from the clearing house. In addition, the clearing house notifies each clearing firm of the margin, or good faith collateral, that must be presented to the clearing house on any open positions held by the clearing firm. This collateral, in the form of cash, T-bills, or letters of credit, must be put up to guarantee that the clearing firm will be able to meet the next day's settlement variation.

When a position is opened, the customer (including floor traders) must put up an amount called *initial margin*—again this represents good faith collateral. The clearing firm, which carries the position on its books and submits the trade in its name to the clearing house, passes on a portion of this amount to the clearing house. The amount of collateral that is passed on equals the *maintenance margin* figure set by the clearing house.

Every day the clearing house calculates each clearing firm's gains or losses on a contract by computing the difference between the day's settlement price (the average of prices during the last 30 seconds of trading) and the previous day's settlement price and then multiplying this figure by the number of outstanding positions. This amount must be paid to or received from the clearing house before trading begins on the following morning.

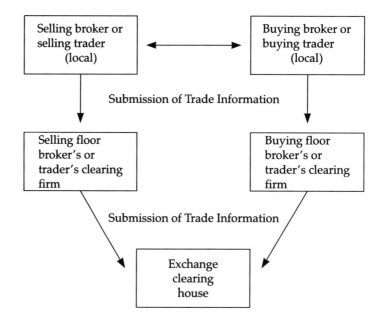

Functions of the Clearing House

1. Matches trade information and verifies that it is a good trade.

2. Passes cash payments from losing clearing firm to winning clearing firm.

3. Collects margin on initiation of any new position from each clearing firm.

4. Acts as ultimate guarantor of performance by each clearing firm to the other clearing firm.

5. Assigns and oversees deliveries when the contract matures.

Figure 8.1 Overview of the Trade Process

The clearing firm must calculate its customer's equity at each day's close as follows:

$$equity = (cash\ contributed\ +\ T\text{-}bills$$
$$+\ amounts\ guaranteed\ by\ letters\ of\ credit)$$
$$+\ unrealized\ gains\ on\ open\ positions$$
$$-\ unrealized\ losses\ on\ open\ positions$$

If the customer's equity level falls below the maintenance margin level, then that customer must wire sufficient funds to the clearing firm in order to bring his equity level back up to the initial margin level.

The manner in which these cash payments between clearing firm and clearing house are effected and the guidelines set for collecting losses and paying gains by the clearing firm to its public customers are sufficiently arcane that I offer an example to clarify the process. To keep things simple, assume that margin is put up only in cash—not in T-bills or by a letter of credit.

The Cash Flows Emanating From a Trade: An Illustration

A June gold futures contract calls for delivery of 100 ounces of gold in June. Initial and maintenance margins are $2,500 and $2,000, respectively. At 11:00 A.M. on a Monday in May, an individual purchases one June futures at $420/oz. At day's end, the contract settles at 416/oz. The customer's unrealized gains and losses for Monday are calculated that afternoon as the difference between the settlement price and the initiating purchase price on 100 ounces of gold (416/oz. − 420/oz.) × 100 oz. = −400. Unrealized gains are zero and unrealized losses amount to 400. Deducting this amount from the 2,500 collected in cash to meet initial margin gives the customer an equity value of 2,100 at the end of the first day.

In Figure 8.2, the amount owed by the customer to his clearing firm is preceded by a minus sign; any amount due the customer from the clearing firm is preceded by a plus sign. The clearing firm that carries this customer's position calculates the customer's loss as the difference between the initiating trade price and the settlement price and passes this 400 loss as settlement variation to the clearing house prior to the beginning of trading on Tuesday morning. Along with this payment of settlement variation to the clearing house goes the maintenance margin payment of 2,000. Any amount paid (received) by the clearing firm to (from) the clearing house is preceded by a minus (plus) sign in Figure 8.2.

After trading ends on Tuesday, the customer's equity is computed. The settlement price has decreased to 400. Therefore, the customer's unrealized loss *(settlement price − trade initiating price)* × 100, increases to 2,000. The cash contribution of 2,500 less the 2,000 unrealized loss results in a 500 equity value. Since the customer's equity has

Margin and Settlement Variation Attached to a Trade*

    Initial Margin = $2,500   (IM)
    Maintenance Margin = $2,000   (MM)

Table of Prices and Cash Flows

	Monday	**Tuesday**	**Wednesday**	**Thursday**
Bought 1 Contract at 11:00 a.m.	$420/oz.			
Sold 1 Contract at 1:00 p.m.			$430/oz.	
Settlement Price	$416/oz.	$400/oz.	$440/oz.	Position Closed

Margin and Settlement Variation Flows between Clearing Firm and Clearing House

			Net
-0-	−2,000 MM − 400 SV	−1,600 SV	+2,000 MM +4,000 SV −1,000 SV
	−2,400	−1,600	+5,000	+$5,000 −$4,000
				+$1,000

Equity and Cash Flows between Customer and Clearing Firm

+2,500 C	+2,500 C	+4,500 C		
− 400 UL	−2,000 UL	+2,000 UG −1,000 UL	Receives Paid in	+$5,500 −$4,500
+2,100 E	+ 500 E +2,000 C +2,500 E	+5,500 E		+$1,000

*IM, MM, SV, UG, UL, C, and E, respectively, denote initial margin, maintenance margin, settlement variation, unrealized gains, unrealized losses, cash, and equity.

Figure 8.2 Cash Flows Emanating from a Trade

dropped below the maintenance margin level of 2,000, the customer is called for additional cash of 2,000—enough to bring equity back up to the initial margin level of 2,500. The customer has now contributed 4,500 in cash.

On Wednesday morning, prior to the day's trading session, the clearing firm settles with the clearing house on the long position. The clearing firm calculates its loss as the difference between Tuesday's settlement price and Monday's settlement price times 100 ounces, which amounts to $(400 - 416) \times 100 = -1,600$. This amount is paid to the clearing house. Notice that whereas the clearing firm calculates settlement variation using the difference between successive settlement prices after the trade's initiation day, the customer's unrealized losses (and gains, if any) are always calculated using the day's settlement price relative to the price at which the trade was opened.

On Wednesday, the customer offsets his long position by selling a June futures contract at 430. That afternoon's settlement price is 440. Though the customer has both a long and a short June futures contract, and so does his clearing firm, they are not offset by the clearing house until after the clearing firm's settlement variation flows are taken care of on Thursday morning. Until then, both the long and the short positions exist simultaneously. Consequently, unrealized gains and losses on both positions are taken into account in computing the customer's Wednesday afternoon equity. The unrealized gain on the long position is the settlement price of 440 less the initial price of 420 times 100. The unrealized loss on the short position is the initiating sales price of 430 less the settlement price of 440 times 100. Combining the calculations ($+2,000$ and $-1,000$) with the total cash contributed by the customer of 4,500 gives an equity value of 5,500.

Thursday morning, the clearing firm has settlement variation flows of 4,000 for the long position, computed as $(440 - 400) \times 100$, and $-1,000$ for the short position, computed as $(430 - 440) \times 100$. In addition, recognizing that the initial position has been offset, the clearing house returns the good faith deposit equal to the maintenance margin of 2,000 to the clearing firm. The clearing firm receives 5,000 on Thursday morning. The positions are now offset. The customer's equity is paid out, and he receives 5,500. His cash contributions amounted to 4,500. His profit is 1,000 ($5,500 - 4,500$)—as it should be, because he offset the contract at 430 that he purchased at 420. The clearing firm's cash flows also net to 1,000 ($-2,400 - 1,600 + 5,000$), as they should, since from the clearing house's point of view, the clearing firm offsets at 430 on Wednesday the contract that was purchased at 420 on Monday.

8.3 Issues in Futures Contract Design: The Supply of the Underlying Security or Commodity

The most frequently offered reason for the existence of a financial futures market is that it provides a low-cost alternative to individuals and firms who have a commercial interest in the actual underlying security and wish to protect themselves against adverse price movements. For example, suppose a security firm holds an inventory of bonds that it wishes to sell to its retail clients. It intends to make money off the markup and not by speculating on the future value of the bond inventory. To protect the value of its inventory against interest rate changes, it sells (shorts) futures. If interest rates rise and the bond inventory declines in value, the bond futures price should also decline, because new contracts will be written at a lower price, reflecting the fact that the underlying security has declined in value. Since the firm is short bond futures, it will make money on them, offsetting the losses on its bond inventory. Of course, if interest rates fall, then the gain on its inventory is offset by its loss on futures. Consequently, the firm has stabilized the value of its inventory by shorting futures. This is called a *short hedge.*

Futures are also used to protect against a loss arising from a price increase. This use of a futures contract is called a *long hedge.* Suppose that a money manager expects pension money to arrive in three months and intends to invest it in bonds. He is concerned that if long-term interest rates fall, the bonds will be more expensive, and this will cause him to effectively receive a lower interest rate than that which is offered today. To counteract this possibility, he locks in today's rate by buying futures contracts. If rates are lower when the cash funds arrive, the bond futures price will rise, for the underlying security has risen in value. These gains on his long futures will allow him to buy more bonds, so that he has effectively obtained his target rate. Of course, if rates rise, then losses on his long futures will prevent him from buying as many bonds as he otherwise could have. Instead of obtaining the higher rate, he ends up with the target rate.

Now, the key to the effectiveness of these hedges is that the bond futures price and the prices of the bonds held in inventory, or the prices of bonds that the fund manager is looking to purchase, move very closely together—almost in lockstep. That is, the essence of obtaining an effective hedge with futures requires that the *basis* (the spot price less the futures price) remains relatively stable. Now we are ready to discuss the essential part of contract design.

Suppose that there are two types of bonds trading. Call them grade 1 and grade 2. You write a futures contract so that only grade 1 is deliverable against the contract. You do not include grade 2 as deliverable, because you believe grades 1 and 2 exhibit high positive price correlation. So if you make only grade 1 deliverable, the futures price will follow grade 1's price, and by virtue of grade 1's positive correlation with grade 2, the futures price and grade 2's price should be positively correlated. Therefore, the futures contract should be a good hedging instrument for a grade 2 bond, even though grade 2 is not deliverable. (This is termed a *cross hedge:* the use of a futures contract to protect the value of a nondeliverable security.)

Unfortunately, because grade 1 bonds are in limited supply, the contract designer will have made a major error. Here is why. A long futures holder gets tricky and buys all outstanding grade 1 bonds. The futures contract is about to expire, and those traders who are short cannot find any grade 1 bonds to deliver. Therefore, to avoid having to pay the default penalties charged by the exchange, the shorts try to buy themselves out, sending the futures price up. During this entire period, the grade 2 bond price remains unchanged. Those who cross-hedged their grade 2 bond inventories by going short futures will suffer a loss on futures and no offsetting gain on their bond inventories. The bond contract has turned out to be an inadequate hedging device.

The exchange, recognizing that this problem was caused by an insufficient supply of the deliverable bond, decides to expand supply to allow both grades 1 and 2 to be acceptable for delivery. Now consider another scenario. Initially, grade 1 is the least expensive to deliver against the contract, so the futures price is expected to follow the price of grade 1. A pension fund manager expects $10 million in three months and intends to invest that money in grade 1 bonds. To lock in today's yield on grade 1 bonds, he buys futures contracts. Unfortunately, as time passes, the yield on the grade 1 bond does not change, but the yield on the grade 2 bond rises significantly. Bond 2 has become the least expensive to buy and deliver by the short. In response, the futures price follows the value of bond 2 as it falls in price. The result is that the pension fund manager loses on the long futures position and must still incur the same costs on the grade 1 bonds that he intends to purchase. This is obviously a bad contract for long hedging.

Thus, the dilemma: Too small a supply of the deliverable security will make the futures contract a bad short hedging instrument. On the other hand, expanding deliverable supply by allowing a heterogeneous group of securities to be delivered will make the contract a bad long hedging instrument. Consequently, the key task when deciding what to trade futures on is finding securities or commodities that are large in deliverable supply and homogeneous in characteristics—like U.S. Treasury bonds and currencies.

Physical versus Cash Delivery: The Necessity of Obtaining a High Positive Correlation between Futures and Spot Prices

In the previous section, an explanation was offered as to why it is important to design a contract so that the futures and spot prices move in the same direction with a high degree of confidence. The exchange believes that in order to obtain this type of futures-spot price behavior, the futures price and the spot price must converge on the contract's expiration day.

A contract that can be satisfied by the short delivering and the long receiving the underlying security will force convergence. To see why, pretend that as the contract nears expiration, when delivery is permitted to begin, the futures price is 100 and the spot price is 98. Clearly, traders will purchase the spot security, hereafter referred to simply as the spot, and simultaneously short the futures contract, knowing that the short futures obligation can be satisfied by physically delivering the spot. Upon delivery, the trader receives 100 and has paid 98, pocketing a certain profit of 2. Pursuit of this arbitrage will force down the futures price and raise the spot price until convergence is achieved. Conversely, if at contract expiration the spot price is 100 and the futures price is 98, traders will attempt to short the spot and purchase the futures contract. Their aim is to take delivery of the spot via the long futures position and then redeliver this underlying security to satisfy the short position in the spot market. The profit from this arbitrage is 2. As this arbitrage is attempted, the spot price will be forced down and the futures price raised until convergence is achieved.

Some spot securities do not lend themselves to delivery. For example, the delivery of $250,000 of the Standard & Poor's 500 stock portfolio would require the delivery of fractional shares—an impossibility. To attempt to deliver a Eurodollar time deposit would be so costly to both long and short that trading in that futures contract would be severely curtailed. But, in such cases, what mechanism could be set in place that would force the convergence of the futures and spot prices at contract expiration? For the contracts just mentioned, the answer was, and still is, cash settlement.

Two activities define the cash settlement procedure:

1. The settlement price on contract expiration day is set equal to the prevailing spot price.

2. Settlement variation is computed using the difference between this expiration settlement price and the previous day's settlement price; or, if the contract position is initiated on expiration day, settlement variation is computed using the settlement price and the initiation price. The settlement variation amount is then transferred between long and short clearing firms through the exchange's clearing house. Outstanding positions are terminated with the payment of settlement variation.

These two procedures ensure convergence. To see this, suppose that five seconds before the close of trading on expiration day the futures price is 100 and the spot price, which is being continuously reported on the electronic screens, is 98. Clearly, everyone will attempt to short futures at 100, or anything above 98, for they see that in five seconds the futures settlement price will be set at the spot of 98, or close to 98. If one can sell at 100 and the settlement price is declared to be 98, then one will receive settlement variation of 2. Consequently, every trader will try to do this, sending the futures price toward the spot price level. Convergence obtains. On the other hand, if the futures price five seconds before the close on expiration day is 98 and the spot price is seen to be hovering around 100, everyone will attempt to buy futures. The futures price will rise until it equals the spot price, resulting in convergence.

Chapter **9**

Pricing Futures, Forwards, and Options on Futures: General Considerations

IN THIS chapter, an argument is presented as to why futures and forward prices might differ. The evidence regarding the practical importance of this argument is then addressed. The empirical results of academic studies and the behavior of practitioners in pricing futures as forwards indicate that forward pricing techniques can be and are used to value futures contracts. The methodology used in pricing a forward contract is introduced. The chapter closes with a section on pricing an option on a futures contract.

9.1 Do Futures and Forward Prices Differ?

The Cox, Ingersoll, and Ross Argument as to Why They Might Differ

The gains or losses on a futures contract are settled in cash daily. Thus, if the futures price rises by day's end, then the long collects and the short pays an amount equal to the dollar value of the futures price change; conversely, if the futures price falls by day's end, the long must pay cash to the short. In contrast, a forward contract price change during the day does not give rise to a cash payment between short and long prior to contract expiration. Bearing this in mind, let us assume that when interest rates rise, the futures price also rises, and when interest rates fall, the futures price falls—that is, interest rates and futures prices are positively correlated.

When there is positive correlation between interest rates and futures prices, it is preferable to be long a futures contract rather than long a forward contract on the same underlying commodity or security, *if both futures and forward carry the same price.* Here's why:

1. Interest rates rise and the futures price rises. (Recall, the assumption is that the interest rate and futures price are positively correlated.) The long futures position gains and the short position loses. Short futures pays long futures in cash at day's end. The long lends this cash at a relatively high interest rate.

2. Interest rates fall and the futures price falls. (Again, recall the positive correlation assumption.) The long futures position loses and the short futures position gains. At day's end, long pays short an amount equal to the day's loss in cash. If the long borrows the money to pay the short, he is doing so at a relatively low interest rate. Or, if long is obtaining the cash from a money market account, the opportunity cost of disinvesting is relatively low.

What we see is that when interest rates rise, the long receives cash that can be lent or invested at relatively high interest rates. When interest rates fall and the futures price falls, long pays cash that can be borrowed at relatively low interest rates. In contrast, no daily cash flows emanate from changes in the price of a forward contract, so there is no financial advantage to being long a forward contract when there is positive correlation between interest rates and futures prices.

It seems reasonable to conclude that when the interest rate and futures prices are positively correlated, there is an advantage to being long a futures contract as opposed to being long a forward contract on the same underlying commodity or security. If the long is at an advantage, then the short is at a disadvantage. The sellers of futures and forward contracts recognize this fact and act accordingly. To be compensated for the relative disadvantage of being short a futures contract, as opposed to being short a forward contract, when the interest rate and the futures price are positively correlated, the seller (short) should demand a higher price from the buyer (long) for the sale of a futures contract than for the sale of a forward contract. Consequently, when the correlation between the interest rate and the futures price is positive, the futures price should exceed the forward price.

Let us examine the other possible interest rate–futures price relationship: a negative correlation between interest rates and futures prices. By reasoning analogous to that presented above, we will conclude that it is preferable to be short a futures contract rather than short a forward contract, *if they both carry the same price*. The reasoning follows.

1. Interest rates rise and the futures price falls. In this case, the short futures position gains and the long futures position loses at day's end. The short futures receives cash from the long futures. The short lends this cash at a relatively high interest rate.

2. Interest rates fall and the futures price increases. In this instance, the short pays the long. If the short borrows money to pay the debt, then he borrows it at a relatively low interest rate. Or, if short obtains the cash from a money market account, his opportunity cost of disinvesting is relatively low.

The above reasoning tells us that when there is a negative correlation between interest rates and the futures price, it would be better to short a futures contract than to short a forward contract on the same underlying commodity or security. The buyers of futures and forward contracts recognize that and act accordingly. To be compensated for being long a forward contract as opposed to being long a futures contract when interest rates and futures prices are negatively correlated, the long should demand a lower price from the short on the purchase of a futures contract than on the purchase of a forward contract.

The above conclusions, which were proved mathematically by Cox, Ingersoll, and Ross (1981), may be summarized as follows:

1. If interest rates and futures prices are positively correlated, then the futures price should be greater than the forward price.

2. If interest rates and futures prices are negatively correlated, then the futures price should be less than the forward price.

Contracts in Which the Cox, Ingersoll, and Ross Price Differential Might Be Observable

Gold futures might be positively correlated with interest rates if the cause of the interest rate rise is inflation. To protect the purchasing power of the dollars to be repaid, lenders, who expect an increase in the inflation rate, ask for compensation from borrowers in the form of a higher interest rate. So, in this case we should see a positive correlation between interest rates and inflation. Gold prices usually respond positively to the expectation of increased inflation. Therefore, a positive correlation between interest rates and the price of gold should result in the price of a futures contract on gold exceeding the price of a forward contract on gold.

In contrast, the futures price of a contract on U.S. Treasury bonds should be negatively correlated with interest rates, since a rise in interest rates generates a fall in bond prices. Therefore, a futures contract on U.S. Treasury bonds should carry a lower price than a forward contract on the bonds.

Can the Cox, Ingersoll, and Ross Price Differential Be Observed in the Market for Futures and Forwards?

One can think of this possible futures-forward price differential, caused by the presumed correlation of futures prices and interest rates and the fact that futures pay settlement variation while forward contracts do not, as a wedge being driven between the futures and forward prices. Now we must ask if this wedge really exists. If it exists, is it of consequential size?

It is difficult to find a commodity or security to study that is free from all other factors that may affect the price differential between futures and forwards. For example, suppose we choose U.S. Treasury bill futures and U.S. Treasury bill forwards in order to study the size of the wedge, if any, caused by the negative correlation between interest rates and U.S. Treasury bill prices. We would quickly discover that differential transaction costs between forward and futures markets would make it difficult to reason that the existence of a wedge supports the Cox, Ingersoll, and Ross theory. Furthermore, in other futures contracts written on commodities or securities, the contracts are designed in such a way that the short is given some advantages at the onset relative to the long; the long knows this and demands a lower futures price than the forward price he would be willing to pay on the same underlying commodity or security. (In Chapter 12, an example using the T-bond futures contract will illuminate this concept). So one must be careful in selecting the appropriate futures contract to investigate. If a wedge is observed, then we must be confident that an unambiguous conclusion can be drawn with regard to the cause of the wedge.

Currency markets seem an appropriate setting in which to consider the wedge question. The transaction costs in both the futures and forward markets are of similar magnitude, and the currency futures contract grants no obvious advantage to the short or to the long. So if a forward price–futures price differential is discovered for the currency market, one could, with some confidence, attribute the differential to the correlation between interest rates and futures prices.

The methodology applied is to check to see if there are actual price differences in the forward and futures markets, and then to see if such differences are consistent in size with the differences predicted by the size of the interest rate–futures price correlation (see Cornell and Reinganum 1981). Researchers first observed that actual futures prices and forward prices are so close that it would be futile to attempt to profit by purchasing the lower-priced instrument and selling the higher-priced instrument. For example, suppose the British pound futures contract price is $1.7000 per pound for delivery on March 17, while the price of the British pound forward contract is $1.6999 per pound. In this case, we could earn a gross profit of $.0001 by purchasing the March forward contract and selling the March futures contract. But this gross profit would pale relative to the costs of setting up and maintaining a trading operation. Additionally, it was demonstrated that the size of the differential between futures and forwards, small as it is, could not be explained in terms of the interest rate–futures price correlation hypothesis. In fact, only a fraction of the small price differential could be accounted for by the interest rate–futures price correlation measured in each of the currency markets. The conclusions from these findings are as follows:

1. The interest rate–futures price correlation is not a significant factor in explaining differences between futures and forward prices.

2. The futures and forward prices of contracts written on the same underlying commodity or security—in this case, currencies—exhibit insignificant differentials.

Of course, since the cleanest studies applied only to the currencies, these conclusions can be drawn only for the currency markets—at least in an academic sense. However, it must be that casual or clinical observations by traders have led them to believe that forwards and futures are essentially the same. Traders must believe this, for they use forward pricing models and techniques to price futures contracts. (Interestingly enough, though traders use forward pricing techniques, they then try to adjust the size of the futures hedge position to mitigate the expected settlement variation. Thus they attempt to make the instrument conform to the pricing model. We will discuss this further in Chapter 11 on Eurodollar futures and in Chapter 12 on T-bond futures.)

9.2 Pricing Forward Contracts

We now illustrate how the riskless arbitrage principle is used to price a forward contract on a security that pays nothing during the life of the contract. The notation is as follows:

S = The current or spot price (price for immediate delivery) of the security underlying the forward contract

F = The forward price, set today, for delivery of the security at expiration; when the buyer receives delivery, he makes a cash payment of F dollars to the seller

i = The annual interest rate (in decimal form)

T = The time to expiration of the forward contract, at which time delivery of the underlying security must be made by the seller of the forward contract to the buyer of the forward contract.

We will argue that the forward price level at which arbitrage cannot occur is

$$F = S(1 + i)^T$$

To prove this, we will consider each of two contrary cases:

$$F > S(1 + i)^T \qquad (9.1a)$$

in which the forward price exceeds the spot price, grossed up by the interest that would be paid to finance the spot purchase of the security, and

$$F < S(1 + i)^T \qquad (9.1b)$$

in which the forward price is less than the spot price, grossed up by the interest that would have to be paid to finance the spot purchase of the security. Our objective is to prove that each case, defined by the pricing inequalities (9.1a) and (9.1b), will lead to a riskless arbitrage opportunity. However, riskless arbitrage opportunities induce transactions that result in a realignment of prices. The prices of forward and spot eventually change so as to nullify the arbitrage opportunity.

Case 1

$$F > S(1 + i)^T \tag{9.1a}$$

The basis for any arbitrage is to sell what is relatively overpriced and to buy what is relatively underpriced. A glance at inequality (9.1a) tells us how we should begin to set up our arbitrage position. We sell the forward at F and buy the spot at S with a loan of S dollars at interest rate i that we must pay back in T years. Our current cash flow amounts to

$$+S - S = 0$$

The first term, $+S$, designates the cash inflow from our borrowings, and the second term, $-S$, represents the cash outflow due to the immediate purchase of the cash security.

Two important items should be noted in setting up this arbitrage:

1. Nowhere in the current cash flows, which sum to zero, does a term representing the sale of the forward contract appear. This is as it should be, for a forward contract entails no transfer of cash from buyer to seller when the contract is first initiated.

2. There is a balance in our positions. By selling the forward contract, we are obligated to deliver the underlying security, but we have protected ourselves by purchasing the underlying security. A short forward position without a counterbalancing long position in the underlying security carries a risk that the spot price may exceed the forward price to be received upon delivery. Should that occur, we would be forced to enter the spot market at the time the forward contract expired and purchase the spot security at a price higher than what the forward contract would pay upon delivery, namely F. This would result in a loss. The balancing transactions of an arbitrage position protect against this occurrence.

A true arbitrage position requires balancing transactions.

Now let us consider future cash flows. At the expiration date of the forward contract, all obligations must be satisfied. So we deliver the security that we have held in fulfillment of our forward sale commitment, receiving F dollars in payment from the buyer of the forward contract and thereby discharging our forward commitment. We must now pay off the loan. The balance on that loan has grown from S dollars, the amount borrowed, to $S(1 + i)^T$ dollars. Did we receive enough money in satisfaction of the forward obligation to repay our loan? That is, is F sufficiently large to cover the balance of $S(1 + i)^T$? The answer is yes. Just look at the initial assumption of this case 1, namely that $F > S(1 + i)^T$. A riskless arbitrage situation arises. Money can be made on zero investment through the sale of the forward and the financed purchase of the spot security. As such transactions continue, the sale of the forward forces F down and the purchase of the spot pushes S up, until the inequality disappears and with it the incentive to arbitrage.

Case 2

$$F < S(1 + i)^T \tag{9.1b}$$

Looking at the inequality tells you how to start to construct the arbitrage. You buy the relatively less expensive side. Consequently, the forward contract is purchased at price F and the security is borrowed and sold for S dollars. The arbitrager invests the S dollars at rate i for T years. Note that the position is balanced. The arbitrager is long the forward contract on the security and short the spot security. (The arbitrager is short the security because he sold a security that he did not own, and thus still owes it to the person from whom it was borrowed.) Furthermore, the position entails zero investment at $t = 0$, since there is an inflow of $+S$ dollars from the sale of the borrowed security, a concurrent outflow of S dollars due to the investment of the sale proceeds, and no cash flow attributable to the purchase of the forward contract.

Now let us consider the cash flows at $t = T$, when the forward contract matures. At that time, the arbitrager takes delivery on the forward contract, paying F and receiving the security, which is then given to the individual from whom it was first borrowed. This obligation is now satisfied. The original investment of S, which has grown to $S(1 + i)^T$, is liquidated and used to pay the price on the forward contract of F. Are net cash flows positive at $t = T$? The arbitrager receives $S(1 + i)^T$ and pays F. Is $F < S(1 + i)^T$? Yes, by the assumption that delineated case 2 (see [9.1b]).

So we see that if $F < S(1 + i)^T$, a riskless arbitrage ensues. Transactions are initiated that alter the relative prices. Since the transactions in this arbitrage entail the purchase of the forward and the sale of the security, these transactions serve to raise the forward price relative to the security price. This behavior continues until F is no longer less than $S(1 + i)^T$.

Conclusion: Because the existence of either $F > S(1 + i)^T$ or $F < S(1 + i)^T$ results in a riskless arbitrage opportunity, these inequalities cannot define a no-arbitrage environment. Therefore, the remaining situation, defined by $F = S(1 + i)^T$, must define the no-arbitrage environment.

9.3 Options on Futures

Description and Pricing

An option on a futures contract differs from an option on the spot instrument in that exercise establishes a position in the futures contract and not the spot. The owner of a call option on a futures contract is granted the right to buy a futures contract at the exercise price. If and when the call is exercised, he receives a long futures position at that exercise price. The writer of the call on the futures contract, upon exercise, receives a short position in the futures contract at the exercise price. At day's end, the long futures position, received by the call owner upon exercise, either receives or pays settlement variation—computed as the difference between that day's settlement price and the price at which the long position was initiated, the exercise price. A similar, but symmetrically opposite, statement can be made with regard to the call writer paying or receiving settlement variation on the short position received on the exercised call. The owner of a put on a futures contract, upon exercise, establishes a short position in the futures contract at the exercise price; the writer of the put receives a long futures position at the exercise price—if and when the put is exercised.

We can apply the binomial option pricing model to value an option on a futures contract. The replicating portfolio consists of n_F futures contracts (the current price of each is F) and B dollars of debt. The numerical values of n_F and B are selected so that the end-of-period value of this portfolio in the up state and in the down state match the values of the option in these states. In the case of a one-period call, the replicating portfolio must be constructed to satisfy

$$n_F(uF - F) + Br = C_u \equiv \max\{0, uF - K\}$$

and

$$n_F(dF - F) + Br = C_d \equiv \max\{0, dF - K\}$$

where u, d, r, and K stand for the same parameters defined in the security option case. Notice that $(uF - F)$ and $(dF - F)$, respectively, represent the settlement variation, in the up and down states on a contract initiated at F. Solving for n_F and B, we obtain

$$n_F = \frac{C_u - C_d}{(u - d)F}$$

$$B = \frac{1}{r}\left[\left(\frac{1 - d}{u - d}\right)C_u + \left(\frac{u - 1}{u - d}\right)C_d\right]$$

Because the futures contract has zero value upon initiation (remember, settlement variation is used to remove all accumulated gains or losses and the contract is repriced as if it had been initiated at the settlement price), the n_F futures contracts in the replicating portfolio have zero value. Consequently, the current value of the replicating portfolio is B. Since the current value of the replicating portfolio represents the present value of the call option's values at expiration, then the replicating portfolio value is also the current value of a European call. Therefore,

$$C = B = \frac{1}{r}\left[\left(\frac{1 - d}{u - d}\right)C_u + \left(\frac{u - 1}{u - d}\right)C_d\right]$$

Notice that the parenthetical expressions that multiply C_u and C_d are both positive, since $u > 1 > d$. (If this does not hold, say if $u > d > 1$ or $1 > u > d$, then either a long or a short position in a futures is a sure winner because an arbitrage opportunity exists.) Furthermore, as in the security option case, these expressions sum to 1. If the futures option is American, then, as in the case of the security option, we must consider the option's value if exercised early. This leads to

$$C = \max\left\{F - K, \frac{1}{r}\left[\left(\frac{1 - d}{u - d}\right)C_u + \left(\frac{u - 1}{u - d}\right)C_d\right]\right\}$$

Extension of this formula to the valuation of a multiperiod futures option is analogous to the methodology used in the security case.

A Numerical Example If $u = 1.5$, $d = 0.5$, $r = 1.25$, $K = 30$, and $F = 70$, then

$$C = \max \left[70 - 30, \left(\frac{1}{1.25} \right) \left(.5 \times 75 + .5 \times 5 \right) \right] = 40$$

In the above example, it is optimal to exercise the call on the futures contract prior to expiration day. Yet for a call on a stock that pays no dividend, it is never optimal to exercise early. Why the difference? In the equity case, remember that the call's time premium receives its value because of two attributes: leverage and insurance. The deeper in-the-money the call is, the lower are the leverage and insurance that it confers. But although these values may shrink toward zero as the stock price continues to rise, they are never less than the leverage and insurance attributes of the underlying stock. So with zero dividends, the time premium of a call on a stock never disappears. But this is not so for the case of a call on a futures contract. To begin with, a futures contract position requires zero investment (only good faith collateral must be put up, such as T-bills), whereas the purchase of an option on a futures contract requires an investment equal to the option premium. This means that the leverage attribute of a long futures contract exceeds that of a long call. It remains true, however, that the call provides more insurance than the long futures contract. But as the futures price rises and the call goes deeper into the money, the insurance value decreases while the discrepancy in the relative amounts of leverage conferred by the futures contract and by the call widens. Eventually, the leverage advantage of the futures contract outweighs the insurance provided by the call, and exercise is forced.

Extension of the Option Pricing Formula to Continuous Time

As the interval between futures price observations shrinks, Black's (1976) formula for a European call on a forward contract becomes appropriate. This gives

$$C = e^{-iT}[FN(d_1) - KN(d_2)]$$

where

$$d_1 = \frac{\left[\ln \left(\frac{F}{K} \right) + \left(\frac{\sigma^2}{2} \right) T \right]}{\sigma \sqrt{T}}$$

$$d_2 = d_1 - \sigma \sqrt{T}$$

Table 9.1   Portfolio Component Values at Expiration

Position	State $F_T \leq K$	State $F_T > K$
Short Call	0	$-(F_T - K)$
Long Put	$(K - F_T)$	0
Long Futures*	$(F_T - F)$	$(F_T - F)$
Loan of $(F - K)e^{-iT}$	$(F - K)$	$(F - K)$
	0	0

*The futures position's value is derived from the sum of settlement variations.

All other symbols have been previously defined. Of course, $\sigma^2 T$ now represents the variance of $\ln(F_T/F)$, where F_T is the futures price on expiration day.

The Put-Call Parity Relation for European Options on Futures

$$C = P + (F - K)e^{-iT}$$

PROOF.   Construct a portfolio consisting of a short call, a long put, a long futures position at price F, and a loan of $(F - K)e^{-iT}$ dollars. The expression for the value of this portfolio's net cash flows at $t = 0$ is $+C - P - (F - K)e^{-iT}$. At $t = T$, when the options expire, there are two states of the world to be examined: $F_T > K$ and $F_T \leq K$. Table 9.1 gives the value of each of the portfolio's positions in each state at expiration.

Since the portfolio has zero value at expiration, it must have zero value at $t = 0$ to prevent riskless arbitrage. Thus $+C - P - (F - K)e^{-iT} = 0$, and the proof is complete.

Chapter 10

Treasury Bill Futures

*I*N THIS CHAPTER, we focus on one of the earliest interest rate futures contracts to be developed that still exists, the three-month Treasury bill futures contract. To understand how and when to use a futures contract and how to price it, one must have some familiarity with the market for the deliverable security, in this case the spot three-month T-bill. Consequently, we begin our discussion with a description of the spot market for T-bills, defining, in the process, the various yield conventions employed. The salient characteristics of the three-month T-bill futures are then listed. The contract's use in locking in a rate for a future period is illustrated. A long (short) hedge is associated with locking in a lending (borrowing) rate. These futures hedges are then contrasted with similar hedges that are constructed solely from spot market transactions—among them, repurchase and reverse repurchase agreements. Finally, with regard to the pricing of T-bill futures, two arbitrage techniques are defined and described: pure arbitrage and quasi arbitrage.

10.1 The Spot Market

The Auction

United States Treasury bills pay no coupon. Instead, interest is earned by the investor on the difference between the price at which the bill is purchased and the face (par) value that is remitted upon the bill's maturity date. Treasury bills are issued with original maturities of three, six, and twelve months (13, 26, and 52 weeks). The three- and six-month bills are auctioned weekly on Monday afternoons and settled (paid for) on the following Thursday. The twelve-month bill is auctioned every fourth Thursday and settles the following Thursday.

The auction process begins with an announcement by the U.S. Treasury specifying the face value of the securities to be auctioned. Bids are accepted in the month prior to the auction date. There are two types of bids: competitive and noncompetitive. A competitive bidder submits a sealed bid in the form of an annualized percentage discount from face value. Obviously, the lower the discount submitted, the greater the bidder's chances of having his bid accepted. The noncompetitive bidder submits a form stating the face value of the securities he wishes to purchase without attaching the price he is willing to pay. The noncompetitive bidder is certain to have his purchase order filled at a discount equal to the average of the winning competitive bids. To assure that every noncompetitive bid is filled, the Treasury officials, prior to the start of the auction, set aside a portion of the issue's face value equal to the total of all noncompetitive bids. For example, if the auction is for $10 billion in T-bills and $2 billion in noncompetitive bids is received, then $8 billion is competitively auctioned. (Each noncompetitive bid is limited to $1 million per auction. Each competitive bid is limited to 35% of the total face value of securities offered.)

The competitive bids are arranged from lowest discount at the top of the list to the highest discount at the bottom. The officials then work their way down the list until all of the securities available to competitive bidders are awarded. The highest discount (lowest dollar price) that is accepted during the auction is called the *stop-out* yield. The weighted average of successful competitive bids is applied to the noncompetitive bids. The difference between the stop-out yield and the average of the competitive bids is called the *tail*. Traders usually use this figure to gauge the strength of the auction. A small tail is interpreted to mean that demand for the issue was strong. Another figure used to gauge the strength of demand is the *cover*, which is the ratio of the dollar amount of all bids divided by the size of the issue. The larger the cover, the stronger the demand.

Spot Pricing and Yield Conventions

The price of a T-bill is quoted as an annualized percent discount from the T-bill's face value. Suppose that the price for a three month bill is quoted as 10%. To calculate the corresponding dollar price for the T-bill, one must substitute the decimal discount (the percent discount divided by 100) and days-to-maturity of the T-bill, as measured from the settlement date,[1] into the following formula:

---

1. U.S. Treasury securities regularly settle on the business day after the trade date.

$$\text{T-bill price} = \text{face value} \times \left[1 - \left(\frac{\% \text{ discount}}{100}\right.\right. \quad (10.1)$$
$$\left.\left. \times \frac{\text{days-to-maturity}}{360}\right)\right]$$

Note that as the discount increases, the price falls. For this example, in which the discount is 10% per year, the corresponding price paid for the three-month T-bill (with 91 days in the three-month segment) and a face value of $1,000,000 is calculated to be

$$\$1,000,000 \left[1 - \left(.10 \times \frac{91}{360}\right)\right] = \$974,722$$

Notice that in deannualizing the discount, it is assumed that the year consists of 360 days.

If you owned the three-month T-bill described in this example and wished to sell it immediately, then you would sell it at the dealer's bid price. Should you wish to purchase the T-bill immediately, you would buy it at the dealer's offer (asked) price. The dealer's bid-asked spread represents the markup on his T-bill inventory. Among its determining factors are (1) the opportunity cost of the funds that the dealer has tied up in inventory, (2) the volatility of T-bill prices, and (3) the opportunity cost of the dealer's labor. When a T-bill has been bought from a dealer, it is said in industry jargon that "the offer was lifted." When a T-bill has been sold to a dealer, one might hear that "the bid was hit."

In order for the dealer to make money, the dollar price asked for a T-bill must exceed the dollar price bid for the same T-bill. Formula (10.1) tells us that the T-bill price and discount are inversely related. Therefore, if the offer or asked price is to exceed the bid price, the discount offered or asked must be less than the discount bid. You will see the following type of quote in the newspaper on a three-month T-bill: 8.25 − .24. The discount bid is 8.25% and the discount asked is 8.24%. The difference, in this case, between the bid and the offer discounts is one basis point. (Recall that a basis point is 1/100 of 1%, or 0.0001 in decimal form.)

The Bond Equivalent Yield on a T-Bill

The discount quoted on a T-bill is not the rate of return that the investor will earn. The reason is that the discount, which is applied to the face value of the T-bill to obtain the dollar interest that will be earned until maturity, does not consider the actual investment made, namely the price of the T-bill. An accepted practice has developed for calculating the rate of return to maturity on a T-bill, which is more often called the *bond equivalent yield.*

The Bond Equivalent Yield for T-Bills Maturing in Six Months or Less   Let T_m denote the days from settlement date to maturity date. The bond equivalent yield, r, for a \$1,000,000 face value T-bill with an asked price of P_A is obtained by dividing the dollar interest to be earned through maturity, \$1,000,000 − P_A, by the dollars invested, P_A, and then grossing up the figure by $365/T_m$ to obtain an annualized equivalent rate of return. Writing the formula out, we have

$$r = \frac{1,000,000 - P_A}{P_A} \cdot \frac{365}{T_m}$$

Note that, in contrast to the formula used for calculating the T-bill price—in which a year is assumed to contain 360 days for purposes of *deannualizing* the discount—in the bond equivalent yield formula, the number of days assumed in the year and used to *annualize* the return is 365.

The Bond Equivalent Yield Formula for U.S. T-Bills with More than Six Months to Maturity   When the time to maturity exceeds six months, the yield, r, is calculated by assuming the T-bill holder receives an interest payment after six months (this is not reality, just an assumption) and then, at maturity, receives the principal plus interest on both the principal and the interest assumed to have been paid after six months. Allowing r to play the role of this interest (rate of return), the above explanation is equivalent to the following mathematical statement:

$$r = \frac{\dfrac{-T_m}{182.5} + 2\sqrt{\left(\dfrac{T_m}{365}\right)^2 - \left(\dfrac{T_m}{182.5} - 1\right)\left(1 - \dfrac{1,000,000}{P_A}\right)}}{\dfrac{T_m}{182.5} - 1}$$

10.2 The Three-Month Treasury Bill Futures: Defining Features

1. A three-month T-bill futures contract calls for delivery of $1,000,000 in face value of a bill maturing in three months (almost always equal to 91 days, but because the maturity date of the deliverable bill may fall on a holiday, the deliverable T-bill may have a maturity of 90 to 92 days).

2. The contract's delivery days are the Thursday, Friday, and Monday following the third Monday of the spot month. (The spot month of a contract occurs when the contract month is also the calendar month.) Trading ends on the day preceding the first delivery day.

3. The T-bill futures contract price is quoted for trading as 100.00 minus the annual discount (in percent) expected to prevail on the three-month T-bills to be delivered on that contract. A quote of 92.00 on the June futures contract means that if you purchased the June and held until delivery, you would have committed to purchase $1,000,000 in face value of three-month U.S. T-bills at an 8% annualized discount. This quote on the T-bill futures contract (100.00 − discount) is called the International Monetary Market (IMM) Index for U.S. T-bills. The International Monetary Market is the name given that division of the Chicago Mercantile Exchange where the three-month U.S. T-bill contract is traded.

Why quote the price of the contract as 100.00 minus the discount, when the spot market quotes T-bill prices simply in terms of the discount? The reasoning is based upon the fact that futures traders who purchase a T-bill contract expect to make money when the price rises. Remember, however, that the discount rate must decline for a rise in the price to occur. So, in order to make this environment compatible with other trading pits and not to confuse futures traders, T-bill futures are quoted as 100.00 minus the discount rate. Thus, when the discount decreases and the T-bill price increases, the IMM Index also increases.

4. The invoice price *(IP)* at delivery, which is what the long pays the short upon receiving the T-bill with T_m days to maturity, is

$$IP = \$1,000,000 \left[1 - \left(\begin{array}{c} settlement\ discount \\ implied\ by\ IMM\ Index \\ on\ last\ trading\ day \end{array} \right) \times \left(\frac{T_m}{360} \right) \right]$$

5. Each basis point move in the IMM Index, such as a move from 92.00 to 92.01 or from 92.00 to 91.99, results in settlement variation

of $25 per contract. If you are long the June T-bill futures and the IMM Index increases from 92.00 to 92.01, or, equivalently, if the implied discount rate on three-month T-bills to be delivered in June decreases from 8.00% to 7.99%, the short pays the long $25 in settlement variation.

10.3 Hedging with Three-Month Treasury Bill Futures

Using a Three-Month T-Bill Futures Contract to Lock in a Three-Month Lending Rate for a Period That Begins at a Future Date

A long position in the June three-month T-bill futures contract is taken on March 28 at an IMM Index value of 92.00. It is retained through the last day of trading, June 20, at which time the contract settles at 94.00. Delivery is received on the next day, Thursday, June 21. First, note that the IMM Index has risen by 200 basis points, so the long has received $5,000 in settlement variation. Second, the invoice price that the long must pay for the three-month T-bill is calculated as

$$IP = \$1,000,000 \left[1 - .06 \times \left(\frac{91}{360} \right) \right] = \$984,833$$

Finally, we calculate the net price as the invoice price less settlement variation received, obtaining

$$\$984,833 - \$5000 = \$979,833$$

Question: Is this price equivalent to having purchased the bills at the 8% discount promised when the June futures contract was bought on March 28? In other words, did the long lock in a price equivalent to an 8% discount? Was this a good hedge? To answer these questions, insert $979,833 into the spot price formula and solve for the corresponding discount rate, d.[2]

---

2. The equivalent discount rate obtained depends on the timing of settlement variation flows. In this example, it is assumed that the $5,000 in settlement variation is received at contract expiration; that assumption increases the similarity between the futures contract and a forward contract.

$$d = (1 - .979833) \times \frac{360}{91} = .07978 = 7.978\%$$

Almost. But why the difference? To obtain an 8% discount, the long would have needed a net price of

$$\$1,000,000 \left[1 - .08 \times \left(\frac{91}{360} \right) \right] = \$979,778$$

The hedger paid a net price of $979,833 and not $979,778. He paid $55 ($979,833 − $979,778) too much. Another way of saying this is that he needed $55 more in settlement variation.

The reason the long hedger fell short of the necessary amount of settlement variation is that a one-basis-point fall on a 91-day T-bill results in a price increase of $25.2777. (Use the spot price formula, (10.1), to convince yourself of this.) However, the settlement variation received is $25 per basis point. This $25 figure is equivalent to assuming that the deliverable T-bill will have 90 days to maturity. (Again use the spot price formula, (10.1), to confirm this.)

So what happened in our long hedging example is that for every basis point drop in the T-bill rate, the long hedger gained $25 in settlement variation but suffered an increase in cost of $25.2777 for the 91-day bill to be purchased. Therefore, for each spot basis point drop, $0.2777 of the increased cost of the T-bill to be purchased was not covered by the hedge. For a 200-basis-point move, this means that $200 \times \$0.2777 \approx \$55$ was not protected by the long hedger. The hedger could have compensated for this deviation by purchasing 91 futures contracts for every 90 three-month T-bills, each with a face value of $1,000,000. But this is such a fine point that it does not merit more attention than we have already given it.

A Short Hedging Example Using T-Bill Futures: Converting a Variable Rate Loan into a Fixed Rate Loan at a Favorable Rate

A firm seeks a $1,000,000 fixed rate loan beginning on the day that the March T-bill futures contract expires, March 20. The bank offers the firm a choice: a one-year fixed rate loan at 11%, or a one-year floating rate loan at the prevailing three-month T-bill yield plus 1.5%, adjustable each quarter.

The firm is aware that the adverse effects of higher T-bill rates can be neutralized by using short futures T-bill positions. It knows that the ensuing higher loan costs due to a rise in rates will effectively be offset by the gains (through settlement variation payments) on the short T-bill futures. Possessing this knowledge, the firm understands that it can take any variable rate loan and change it into a fixed rate loan. At present, the current three-month T-bill discount is 7.75%, and the discount rates implied by the June, September, and December futures contracts are 8.00%, 8.25%, and 8.50%, respectively. The corresponding annualized interest rates are presented in Table 10.1.

Using short positions in the appropriate T-bill futures contract months to lock in the interest rates of 8.28%, 8.54%, and 8.81% at the loan's initiation (March), the firm transforms the variable rate loan into a fixed rate loan at a projected one-year cost of

$$\left[1 + (.0802 + .015)\left(\frac{92}{365}\right)\right] \times \left[1 + (.0828 + .015)\left(\frac{91}{365}\right)\right]$$
$$\times \left[1 + (.0854 + 0.015)\left(\frac{91}{365}\right)\right] \times \left[1 + (.0881 + .015)\left(\frac{91}{365}\right)\right]$$
$$= 1.1029$$

If the firm borrows one dollar for one year, rolling over the principal and interest owed each quarter, it must repay the dollar plus 10.29 cents. Therefore, the effective interest rate is 10.29%. Since this rate is superior to the 11% on the conventional fixed rate loan, the firm opts for the variable rate loan, borrowing $1,000,000 at (8.02% + 1.5%) × 92/365 for the first quarter and simultaneously selling one June T-bill futures contract, one September T-bill futures contract, and one December T-bill futures contract (a *strip* of three futures).

Table 10.1   Three-Month T-Bill Rates

Month of Maturity	Discount	Bond Equivalent Yield*
March (Spot)	7.75%	8.02%
June (Futures)	8.00%	8.28%
September (Futures)	8.25%	8.54%
December (Futures)	8.50%	8.81%
*Assuming 92 days in the first quarter, 91 days in each subsequent quarter, and 365 days in a year.		

Having explained what to do to transform a variable rate loan into a fixed rate loan, let us try to obtain a sense of what happens if rates change. Note that the succeeding interest rate scenario is one of an infinite number of possible scenarios, so its presentation is meant only to provide a sense of how the cash flows from the futures act to provide a rate close to the 10.29% that was projected at the outset of the loan. Suppose all discount rates immediately rise by 200 basis points. This means that each contract immediately provides settlement variation of $25 \times 200 = \$5,000$. The set of new T-bill rates is given in Table 10.2.

Taking account of settlement variation flows, the effective borrowing rate may be calculated as an internal rate of return, R, that satisfies

$$
1,000,000 = -15,000
$$

$$
+ \ 1,000,000 \left[\frac{(0.0802 + 0.015)\left(\frac{92}{365}\right)}{(1 + R)^{0.25}} + \frac{(0.104 + 0.015)\left(\frac{91}{365}\right)}{(1 + R)^{0.5}} \right.
$$

$$
+ \frac{(0.1067 + 0.015)\left(\frac{91}{365}\right)}{(1 + R)^{0.75}} + \left. \frac{(0.1094 + 0.015)\left(\frac{91}{365}\right) + 1}{(1 + R)^{1.00}} \right]
$$

The solution is $R = 0.1025$; a bit lower than the expected 0.1029. However, if the interest rate changes took place just prior to the June futures expiration, then settlement variation would be collected three months later. This means that settlement variation of $15,000 would be received in June, raising the effective one-year borrowing rate, R, to 0.1034. (Apart from the timing of settlement variation, one can suggest several reasons for obtaining a figure different from 10.29%. Among them are that we hedge $1,000,000 each quarter rather than $1,000,000 plus accumulated interest, and we use one 90-day contract

Table 10.2 Three-Month T-Bill Rates after a 200-Basis-Point Increase

Month of Maturity	Discount	Bond Equivalent Yield
June	10.00%	10.40%
September	10.25%	10.67%
December	10.50%	10.94%

each quarter and do not adjust for the actual number of days that the hedge will run.)

A Summary Note on Hedging with Futures

1. When you purchase a June T-bill futures contract at an implied discount of 8%, you lock in an 8% lending rate for the June–September period. The reasoning is as follows. If, by June, the three-month T-bill rate drops to 6%, the invoice price paid at delivery is calculated using 6%, which exceeds the invoice price that you expected to pay—the price corresponding to the 8% discount upon the contract initiation date. However, the settlement variation earned offsets the unanticipated higher costs, so that you do, in effect, pay a price upon delivery that is equivalent to receiving an 8% discount. Of course, if the three-month T-bill discount rate rises to 10% by June, you pay a lower invoice price, calculated using 10% instead of the anticipated 8%; however, this reduction in cost is offset by the 2% loss in settlement variation. So, again, you effectively pay a price equivalent to 8% for the three-month bills received at delivery.

Consequently, even though the invoice price will almost surely differ from the price, P_F, implied by the futures at the trade date, you gain or lose sufficient funds in settlement variation to assure that you have locked in P_F. Essentially, the invoice price at delivery plus settlement variation earned or paid prior to delivery equals P_F, the price implied by the IMM Index at the time the contract was purchased, where

$$P_F = \$1{,}000{,}000 \left[1 - \left(\begin{array}{c} \text{discount implied} \\ \text{by IMM Index} \\ \text{on trade date} \end{array} \right) \times \frac{91}{360} \right]$$

2. A symmetric argument can be offered to explain that when you short a June T-bill futures at an implied discount of 8%, you lock in a borrowing rate for the June–September period. If you sell at an implied rate of 8%, then at delivery you receive an invoice price, plus or minus settlement variation, that is equivalent to the trade date price using 8% in the P_F formula. In effect, the bills are sold for P_F dollars no matter where the IMM Index settles on the expiration date of the contract.

We have illustrated how three-month T-bill futures can be used to lock in a lending rate for a future period in a procedure called a long hedge. We have also demonstrated how T-bill futures can be utilized to effectively eliminate the uncertainty in future borrowing costs, in a procedure termed a short hedge. We now demonstrate that both types of hedges, long and short, are theoretically achievable strictly through the use of cash (spot) market instruments. The question that should arise after the following section is, Then why do we need a futures contract? The answer—which will be provided with a bit more detail—is, Because the transactional cost of effecting such hedges is lower in the futures market than in the cash market.

10.4 Alternative Hedges Using Spot Instruments

Illustration: Using Cash (Spot) T-Bills to Lock in a Three-Month Lending Rate, Three Months from Today

Suppose that today, at $t = 0$, the objective is to lock in a three-month lending rate beginning three months from today. This could be accomplished in the following manner. Today, sell short a spot three-month T-bill having a face value of $1,000,000 at a price P_3. Use the money generated from the short sale to buy six-month T-bills at a price of P_6 per $1,000,000 in face value. The number of six-month T-bills purchased is P_3/P_6. Note that the money needed to purchase the six-month T-bills is provided by the short sale of the three-month T-bill. The set of transactions is self-financing—that is, net investment is zero. This set of transactions has this feature in common with a futures position. There is no net inflow or outflow of cash at the initiation of the futures contract or in this set of spot transactions.

Three months later, at $t = 3$, the three-month T-bill matures. The entity from which it was borrowed expects to receive a dollar amount equal to the bill's face value, $1,000,000. Consequently, the short position must be covered by paying $1,000,000 to the entity from whom the bill was borrowed. It is important to observe that at $t = 3$ a net cash flow occurs. It is an outflow equal to $1,000,000. Recall that prior cash flows netted to zero. Finally, six months from the initiation of the set of transactions, that is, at $t = 6$, P_3/P_6 six-month T-bills mature. Since each T-bill pays $1,000,000 upon maturity, the cash inflow at $t = 6$ is $(P_3/P_6) \times \$1,000,000$. Table 10.3 summarizes the transactions and cash flows.

Table 10.3 Transactions and Cash Flows

Time	Three-Month T-Bill	Six-Month T-Bill
$t = 0$	Sell a three-month T-bill with a face value of $1,000,000 at a dollar price of P_3.	Purchase P_3/P_6 six-month T-bills, each with a face value of $1,000,000, at a per-unit price of P_6.
	Net cash flow at $t = 0$ amounts to $+P_3 - (P_3/P_6)P_6 = 0$	
$t = 3$	Pay $1,000,000 to cover short sale of the three-month T-bill.	
$t = 6$		Receive (P_3/P_6)1,000,000 on the six-month bills held.

An outflow at $t = 3$ and an inflow at $t = 6$ looks precisely like a three-month loan or three-month investment: a cash outflow followed by a cash inflow. If we let $r_{3,6}$ denote the annual implied interest rate to be earned on this loan between $t = 3$ and $t = 6$ and $T_{3,6}$ denote the number of days from the end of the third month to the end of the sixth month, then $r_{3,6}$ satisfies

$$1,000,000 \left[1 + r_{3,6} \left(\frac{T_{3,6}}{365} \right) \right] = \left(\frac{P_3}{P_6} \right) 1,000,000$$

What the equation says is that an investment of $1,000,000 at time $t = 3$ is repaid with interest at $t = 6$, where the payment of interest and principal amounts to $(P_3/P_6) \times$ $1,000,000. (The convention is to divide by 365 when deannualizing an interest rate.) This rate $r_{3,6}$, the implicit annualized lending rate that relates the cash outflow at $t = 3$ to the cash inflow at $t = 6$, is locked in at $t = 0$. This is evident, since no new transactions occurred after $t = 0$. All that was done was to satisfy the short obligation to return the bill or its equivalent in cash at $t = 3$, and then simply wait an additional three months for the payoff from the long six-month T-bills maturing at $t = 6$. This set of transactions results in fixing a three-month rate today on a three-month loan that is to commence in three months—just like a long futures position.

In a similar fashion, a three-month borrowing rate, commencing in three months, can be fixed today by shorting a six-month bill and using the proceeds to purchase three-month bills. This set of transactions will provide a cash inflow at $t = 3$ and an outflow at

$t = 6$. Of course, theoretically, we are not restricted to using this methodology to lock in a three-month rate, three months from today. For example, using T-bills that have four and six months left to maturity, two-month rates commencing four months from today can be fixed today.

If one can essentially form equivalent futures positions with cash market instruments, why has a futures market been able to flourish? The reason is that the costs of transacting in the cash market exceed transaction costs in the futures market. To be specific, let us return to the example just discussed, in which it was demonstrated that one could use a combination of long and short spot T-bill positions instead of futures positions to lock in a lending rate. Recall that a spot T-bill was shorted and not covered until it matured. At maturity, it was assumed that a payment of the face value of $1,000,000 would fully satisfy the entity from which the bill was borrowed. In practice, an additional payment equal to an agreed-upon number of basis points on the price P_3 must be made. For example, if the premium was set at 50 basis points, a rate usually associated with borrowing a T-bill for a few weeks, then the short satisfies his obligation by paying $1,000,000 + (0.005/4)P_3$. (Note that the 50 basis point figure is deannualized in the calculation to conform with the three-month period over which the security was borrowed.) However, it would be remarkable if one were permitted to borrow a three-month T-bill for the full three months. At some point during its life, that T-bill usually becomes quite valuable to the owner, as traders will want to borrow it to maintain a short position. At that point, the premium might climb far above 50 basis points. Therefore, to obtain agreement from the owner of the three-month T-bill that it will not be called back prior to its maturity date, a fixed premium must be paid that is considered extraordinarily high—say, 200–300 basis points. Finally, one must consider that the entity from which the T-bill was borrowed will not permit the use of the full sale price, P_3, by the short—recall that in the illustration, P_3 dollars were used to purchase the six-month T-bills. A small fraction of that cash amount, termed a haircut, must be put up with the owner of the T-bill as collateral. These costs of shorting tend to make any set of cash transactions that aims to emulate a futures position relatively expensive. We have just touched upon the single most important reason for the existence of futures markets: lower transaction costs than cash markets.

Yet before the advent of futures markets, cash market participants would, on occasion, wish to lock in a three-month lending rate for some time period in advance. They were able to do so in a relatively cost-efficient manner compared to the transactions just described. But before turning to a description of such a transaction, we must introduce the instruments known as *repurchase agreements* and *reverse repurchase agreements*.

Repurchase Agreements ("Repos")

A government securities dealer who owns U.S. government fixed income securities finds another business entity who has funds to invest overnight. The dealer sells to this business entity $1 million face value of six-month T-bills at the current price of P_6. Payment is made in federal funds[3] to the dealer's bank against the delivery of the securities—also transferred by wire. At the time the dealer sells the securities, he agrees to repurchase them the next day at a higher price. Thus the buyer of the securities is, in effect, extending the dealer a one-day loan collateralized by the dealer's securities.[4]

The difference between the repurchase and sale prices in a repo amount to the interest that the dealer pays on the loan. The interest rate is quoted as an annualized rate and is, of course, called the *overnight repo rate* for U.S. T-bill securities. To deannualize this repo rate, one assumes that the year consists of 360 days and then multiplies the annual repo rate by $1/360$ to obtain the appropriate repo rate for an overnight loan. It follows that the repurchase and sale prices of the repo transaction are related by

$$repurchase\ price\ =\ sale\ price\ \times\ \left(1\ +\ \frac{R_P}{360}\right)$$

where R_P denotes the annualized overnight repo rate. If the repo is written for a period longer than a day, then to deannualize the repo rate, multiply it by the days in the period and divide by 360. Repo agreements that extend for at least 30 days are referred to as *term repos*.

---

3. Payments and security deliveries are accomplished by transmitting instructions over the Federal Reserve's wire. Funds and securities are transferred among the accounts of Federal Reserve member banks through book entry credits and debits.

4. On a repo, the lender of money asks for a collateral cushion in that the amount of money lent is less than the market value of the securities received as collateral. The percentage difference is called the haircut. The haircut varies with the maturity of the security and with the volatility of the market. A recent schedule showed a haircut range of 10 basis points (bps) for an overnight repo to 75 bps for a three-month repo.

Reverse Repurchase Agreements ("Reverse Repos")

A reverse repo is a technique often used to borrow securities. First the dealer finds an investor who has the desired securities. Then the dealer purchases the securities from the investor and simultaneously agrees to resell the same securities to the investor on the next day. In essence, the dealer extends the investor a loan with the desired security as collateral. The difference between the resale price and the purchase price represents the interest earned by the dealer on the loan.

The relevant rate is called the *overnight reverse repo rate* for U.S. Government securities. The same procedure used to deannualize the repo rate applies to the reverse rate. Assume that there are 360 days in a year and multiply the reverse rate (in decimal form) by the length of the loan in days divided by 360. It follows that the resale and purchase prices for an overnight reverse are related by

$$resale\ price\ =\ purchase\ price\ \times\ \left(1\ +\ \frac{R_V}{360}\right)$$

where R_V denotes the annualized overnight reverse repo rate in decimal form. A reverse agreement that extends for at least 30 days is called a *term reverse.*

Some Features of Repos and Reverses

Which rate would you expect to be higher, R_V or R_P? Since the dealer's repo desk acts like a bank, lending and borrowing on collateral, one should expect its lending rate to exceed its borrowing rate. Since the repo desk lends at R_V and borrows at R_P, you will see that R_V exceeds R_P. There are exceptions. If the dealer needs a specific security to cover an uncomfortable short position, the R_V offered for that particular loan on that security may be several hundred basis points below the repo rate.

Another point worth understanding relates to the Federal Reserve Board's use of repos and reverses in conducting open market operations. When the Fed wishes to increase the money supply for short time periods, one to seven days, it will often do so by purchasing U.S. Treasury securities from the various dealers and simultaneously entering into an agreement to resell those securities in one to seven days; the exact number of days is specified at the onset of the transaction. In this way, the Fed increases bank reserves by the amount paid for the securities until the time arrives when the securities are resold to dealers.

Because the Fed is purchasing securities with an agreement to sell them, this set of transactions can be characterized as the Fed undertaking a reverse repo position. However, in the terminology of Wall Street, "the Fed is doing repos." Why? Because all transactions between the Fed and the government dealers are viewed from the government dealers' point of view. In this case, when the Fed is first purchasing, then reselling securities, the dealers are, in turn, first selling and then repurchasing the securities. The government dealers, in response to the Fed's actions, are doing repos. It is because the market views all actions from the dealers' perspective that, when the Fed is in reality doing reverses, it is said to be doing repos. So remember, when the announcement is made that the Fed is doing repos, it is the dealers who are doing repos with the Fed.

When the Fed wishes to contract the money supply, it often sells U.S. Treasury securities to dealers under an agreement to repurchase those same securities in one to seven days; again, the exact maturity is specified upon the initiation of the transaction. While the Fed is doing repos, the dealers are doing reverses—buying from the Fed under an agreement to resell. So, when the Fed undertakes the set of transactions that begins with a security sale and ends with a repurchase, the Fed, while doing repos, is said to be doing reverses, because the market's view is from the dealer's vantage point. By the way, a phrase more often used than "the Fed is doing reverses" is "the Fed is doing matched sales." In this instance, *matched sales* is a synonym for *reverses*.

Locking in a Three-Month Lending Rate, Three Months in Advance, by Using Repos

Using a three-month term repo today, one can lock in a three-month lending rate beginning in three months. Suppose one purchases a six-month T-bill with a face value of $1,000,000 at a price of P_6. To finance this purchase, repo the T-bill for three months, receiving P_6 on the repo and incurring an obligation to pay $P_6(1 + R_P/4)$ in three months, when the T-bill will be returned. (For simplicity, we have assumed that there are 90 days in the three-month period, so deannualization of R_P, which now is used to symbolize the three-month repo rate, results in $R_P(90/360) = R_P/4$.) So today, call it $t = 0$, P_6 is paid for the T-bill, but P_6 dollars are received on the repo, so that the net cash flow at $t = 0$ is zero—just as in the initiation of a futures contract.

Three months later, at $t = 3$, the bill must be repurchased at a cost of $P_6(1 + R_P/4)$. So at $t = 3$ a cash outflow occurs. Finally, six months after the T-bill was purchased, it matures and pays its face value. So at $t = 6$ a cash inflow occurs equal to $1,000,000.

To recapitulate: At $t = 0$, a six-month T-bill is purchased and repoed-out for three months, resulting in a net cash flow of zero. At $t = 3$, the repo is concluded with the repurchase of the T-bill, resulting in a cash outflow of $P_6(1 + R_P/4)$. Finally, at $t = 6$, the T-bill maturity date, a cash inflow equal to $1,000,000 occurs. No cash flow occurs for the first three months; a cash outflow, known today, equal to $P_6(1 + R_P/4)$ occurs in three months (at $t = 3$); a cash inflow equal to $1,000,000 is received in six months (at $t = 6$). What has just been described is a three-month loan beginning in three months, where all cash flows are known with certainty today.

If all future cash flows are known with certainty today, then the interest rate implied by the relative amounts lent at $t = 3$ and received at $t = 6$—label that annualized rate $r_{3,6}$—is defined by and can be calculated from

$$P_6\left(1 + \frac{R_P}{4}\right)\left[1 + r_{3,6}\left(\frac{T_{3,6}}{365}\right)\right] = \$1,000,000$$

This rate $r_{3,6}$ equates, after the appropriate deannualization, the amount lent with the amount received. Note that $T_{3,6}$ is used to symbolize the number of days from the end of the third month to the end of the sixth month. In addition, since the interest rate is considered to be a rate of return, we follow standard practice and use 365 days to deannualize.

10.5 Pure Arbitrage Strategies Using T-Bill Futures

Recall that P_F, R_P, R_V, and P_6, respectively, denote the price of a three-month T-bill that can be locked in today by using the T-bill futures, the appropriate annualized repo and reverse rates for the period of the loan, and the price today of a six-month T-bill having a face value of $1 million. The following two situations are viewed from the dealer's point of view.

Case 1

$$P_F > P_6 \left(1 + \frac{R_P}{4}\right)$$

This inequality means the futures contract is relatively overpriced. We will see why shortly. To take advantage of this situation, sell today (at $t = 0$) the futures contract that expires in three months (at $t = 3$), locking in an effective invoice price of P_F. But this is a risky position, for if rates fall sharply, the losses to this short position will be appreciable. Therefore, the next step is to balance the position by going long the six-month spot T-bill at a cost of P_6 dollars. You are now committed to delivering a three-month T-bill in three months, but in three months the six-month T-bill you purchased today will be a three-month T-bill that is deliverable on the futures contract at $t = 3$. You have now converted your risky position into a riskless position. You have a balanced position.

There is only one problem. You have a net cash outflow of P_6 at $t = 0$. (Recall that zero cash flows are associated with the initiation of a futures position.) But pure arbitrage means a balancing of positions and zero net cash flows. To achieve a zero net cash flow, you repo out the six-month T-bill for three months, receiving P_6 dollars at $t = 0$. You use this money to pay for the six-month T-bill purchased earlier that day. (The settlements on the bill purchased and repoed out occur simultaneously, at the close of the next business day.) The position's net cash flow at $t = 0$ is now zero.

At $t = 3$, three months later, the repo must be unwound. You pay the counterparty $P_6 (1 + R_P/4)$, and the counterparty returns the T-bill, which now has three months remaining to maturity. You deliver this T-bill on the short futures position and receive P_F dollars from the long futures holder. All obligations have been satisfied.

Has a profit been made? Revenues amount to P_F. Costs are $P_6(1 + R_P/4)$. The profit is $P_F - P_6(1 + R_P/4)$. This quantity is positive by the assumption that defined this case, $P_F > P_6(1 + R_P/4)$. Consequently, when this condition is observed, a sure profit on zero investment can be effected. Therefore, the futures contract is relatively overpriced.

Case 2

$$P_F < P_6\left(1 + \frac{R_V}{4}\right)$$

This inequality means that the T-bill futures contract is relatively underpriced. We will see why. Proceeding on this assumption, buy today (at $t = 0$) the futures contract that expires in three months (at $t = 3$), locking in an effective invoice price of P_F. However, this position is risky, so the next step is to balance it with a short position. This is accomplished by reversing in a six-month T-bill for three months and immediately selling it. Since you no longer have the T-bill that you, as dealer, must return in three months in order to complete the reverse, you are short this bill. But your position is balanced, for in three months you will take delivery on the long futures of a three-month T-bill which you will redeliver to satisfy the reverse. Therefore, your short position is covered. Additionally, you have satisfied the zero investment requirement of pure arbitrage, for at $t = 0$, no cash is paid on the futures position, an amount equal to P_6 dollars is paid out on the reverse, but this same amount is received on the sale of the T-bill that was reversed in.

At $t = 3$, all obligations must be satisfied. A three-month T-bill is obtained by taking delivery on the expiring futures and P_F is paid. This T-bill is then redelivered to the counterparty of the reverse agreement, and you receive $P_6(1 + R_V/4)$.

Did you make money? Is $P_6(1 + R_V/4) > P_F$? Yes, because this condition was assumed when defining the market situation for this case. Consequently, when $P_F < P_6(1 + R_V/4)$ is observed, a sure profit on zero investment can be earned. The futures contract is relatively underpriced.

10.6 Quasi Arbitrage

A situation may arise in which a portfolio manager recognizes an opportunity to create a security that has identical future cash flows to a security held in his portfolio. If the created (synthetic) security can be manufactured at a lower price than the market price of the security held in the portfolio—referred to as the conventional security to avert confusion—then the latter should be sold and the synthetic purchased. A net gain equal to the difference in prices is obtained.

The replacement of a conventional security with a lower-cost synthetic is called a quasi arbitrage. Notice how it differs from a pure arbitrage: (1) Instead of a zero investment, a quasi arbitrage always entails a positive investment; (2) where the pure arbitrage balances a long against a short position, the quasi arbitrage is always characterized by a net long position. Two examples are presented that use the three-month T-bill futures contract to create the synthetic security.

In this first example, a long position in a six-month T-bill is created. A conventional six-month bill pays $1,000,000 at maturity and nothing prior to that time. Recall that our objective is to match the future cash flows of the conventional T-bill. Start at $t = 6$. The conventional T-bill's final and only cash flow is $1,000,000. What must we have at $t = 3$ in order to receive $1,000,000 at $t = 6$? Taking delivery on an expiring T-bill futures contract at $t = 3$ will give us a spot three-month T-bill with a $1,000,000 face value maturing at $t = 6$. So the first thing to do is to purchase today (at $t = 0$) a T-bill futures contract expiring at $t = 3$ and take delivery of a three-month T-bill at that time. However, if we are to take delivery at $t = 3$ on that futures contract, we must have funds available at $t = 3$ to pay the P_F dollars required of the long.

The original six-month cash flow matching problem has now been reduced to a three-month problem. In particular, how do we generate the P_F dollars needed at $t = 3$ to satisfy delivery? We buy three-month T-bills at $t = 0$. How many? Since each three-month bill pays $1,000,000 when it matures at $t = 3$, and we need P_F dollars at the time, then we buy $P_F/1,000,000$ three-month bills at $t = 0$. (Notice that multiplying the number of bills, $P_F/1,000,000$, times the $1,000,000 that each pays upon maturity gives the required P_F dollars.) We have found the strategy that synthetically creates a six-month T-bill: buy, at $t = 0$, one futures contract expiring at $t = 3$ and simultaneously purchase, at $t = 0$, $P_F/1,000,000$ three-month spot T-bills. The cost of the synthetic six-month bill is equal to the cost of the long futures contract (zero) plus the cost of $P_F/1,000,000$ three-month bills, which is $(P_F/1,000,000)P_3$. If this number is less than P_6, undertake the quasi arbitrage.

In this next example, a long position in a three-month bill is created. Since the conventional three-month T-bill pays $1,000,000 at $t = 3$, that is the amount that the synthetic must produce at $t = 3$. Suppose that at $t = 0$ we sell a futures contract that expires at $t = 3$, and buy a six-month T-bill. We intend to make delivery of a three-month T-bill at $t = 3$. We will be paid P_F upon delivery. But to replicate the $1,000,000 payment of the conventional three-month bill, we need to sell $1,000,000/P_F$ futures contracts. Since each futures contract will pay P_F dollars upon delivery, the total flow from the $1,000,000/P_F$ futures contracts amounts to $1,000,000—precisely what we want. To deliver on $1,000,000/P_F$ futures contracts at $t = 3$, we need to purchase $1,000,000/P_F$ six-month T-bills at $t = 0$.

To recap, the synthetic three-month T-bill is formed by purchasing $1,000,000/P_F$ six-month T-bills at a total cost of $(1,000,000/P_F)P_6$ and selling the same number of futures contracts at a cost of zero. The cost of the synthetic three-month T-bill amounts to $(1,000,000/P_F)P_6$. If this amount is less than P_3, execute the quasi arbitrage by selling the three-month bill out of the portfolio and purchasing the synthetic for a net gain.

While quasi-arbitrage strategies are interesting in themselves, they also point out a characteristic of futures. This characteristic is of paramount importance in the use of futures in managing a portfolio's risk. Recall that in the first example, the combination of three-month bills and a long futures contract replicated a long six-month bill position. The purchase of a futures contract served to lengthen the maturity of the portfolio. In that example, the long futures contract effectively lengthened the three-month bill position into a six-month bill. In the second example, a long position in six-month T-bills was transformed into a spot three-month T-bill through the sale of futures contracts. The sale of the futures contracts served to shorten the maturity of the portfolio.

Chapter **11**

Eurodollars

W*E BEGIN* this chapter with a description of the spot market for Eurodollars, move on to the defining characteristics of the Eurodollar futures contract, and then give examples of a futures hedge and an arbitrage. Discussion follows of how a forward rate agreement (or simply a "forward") might be used to achieve the same ends as the Eurodollar futures. We then turn to a demonstration of how a string of successive futures contracts—a strip—can be used to replicate a zero-coupon spot instrument; this notion is central to the pricing of interest rate swaps. The chapter concludes with a somewhat detailed examination of how traders, who hedge with futures, attempt to neutralize the effects of settlement variation in order to make a futures contract behave like a forward contract. A conclusion of this analysis is that, in a no-arbitrage environment, the Eurodollar rate implied by a futures contract must exceed that quoted for a forward contract on Eurodollars.

11.1 The Spot Market

A Eurodollar deposit is a dollar deposit in a bank outside the United States. A portion of these deposits take the form of Eurodollar Certificates of Deposit, but this part of the market is small and thinly traded. For all intents and purposes, the Eurodollar market is a time deposit market in which early withdrawal of principal results in loss of interest.

The Eurodollar market has exhibited extraordinary growth. From the early 1960s to the beginning of the 1990s, Eurodollar deposits have increased from under $10 billion to over $3 trillion. The center of this market is London. A number of reasons are offered for this growth phenomenon: (1) the habitual weakness of sterling made the dollar the currency of choice for international trade; (2) Russia and its allies had to carry dollar balances in order to conduct trade and were reluctant to leave those balances on deposit with domestic U.S. banks; (3) deposit rate ceilings existed on domestic accounts, while none were imposed on Eurodollar accounts; (4) the Federal Deposit Insurance Corporation (FDIC) levied an insurance premium on domestic time deposits but not on Eurodollar deposits; (5) initially, there was no reserve requirement on Eurodollar deposits. There is still no reserve requirement on net Eurodollar borrowings (deposits received less loans made).

In the Eurodollar market, deposit maturities range from overnight to five years. Eurodollar rates are quoted in increments as small as thirty-seconds, although one rarely sees a cut finer than a sixteenth. Eurodollar rates are quoted on an annual basis and deannualized, when appropriate, by assuming 360 days in the year. The rate at which a London bank is willing to lend Eurodollars to another London bank is known as the *offer rate* for that maturity. The rate that a London bank is willing to pay for a time deposit—that is, to borrow Eurodollars—is referred to as the *bid rate* for that maturity. When lending to another bank (called a *placement*), credit risk and, for that matter, country risk are controlled by setting a limit on the amount that the bank will lend to another bank. Receiving (borrowing) Eurodollars from another bank is referred to as "taking Euros." The settlement date or delivery date for a Eurodollar deposit, also known as the *value date* or *spot date,* occurs two business days after the trade date. The deposit's maturity is measured from the value date, and interest begins to accrue as of that date.

The acronym LIBOR stands for the London Interbank Offer Rate. It is used on settlement dates of Eurodollar forwards and swaps as a reference rate to calculate the cash payments due on the contracts. It is provided by the British Bankers Association (BBA). The methodology applied by the BBA in computing the reference rate is to provide a BBA-designated information vendor, such as Telerate, with a list of sixteen banks. At 11:00 A.M. London time, Telerate collects each bank's perception of the Eurodollar offer quote for each deposit maturity. For each maturity class, the two highest and two lowest quotes are discarded and the remaining quotes averaged.

For reasons not quite apparent, banks operating in the Eurodollar market tend to compartmentalize their Eurodollar activities. This practice may have arisen because no reserve requirement was imposed on Eurodollar deposits, or perhaps because of banking regulation differences between the United States and foreign countries. Whatever the reason for this practice, Eurodollar assets and liabilities are managed apart from the bank's other assets and liabilities. The management of the bank's Eurodollar assets and liabilities is known as "running the Eurodollar book." If the book's assets have a maturity that is greater than (less than) the maturity of its liabilities, the manager is said to be running an open (closed) book. If the Eurodollar assets and liabilities have the same maturity, the book is said to be matched. An open (closed) book is a bet that rates will fall (rise). A matched book is insensitive to rate changes.

11.2 Defining Features of the Eurodollar Futures Contract

1. Each futures contract is for a Eurodollar time deposit having a principal value of $1 million with a three-month maturity.

2. The futures price is quoted in terms of the International Monetary Market (IMM) Index for three-month Eurodollars, which is 100.00 minus the yield that traders expect to prevail on three-month time deposits on the contract's expiration day. For example, an Index value of 90.00 implies an (add-on) yield of 10%.

3. The minimum fluctuation in the Eurodollar IMM Index is 0.01. Since this is 0.01%, the equivalent yield change is one basis point, 0.0001. A change of 0.01 in the Index is worth $25 in settlement variation.

4. Trading in a Eurodollar futures contract terminates at 3:30 P.M. London time on the Monday preceding the third Wednesday of the spot month, the month in which the contract expires.

5. The delivery mechanism is cash settlement. Recall that this means that on the last day of trading in the spot month, a futures settlement price is declared that is equal to the current spot price. If that settlement price is higher (lower) than the previous day's, the long receives (pays) settlement variation from (to) the short. Subsequently, all outstanding positions are erased.

Since Eurodollar spot trading does not occur at one location, it is difficult to identify a unique spot rate to which the final future settlement rate will be equated. The Chicago Mercantile Exchange employs the following sampling procedure to determine the settlement rate and, equivalently, the settlement price of 100.00 less the settlement rate. From a list of banks that are deemed to constitute the prime banks in the Eurodollar market, twenty are randomly selected. At a randomly selected time within 90 minutes of the close, each bank is called and asked for its perception of the offer quote on three-month Eurodollars. Of these twenty responses, the four highest and four lowest quotes are ignored, and the remaining quotes are averaged. The entire process is repeated at the close of trading in the contract; another average quote is obtained. The two averages are then averaged to arrive at a settlement rate. This percentage value is subtracted from 100.00 to obtain the final Eurodollar futures settlement price.

Why employ such an elaborate sampling technique—random times, random lists, ignoring highs and lows, etc.? The Chicago Mercantile Exchange must prevent market manipulation. If traders believe that someone can alter the final outcome to reap extra profits, the contract will die. The CME's concern can be summarized in a brief paradigm. Suppose a large bank has a huge long Eurodollar futures position. If the bank can push the spot rate down as the contract closes, the bank stands to reap large profits at the expense of traders playing the game fairly. The bank may attempt to achieve this goal not only by giving a low offer quote (anyway, it will be thrown out); but it may choose to lend funds at the close at a very low rate, pushing the entire market down. Then every bank's quote will be low. The manipulating bank reasons that the money it will lose on the off-market rate offered on spot loans will be more than offset by the profits on its outsized futures position. To counter this possibility, the CME tries to make such a ploy expensive. It does so by essentially using the last 90 minutes of trading to calculate its settlement price. This means that the bank intending manipulation must keep the market at an uneconomically low rate for 90 minutes.

11.3 A Hedging Example

A Eurodollar manager, running an open book, is concerned that interest rates may rise by the time he must refinance his assets. The refinancing, which will occur on the date that the March Eurodollar futures contract expires, will necessitate borrowing 100 million Eurodollars for three months. The March three-month Eurodollar futures contract is trading at 92.00—the implied three-month rate is 8%. A refinancing rate of 8% is acceptable to the manager. To hedge against the possible rate rise, he sells 100 March Eurodollar futures contracts.

On the date that the March contract expires—coincidentally, the refinancing date—the three-month Eurodollar rate is 11%; the March futures settlement price is computed to be 89.00. Consequently, the manager must borrow 100 million Eurodollars at 11%, resulting in an increased borrowing cost of 3% or $750,000 ([0.03/4] × $100,000,000). (Notice that the 3% increase in rate had to be deannualized to reflect the fact that the increased cost would be borne for only one quarter of a year.) However, since the March Eurodollar futures contract settles at 89.00, the settlement variation on the 100 short futures contracts equals $750,000 ($25/bp × 300 bps × 100 contracts). The gain on the short futures serves to offset the unanticipated increase in financing costs.

11.4 A Pure Arbitrage Example

The numbers are fictitious, but the following arbitrage did occur. It took place over a period extending several months after the opening of the Eurodollar futures contract.

We borrow Euros for six months at an annual rate of 7%, or 3.5% for six months, lend that money for three months at 6%, 1.5% quarterly, and simultaneously lock in the three-month lending rate three months from today by purchasing the futures contract at 84.00—a 16% annual rate and 4% quarterly. In short, we borrow money for six months at a cost of 3.5%, lend that money for three months at 1.5%, and then roll it over upon maturity, lending it for an additional three months at 4%. We have borrowed for six months at 3.5% and lent for two successive three-month periods at a total rate of 5.5% (1.5% + 4%). This is a rough calculation, but it points to the essentials.

It is important to recall why the purchase of the Euro futures contract at 84.00 locks in the 16% annual lending rate on expiration day. If the three-month rate has risen to 20%, then in three months we can lend at the higher 20% rate, but will have lost 4% in settlement variation, because the IMM Index has dropped from 84.00 to 80.00. The net rate locked in is 16%. On the other hand, suppose the three-month rate has dropped to 12%. Then the gain in settlement variation is 4%, because the IMM Index has risen from 84.00 to 88.00. Again the net rate is 16%.

The arbitrage should be presented with a bit more attention to detail. For example, when we purchase the futures contract to lock in a 16% three-month rate, the contract is on a 1 million Eurodollar deposit. Since we are intending to hedge the rate on a 1 million deposit three months from today, we must plan on having 1 million Eurodollars to invest in three months. We will earn 1.5% on our first three-month deposit, and we want to have 1 million at the end of that period. So less than 1 million must be borrowed today. Specifically, we borrow 1,000,000/1.015 for six months, and invest it at 1.5% for three months, resulting in the desired balance of 1 million. This is reinvested at the 4% rate for the second three-month period. The amount accumulated after six months is 1,040,000 Eurodollars. The amount owed on the 1,000,000/1.015 Euros borrowed for six months is 1,019,704 ([1,000,000/1.015] × 1.035). The net gain on a balanced, zero investment position is $20,296.

What is a "fair" price for a Eurodollar futures contract? A price at which it does not pay to undertake a pure arbitrage like the one described above. Given the spot rates of the previous example, a no-arbitrage futures price would be 92.12.

11.5 Forward Rate Agreements (FRAs)

Like Eurodollar futures, a forward rate agreement (FRA) can be used to lock in Eurodollar lending and borrowing rates or to speculate on the future level of rates. An FRA is an over-the-counter contract between buyer and seller, wherein the buyer commits to pay the seller the contract rate on a notional sum over the stipulated future period. Information on the starting date (also the settlement date) and the length of the designated future loan period are provided in the manner in which the FRA is quoted. For example, a dealer quote of 7.95–8.00 on a 2 × 5, 10-million-Eurodollar FRA means that the future loan period begins two months from today and lasts for three months; the notional sum is $10 million, and the FRA can be purchased from the dealer at a contract rate of 8.00% or sold to the dealer at a contract rate of 7.95%. The $10 million notional sum is not lent or borrowed; rather it is used to calculate the cash payment between buyer (seller) and dealer necessary to ensure that the buyer (seller) has locked in the contract rate agreed to by the dealer.

By purchasing an FRA, the buyer has locked in a borrowing rate for that future period equal to the contract rate. Here's why. Suppose the 2 × 5, 10-million-Eurodollar FRA is purchased at 8% and the benchmark rate is three-month LIBOR. Two months later, on settlement day, three-month LIBOR is 10%. On that first day of the three-month period, the buyer of the FRA receives a cash payment from the seller equal to the present value of the increase in borrowing costs. This amount is computed as

$$\left[\frac{1}{1 + .10\left(\frac{91}{360}\right)}\right] \times .02 \times \frac{91}{360} \times \$10,000,000 = \$49,309$$

Since the buyer must now borrow for three months at 10% rather than at the anticipated 8%, the increase in borrowing costs is $50,556. But this amount is precisely the future value of the cash settlement of $49,309 paid on the first day of the loan period. Consequently, the FRA buyer has locked in 8% as a borrowing rate.[1]

Conversely, if LIBOR falls to 6% on settlement day, the buyer makes a cash payment to the seller of

$$\left[\frac{1}{1 + .06\left(\frac{91}{360}\right)}\right] \times .02 \times \frac{91}{360} \times \$10,000,000 = \$49,800$$

Although the buyer of the FRA, seeking to lock in an 8% rate, can borrow at 6%—a lower rate than anticipated—the cash payment from buyer to seller will bring the effective borrowing rate back up to 8%. A similar exercise can be performed to demonstrate that a seller of a 2 × 5 FRA at 7.95% locks in a 7.95% three-month lending rate.

The FRA looks just like an OTC forward contract. If the spot price is higher than the contract price at expiration, the long forward position has a positive value. If the spot is lower than the contract price, the long forward position is a loser. Substitute interest rates for prices in the above sentences, and you see that we are describing the profit profile of an FRA.

Because an FRA is an OTC instrument, it can be tailored to please the buyer or seller with regard to starting date, loan period, and nominal amounts. In contrast, the Eurodollar futures contract is written on a nominal amount of 1 million on a three-month Eurodollar

---

1. This example assumes that the new three-month Eurodollar borrowing rate and three-month LIBOR are the same. In fact, because LIBOR is computed as an average of offer rates at 11:00 A.M. London time, the actual borrowing rate may differ from LIBOR.

deposit and has a fixed expiration date in each of four months—March, June, September, and December. Though the FRA is a more flexible instrument than the Eurodollar futures, it trades in a less liquid market. Furthermore, the creditworthiness of an FRA depends on the capital base of the counterparties. In contrast, the CME guarantees performance on the Eurodollar futures.

11.6 Replicating a Zero-Coupon Instrument with a Eurodollar Strip

When we turn in Part III to the subject of interest rate swaps, we will see that strips of Eurodollar futures play an integral part in the valuation of existing swaps and the pricing of new swaps. A Eurodollar strip is defined as the purchase or sale today of a sequence of futures contracts that have successive expiration dates. A strip can be used to lock in a lending rate or a borrowing rate for a time period equal to the length of the strip.

Suppose an investment manager expects to receive $1,000,000 on the date that the March Eurodollar futures expires. His objective is to invest the money for one year in the Eurodollar market. He is concerned that rates may fall by March. A long Eurodollar strip is one way of meeting his objective. Whether it is best depends, of course, on the prices of alternative instruments.

At present, in February, the March, June, September, and December futures are trading at 92.00, 88.00, 84.00, and 80.00, respectively. Clearly, the March–June interest rate can be fixed today on the forthcoming $1,000,000 by purchasing a March Eurodollar future. The rate locked in is 8% annually, equivalently 2% for the March–June quarter. If in March the three-month Eurodollar rate has fallen to 6%, then a 1.5% rate of return will be earned over the March–June period on the $1,000,000 spot investment, i.e., a dollar amount equal to $15,000. But this spot return is enhanced by the settlement variation earned on the March futures contract, which comes to $5,000 (200 bps × $25/bp). The effective return is 2% ([15,000 + 5,000]/1,000,000). If, instead, the three-month Eurodollar rate has risen to 10%, the $1,000,000 spot investment would earn 2.5% quarterly, providing a dollar return of $25,000. However, from this dollar return, the settlement variation loss amounting to $5,000 (200 bps × $25/bp) must be subtracted. The effective investment rate for the March–June period is again 2% ([25,000 − 5,000]/1,000,000).

Looking ahead to June, the spot three-month investment will have accrued to $1,020,000 and must be reinvested. The 12% three-month rate for the June–September interval can be locked in today on that amount by purchasing 1.02 June Eurodollar futures today. If by June the Eurodollar rate has fallen to 8%, i.e., 2% quarterly, then the spot investment of $1,020,000 will earn $20,400 over the subsequent three months. However, the settlement variation gain on the 1.02 futures provides an additional $10,200 (1.02 × 400 bps × $25/bp). The total dollar return for this second three-month interval amounts to $30,600, implying a 3% (30,600/1,020,000) quarterly return or 12% annual return. A symmetrical exercise demonstrates that 3% is again locked in if rates happen to be higher in June.

Extending the foregoing reasoning, to lock in a reinvestment rate today for the September–December period on the resulting $1,050,600 September balance, purchase 1.02 × 1.03 September contracts today. This action locks in a 4% quarterly rate on that balance. And to fix the final quarter's (December–March) reinvestment rate at 5% on the December balance of $1,000,000 × 1.02 × 1.03 × 1.04, purchase 1.02 × 1.03 × 1.04 December contracts today.

Therefore, to fix a one-year investment rate today of 14.73%, a Eurodollar strip is purchased composed of one March contract, 1.02 June contracts, 1.02 × 1.03 September contracts, and 1.02 × 1.03 × 1.04 December contracts. This simple exercise demonstrates that the return on a long-dated, zero-coupon instrument can be replicated by stringing together a series of futures contracts, forming a strip. In this example, an equivalent instrument was created that paid $1 one year from the initial investment date in March and nothing before that date. Its initial value would be $1/1.1473 = $0.8716.

11.7 A Hedging Subtlety in Using Eurodollar Futures

When futures and forwards were compared in Chapter 9, a theory was presented as to why settlement variation on futures might drive a wedge between futures and forward prices. It was pointed out that empirical evidence from currency futures markets did not support this wedge theory, because differences between futures and forward prices in these markets appeared statistically insignificant. Furthermore, either because of such empirical evidence or because of the knowledge gained from watching such instruments trade, academics and traders tend to price futures using forward pricing models. To make the futures instrument consistent with the pricing technique, traders attempt to adjust the size of their futures hedges to neutralize any effects of settlement variation. Their objective is to make the futures gain or loss, taking into consideration settlement variation, equal to the forward contract's gain or loss.

To understand how this is attempted, let the goal be to lock in a lending rate for the three-month period that ends T days from today. Trading on the futures contract terminates on the date that this three-month loan period commences. The rate to be locked in is equal to today's implied three-month Eurodollar futures rate. Today's implied futures rate is r_0 (annualized), and that rate will change by day's end to r_1. At the start of the day, funds can be lent or borrowed for T days at a daily rate of R_T; the daily rate that will apply tomorrow for the subsequent $T - 1$ days is R_{T-1}. (All rates are in decimal form.) If h symbolizes the number of Eurodollar futures used in constructing the hedge, then, to lock in a three-month lending rate for the future three-month period, h is selected to satisfy the following equation:

$$\frac{r_1}{4} + h\left[\left(\frac{r_0 - r_1}{4}\right)\left(1 + R_{T-1}\right)^{T-1}\right] = \frac{r_0}{4} \qquad (11.1)$$

The terms on the left-hand side of the equation represent the sum of money to be earned on \$1 lent over the three-month period following the contract's termination—assuming rates do not change after today. The first term represents the earnings at the new rate, r_1, and the second term represents the accrued earnings or costs through day T from today's settlement variation. If the value of this second term can be made equal to $(r_0 - r_1)/4$, the value of the forward's payment at the end of the three-month loan period, then the futures payoff will be identical to that of a forward. The term on the right-hand side of the equation represents the loan income that we attempt to lock in for that forthcoming three-month period—essentially the initial futures rate of r_0. (Note that since all rates are stated on an annual basis, they must be deannualized to make them applicable for our three-month lending/borrowing period.)

Traders do not know today what R_{T-1} will be tomorrow. But, assuming that $R_{T-1} = R_T$, then the h value that satisfies this equation is $h = 1/(1 + R_T)^{T-1} = 1/(1 + R_{T-1})^{T-1}$. Consequently, if the rate at which funds may be reinvested or borrowed remains constant over the life of the hedge, choosing a hedge ratio of $h = 1/(1 + R_T)^{T-1}$ reduces the left-hand side of the equation to $(r_0/4)$—exactly the return that could be locked in with a forward contract. If this hedging methodology locks in r_0 in the face of a rate change today, then it can be reapplied tomorrow to continue to ensure that r_0 will be obtained in the face of future rate changes.

Notice that this hedging prescription means that, for each forward contract used to hedge interest rate risk, less than one futures contract will be used to achieve the same goal. This is referred to as *tailing the hedge*. The intuition is that if one earns (loses) settlement variation on a futures contract equal to $(r_0 - r_1)/4$, and it accrues to $[(r_0 - r_1)/4](1 + R_{T-1})^{T-1}$ by the end of the loan period, then profits (losses) on the futures contract will exceed profits (losses) on the forward. This is because the profits (losses) on the forward, valued at the end of the loan period, are exactly equal to the amount implied by the rate difference $(r_0 - r_1)/4$.[2] Therefore, we wish to reduce the futures gains (losses) that emanate from the settlement variation received (paid) today. This is done by purchasing $1/(1 + R_T)^{T-1}$—which equals $1/(1 + R_{T-1})^{T-1}$, given $R_T = R_{T-1}$—futures contracts instead of one futures contract, so that the accrued settlement variation is

$$\left[\frac{1}{(1 + R_{T-1})^{T-1}}\right]\left(\frac{r_0 - r_1}{4}\right)(1 + R_{T-1})^{T-1} = \frac{r_0 - r_1}{4}$$

All of this works if, indeed, the reinvestment/borrowing rate, R_T, remains constant over the remainder of the hedge period. If it does not, as will almost surely be the case, then if futures and forward contracts carry the same price at the outset, when the rate is r_0, the forward contract will be a dominant long hedging instrument. To see this, suppose that we choose $h = 1/(1 + R_T)^{T-1}$, and interest rates rise so that $r_1 > r_0$ and $R_{T-1} > R_T$, say $(1 + R_{T-1})^{T-1} = (1 + R_T)^{T-1} + \epsilon$, where $\epsilon > 0$. Then the left-hand side of equation (11.1) can be rewritten as

$$\frac{r_1}{4} + \left[\frac{1}{(1 + R_T)^{T-1}}\right]\left\{\left[\frac{r_0 - r_1}{4}\right]\left[(1 + R_T)^{T-1} + \epsilon\right]\right\} =$$

$$= \frac{r_1}{4} + \frac{r_0 - r_1}{4} + \left[\frac{1}{(1 + R_T)^{T-1}}\right]\frac{(r_0 - r_1)\epsilon}{4}$$

$$= \frac{r_0}{4} + \left[\frac{1}{(1 + R_T)^{T-1}}\right]\frac{(r_0 - r_1)\epsilon}{4}$$

---

2. Remember from the FRA discussion that the payoff that comes at the beginning of the relevant loan period equals the present value of the end-of-period interest income lost or gained. This end-of-period amount is $(r_0 - r_1)/4$.

Because $r_1 > r_0$, the return earned is less than r_0, the lending rate locked in via a forward contract.

On the other hand, suppose that with a futures position of $h = 1/(1 + R_T)^{T-1}$ rates fall so that $r_1 < r_0$ and $R_{T-1} < R_T$. Assume that $(1 + R_{T-1})^{T-1} = (1 + R_T)^{T-1} - \epsilon$, where $\epsilon > 0$. Then the left-hand side of equation (11.1) reduces to $r_0/4 - [(r_0 - r_1)/4]\epsilon/(1 + R_T)^{T-1}$. Since $r_1 < r_0$, the lending rate locked in will again be less than r_0, the rate that can be obtained with a forward contract.

Consequently, if the futures and forward command the same price at the outset, r_0, the forward contract will dominate the futures contract as a long hedging instrument. The intuitive reason for this is that the profit profile of the forward contract is convex, while the profit profile of the futures contract is linear—always paying \$25 per basis point, independent of the level of the interest rate. To make the long hedger indifferent between a futures contract and a forward contract, the futures rate must exceed the forward rate. Now suppose we view the entire process from the short hedger's point of view. If the futures and forward contracts are both initially priced at r_0, the borrowing rate that will result with a futures hedge will be less than the one that can be obtained with a forward contract. Although the forward is convex for the long hedger, it is concave for the short hedger and thus loses to the linearity of the futures profit profile. For the short hedger to be indifferent between futures and forwards, the futures rate must exceed the forward rate. If both futures and forwards carried the same rate, r_0, a riskless arbitrage would be to short the futures and buy the forward. Thus, in a no-arbitrage environment, the futures rate must exceed the forward rate.

Chapter *12*

U.S. Treasury Bond and Note Futures

*I*N KEEPING with our adopted mode, we begin with a description of the spot market for U.S. Treasury bonds (T-bonds) and Treasury notes (T-notes). These sections focus on the Treasury auction and spot market conventions with respect to security delivery and price and yield quotes. The role of the Government Securities Clearing Corporation (GSCC) in clearing spot market transactions in Treasuries is examined. As in previous chapters, the salient features of the Treasury bond and note futures contracts are delineated. A discussion of no-arbitrage pricing, hedging, and optimal delivery time, assuming only one deliverable bond, follows. Next, our view is expanded to include pricing and hedging questions when more than one T-bond (T-note) is eligible for delivery, as in reality. The chapter concludes with an examination of the options embedded in the T-bond (T-note) futures contract and available to the short.

12.1 The Spot Market

At the end of each month, the U.S. Treasury auctions and issues a two-year note and a five-year note. At the beginning of February, March, August, and November, the Treasury auctions, on successive days, a three-year note and a ten-year note for issue (and settlement on the fifteenth of those months). On the third day of the February and August auctions, a 30-year bond is auctioned for settlement on the fifteenth of the month. Beginning in 1985, new issues did not contain a call feature. Since 1986, all notes and bonds have been issued in book entry form—no certificates of ownership are issued. Coupons are paid semiannually. The first payment date occurs six months after the issue date. On each payment date, one-half of the annual coupon is remitted to the bond holder. The structure of the 3-year, 10-year, and 30-year bond auctions is similar to the T-bill auctions. The amount needed to satisfy noncompetitive bidders is set aside. Competitive bids on the remaining part of the new issue are received in the form of yields, representing the coupon that the bidder wishes to be paid on the issue. These bids are ordered from lowest to highest. The Treasury officials work their way down the list until the amount available for competitive bidding is exhausted. The highest yield at which a bid is accepted is called the *stop-out yield*. The Treasury then sets the coupon rate to the nearest one-eighth of a percent of the weighted average of the competitive yields accepted—the weights being the face values of the competitive bids as fractions of the total face value subject to competitive bidding.

Each competitive bidder pays a price equal to the discounted value of the coupons (which is known after the coupon rate has been determined) plus the face value. The discount rate applied for each bidder in determining the price to be paid is the yield submitted by that bidder and accepted by the Treasury. Those who submitted high price bids (low yields) will pay a premium for their portion of the issue; those submitting low price bids (high yields) will purchase the notes or bonds at a discount. For noncompetitive bidders, the price paid is found by discounting the coupon set by the weighted average of competitive bids. The price is either 100.00 or less. The reason it might be less is that the coupon is set to the nearest eighth that will produce a price of par or less when discounted at the average yield. The auction terms *tail* and *cover* carry the same meanings as in the Treasury bill auctions.

In 1992, the Treasury began experimenting with a different type of auction structure for the two- and five-year note issues. All the steps previously described for the three- and ten-year note auctions and the bond auction apply, except that all winning competitive bidders receive their bonds at the same price, no matter what they bid. After the stop-out yield has been determined, all winning competitive bidders are assigned this highest yield (lowest price) as if they had indeed bid it. So all are rewarded with the lowest price, and the coupon is set at the stop-out yield. (If the stop-out yield cannot be expressed exactly in eighths, then the coupon is set to the nearest eighth below the stop-out yield.) Clearly the highest bidder (lowest bid yield) will end up paying less for the bonds than the dollar amount commensurate with his bid yield. Won't the Treasury receive less for the sale of those issues under this type of allocation, called a *competitive auction* by economists and called a *single-price auction* by the Fed, as opposed to the traditional Treasury's auction, called a *discriminatory auction* by economists and called a *multiprice auction* by the Fed? Not necessarily. No matter how high (low) the price (yield) bid by an individual is, if he wins, he gets his bonds at the stop-out yield (lowest price). Consequently, this auction type will tend to raise the entire demand schedule for the issue, thus it results in a lower stop-out yield. If the stop-out yield is sufficiently lower, the total revenues received by the Treasury under this competitive or single-price auction will exceed those obtained from the discriminatory or multiprice auction. The experiment continues.

In the secondary market, T-note and T-bond prices are quoted as a percentage of face value, with a typical increment of $\frac{1}{32}$, but sometimes down to $\frac{1}{64}$. For example, a price quote of 92.10 on $1 million of face value translates into a dollar figure of $923,125 ($[(92^{10}/_{32})/100] \times$ $1,000,000$).

Regular settlement on T-notes and T-bonds occurs one business day after the trade date. Trades that are scheduled for settlement more than one business day after the trade date are called *forward trades*. The most common type of forward trade is a *when issued* (WI) trade. The WI label describes the market for Treasury securities that have been announced but not yet auctioned. The WI period extends from announcement to issue day. During this period, the to-be-issued security is traded on a yield basis, where the yield paid reflects the expected coupon on the new issue. The buyer's invoice price upon issue is calculated by discounting the then-known coupon and principal by the yield agreed to in the WI trade.

If, on settlement day, the seller *fails to deliver* the securities to the buyer, then the buyer is entitled to the coupon interest measured from the settlement day. Even though the buyer has not received and therefore has not paid for the securities, the buyer receives the interest income on the securities as if delivery and payment had been made. In addition, since the buyer does not pay for the securities until actual delivery, he earns interest on the funds he would have used in payment. Since the coupon interest and the interest on the money set aside to pay for the securities is earned by the dealer, who has not received the securities on settlement day, the dealer is not unhappy about the failure to deliver by the counterparty to the trade.

The note or bond price quoted on electronic screens or in the newspapers is called the *clean price* or net price. The 92.10 price used earlier was a clean price quote. In addition to paying the clean price on settlement day, the buyer must, in addition, pay to the seller that part of the next coupon payment that the seller is deemed to deserve. For example, if the time period from the last coupon date to the forthcoming coupon date consists of 182 days, and the settlement date occurs 91 days subsequent to the last coupon payment, then the seller is deemed to be entitled to 91/182 or one-half of the next coupon payment, for he held the security for half the period for which that coupon payment is being made in satisfaction of the bond interest owed. The bond buyer will receive the entire coupon payment on the next payment date, but, upon settlement day, that portion of the next coupon earned by the seller must be paid to the seller by the bond buyer. This payment is called *accrued interest*. Denoting the number of days from the last coupon date to settlement date by t_{is}, the number of days in the current coupon period by N_d, and the annual coupon rate by c, the accrued interest, AI, per \$1 of the security's face value is calculated as

$$AI = \left(\frac{c}{2}\right)\left(\frac{t_{is}}{N_d}\right)$$

In order to calculate the clean price, the gross price of the security must first be calculated. Letting P_g, y, t_{sc}, and n, respectively, denote the bond's (note's) gross price, its yield to maturity, the number of days from settlement to the forthcoming coupon date, and the number of future coupon payment dates, the formula that relates the gross price to the yield to maturity on a bond that has \$1 of face value is

$$P_g = \frac{1}{\left(1 + \frac{y}{2}\right)^{t_{sc}/N_d}} \left[\sum_{k=1}^{n} \frac{\frac{c}{2}}{\left(1 + \frac{y}{2}\right)^{k-1}} + \frac{1}{\left(1 + \frac{y}{2}\right)^{n-1}} \right]$$

The gross price is defined as the present value of all future cash flows discounted back to the settlement date. The clean price, P_c, is defined and calculated as the gross price less accrued interest, $P_c = P_g - AI$.

12.2 Clearing and Settling Trades in U.S. Treasury Securities: The Government Securities Clearing Corporation (GSCC)

The Government Securities Clearing Corporation (GSCC) performs functions for U.S. Government debt securities analogous to those performed by futures and option clearing entities for futures and option contracts. GSCC electronically compares trades, nets each member's buys and sells in order to reduce deliveries, guarantees performance by the parties to the trade by assuming the role of buyer to the selling member and of seller to the buying clearing member, collects margin (good faith collateral), and marks-to-market daily each net position to offset the risk of a member not performing the delivery and payment obligations assumed in the trades. Should insolvency befall a member, GSCC uses all of its financial resources and, if necessary, those of the solvent members to meet the financial obligations of the defaulting member. The classes of securities accepted by GSCC for clearing extend beyond U.S. Treasury securities and include the debt securities of the World Bank, the Student Loan Marketing Association, the Federal National Mortgage Association, and the Federal Home Loan Mortgage Corporation, among other U.S. government–sponsored agencies.

Securities acceptable by GSCC for netting must be eligible for settlement over the Fed wire. Delivery and payment are simultaneous. This means that on settlement day, the buyer's bank credits his securities statement an amount equal to the face value of the transaction and debits his money account an amount equal to the invoice price of the transaction. The opposite entries are made by the seller's bank. The money credits and debits received over the Fed wire are referred to as Fed funds or same-day funds, for no float is attached to these money transfers. GSCC clears both regular way trades (settlement occurs on the following business day) and forward trades.

The comparison stage of the clearing process consists of matching data submitted by the long and short sides of a trade. The trade data set is composed of, among other things, an indicator as to whether the submitting party bought or sold, a security identification in the form of a CUSIP (Committee for Uniform Securities Identification Procedures) number, the trade's face value, the money to be exchanged in the trade, the trade and settlement dates, and the identification of the participants to the trade. If the data submitted by the counterparties to the trade match, then the trade is declared to have cleared and becomes a binding contract between the participants. This occurs by 2:00 A.M. on the day following the trade day. The data for unmatched trades are returned to the submitting parties with the presumption that they will attempt to reconcile their differences quickly and resubmit the edited trade data to GSCC for another comparison.

Once cleared, the trade is eligible for netting. The netting stage involves offsetting a member's buys and sells in a particular security class for a specific settlement date. The purpose is to minimize the number of deliveries. A member's net long (short) position in a security represents the face value (often referred to as the *par value* by GSCC) of the security that the member will receive from (deliver to) GSCC. Any delivery or receipt of securities between GSCC and a member must be made against simultaneous receipt or delivery of Fed funds.[1]

After netting, the amount of securities to be delivered or received can no longer be identified with a specific trade and consequently cannot be assigned a particular trade price, so GSCC assigns a *system price* to all deliveries. The system price is calculated as a weighted average trade price for that security; the weights are the face values of the various trades. The prices and weights are taken from trades in that security from the most recent trade date. When GSCC receives securities from a net short member, it wires that member an amount of funds equal to the system price for that security plus accrued interest per dollar of face value; the system price plus accrued interest is referred to as the *system value* of that security. Conversely, when GSCC delivers securities over the Fed wire, it receives the system value of those securities from the net long member. But the trades did not occur at the system value. To reconcile the difference between a trade value and the system value, GSCC enters into a transaction adjustment payment (TAP) with each member.

An example might help to clarify these terms and concepts. Suppose only three members, A, B, and C, trade in a given security for settlement on a set day. Member B buys one unit of the security from A at 94 and sells it to C at 98. Accrued interest is zero on settlement day. The security's system price is 96, and, because accrued interest is zero, the system value is 96. Since B is both a buyer and a seller of one unit of the security, B's net is zero and B has no delivery obligation. Member A delivers the security to GSCC and receives 96 in Fed funds. GSCC delivers the security to C, receiving 96 in Fed

---

1. Up to this point in the description, GSCC's functions correspond to those of a futures clearing house. But here there is a difference. On settlement day, GSCC legally interposes itself as the counterparty to the delivering member and the counterparty to the receiving member. GSCC takes delivery and redelivers securities; it receives payments and makes payments. On a number of futures contracts the clearing house does not interpose itself in the delivery process; rather it oversees the process. The delivery is made by the seller directly to the facility of the assigned buyer, and the buyer makes a direct payment to the seller's bank. This is how it works in the Chicago Mercantile Exchange's T-bill contract and the Chicago Board of Trade's T-bond and T-note contracts. With regard to its currency contracts, the Chicago Mercantile Exchange, like GSCC, does interpose itself directly in the delivery and payment process.

funds from C. Member A is entitled to the sale price of 94. The system value of 96 received by A less A's debit TAP to GSCC of 2 equals 94. Member C is obligated to pay the purchase price of 98. Since the system payment made by C upon delivery was 96, its debit TAP to GSCC must be 2. Because B bought at 94 and sold at 98, its credit TAP from GSCC is 4, the sum of A's and C's TAPs to GSCC.

To deal with the risk that a member might not pay the money owed or deliver the securities due, GSCC requires that a member post an amount of collateral that is determined by the following formula: 125% of the member's average daily funds settlement (debit or credit), based on data from the most recent 20 days, plus the maximum of (1) the member's average daily margin over the prior 20 days, taking into account margin reductions due to risk-reducing positions (referred to as *offsets* by GSCC); (2) 100% of today's daily margin, including risk-reducing positions or (3) 50% of today's daily margin, ignoring risk-reducing positions. Collateral may take the form of cash, Treasury securities, letters of credit from approved banks, or a combination of these.

Example of a Margin Calculation for Two Particular Positions

After the netting process has been completed, member A is obligated to deliver bonds with a system value of $14 million that have a maturity of 25 years and to receive bonds with a system value of $12 million that have a maturity of 10 years. The margin requirement on this position, which will enter into the subsequent 20-day average calculation, is computed in the following manner. First, both positions are margined, ignoring the risk-reducing effects of having both securities in the same portfolio. The margin required for each position is based on the application of a percentage figure for that maturity, called a *margin factor* by GSCC, to the system value of the position. This provides a dollar margin figure for each position. This margin amount is intended to cover one day's change in the value of the position.[2] For the 25- and 10-year Treasuries, the margin factors are 1.45% and 0.935%, respectively. Applying these factors to the system values of the obligations leads to an initial margin calculation of $(0.0145 \times \$14,000,000) + (0.00935 \times \$12,000,000) = \$315,200$. Since

---

2. The margin factor is selected so that the resulting collateral required would have covered at least 95% of past one-day value changes in the security.

this calculation ignores the risk-reducing effects of having both security positions in a portfolio, the resulting margin figure is excessive.

The second step is to compute the margin credit that is to be deducted from this gross margin figure. If the member's net short and long positions were in the same maturity class, then a credit of 12 million times the class margin factor would be deducted from the margin calculation of the short side and an identical amount would be deducted from the margin calculation for the long side. Thus, if the member had a 14 million short obligation of 25-year bonds and a 12 million long obligation of 20-year bonds (instead of the 12 million of 10-year Treasuries), both would be placed in the same maturity class and given the same margin factor by GSCC. The initial margin would be $(0.0145 \times 14) + (0.0145 \times 12)$, and the margin credit would amount to $(0.0145 \times 12) + (0.0145 \times 12)$, resulting in a net margin (a margin with offsets) of $0.0145 \times 2,000,000$. Here, as expected, the long position served as a complete offset to 12 million of the 14 million short position for purposes of the margin calculation.

However, in our example of the 25- and 10-year Treasuries, the two bonds are not considered by GSCC to be in the same maturity class, so a full deduction is not permitted. Instead, part of the full credit is disallowed. In this example, 20% of the margin reduction that would result from a full margin credit is disallowed. The 20% is termed the *disallowance factor* for these two security classes. The credit calculation is reduced to $[(0.0145 \times \$12,000,000) + (0.00935 \times \$12,000,000)](1 - 0.2) = \$228,960$. This amount is subtracted from the initial margin calculation to arrive at a "margin with offsets" figure of $86,240.[3]

Finally, the margin with offsets number is compared to 50% of the initial margin number. In this case the latter calculation yields $0.5 \times \$315,200 = \$157,600$. Since the latter amount exceeds the margin with offsets amount, the relevant margin figure is $157,600.

12.3 The Treasury Bond Futures Contract: Defining Features

1. The contract requires delivery of $100,000 face value (par) of bonds with at least fifteen years to call, if callable, or fifteen years to maturity, if not callable.

---

3. This 20% disallowance factor recognizes a fairly high positive correlation between the prices of the 10- and 25-year bonds. The disallowance factor for a long position of six-month bills and 25-year bonds is 100%, resulting in a zero credit to the initial margin figure.

2. The futures price is quoted as a percentage of par with a minimum increment of $\frac{1}{32}$, worth \$31.25 in settlement variation. A quote of 98-07 means $98\frac{7}{32}\%$ of par (\$100,000).

3. Upon delivery, the short invoices the long an amount equal to the conversion factor *(cv)* for the bond delivered times the futures settlement price (in decimal) times \$100,000, plus the accrued interest on that particular bond. The conversion factor for the delivered bond is calculated as the clean price of the bond per \$1 of face value, using a yield to maturity of 8% as the discounting rate and a time to maturity (or time to call, if callable) calculated from the first day of the delivery month to the maturity (callable) date. Fractions of a year are rounded down to quarters. So, for computational purposes, fifteen years and five months becomes fifteen years and one quarter.

Suppose short delivers an 8% coupon bond. Then, using the prescribed 8% discount rate, the clean price per dollar of face value is \$1.00. So the conversion factor is 1.00 for an 8% coupon bond. This means the invoice price when delivering an 8% bond is

$$1.00 \times \frac{F}{100} \times 100{,}000 + \text{AI}$$

where *F* is the settlement futures price on the day delivery is declared by short. To simplify the remainder of this discussion, assume that only \$100 of face value is delivered on any bond, and, for the time being, ignore accrued interest. Then the invoice price for an 8% bond is simply *F*.

Let us attempt to give an intuitive explanation of this delivery invoicing method. Consider the delivery of an 8% perpetuity or a 16% perpetuity; they never mature. The conversion factor for the 8% perpetuity is 1.00 and that for the 16% perpetuity is 2.00.[4] The respective invoice prices on \$100 of face value, ignoring accrued interest, are, respectively, *F* and 2*F* for the 8% and 16% bonds. So the short gets paid twice as much if he delivers 16s as he would if 8s are delivered. But this makes sense, for a 16 contains two 8s. Consequently, the conversion factor, which is 2.00 for the 16s (perpetuities) and 1.00 for the 8s, measures the quantity of 8s contained in the bond being delivered. The invoice price—futures price times conversion factor—

---

4. The perpetuity price, assuming for simplicity an annual coupon, is the coupon rate divided by the discount rate. In these conversion factor calculations, the discount rate is always 0.08.

can then be interpreted as the price of an 8, *F*, times the quantity of 8s.

4. Notice of delivery by short must be given to the Chicago Board of Trade (CBOT) Clearing Corporation two days prior to the delivery date. This date is called *position day*, and the CBOT must be notified of delivery by 8:00 P.M. (CST) on position day.

5. By 2:00 P.M. (CST) on the day before delivery day, called *intention day*, short must state precisely which bond will be used for delivery.

6. On delivery day, any day of the spot (delivery) month, short must transfer bonds to long, and long must pay for the bonds in Fed funds before 1:00 P.M. (CST).

7. The daytime trading session starts at 7:20 A.M. (CST) and ends at 2:00 P.M. (CST).

8. No trades may be made during the final seven business days of the spot (delivery) month.

The 2-, 5-, and 10-year T-note contracts are identical in structure to the T-bond contract, except that only T-notes with maturities between 1 year, 9 months and 2 years may be delivered on the 2-year T-note contract, only maturities between 4 years, 3 months and 5 years, 3 months may be delivered on the 5-year T-note contract, and only T-notes with maturities between 6½ and 10 years may be delivered on the 10-year T-note contract. The minimum price increments on the 2-, 5- and 10-year T-note contracts are 1/128, 1/64, and 1/32, respectively. Whereas the 5- and 10-year T-note contracts require delivery of $100,000 face value of acceptable T-note maturities, the 2-year T-note contract requires delivery of $200,000 face value of acceptable T-note maturities. Because the contracts are economically similar, the following analysis focuses on the T-bond futures contract, the Treasury futures contract with the highest daily volume.

12.4 Futures Pricing, Hedging, and the Optimal Time to Deliver for the Case of Only One Deliverable Bond

No-Arbitrage Pricing

More than thirty bonds are deliverable on the T-bond futures contract. However, to make some points essential to an understanding of the contract's pricing and uses, let us begin with a simpler environment. We assume only one bond is deliverable. We also abstract from the two-day waiting time between position day and delivery day.

Define P_0, AI_0, and F_0, respectively, as the bond's clean price, its accrued interest, and the futures price at $t = 0$; T is the number of days to expiration of the futures contract; AI_T represents the bond's accrued interest at $t = T$; $c/2$ is the coupon payment that might occur at $t = t'$, where $0 \leq t' \leq T$; cv symbolizes the bond's conversion factor, as measured from $t = T$ to the bond's maturity date—at least fifteen years away—and r and r_v, respectively, denote the overnight repo and reverse rates, assumed to be constant and representing *one-day* interest rates. There are two types of pure arbitrages.

1. Sell the futures, buy the bond, and, to achieve zero net investment, repo it out. These transactions result in the following profit, π, expression:[5]

$$\pi = cvF_0 + AI_T - (P_0 + AI_0)(1 + r)^T + \frac{c}{2}(1 + r_v)^{T-t'}$$

The first two terms on the expression's right-hand side represent the invoice price upon delivery of the bond at $t = T$; the third term is the amount that the arbitrager must pay to close out the repo at $t = T$ and, in return, receive back the bond that is to be delivered on the short futures at $t = T$; the last term is the amount that the coupon payment, received at t', will accumulate to at T. The funds received from the coupon payment, $c/2$, are lent out at the reverse rate. The no-riskless-arbitrage condition requires that $\pi \leq 0$. Consequently,

$$F_0 \leq \frac{1}{cv}\left[(P_0 + AI_0)(1 + r)^T - \frac{c}{2}\left(1 + r_v\right)^{T-t'} - AI_T\right] \quad (12.1)$$

represents a no-arbitrage *upper bound* on the futures price. If the futures price exceeds the value of the expression on the right-hand side of (12.1), then a riskless profit on zero investment is available.

---

5. Realistically, the arbitrager would lock in his borrowing (repo) and lending (reverse) rates at $t = 0$. So the overnight rates in the profit expression should be replaced by the repo and reverse rates for T days. We could develop the material in this fashion, but it is more cumbersome, and the points with respect to hedging and delivery contained in the following sections are more easily made using the overnight financing rates.

2. Buy the futures, reverse in the bond, and sell it, achieving a balanced position on zero investment. The profit expression that corresponds to this set of transactions is

$$\pi = (P_0 + AI_0)(1 + r_v)^T - \frac{c}{2}(1 + r)^{T-t'} - cvF_0 - AI_T$$

The first term represents the revenues received at $t = T$ when the reverse is unwound, the bond is returned, and the dealer receives the money lent out at $t = 0$ plus interest; the money needed to finance this reverse at $t = 0$ is obtained by selling, at $t = 0$, the bonds obtained through the reverse. The individual from whom the dealer reversed in the bonds is entitled to any coupon payments during the term of the reverse. So the dealer must pay $c/2$ at $t = t'$. To make this payment he makes arrangements to borrow $c/2$ at t', at the repo rate, and pays back an amount equal to the second term of the π expression. The last two terms represent the effective price that the dealer, as long, must pay when receiving the bond on the futures delivery; this bond will be redelivered to satisfy the reverse. The no-arbitrage condition requires that $\pi \leq 0$. This implies that the *lower bound* on the futures price is

$$F_0 \geq \frac{1}{cv}\left[(P_0 + AI_0)(1 + r_v)^T - \frac{c}{2}(1 + r)^{T-t'} - AI_T\right] \quad (12.2)$$

If $r = r_v$ then (12.1) and (12.2) provide identical expressions for the upper and lower bounds. Upper and lower bounds converge, and

$$F_0 = \frac{1}{cv}\left[(P_0 + AI_0)(1 + r)^T - \frac{c}{2}(1 + r)^{T-t'} - AI_T\right] \quad (12.3)$$

In the next two sections, expression (12.3), arising from the no-arbitrage condition and the approximation that $r = r_v$ will be used to draw some conclusions with regard to hedging this single bond and the best time to deliver it.

Hedging the Bond

A second glance at the π expression from which (12.3) is obtained brings some questions to mind. For example, we know from the

T-bond contract's description that the invoice price equals the product of the conversion factor and the final futures price, F_T, plus the accrued interest. So how can we assume a futures price of F_0 in the profit expression and the subsequent pricing equations? Furthermore, how can we write down a pricing relation that derives its form from a no-arbitrage, zero-profit position and ignores an important source of profits or losses, namely the interest flows associated with borrowing or lending due to daily settlement variation? In sum, how can we legitimately assume forward pricing for this futures contract? The answer is that hidden behind the futures price derivation is the assumption that we have a hedge ratio, number of futures contracts per unit of the spot bond, that eliminates these problems and permits us to price the T-bond futures contract as a forward contract.

What hedge ratio allows us to price the futures as a forward? If we own the bond and sell a forward to hedge it, then we have transformed a long maturity security into a short-term investment that pays r. So the futures hedge ratio selected should provide an overall rate of return of r to the hedged position in order to achieve equivalency between futures and forwards.

Consider a two-period hedge. If we hedge correctly with futures, the hedged position's value at the end of the second period, $t = 2$, should be the position's initial value at $t = 0$ times $(1 + r)^2$. Furthermore, if we hedge correctly, then the futures and forwards look alike, and the futures price can be assumed to satisfy the forward pricing equation at the beginning of each period. That is, at $t = 0$,

$$cvF_0 + AI_T = (P_0 + AI_0)(1 + r)^T - \frac{c}{2}(1 + r)^{T-t'} \qquad (12.4)$$

At $t = 1$,

$$cvF_1 + AI_T = (P_1 + AI_1)(1 + r)^{T-1} - \frac{c}{2}(1 + r)^{T-t'} \qquad (12.5)$$

And at $t = 2$,

$$cvF_2 + AI_T = (P_2 + AI_2)(1 + r)^{T-2} - \frac{c}{2}(1 + r)^{T-t'} \qquad (12.6)$$

where it is assumed that the coupon is paid after $t = 2$, i.e., $t' > 2$, and F_1, F_2, P_1, P_2, AI_1, and AI_2 are the futures price, bond price, and accrued interest at $t = 1$ and $t = 2$, respectively.

Let h_0 be the number of futures used in the construction of the hedge at $t = 0$. Then at $t = 1$, h_0 must satisfy

$$h_0(F_1 - F_0) + P_1 + AI_1 = (P_0 + AI_0)(1 + r) \qquad (12.7)$$

The first term is the settlement variation. The next two terms represent the gross value of the bond at $t = 1$. So the left-hand side of the equation represents the value of the hedged position at $t = 1$. The right-hand side represents the $t = 1$ value of the bond's gross price if these funds were invested at the short-term rate, r. Use (12.4) and (12.5) to obtain

$$(F_1 - F_0) = \frac{1}{cv}\left[\begin{array}{l} (P_1 + AI_1)(1 + r)^{T-1} \\ - (P_0 + AI_0)(1 + r)^T \end{array} \right] \qquad (12.8)$$

Use (12.8) to substitute into the left-hand side of (12.7). This gives

$$\left(\frac{h_0}{cv}\right)[(P_1 + AI_1)(1 + r)^{T-1} - (P_0 + AI_0)(1 + r)^T]$$
$$+ P_1 + AI_1 \qquad\qquad = (P_0 + AI_0)(1 + r) \qquad (12.9)$$

Select

$$h_0 = \frac{-cv}{(1 + r)^{T-1}} \qquad (12.10)$$

and (12.9) is satisfied. So the number of futures contracts to sell against one unit (face value) of the bond is given by (12.10).

Let h_1 be the number of futures to sell at $t = 1$. Then at $t = 2$, h_1 must satisfy

$$h_1(F_2 - F_1) + P_2 + AI_2 + h_0(F_1 - F_0)(1 + r) \qquad (12.11)$$
$$= (P_0 + AI_0)(1 + r)^2$$

Except for the last term on the left-hand side of this equation, all the other terms have their counterparts in equation (12.7), the equivalent equation at $t = 0$. The extra term represents the settlement variation received or paid at $t = 1$, which is then lent or borrowed at rate r for an additional period. Use equations (12.5) and (12.6) to obtain an expression for $F_2 - F_1$. Substitute it into the left-hand side of (12.11). Then choose

$$h_1 = \frac{-cv}{(1 + r)^{T-2}} \tag{12.12}$$

The left-hand side of (12.11) reduces to $(P_0 + AI_0)(1 + r)^2$, the desired result.

In general, with T periods to contract expiration, the correct number of futures to sell per unit of spot is given by (12.10). This number will usually be different than the old fashioned one-to-one hedge. The absolute value of the difference between the absolute value of h_0 and 1 is called the *tail of the hedge*.

$$tail = \left| \left| \frac{-cv}{(1 + r)^{T-1}} \right| - 1 \right|$$

Only one bond can be delivered on a bond contract. Therefore, if the short (long) hedge requires more than one contract, buy (sell) the tail prior to delivery, and deliver on one contract. If the short (long) hedge requires less than one contract, sell (buy) the tail and deliver on one contract.

When to Deliver

When should the short choose to deliver—at the beginning of the spot month or at its end? Assume the contract is in the spot month, and abstract from the one-day settlement delay in the spot market and the two-day delivery delay in the futures market. No coupon is paid in the spot month. A trader buys the bond, sells the futures, and immediately delivers. His profit today, at $t = 0$, is

$$\pi_0 = (cv)F_0 + AI_0 - (P_0 + AI_0) = cvF_0 - P_0$$

If instead he waits to deliver tomorrow, at $t = 1$, his profit is

$$\pi_1 = (cv)F_0 + AI_1 - (P_0 + AI_0)(1 + r)$$
$$= \pi_0 + (AI_1 - AI_0) - (P_0 + AI_0)r$$

If $AI_1 - AI_0 > (P_0 + AI_0)r$, then $\pi_1 > \pi_0$, and it is worthwhile to delay delivery. (Remember F_0 was locked in at the time of sale—assuming the appropriate hedging policy.) So if the coupon income of the bond exceeds the cost of financing the bond, then delivery should be delayed. Inductively applying this type of argument, one arrives at the conclusion that if the coupon income exceeds financing costs, the trader should deliver at month end.

The difference between the coupon income and financing costs is referred to as the *carry* of the futures contract. If the difference is positive (negative), the futures contract is said to have positive (negative) carry. If the difference between the spot price and the product of the conversion factor and the futures price equals the contract's carry, the futures contract is said to be at *full carry*.

12.5 Several Deliverable Bonds: Identifying the Cheapest-to-Deliver (CTD)

Of the many bonds that are deliverable, the futures contract will be priced off of the bond that will provide the greatest profit if delivered, also known as the *cheapest-to-deliver* (CTD). Since the futures price is closely tied to the price of the CTD, changes in the futures price will most closely reflect the price moves of the CTD. We now turn to the identification of the CTD bond.

The Implied Repo Rate

The CTD bond is the one that maximizes the return to buying the spot bond, carrying the bond to delivery, and then delivering the bond into the futures contract. The rate of return earned by purchasing, carrying, and delivering the jth bond is defined by the rate, IRR_j, that equates the cost of the short hedged position to its revenues—the futures invoice price plus any coupon paid.[6] Note that the cash bond position is not financed.

$$(P_{j,0} + AI_{j,0})(1 + IRR_j)^T = cv_j F_0 + AI_{j,T} \qquad (12.13)$$

$$+ \frac{c_j}{2}(1 + r_v)^{T-t'}$$

---

6. We know that $cvF_0 + AI_T$ is not the invoice price paid upon delivery, for that price is calculated as of position day using F_T in lieu of F_0. However, the effective invoice price is $cvF_0 + AI_T$ because when settlement variation from the hedge is added to $cvF_T + AI_T$, the result is $cvF_0 + AI_T$. It is this latter quantity that is of prime importance to the hedger, and so we will continue to refer to it as the invoice price, unless otherwise stated.

The subscript j has been added to the previously defined symbols to identify them as belonging to bond j. Solving for IRR_j gives

$$IRR_j = \left[\frac{cv_j F_0 + AI_{j,T} + \frac{c_j}{2}(1 + r_v)^{T-t'}}{P_{j,0} + AI_{j,0}} \right]^{1/T} - 1 \qquad (12.14)$$

One can rearrange this equation to make it look like (12.3), except that IRR_j plays the role of r. Consequently, the hedged rate of return on bond j, IRR_j, is called the *implied repo rate*. The name *implied repo rate* also has some intuitive appeal. If one can earn IRR_j on the hedged bond, then one should be willing to pay up to IRR_j to finance it. Thus the break-even repo rate that could be paid on financing bond j is its implied repo rate. Since the bond with the highest rate of return (implied repo rate) is the most profitable, then that bond is cheapest-to-deliver.

The above analysis focuses on an overnight implied repo rate for bond j. Often, the implied repo rate that is calculated corresponds to the term of the financing period, T days. In that case, bond j's implied repo rate, $IRR_{j,T}$, for T days is given by

$$IRR_{j,T} = \frac{\frac{360}{T}\left\{ cv_j F_0 + AI_{j,T} + \frac{c_j}{2}\left[1 + r_{v,T-t'}\frac{(T - t')}{360} \right] \right\}}{(P_{j,0} + AI_{j,0})} - 1 \qquad (12.15)$$

To obtain (12.15), simply replace $(1 + IRR_j)^T$ of (12.13) with $1 + (IRR_{j,T})T/360$, note that the $(1 + r_v)^{T-t'}$ is altered to $(1 + r_{v,T-t'}(T - t')/360)$, and solve. The only change in notation is the addition of a subscript $T - t'$ to the reverse rate symbol to identify it as the forward reverse rate that applies to $T - t'$ days. The bond with the highest $IRR_{j,T}$ is cheapest-to-deliver.

The Implied Futures Price as a Means of Determining CTD

The implied futures price (IFP) for bond j, IFP_j, is the futures price that provides zero profit on the purchase, carry, and delivery of bond j. If overnight repo financing is assumed, then for bond j, IFP_j satisfies

$$(cv_j)IFP_j + AI_{j,T} - (P_{j,0} + AI_{j,0})(1 + r)^T \qquad (12.16)$$
$$+ \frac{c_j}{2}(1 + r_v)^{T-t'} = 0$$

In (12.16) IFP_j plays the role of the futures price. Solving (12.16) for IFP_j gives

$$IFP_j = \frac{(P_{j,0} + AI_{j,0})(1 + r)^T - \frac{c_j}{2}(1 + r_v)^{T-t'} - AI_{j,T}}{cv_j} \qquad (12.17)$$

The bond with the lowest implied futures price will be CTD, for at that futures price, any other bond will, upon delivery, provide a negative profit. For example, suppose there are two deliverable bonds, $j = 1,2$; $IFP_1 = 100$, and $IFP_2 = 90$. If the actual futures price, F_0, equals 95, then the delivery of bond 1 is a loser, for it requires a futures price as high as 100 to break even. However, bond 2 requires a futures price of only 90 to break even. Any futures price above 90 provides a profit upon the delivery of bond 2. So bond 2, the one with the lowest implied futures price, is CTD.

A Delivery Period Approximation for the Implied Futures Price

You buy the jth bond, sell the futures, and notify the CBOT's clearing house that you plan to deliver two days from today—position day. Next day, you settle on the cash bond and inform the clearing house about the bond's coupon and maturity. This occurs on intention day. One day later, delivery day, you send the bond to the long and receive payment equal to the invoice price. Between intention day, when you settled on the cash bond and provided the clearing house with the bond's features, and delivery day, you earn one day's accrued interest and pay one day's financing cost. Over the two-day period, the jth bond's implied futures price satisfies

$$cv_j(IFP_j) + AI_{j,2} - (P_{j,0} + AI_{j,0})(1 + r) = 0$$

where $P_{j,0} + AI_{j,0}$ represents the bond's cost locked in at $t = 0$ and paid for one day later, at $t = 1$. $AI_{j,2}$ represents the accrued interest that constitutes part of the invoice price. Because $P_{j,0} + AI_{j,0}$ is not paid until $t = 1$, settlement day, $AI_{j,2} - AI_{j,0}$ is one day's accrued interest. Now

$$IFP_j = \frac{P_{j,0} - [(AI_{j,2} - AI_{j,0}) - r(P_{j,0} + AI_{j,0})]}{cv_j}$$

The bracketed term represents one day's carry. If this is considered small enough to ignore, then the jth bond's implied futures price during the delivery period may be approximated by

$$IFP_j \approx \frac{P_{j,0}}{cv_j} \tag{12.18}$$

When the bond contract first began trading, in 1977, there were no desktop computers, nor were there news services that identified the CTD bond on an electronic page. So traders used the approximation to get a quick, and fairly accurate, picture of which bond was CTD and which bonds were likely to become CTD. The bond with the lowest $P_{j,0}/cv_j$ ratio was identified as CTD. With modern portable computing capabilities, the approximation is no longer necessary to identify the CTD. But it remains a useful tool for explaining some of the more arcane concepts of pricing T-bond futures. We will make use of this approximation in Section 12.7 to explain the value of the options available to the short seller of the futures contract. However, before doing so, we discuss the use of a futures contract to hedge a deliverable bond that is not CTD.

12.6 Hedging a Non-CTD Bond

We know how to hedge the CTD bond. Sell $cv/(1 + r)^{T-1}$ dollars in the futures market for each dollar of the cash bond's face value. Now all we need to do is to figure out how many units, x, of the CTD bond to short for each unit of the bond we hold and wish to hedge—refer to it as the I (inventoried) bond. Once x is ascertained, then the number of futures to hedge against a unit of the I bond equals $[cv/(1 + r)^{T-1}]x$. This can be seen by viewing this product dimensionally.

$$\left[\frac{cv}{(1 + r)^{T-1}}\right]x = \left(\frac{\text{futures units}}{\text{CTD units}}\right) \times \left(\frac{\text{CTD units}}{I \text{ bond units}}\right) \quad (12.19)$$

$$= \text{futures sold per } I \text{ bonds held}$$

Methods for Determining x

A Method for Small, Parallel Shifts in the Yield Curve   Set up a portfolio with value V containing one unit of the I bond, price P_I, and a short position of x units of the CTD bond, price P_{CTD}. Then calculate the price change of the portfolio, using the differential notation d($\cdot$) to denote the change in a variable.

$$dV = dP_I - xd(P_{CTD})$$

Choose x so that $dV = 0$. Then

$$x = \frac{dP_I}{dP_{CTD}}$$

The prevailing academic approach is to transform this ratio into a variable that is more familiar to interpretation and measurement. Assume that the yield curve is flat in the y_I and y_{CTD} region, so $y_I = y_{CTD} \equiv y$. Then

$$x = \frac{\left(-\dfrac{dP_I}{dy}/P_I\right)P_I}{\left(-\dfrac{dP_{CTD}}{dy}/P_{CTD}\right)P_{CTD}} = \frac{D_I P_I}{D_{CTD} P_{CTD}} \quad (12.20)$$

where D_I stands for $(-dP_I/dy)/P_I$ and is called the modified duration of the I bond. Similarly, D_{CTD} symbolizes the modified duration of the cheapest-to-deliver bond. It can be demonstrated that

$$D = \frac{1}{(1 + y)}\sum_{i=1}^{n} \frac{t_i CF_i}{(1 + y)^{t_i}}\bigg/ P \quad (12.21)$$

where t_i, CF_i, n, y, and P, respectively, denote the time (measured in years) to the ith cash flow, the ith cash flow, the number of forthcoming cash flows, the yield to maturity and current bond price. Calculate D_I and D_{CTD} using (12.21), and then substitute these values into (12.20) to obtain x. Use x in expression (12.19) to obtain the number of futures to sell. The reason the hedge ratio is accurate for only small changes in y is because calculus was used to arrive at the algebraic expression for x.

A Linear Regression to Determine x　Regress the change in the I bond's price on the change in the price of the CTD bond. The slope coefficient, which can be interpreted as dP_I/dP_{CTD}, provides an x estimate. While this technique for finding x may be considered superior to that provided in the prior section because it takes into account large price changes, it can also be viewed as inferior because it derives an x value from past data that may no longer describe the current tenor of the market.

Sensitivity Analysis to Determine x　Increase both bond yields, y_I and y_{CTD}, by 100 bps and then decrease them from the current levels by 100 bps. Calculate prices at these new yield levels. Compute the increase and decrease in price for each bond. Average these price changes for each bond. This gives an estimate, using realistic yield changes, of dP_I and dP_{CTD}. Divide the number obtained for dP_I by that obtained for dP_{CTD}. This provides an x estimate. Traders prefer this method, although they examine the price changes for many scenarios of future yield levels.

12.7 Options Implicit in the T-Bond Futures Contract

If the futures contract is priced off of the CTD bond, one might reasonably conclude that the futures price should equal the implied futures price (IFP) of the CTD. Not so. With rare exception, the futures price is less than the IFP of the CTD bond. This means that a short hedger who is long the CTD bond and simultaneously short the correct number of futures will lose money if he carries the bond into the spot month and delivers. To not lose money on carry and delivery, the futures price must be greater than or equal to the IFP.

The reason that the futures price often rests below the implied futures price for any one of the deliverable bonds is that the short has several options embedded in the futures contract. The long futures trader knows this and charges the short by requiring a futures price that is lower than the short's break-even price (the IFP).

The Quality Option or CTD Option

The possibility that some other bond becomes CTD and the short's right to choose that bond for delivery produces an option that can be quite valuable. To clarify this point, an example, somewhat stylized but sufficiently substantive, is presented. The pricing of the quality option is then discussed.

The Payoff to the Quality Option: An Example   Assume that a trading period within the delivery month is observed. Therefore, bond j's implied futures price may be taken as P_j/cv_j. Only two bonds are deliverable. Additionally, assume that long neglects to charge short for any option embedded in the futures contract. The last assumption means that the futures price will equal the value of the implied futures price of the CTD; i.e., the futures price equals min $\{P_j/cv_j\}$ over all j. Table 12.1 provides the spot price (in decimal) and each bond's conversion factor for each of two successive days. The futures price on each day equals the lowest implied futures price. Its value is italicized.

A short position initiated at the first day's settlement price of 100 and settling at 80 on the second day would earn 20 in settlement variation. Note that the CTD bond has changed over this time period. (Because we are considering only a short speculator selling one contract, we do not concern ourselves with the appropriate hedge ratio.)

Table 12.1   Value in the CTD (Quality) Option

Bond 1	Day 1	Day 2
Price (P_1)	125	101.25
Conversion Factor (cv_1)	1.25	1.25
$IFP_1 = P_1/cv_1$	*100* (CTD)	81
Bond 2		
Price (P_2)	101	80
Conversion Factor (cv_2)	1.00	1.00
$IFP_2 = P_2/cv_2$	101	*80* (CTD)

Suppose only bond 1 was deliverable, then the settlement variation earned would amount to 19, since the futures price on day 2 must settle at the IFP of the only deliverable bond, namely bond 1. Consequently, there is value to the short in having a choice of bonds to deliver—as long as there is a positive probability that a different bond will become CTD.

Considerations in Pricing the Futures Contract in Light of the Quality Option   At what price should the futures contract trade once the long recognizes that short owns the quality option? To answer this, compare two alternatives on two successive delivery days: (1) long futures and (2) long bond 1 plus short a call that gives the call's owner the right to call away bond 1 in exchange for bond 2. (Recall the exchange option discussed in Part I.) Table 12.2 compares the composition of these two alternatives on day 2.

Table 12.2 demonstrates that on day 2 the two alternatives result in equivalent positions, whether bond 1 remains CTD or bond 2 becomes CTD. Therefore, the positions on day 1 must be equivalent. Consequently, we infer that

$$\begin{aligned} \textit{long futures} = \ &\textit{implied futures price} \\ &\textit{of the current CTD bond} \\[6pt] -\ &\textit{value of an option to exchange the bond} \\ &\textit{that becomes CTD for the current CTD bond} \end{aligned}$$

We have already discussed a general methodology for the valuation of the exchange option (see Part I). But this was for the case of two stocks whose price ratio obeyed a multiplicative binomial. For

Table 12.2   Identifying the Quality Option

	Position on Day 1*	Position on Day 2	
		Bond 1 is CTD	Bond 2 is CTD
Alternative 1	Long Futures	Bond 1	Bond 2
Alternative 2	Long bond 1 plus short an option granting the option owner the right to call away bond 1 in exchange for bond 2.	Bond 1	Bond 1 + (bond 2 − bond 1)** = bond 2

*Bond 1 is CTD on day 1.

**Bond 2 is CTD on day 2. Therefore the call owner exercises, delivering bond 2 in exchange for bond 1.

options on interest rate instruments, care must be taken to ensure that the underlying bond prices are arbitrage-free. The practice is to then apply, iteratively, the no-arbitrage condition discussed in Part I to the exchange option's payoffs. (See Part I for this technique applied to the valuation of interest rate options.)

Whether the T-bond futures contract is overvalued (undervalued) depends on whether the quality option (exchange option) given to the short futures position is undervalued (overvalued). If, after applying a model to value the quality option, it is determined that the futures contract is undervalued (the quality option is overvalued), then long futures positions should be substituted for all or some of the spot bonds held in a fixed income portfolio. If, at a later date, the quality option is determined to be undervalued, then the long futures position has become overvalued, and it should be sold and replaced with spot bonds. This strategy is often followed.

The Wild Card Option

We reasoned earlier that in a positive carry market, i.e., when coupon interest exceeds financing cost, the short hedger should delay delivery until the last possible day of the spot month. However, in arriving at this conclusion, we ignored the fact that another embedded option, named the *wild card*, is held by the short. This option is used when the spot price of the CTD bond exhibits a large change after the futures market has closed for the day. The use (exercise) of the wild card option in such circumstances results, in a positive carry market, in the early delivery by the short hedger of the CTD bond. The following examples provide situations in which this might occur. In these examples, we ignore two complicating factors:

1. The precise hedge ratio should be $cv/(1 + r)^{T-1}$. However, ignoring $1/(1 + r)^{T-1}$ makes the factors driving the wild card easier to focus on; additionally, during the delivery period, $1/(1 + r)^{T-1}$ is very close to 1.

2. Calculations involving the accretion of accrued interest versus financing cost will not be made. To do so would divert attention from the important factors that drive the wild card. However, if you had the responsibility to decide whether to exercise the wild card and to show net profits emanating from the decision, you perform a side calculation and add it to (subtract it from) the type of profit computations in the following examples. All prices will be presented in decimal, not thirty-seconds.

Example 1 The CTD bond, with conversion factor of 1.5, is priced at 151 at 2:00 P.M. CST, when the futures market is closed. The futures settlement price is 100. You hold $1 million in face value of the CTD and are short 15 futures. Recall the simplified hedge ratio is now cv = 1.5. So $1.50 is sold in the futures market for each $1 in face value of the spot. Therefore, $1.5 million must be shorted in the futures market, i.e., 15 contracts.

If you chose to deliver your spot inventory, you would first rid yourself of the 5-contract tail by purchasing 5 futures at the settlement price—remember the futures position has zero value because of settlement variation, so this does not entail a gain or a loss. You would then deliver your bond inventory of $1 million face value into the 10 futures contracts, each requiring the delivery of $100,000 face value of bonds. Clearly you would suffer a loss equal to $1,510,000 − (1.5 × 10 × $100,000) = $10,000. Obviously, this is not the type of delivery you should choose. At the very least you would wait until month end, when the accumulation of positive carry would serve to minimize this sort of loss.

But suppose that after the futures market closed for the day and while the spot market remained open, the spot price of the CTD fell from 151 to 146.50. Now two choices are open to you.

1. You do nothing and wait until tomorrow. Assuming the difference between tomorrow's spot price and cv times tomorrow's futures price, F_1, called the *basis* by bond traders, is the same as it was today, 1.00, then on tomorrow's opening of the futures market, F_1 must satisfy

$$146.50 - 1.5F_1 = 1$$

So

$$F_1 = 97.00$$

Then the loss on the spot position is $0.045 \times \$1,000,000 = \$45,000$, but this is offset by the settlement variation on the short 15 futures of $45,000 ($3,000 × 15). So retaining the hedge is a wash.

2. You exercise the wild card option. By 8:00 P.M. CST, you notify the CBOT clearing house of your intention to deliver on all 15 contracts. That afternoon, prior to the close of the spot market, you

purchased an additional $0.5 million in face value of the CTD bond at the new price of 146.50. The cost was $732,500. Add this to the original value of the $1 million face value in CTD bonds already held, $1,510,000, for a total spot bond cost of $2,242,500. The futures invoice price is calculated using the 2:00 P.M. settlement price of 100.00. Thus, upon delivery on all 15 futures, you receive $2,250,000 (15 × 1.5 × $100,000). The profit upon exercise is $7,500. This second choice, to exercise, dominates the first, not to exercise. You have exercised the wild card, delivered prior to month end, and made a profit.

The factors that made a profit possible were a hedge ratio that exceeded one, because $cv > 1$, and a sufficiently large spot price drop after the close of the futures market. Not any spot price drop will do. If the spot price fell by 1.00 instead of 4.50, then the cost of the additional $0.50 million in face value would be $750,000. The total cost of the bonds would be $2,260,000, exceeding the invoice receipts of $2,250,000—still calculated at that day's settlement price. In this case, the wild card would not be exercised. Wait for the next day, and see what happens.

Example 2   The CTD has a cv equal to 0.5, and its spot price at the time the futures market settles is 50. The futures settlement price is 98. Your hedge ratio is 0.5, so for a $1 million face value spot position, you are short 5 contracts. If you wished to deliver at these prices, you would rid yourself of the tail by selling an additional 5 contracts. Delivering on 10 contracts results in a loss of $500,000 − (.5 × $98,000 × 10) = $10,000. It would be better to wait and allow the accumulation of positive carry to attenuate the delivery loss.

But suppose that after the close of the futures market and while the spot market remained open, the spot price rose from 50 to 53. Now two choices are available to you.

1. You do nothing and wait until tomorrow. Assuming the difference between tomorrow's spot price and the product of cv and tomorrow's futures price, F_1, is the same as it was today, 1.00,[7] then at tomorrow's opening, F_1 must satisfy

$$53 - .5F_1 = 1.00$$

---

7. Depending upon your experience, you can make some other assumption about this difference and continue with the analysis.

So

$$F_1 = 104$$

Then the gain on the spot position is $0.03 \times \$1,000,000 = \$30,000$, which is offset by the loss on the short futures position of $5 \times \$6,000 = \$30,000$. So, under these assumptions, you break even by waiting.

2. You exercise the wild card by delivering half of your inventory of $1 million face value on the 5 short contracts, and sell the remaining half of the inventory in the spot market at the new price of 53. Your total investment amounted to $500,000 on $1 million dollars face value of bonds. When delivering on 5 futures, you receive $5 \times 0.5 \times \$98,000 = \$245,000$. The receipts from the spot sale of the remaining $0.5 million of bonds amounts to $0.53 \times \$500,000 = \$265,000$. The total receipts of $510,000 exceed the cost of $500,000, resulting in a profit of $10,000. Better than the first choice, so you exercise.

It was worthwhile to exercise the wild card because the spot price increase, after the close of the futures market, was sufficiently large. A spot price increase of only one-half point, to 50.5, would have changed total receipts to $497,500 ($245,000 + $252,500), an amount that is less than the $500,000 cost. In this event, it would be better not to exercise.

The Switch Option

During the last seven business days of the delivery month, the futures contract does not trade. Its price is fixed as of the last trade date. Recall that the quality option pays off through a decline in the futures price, which is driven by a change in the CTD bond. After the trading period expires, the quality option becomes an option to switch to a bond that is cheaper to deliver, and short makes his money on the delivery and not through a drop in the futures price. This distinction of how a change in the CTD results in profits to the short implies another option classification, the *switch option*.

Fixing the settlement price at the expiration of trading, while seven business days remain in the delivery month, has one immediate implication: hedge ratios must be adjusted. Since there is no concern about the size of settlement variation payments relative to the price moves of the bond being hedged, there is no need for a tail on the hedge. Therefore, the correct hedge ratio for those last seven business days of the delivery month is one to one and not $cv/(1 + r)^{T-1}$. Once the tail is removed, the wild card option is gone. So upon the conclusion of trading, both the quality and wild card options expired. What remains is the switch option, whose life extends over those last seven business days of the delivery month. On that last trading day, the futures price will settle below the implied futures price of the CTD bond, because of the existence of this switch option.

To explain the switch option is straightforward. Immediately after trading concludes, you are short one futures and long the CTD bond. If during the next (and last) seven business days of the delivery month, another bond becomes CTD, switch into it and carry to the last delivery day—if carry is positive. To illustrate, consider the following simple example.

Suppose the settlement futures price, conversion factors, spot prices, and carry are such that the delivery of bond 1 loses 0.25 points, while the delivery of bond 2 loses 0.375 points. Two days after the last trading date, the yield curve changes, causing bond 1's price to fall by 0.875 and bond 2's price to fall by 1.5. You sell bond 1, incurring a loss of 0.875, and purchase bond 2 to deliver into the futures contract. Prior to the yield curve change, the delivery of bond 2 entailed a loss of 0.375. But that was at the old spot price. At the new, lower spot price, there is now a gain from delivering bond 2 equal to $-0.375 + 1.5 = 1.125$. Remember that the futures price is fixed.[8] Deduct the loss of 0.875 incurred from the sale of bond 1 and the net profit from switching is 0.25. A similar example can be offered to demonstrate the value of the switch option if the yield curve were to shift down.

---

8. Carry will change because the cost of financing bond 2 has changed—another side calculation.

Chapter **13**

The Standard & Poor's 500 Stock Price Index Futures Contract

*T*HE FUTURES contract on the S&P 500 Stock Price Index is the most widely used equity futures contract. The calculation of the Index is explained in the first section of this chapter. The following section lists this futures contract's important features. A relation for the S&P futures price relative to the spot Index is identified through two quasi-arbitrage examples. The chapter concludes by demonstrating how this contract might be employed to hedge a stock portfolio against unexpected market fluctuations.

13.1 The S&P 500 Index: The Spot

An understanding of the S&P 500 Index can be imparted through an explanation of how it is formed. The first step in composing the Index at time T is to multiply the number of outstanding shares, N_{iT}, of the ith stock by the price per share, P_{iT}, and sum over all 500 stocks. Repeat this procedure again using the shares outstanding at T, N_{iT}, but multiply by the price per share at time 0, the base period—soon to be defined—and again sum over all 500 stocks. Next divide the first sum by the base period sum, and define this ratio as I_T/I_0. That is,

$$\frac{I_T}{I_0} = \frac{\displaystyle\sum_{i=1}^{500} N_{iT}P_{iT}}{\displaystyle\sum_{i=1}^{500} N_{iT}P_{i0}}$$

The base period selected by Standard & Poor's was 1941–1943. The denominator on the right-hand side of the foregoing equation is calculated as the average of these sums over that base period. If I_0 is assigned a value, then the equation gives us a value for I_T. S&P arbitrarily set $I_0 = 10$. The resulting I_T value is called the S&P Index.

13.2 The S&P 500 Stock Index Futures: Defining Characteristics

The futures on the spot S&P 500 Index permits the long (short) to buy (sell) the value of the futures S&P Index, usually numerically different from the spot S&P Index—except at contract expiration. The contract's defining features are presented here.

1. The Chicago Mercantile Exchange gives the contract a nominal value of 500 times the futures Index level. This is done to define the dollar size of the contract, which is necessary for setting appropriate margin levels. However, for application purposes, it is more productive to think of an S&P futures contract as being written on 500 units of the underlying S&P Index, each of which is being traded for settlement at some future date at the current contract price.

2. The minimum fluctuation in the futures price is 0.05 Index points, worth $25 in settlement variation. Therefore, a change of one full point is worth $500 in settlement variation.

3. Delivery is by cash settlement. The contract expires at 2:30 P.M. CST on the Thursday preceding the third Friday of the spot month. The final settlement price is based upon the prices of the 500 stocks on the New York Stock Exchange's Friday opening, and is set equal to the computed S&P 500 Index using those opening prices. Settlement variation on a position initiated before that Thursday is then calculated using the difference between this final settlement price and Wednesday's settlement price. On positions initiated during Thursday's trading session, settlement variation is computed using the difference between the final settlement price and the trade-initiating price. After payment of this final day's settlement variation, contract positions are erased from the books.

13.3 Index Arbitrage: Pricing Implications

Given the spot Index level, what should the futures price be? Examination of two quasi-arbitrage situations will provide the answer.

In both situations, the S&P futures contract is discussed as being written on a single unit of the spot Index. This means that if the spot Index is quoted as 465.00, then, hypothetically, you buy a share for $465 in a fund that contains every one of those 500 stocks.[1]

Situation 1

Consider a fund manager whose objective is to match the performance of the S&P 500. He manages a passive fund, in this case, an S&P Index fund. There are two strategies open to him.

A. Buy the stocks of the S&P 500 Index in the correct proportions, or

B. Place the same amount of money in T-bills, and use them to collateralize the purchase of S&P 500 futures.

Suppose the current spot Index level is 100.00, the price of the S&P futures that expires in one year is 99.00, the one-year T-bill rate is 8%, and the annual dividend yield on the S&P stock portfolio is 4%. In these circumstances, which strategy should the passive fund manager follow? Table 13.1 compares the two strategies for a ±10% one-year change in the spot Index.

Table 13.1 Rates of Return on Alternative Index Matching Strategies

				S&P Spot Level Changes	
Strategy	Position	Return Type		+10%	−10%
A.	Long Spot Portfolio	Capital Gain		+10%	−10%
		Dividend Yield		+4%	+4%
			Net Return of Strategy A	+14%	−6%
B.	Long Spot T-Bills	Interest		+8%	+8%
	Long S&P Futures	Capital Gain		+11%*	−9%**
			Net Return of Strategy B	+19%	−1%

* +[(110 − 99)/100]
** +[(90 − 99)/100]

---

1. Of course, to buy the Index with $465 one would need to purchase a fraction equal to 465/(*S&P portfolio value*) of each company's total shares.

In both an up market and a down market, the long futures–long T-bill strategy dominates the spot portfolio. This is because the futures contract is underpriced.

Instead of 99, insert a price of 104 into the analysis presented in Table 13.1. Except for the returns attributable to the futures long position, 6% ([110 − 104]/100) in an up market and −14% ([90 − 104]/100) in a down market, all other component returns remain the same. The net return for strategy B drops to 14% in an up market and −6% in a down market. The manager would be indifferent between strategies A and B.

This is part of the "index arbitrage" that the newspapers write about, where reference is made to futures on other equity indices as well as the S&P 500. The journalists' concern, however, is not whether the passive fund manager is using futures to provide a superior return to his investors, but rather the effect of this arbitrage on the stock market's volatility. The newspaper argument goes something like this: (1) To take advantage of the underpriced futures contract, the index manager must sell his stock portfolio, depressing the stock market. (2) Since the futures contract provides greater liquidity than the spot market, speculators and hedgers will move to sell futures, once again driving the futures price below the spot. (3) The index fund manager repeats step 1. So, journalists argue, futures underpricing leads to a sequence of actions that depresses the stock market.

Situation 2

Consider a manager of a "near cash" portfolio, such as the money market funds offered by banks and brokerage firms. Part of his portfolio is invested in T-bills—to make it simple, one-year T-bills. He has a choice of two strategies:

C. Buy T-bills, or

D. Buy the spot S&P portfolio and sell S&P futures against that portfolio.

The latter strategy is known as a synthetic T-bill. Except for an initial futures price of 109.00 on a futures contract expiring in one year, all the data of situation 1 apply. Table 13.2 presents the rates of return on these alternative strategies in an up and a down market.

In both market environments, strategy D outperforms strategy C. The synthetic T-bill dominates the real T-bill. The reason is that the

Table 13.2 Rates of Return on Alternative T-bill Matching Strategies

				S&P Spot Level Changes	
Strategy	*Position*	*Return Type*		*+ 10%*	*− 10%*
C.	Long T-Bills	Interest		+8%	+8%
			Net Return of Strategy C	+8%	+8%
D.	Long Spot S&P	Capital Gain		+10%	−10%
		Dividend Yield		+4%	+4%
	Short S&P Futures	Capital Gain		−1%*	+19%**
			Net Return of Strategy D	+13%	+13%
*− [(110 − 109)/100]					
** − [(90 − 109)/100]					

futures contract is overpriced. Clearly, in this environment, the money manager prefers D to C. He will sell his T-bills, buy the S&P portfolio, and simultaneously sell futures. This is the other part of the "index arbitrage" reported in the financial pages. Try an initial futures price of 104, and you will see that the synthetic T-bill's return drops to 8%.

At a futures price of 104 neither the passive fund manager nor the money manager has an incentive to switch from the spot security into a synthetic security formed by using futures. The no-arbitrage futures price is 104, given the spot Index, T-bill rate, and dividend yield levels of the example. Now if we multiply the spot price by the sum of one plus the difference between the T-bill rate and the dividend yield, we get 104 [100 × (1 + 0.08 − 0.04)]. We can prove, in a rigorous fashion, that this type of calculation will always provide the no-arbitrage S&P futures price, but the examples just presented should be convincing. Therefore, in general,

$$S\&P \text{ futures price } = S\&P \text{ 500 spot price}$$
$$\times (1 + T\text{-bill yield } - dividend \text{ yield})$$

If the futures contract expires in less than one year, then to obtain the no-arbitrage futures price, deannualize the T-bill and dividend yields.

The futures pricing relation given in the previous paragraph is an approximation. The S&P dividend yield was assumed to be earned on the futures contract's expiration day. But dividends are paid throughout the life of the contract, with many of the stocks' quarterly dividend dates grouped in February, May, August, and November. A more precise pricing relationship must take into account the discrete payments of dividends throughout the contract life. When this is done, the pricing relationship becomes

$$F = S(1 + r_T)^T - \sum_{t=0}^{T} D(t)(1 + r_{T-t})^{T-t} \qquad (13.1)$$

where r_{T-t} now denotes the *one-day* yield of a $(T - t)$-day T-bill starting at $t (= 0, 1, \ldots, T)$ and $D(t)$ represents the dollar dividend paid at t on one unit of the S&P 500 Index. Notice that the dividends received are assumed to be reinvested at the T-bill rate.[2]

The relationship is straightforward to prove. Just look for the futures price that will make the Index fund manager indifferent between his alternative strategies, or perform the same exercise from the money manager's viewpoint. Both cases will result in the same no-arbitrage price, given by (13.1). For example, the Index fund manager is indifferent between the two alternative strategies when the wealth at T from holding one unit of the spot Index is equal to the wealth at T from investing the current value of that unit in T-bills and using those bills to collateralize the purchase of a futures contract written on one unit of the spot. Thus, at $t = T$,

$$S_T + \sum_{t=0}^{T} D(t)(1 + r_{T-t})^{T-t} = (F_T - F) + S(1 + r_T)^T \qquad (13.2)$$

The left-hand side of (13.2) represents the spot unit's value at T, the final price of an S&P unit plus its dividend return. The right-hand side represents the settlement variation from the long futures position plus the value of investing S dollars in T-bills for T days. Cash settlement at contract expiration requires that $F_T = S_T$. The remaining terms can be rearranged to obtain equation (13.1).

---

2. Except for the T-day T-bill rate that can be observed today, r_T, the other r_{T-t} rates for $t = 1, \ldots, T$ are random variables. However, they can be locked in today through a long hedge using T-bill futures and T-bill forwards. Strictly speaking, the dividends, $D(t)$, for $t = 1, \ldots, T$ are also random variables, whose values cannot be hedged. Nevertheless, as a group their values are surprisingly predictable.

13.4 Hedging with the S&P Futures Contract

In this section, exposition of the hedging technique can be simplified by assuming that the interest rates appearing in the pricing equation all equal r. Thus equation (13.1) is rewritten as

$$F = S(1 + r)^T - \sum_{t=0}^{T} D(t)(1 + r)^{T-t} \qquad (13.3)$$

Consider hedging one unit of the spot Index with a futures contract written on one unit. The guiding principle is that a hedge position should return the riskless rate, r. Use equation (13.3) and follow the proof used in obtaining the number of T-bond futures needed to hedge the cheapest-to-deliver bond, and you will find that the hedge ratio, h_0, at $t = 0$ with T days to expiration, is

$$h_0 = \frac{1}{(1 + r)^{T-1}}$$

This is the hedge ratio for one unit of the spot. The actual S&P futures contract contains 500 units of the spot. How do we implement our hedge result? Suppose you wish to short hedge a spot S&P portfolio with a $1 million current value. The current S&P 500 spot price is 400. Then the portfolio contains 2,500 units of the spot. For each unit of the spot, you must sell $1/(1 + r)^{T-1}$ units in the futures market. Since you hold 2,500 spot units, this requires a sale of $2,500/(1 + r)^{T-1}$ units in futures. Each futures contract contains 500 units. So you must sell $[2,500/(1 + r)^{T-1}]/500 = [5/(1 + r)^{T-1}]$ futures contracts short in order to effect the hedge. So if n is the number of actual S&P 500 futures contracts to use in the hedge, then

$$n = \left(\frac{1}{(1 + r)^{T-1}}\right) \frac{market\ value\ of\ the\ spot\ S\&P\ portfolio}{(500 \times spot\ index\ value)} \qquad (13.4)$$

To hedge a non-S&P portfolio with the S&P futures, reason as follows. How large an S&P spot portfolio must we sell short to hedge the value, V, of the non-S&P portfolio? Let R_s and R_p, respectively, denote the rates of return of the S&P and non-S&P portfolios. Both have value V. If x represents the number of S&P portfolios, each with value V, to sell short, then the hedged portfolio's rate of return, R_h, is

$$R_h = R_p - xR_s \tag{13.5}$$

Choose x to minimize the variance of R_h, which is given by

$$\sigma_h^2 = \sigma_p^2 + x^2\sigma_s^2 - 2x\sigma_{ps} \tag{13.6}$$

σ_p^2, σ_s^2, and σ_{ps} symbolize the variances of R_p and R_s and the covariance between these two rates of returns. Taking the derivative of (13.6) with respect to x, setting it equal to zero, and solving for x gives

$$x = \frac{\sigma_{ps}}{\sigma_s^2} \tag{13.7}$$

The ratio in (13.7) defines the "beta," β, of the portfolio, i.e., the sensitivity of the portfolio's rate of return to changes in the S&P rate of return.

So here is what we know. To hedge V dollars of a non-S&P portfolio, $\beta \neq 1$, sell short βV dollars of an S&P portfolio. But we know from the analysis that preceded (13.4) that this is equivalent to selling βn futures, where n is calculated by substituting V for the market value of the S&P portfolio in (13.4).

PART III

Interest Rate Swaps

Chapter **14**

Basics

$W_{E \; BEGIN}$ with a description of the most elementary interest rate swap, the *generic interest rate swap*. Central to this discussion is an understanding of the swap dealer's pricing schedule, the total cost savings that might be shared by all parties to the swap, and why the terms of the swap are ostensibly insensitive to the party's credit rating. In light of the wide acceptance of swaps, academics have endeavored to sort out the interest rate swap's real benefits from those that are illusory; we cover this topic as well. The chapter ends with a listing and some discussion of swap terms and market conventions.

14.1 Swaps and Risk Management

Interest rate risk management by a financial institution normally focuses on the relative sensitivities of asset and liability market values to changes in interest rate levels. Variations in the level and/or structure of interest rates can cause the market value of the firm's assets to fall by more or rise by less than the market value of its liabilities. The result is a decrease in the firm's market equity value. The institution will seek to manage the relative interest rate sensitivities of its assets and its liabilities. This is known as *managing the gap*. We have encountered the gap management problem already. Recall the Eurodollar manager attempting to match up his book through the use of futures. Though financial futures can be of assistance in the gap management problem, none address this problem as directly and cleanly as the interest rate swap.

An interest rate swap may be described as a bilateral agreement to exchange a sequence of interest rate payments based upon a principal amount that is never exchanged—a notional principal. In the most popular interest rate swap, commonly called a generic or *plain vanilla* swap, one party is obligated to make payments on designated dates, calculated by applying a fixed rate to a notional principal, while the counterparty makes payments on specified dates, calculated by applying an agreed-upon floating rate to the notional principal. If the prespecified periodic payment dates coincide, then, to the extent that the two payments offset, a net payment is made; the direction of the payment is determined by the relative values of the fixed and floating rates that are pertinent to that payment date.

From the above description, the reasons for undertaking an interest rate swap can be readily deduced. One economic entity has floating rate assets and fixed rate liabilities, while another entity has fixed rate assets and floating rate liabilities. The management of these opposite asset-liability gaps can be efficiently addressed through a fixed-for-floating rate swap, for a swap allows an entity to hedge itself exactly against any interest rate risk on any cash flow structure. The first entity swaps its fixed rate debt payments for floating rate debt payments, while the second swaps its floating rate payments for fixed rate payments. The economic outcome of the swap is to trade the first entity's fixed debt service for floating debt service and thus match the interest rate sensitivity of its debt to that of its assets. The second entity has transformed its floating rate debt service to fixed rate debt service and matched the interest rate sensitivity of its debt to that of its assets.

Interest rate futures, forwards, and options provide alternative means of gap management. However, the application of these instruments to this risk management problem focuses on matching the value sensitivity of the derivative instruments selected to the value sensitivity engendered by the gap. Such replicating techniques are usually robust for small changes in interest rates, but leave something to be desired for larger rate changes. In contrast, the swap is out to match, period by period, the entity's asset and liability cash flows—with, of course, some spread for profits. Logically, futures, forwards, or options may, at any particular time, be deemed to be a superior hedging instrument because they may be mispriced. However, the size of the interest rate swap market provides strong evidence that for long-dated hedges, swaps provide a precise means of mitigating the asset-liability gap risk at an affordable cost.

14.2 An Illustration of the Generic Swap: Fixed-for-Floating

A firm with a AA credit rating, call it AA, seeks five-year floating rate financing at a rate based on six-month LIBOR. Another firm with a BBB rating, call it BBB, seeks five-year fixed rate financing. AA can borrow in the five-year market at 5.30% fixed and floating at six-month LIBOR. BBB can borrow in the five-year fixed rate market at 6.20% and floating at six-month LIBOR plus 0.5%.

A swap dealer familiar with the needs of both these firms has a swap pricing schedule for AA firms and another schedule for BBB firms. The five-year (fixed) swap rates that the dealer offers AA against six-month LIBOR are presented in Table 14.1.

This part of the pricing schedule presented in Table 14.1 says that if AA enters into a five-year swap with the dealer, then AA can choose to pay the dealer (dealer receives) on a semiannual basis the current five-year U.S. Treasury note rate plus 52 basis points and receive six-month LIBOR on the semiannual payment dates. Conversely, AA could receive from the dealer (dealer pays) the current five-year U.S. Treasury note rate plus 50 basis points and pay the dealer six-month LIBOR.

Since AA wishes to end up with a floating rate liability, it is interested in a swap where the dealer pays the fixed rate to AA, and AA pays the dealer six-month LIBOR. AA, being a knowledgeable player, knows what it must do. Noting that the five-year T-note rate is 5.00%, it issues $100 million of five-year fixed rate debt, which pays semiannual coupons at an annual rate of 5.30%. The firm immediately enters into a swap with the dealer in which the dealer pays AA 5.50% per year and receives six-month LIBOR from AA on a notional principal of $100 million. The firm's net borrowing cost is the difference between the fixed rate it pays (5.30%) and the fixed rate it receives (5.50%) plus six-month LIBOR. This amounts to LIBOR-20 bps, which is less than what AA would have to pay to borrow directly in the floating rate market—i.e., six-month LIBOR.

Coincidentally, BBB approaches the dealer to swap floating for fixed. BBB has just borrowed $100 million in the six-month Eurodollar market at six-month LIBOR plus 50 bps. This part of the dealer's

Table 14.1 The 5-Year Swap Entry in the Dealer's Pricing Schedule for AA Firms

Swap Maturity	*Dealer Pays*	*Dealer Receives*
5 Years	5-Year Treasury Note Rate + 50 bps (s.a.)*	5-Year Treasury Note Rate + 52 bps (s.a.)
versus 6-month LIBOR.		
*The abbreviations *bps* and *s.a.* stand for basis points and semiannual, respectively.		

pricing schedule, pertaining to five-year swaps for BBB, is presented in Table 14.2. It is different than that shown to AA, for BBB is, by definition, not as good a credit risk.

BBB enters into a five-year swap with the dealer in which the dealer pays six-month LIBOR to BBB and receives from BBB semiannual payments at the annual fixed rate of 5.54% on $100 million notional principal. BBB's net cost of funds is 6.04% fixed, calculated as the difference between the floating rate at which it borrows in the external market and the one it receives from the swap dealer (LIBOR + 0.5% − LIBOR) plus the fixed rate paid to the swap dealer (5.54%). This fixed rate of 6.04%, achieved through the swap, is less than the fixed rate of 6.20% that it would pay if it issued a five-year note.

The dealer's profit is calculated by bringing together all of the dealer's payments to and receipts from AA and BBB.

$$dealer's\ profit\ =\ (+LIBOR\ -\ 5.50\%)\ +\ (5.54\%\ -\ LIBOR)\ =\ 4\ bps$$

The first parenthetical term represents the net from AA and the second the net from BBB. This 4 bps profit on the $100 million notional principal represents the swap rate spread between what the dealer receives from BBB and what he pays AA on the fixed side.

Notice that the sum of the gains to all of the swap's parties, including the dealer, amounts to 40 bps (20 for AA + 16 for BBB + 4 for the dealer). This amount exactly equals the fixed rate differential between AA and BBB, 90 bps, less the floating rate differential between AA and BBB, 50 bps. These rate differentials are called *quality spreads.* So the gain from the swap to all parties equals the quality spread of these two firms in the fixed rate market less the quality spread in the floating rate market. Be careful not to confuse the term *quality spread,* which refers to the fixed or floating rate differential between two firms having different credit levels, with the swap's *spread,* which

Table 14.2 The 5-Year Swap Entry in the Dealer's Pricing Schedule for BBB Firms

Swap Maturity	Dealer Pays	Dealer Receives
5 Years	5-Year Treasury Note Rate + 48 bps (s.a.)*	5-Year Treasury Note Rate + 54 bps (s.a.)
versus 6-month LIBOR.		

*The abbreviations *bps* and *s.a.* stand for basis points and semiannual, respectively.

refers to what the dealer is willing to pay or receive above Treasury rates.

By undertaking the swap, both AA and BBB seem to come out ahead. Whether such gains are real or illusory is a subject that has occupied a number of academics and practitioners. In Section 14.4, more will be said about the economic benefits conferred by a swap. With regard to this example, a few points should be made immediately.

Is the dealer mispricing the swap to BBB? After all, for BBB's fixed rate debt the market requires 120 bps over the T-note rate, while the dealer asks only 54 bps. Of course, if BBB defaults and rates have risen, the dealer is no worse off. He can pay off BBB's in-the-money swap at its fair market value. However, if BBB defaults when rates are lower, the dealer is harmed. He must replace the receive fixed–pay LIBOR swap at a lower fixed rate. The dealer risks a loss should BBB default, and yet the swap appears underpriced relative to the market rate for BBB's debt.

There are some features of the swap agreement that serve to explain this ostensible underpricing. First, BBB, which has borrowed floating and swapped for fixed, has not exactly replicated a fixed rate loan. BBB must reborrow the principal amount every six months, which is not the case in a fixed rate external borrowing. Because the swap does not endow BBB with the same degree of liquidity as a fixed rate external loan, BBB should be willing to pay more for external fixed rate financing than it would for the conversion to fixed payments through a swap. Second, on external fixed rate borrowing, the lender's risk relates to both interest and principal payments. The swap dealer's risk relates only to interest payments; more precisely, if the payment dates for fixed and floating coincide, that risk relates to the difference in interest payments. Third, the dealer will often require collateral from BBB in the form of high-grade securities. Fourth, swaps with longer maturities may contain credit triggers. If a swap party's credit rating falls below BBB (investment grade), the opposite party has the right to demand an immediate cash payment sufficient in size to enable it to replace the swap with one offered by an investment-grade counterparty.

The fact that a swap party is not exposed to principal risk, may require collateral from the counterparty, and may impose a credit trigger on the swap makes BBB a better credit risk to the swap dealer than BBB is to the external debt market—thus, the appearance that the swap is underpriced. Because of these factors, we can also understand why the dealer's swap spread against BBB, 48–54 bps, is not far different than that shown AA, 50–52 bps.

14.3 A Comment on Limited Two-Way Payment (LTP)

Until the late 1980s, swap contracts were written in a manner that favored the stronger credit counterparty. To explain this aspect of prior swap agreements, assume that BBB's swap with the dealer has a positive market value. For example, there could be one remaining payment date on which BBB would receive LIBOR, set at 8.25%, and would pay the fixed rate of 5.54% to the dealer. The swap has positive value to BBB. However, at this time, BBB cannot meet its interest payments on other debts, so it declares bankruptcy. The swap agreement is terminated. If both parties had agreed to the LTP clause in the International Swaps and Derivatives Association (ISDA) standard swap agreement, the dealer would have had the right to walk away from BBB and pay nothing. On the other hand, if the swap instead had a negative value to BBB (positive value to the dealer), say, if LIBOR was at 3% with a fixed rate of 5.54% for the last payment date, then BBB would have been obligated to make good his swap's debt to the dealer. In short, under LTP, if the insolvent party's swap position has positive value, its claim against the counterparty is zero; if the swap has positive market value to the solvent counterparty, then that amount is to be accepted as the solvent party's claim against the insolvent party in bankruptcy proceedings.

In June 1992, ISDA's standard swap agreement was rewritten to permit a choice in handling a swap's termination payments in the event of a party's insolvency. The alternative is called Full Two-Way Payment (FTP). If FTP has been agreed to in the swap contract, then in the event of a swap party's insolvency and consequent swap termination, the party whose swap position has a negative value has a contractual obligation to pay the counterparty.

The principal justification for incorporating the LTP clause in the standard contract and thus agreeing not to pay an insolvent party what is owed to him in the swap, was that the solvent party might be owed other sums by the insolvent party stemming from non-swap transactions. If the solvent party had agreed to pay what it owed on the swap, it would lose its bargaining power in its attempt to collect non-swap-related debts. This was the intent of requiring the LTP clause, not to garner a windfall gain for the solvent, but losing, swap party in the event of the counterparty's insolvency.

Although this remains a strong consideration when initiating a swap agreement, ISDA's members have come to the conclusion that "the efficiency of the market is promoted by providing certainty that future cash values of the terminated transactions can generally be realized even by defaulting parties" (see International Swap Dealers Association 1992a). In addition, capital requirement rules that apply to a bank's swap positions have been altered so that all swaps written under one master agreement can be netted prior to the calculation of the capital requirement, if FTP is the accepted clause. This adds to the attraction of selecting FTP.

14.4 Real versus Illusory Benefits to the Swap Parties

If one assumes that there are no cost savings to effecting a swap, then Turnbull (1987) has proved that not all parties to a swap can benefit. His method of proof consists of assuming that all three parties to the swap, AA, BBB, and the dealer, benefit. This assumption is imposed as three present value conditions: the present value of the swap's cost is less than the present value of external financing, both to AA and to BBB, and the present value of the dealer's intermediation profits is positive. Turnbull shows that these present value conditions imply a contradiction. Consequently, unless external cost savings can be garnered by the swap's end users, AA and BBB, the swap cannot make everyone better off.

Obviously, since the value of outstanding interest rate swaps has grown to about $5 trillion, they must provide some benefit, either in the form of direct cost savings or by serving as a more efficient risk-reduction tool relative to other financial instruments. Below are some of the points raised with regard to the economic benefits of swaps. Smith, Smithson, and Wakeman (1988) and Litzenberger (1992) address these issues.

Illusory Benefits

Comparative Advantage The credit quality spread between AA's fixed rate and BBB's fixed rate is greater than their quality spread in the floating rate market. This difference in quality spreads is viewed as AA having an absolute advantage in both fixed and floating markets, while BBB holds a comparative advantage in the floating market. AA recognizes its comparative advantage in the fixed market. Thus the basic reason for trade exists—in this case, a trade of payments. While each country's resources in the traditional trade setting are assumed to be scarce and immobile, the resources in the swap market—capital available to credit classes—are plentiful and mobile. As capital chooses to flow to the swaps markets in lieu of other financial markets, financial arbitrage should eliminate any gains attributable to the comparative advantage analogy.

Intermarket Arbitrage Opportunities Bicksler and Chen (1986) contend that the difference in the quality spreads is due to relative mispricing in the fixed and floating markets; consequently, swaps are used to arbitrage these markets. First note that a difference in quality spreads need not imply mispricing. Consider a two-period example in which one firm, A, is considered riskless and the other, B, is risky. The tree of one-period rates is presented in Figure 14.1, where the probabilities of an up move and of a down move in interest rates are both 0.5.

Firm A can borrow floating at the one-period interest rate or it can borrow fixed at a par coupon rate, R_A, that must satisfy

$$\frac{R_A}{1.05} + 0.5\left[\frac{1 + R_A}{(1.05)(1.10)}\right] + 0.5\left[\frac{1 + R_A}{(1.05)(1.02)}\right] = 1$$

Then $R_A = 5.41\%$.

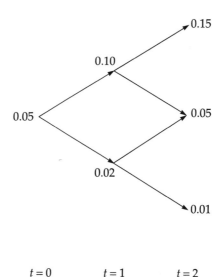

$$t = 0 \qquad t = 1 \qquad t = 2$$

Figure 14.1 Two-Period Interest Rate Tree

Assuming that the risky firm is bankrupt in the state described by a one-period rate of 1%, then R_B must satisfy

$$\frac{R_B}{1.05} + 0.5\left[\frac{1 + R_B}{(1.05)(1.10)}\right] + 0.25\left[\frac{1 + R_B}{(1.05)(1.02)}\right] = 1$$

And $R_B = 20.61\%$.

Finally, the margin, m_B, over the one-period rate that firm B must pay to borrow floating is determined by

$$\frac{0.05 + m_B}{1.05} + 0.5\left[\frac{1.10 + m_B}{(1.05)(1.10)}\right] + 0.25\left[\frac{1.02 + m_B}{(1.05)(1.02)}\right] = 1$$

The solution is $m_B = 14.71\%$.

The fixed rate quality spread is 15.20%, while the floating rate quality spread is 14.71%. The markets have not mispriced the debt instruments, yet there is a quality spread differential. A differential does not necessarily imply mispricing. However, if there is mispricing, then arbitrage should lead to decreasing swap volume as mispricing is eliminated. Swap volume continues to increase.

Underpriced Credit Risk In a special case of the existence of arbitrage opportunities, the credit risk associated with the floating rate loan is underpriced. See Smith, Smithson, and Wakeman 1988, 1990. It is argued that this will initially increase the use of swaps. Eventually, the increased demand for external floating rate debt by the lower-rated firm and that for external fixed rate debt by the higher-rated firm will raise the floating rate quality spread and lower the fixed rate quality spread. As these spreads converge, swap volume should diminish. Again this is contrary to what has occurred.

Real Benefits

A Swap as a Low-Cost Hedging Instrument of Long-Dated Risks Essentially, swaps may allow firms to hedge long-dated interest rate risks at lower costs than that which accompany the use of futures and forwards. First, a swap contract, like a forward contract, can be fashioned quite flexibly. Second, the market for futures contracts that mature in seven or more years is illiquid. The same applies to the forward market beyond two years. Third, futures or forward contracts must be used in strips, and there are no quantity discounts per transaction.

Information Asymmetries Arak et al. (1988) reason that a firm that believes its credit risk is lower than the market's assessment of that risk may borrow floating externally, say at LIBOR + 1%, and swap into fixed to avoid any interest rate risk. As the market learns of the true nature of the firm's credit risk, the LIBOR margin is reduced, say to 0.25%. The firm has realized gains of about 0.75% per year that serve to reduce its fixed borrowing cost. Note that if the firm waits until the market recognizes its true credit risk, interest rates may be higher, which may more than offset the potential savings. However, if the firm now borrows fixed externally, it locks in that rate and cannot achieve the cost savings from the market's gaining knowledge of its true credit risk.

Overpriced Callable Bonds Due to an Underpricing in the Implicit Call Option It is believed that the market has been underpricing the call option in corporate debt. Corporations realize this and sell the option part of a bond as an option on a swap to pay fixed. The corporation is left with cheap noncallable fixed debt, which it swaps into the desired floating rate debt, achieving a net savings.

14.5 Some Terminology, Definitions, and Attendant Points

1. When the floating rate equals LIBOR plus some percentage, then the floating rate is said to be equal to LIBOR plus a *margin*. In our generic swap example (see Section 14.2), BBB's margin is 0.5% and that of AA is zero. A positive margin is described as "a margin over LIBOR"; a negative margin is referred to as "a margin under LIBOR." When the margin is zero, then the borrower is paying and the lender is receiving LIBOR "flat."

2. If a party that enters into the swap pays fixed and receives floating, that party is said to have bought the swap. Conversely, if a party to a swap receives fixed from and pays floating to the dealer, that party is said to have sold the swap.

3. The *trade date* is the date on which the parties agree to the swap. The *effective date* or *value date* is when the initial fixed and floating payments begin to accrue. For swaps involving Eurodollar

rates, this is usually two London business days subsequent to the trade date. The date two business days after the trade date is called the *spot date.*

4. The length of the swap's life, that is, the time from the effective date to the maturity date, is referred to as the swap's *tenor.*

5. The floating rate level is first set on the trade date and then reset at specified intervals. If the generic swap of our example trades on 2/15/94, its effective date (value date) is 2/17/94. The first payment is scheduled for 8/17/94. The second payment is scheduled for 2/17/95. The six-month LIBOR level relevant for that second payment date is set on 8/15/94, since the first reset date occurs two business days prior to the first payment date. The second reset date occurs two days prior to the second payment date and applies to the third payment, and so on (see Figure 14.2).

6. In resetting the floating rate, reference is made to a quote on the agreed-upon rate from a source such as Telerate or Reuters. For swaps involving LIBOR, the 11:00 A.M. London time LIBOR is normally used.

7. The swap's sequence of floating rate payments is called the *floating leg.* Its sequence of fixed payments is known as the *fixed leg.*

8. The term a *front stub period* is used to describe the time from value date to first payment date, if the length of that period is different (generally shorter) from the subsequent payment periods. A *back stub period* is the term attached to the last payment period, if the length of that period is different (generally shorter) from the preceding payment periods.

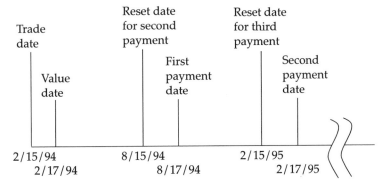

Figure 14.2 Critical Dates in a Swap

9. The *swap spread* is the spread over the T-note rate that corresponds to the maturity of the swap. In our swap example, the spread for AA is 50–52 bps.

10. The *par swap rate* is the fixed rate at which the swap has zero present value.

11. The International Swaps and Derivatives Association (ISDA) was formed in 1985 with the aim of standardizing swap contract language in order to cut the costs of initiating swaps and facilitate their transfer. This makes it easier for the swap dealer to take a position even though a counterparty to that swap is not waiting in the wings.

Among the standards set by ISDA are the calendar dates considered eligible to be payment dates and alternate methods for determining the fixed rate day count fraction, i.e., the number of days between the preceding payment date and the forthcoming payment date divided by the number of days in the year. The fixed rate day count fraction (FIDCF) is used to deannualize the swap's fixed rate and then is multiplied by the notional principal to obtain the fixed rate payment. That is,

fixed rate payment = fixed rate × FIDCF × notional principal

The floating rate payment is computed as

floating rate payment = floating rate × FLDCF × notional principal

where *FLDCF* denotes the floating rate day count fraction. The floating rate day count is calculated as the number of days between the preceding and the forthcoming payment dates divided by 360. For a floating rate leg at six-month LIBOR, where the preceding payment date was 8/17/94, the last reset date was 8/15/94, and the forthcoming payment date is 2/17/95 (a business day), the floating rate day count fraction is 184/360.

12. The various fixed rate day count conventions are described here.

   a. *Actual/365* (Fixed): The numerator is calculated as the actual number of days between the previous fixed payment date and the forthcoming fixed payment date, including the date on which the previous payment was made but excluding the date on which the forthcoming payment is to be made. The parenthetical *Fixed* means that exactly 365 days are to be assumed in a year; even a leap year is assumed to have 365 days. If the successive payment dates are 2/17/94 and 8/17/94, then the fractional day count applied to the swap's fixed rate is 181/365.

b. *Actual/Actual:* Same as in actual/365, except the denominator becomes 366 in a leap year. Day counts for calculation periods that cross into (out of) a leap year are prorated. For example, if the calculation period consists of 61 days in 1995 and 30 days in 1996, a leap year, then the fixed payment is calculated as [(61/365) × *coupon* + (30/366) × *coupon*] × [*notional principal*].

c. *Actual/360:* The numerator is computed as in actual/365 and in actual/actual, and then divided by 360, the assumed number of days in the year.

d. *30/360:* Under this convention, the fixed rate day count fraction is computed by calculating the number of days between successive payment dates, assuming 30 days in each month, including the prior payment date and excluding the forthcoming payment date, and dividing by 360. For the consecutive payment dates of 2/17/94 and 8/17/94, the number of days in this calculation period is computed to be 14 (includes the last payment date) + (5 × 30) + 16 (does not include next payment date) = 180. The corresponding fixed rate day count fraction is 180/360.

There are a few exceptions that one must be aware of in the application of the 30/360 convention.

(i.) If the day before the forthcoming payment date is the 31st of a month but the prior payment date is not the 30th or the 31st of the month, then the last month before the payment date is not shortened to 30 days for the purpose of calculating the fixed rate day count fraction.

Illustration: 3/1/94–9/1/94. To calculate the fixed rate day count fraction under the 30/360 convention, the number of days in the period including 3/1 but excluding 9/1 must be counted. Therefore, the calculation period extends from 3/1/94 to 8/31/94. Applying the exception to the rule, the number of days in the period is (5 × 30) + 31 = 181, and the corresponding fixed rate day count fraction is 181/360.

(ii.) If the day prior to the next payment date is the last day of February, either the 28th or the 29th, then the month of February is not extended to 30 days for computational purposes.

Illustration: 9/1/94–3/1/95. To obtain the fixed rate fractional day count, calculate the number of days contained in the period 9/1/94–2/28/95. According to the exception to the 30/360 rule, the number of days equals $(5 \times 30) + 28 = 178$, and the fixed rate day count fraction is 178/360.[1]

e. 30E/360 (Eurobond Basis): The fraction is computed just as in the unexceptional cases of d, apart from a new exception. In the case of the last payment period, if the swap's maturity date is the last day of February, then February is not lengthened to 30 days.

13. Eligible payment date conventions: If the scheduled payment date is not a banking day, then a rule must be adopted to provide an alternate payment date.

a. Modified Following Business Day: If a payment is scheduled to fall on a banking holiday (weekends apply), then, if the next business day is in the same month of the scheduled payment date, that next business day becomes the payment date. If the next business day occurs in the following month, then the preceding business day becomes the payment date.

b. Following Business Day: If the swap's scheduled payment day occurs on a banking holiday, then the next business day becomes the payment date, whether that next business day is in the same month or in the following month.

c. Preceding Business Day: If the swap's scheduled payment day occurs on a banking holiday, then the preceding business day becomes the payment day, whether or not it falls in the same month as the scheduled payment date.

---

1. Notice that the two illustrations deal with two adjacent periods that together encompass a full year, yet the two day count fractions, 181/360 and 178/360, do not add to one. This means that the full fixed rate may not be received if the ISDA rules are strictly adhered to. To ensure that the full fixed rate is received in such circumstances and to avoid misunderstandings once the swap is under way, firms will often write into the contract the *dollar* amounts to be transferred on the fixed leg for each payment date.

14. To convert a bond equivalent yield, R_{365}, computed using actual/365, to a money market yield, R_{360}, computed using actual/ 360, the formula $R_{360} = R_{365} (360/365)$ is employed. With this formula in mind, recompute the gains to AA and BBB in our swap example. AA's net borrowing cost from the swap was LIBOR-20 bps. But the 20 bps came from the difference in the two bond yields, 5.50% and 5.30%. Since LIBOR is a money market rate, deannualized using 360 days in a year and not 365, then the 20 bps must be multiplied by 360/365 to obtain a more accurate measure of the effective floating rate. Performing this calculation gives LIBOR-19.73 bps. BBB's borrowing cost turned out to be 6.04% fixed, which is the sum of 5.54% plus the 50 bps difference in the floating borrowing rates. But the 50 bps is part of a money market rate. Strictly speaking, before it can be added to the bond equivalent yield of 5.54%, it must be converted. Multiplying the 50 bps by 365/360 gives 50.69 bps, for an all-in-fixed cost to BBB of 6.0469%.

Chapter *15*

Swap Pricing and Hedging

THE THEME of this chapter is the pricing and hedging of generic swaps. How does the swap dealer determine the fixed rate to pay or receive against the floating LIBOR payments? Once a swap agreement has been reached, how does the dealer manage the swap's market risk until another party is found who wishes to initiate a swap opposite to the one on the dealer's books? Should a client wish to exit a swap prior to maturity, how does the dealer value the existing swap in order to arrive at the compensating payment to be made to or received from the client? We address these questions first by noting that a swap's objectives can be accomplished through the use of Eurodollar futures, and then by examining the pricing and hedging of a simple swap—that is, a swap whose reset dates coincide with the expiration dates of the Eurodollar futures contract. The subject area is then broadened to include swaps whose reset dates do not coincide with the expiration of the Eurodollar futures, the valuation of off-market swaps and long-dated swaps. The remaining part of the chapter contains a presentation of a T-note futures–swap arbitrage that was undertaken in early 1985.

15.1 A Relationship between Eurodollar Futures and Swaps

In the discussion of Eurodollar futures, it was shown how individual Eurodollar futures contracts or strips of such futures contracts could be used to fix future borrowing and lending rates. For example, suppose it is March 14, the day when the March Eurodollar futures contract expires. All Eurodollar time deposit rates through the six-month maturity are 8%. The June futures contract, which expires in exactly three months, on June 14, is trading at 92.00, implying a three-month yield of 8% annually. An 8% borrowing rate on $1 million for the forthcoming six-month period can be locked in today by borrowing $1 million for three months at 8% and simultaneously selling one June futures at 92.00. On June 14, you pay 2%, the deannualized three-month spot rate, on the $1 million borrowed—8% annually.[1] Suppose three-month rates have risen to 12% annually. Then, on the rollover borrowing of $1 million for the second three-month period, June–September, you will pay 3%. However, the settlement variation received on the short futures position will bring the effective borrowing rate for the June–September period back down to 2% (8% annually). If, instead, on June 14 the three-month borrowing rate has dropped to 4%, then you will pay 1% on the rollover borrowing for the June–September period. Once again, settlement variation on the June futures contract will bring the effective borrowing rate back to 2% (8% annually). We see that on March 14, a six-month borrowing rate for the March–September period has been fixed: 8% spot for the first three months and 8% fixed by a Eurodollar futures hedge for the second three months.

Instead of this futures hedge, you borrow $1 million floating for six months and enter into a six-month swap from which you receive quarterly floating rate payments and pay a quarterly fixed rate set at 8% annually. On June 14, the first payment date, there will be a net cash flow of zero on the swap. The floating rate for the first three months is set at 8% and the fixed rate on the swap is 8%; the floating payment to be received is entirely canceled by the fixed payment to be made. Your only cash flow on that date is the 8% (2% deannualized) to be paid on the $1 million borrowed in the external market at the then-existing three-month LIBOR rate of 8% annually. On June 14, three-month LIBOR has risen to 12% annually. So you pay, on September 14, 3% on $1 million (12% annually). However, on September 14, the swap pays you the June 14 LIBOR rate of 12% on $1 million, exactly offsetting the cost of your external loan payment. In return, you pay your swap counterparty 8% fixed on an annual basis. If, instead, three-month LIBOR is lower on June 14, say 4%, then you receive 4% on the swap, which cancels the 4% that you pay on the external borrowing. The net is again 8% annually. This six-month swap has fixed an 8% annual rate for the six-month period.

---

1. To stress the equivalency of the Eurodollar futures and swap markets in the simplest manner, the two days difference between trade and value dates in both Eurodollar and swap markets is ignored.

The swap and the futures hedge have achieved the same objective. In an analogous manner, we can reason that fixed rate borrowing can be transformed into floating rate borrowing by the purchase of Eurodollar futures or through a fixed-for-floating swap. Consequently, it is not surprising that the prices of Eurodollar futures are used to price a swap. Nor should it come as a surprise that dealers use Eurodollar futures to hedge a swap until a counterparty to the swap is found.

15.2 Pricing a Simple Swap: The Case of an International Monetary Market (IMM) Swap

A corporation wishes to enter into a $100 million swap with a dealer in which the dealer will receive the fixed rate quarterly and pay three-month LIBOR quarterly. The trade occurs on 2/14/94, the effective (value) date is 2/16/94, and the swap's maturity date is 3/20/96. The swap's payment dates occur two business days after each successive IMM Eurodollar contract expires. The futures expiration date is the day upon which the swap's floating rate is reset. It is set equal to the rate implied by the futures contract on that date and applies to the payment period that begins two business days after the contract expires and ends two business days after the next futures contract expires. See Figure 15.1. The fixed rate day count and floating rate day count fractions are both actual/360. Because of the payment timing and pricing features, this swap is labeled an *IMM swap*.

Table 15.1 contains the relevant interest rate data for determining the swap's fixed rate, that is, for pricing a swap. Column 1 starts with the trade date of 2/14/94. It is on this date that the floating rate is

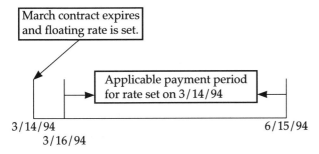

Figure 15.1 Reset Date and Subsequent Payment Period

Table 15.1   Futures Prices, Implied Forward Rates, and the Stub Rate for the IMM Swap

(1) Reset Date	(2) Payment Date	(3) Day Count*	(4) Futures Price on Expiration (Reset Day)	(5) Implied Futures Rate	(6) Discount Factor
	2/16/94***				
2/14/94**	3/16/94	28		3.35%****	0.9974
3/14/94	6/15/94	91	96.35	3.65%	0.9883
6/13/94	9/21/94	98	96.02	3.98%	0.9777
9/19/94	12/21/94	91	95.68	4.32%	0.9671
12/19/94	3/15/95	84	95.28	4.72%	0.9566
3/13/95	6/21/95	98	95.10	4.90%	0.9440
6/19/95	9/20/95	91	94.86	5.14%	0.9319
9/18/95	12/20/95	91	94.65	5.35%	0.9195
12/18/95	3/20/96	91	94.39	5.61%	0.9066

*Day count between prior payment date and current payment date
**Trade date
***Effective date
****Stub rate

set for the first payment period, which begins on 2/16/94, the effective date, and ends on 3/16/94. The first payment period is not equal to a full quarter and so is a stub period. The floating rate set for this period is referred to as the *stub rate* and is the spot market rate corresponding to the length of the stub period. The second entry in column 2, 3/16/94, is the first payment date; the discount rate to be applied to any cash flow to be received on that date is the rate that can be locked in through that date. For this stub period, the rate is 3.35%, and the corresponding discount factor is calculated as 1/[1 + 0.0335(28/360)] = 0.9974. In the calculation of the discount factor, the rate is deannualized by the actual number of days in the period divided by 360. This is the deannualization method usually applied to Eurodollar rates. For the next payment period, a rate of 3.65% is set off of the March Eurodollar futures contract on 3/14/94, the contract's expiration date.

We know from our discussion of hedging with Eurodollar futures that placing one dollar in the spot instrument and buying the appropriate number of futures contracts is equivalent to purchasing a zero-coupon bond. Therefore, we can lock in a rate from the current date to each payment date. For example, if you placed \$1 in the spot instrument for one month and locked in the reinvestment rate through the purchase of the March Eurodollar futures, your \$1 would grow to $[1 + (0.0335)(28/360)][1 + (0.0365)(91/360)]$.[2] Consequently, the amount that would be needed on the effective date in order to have \$1 on 6/15/94 is

$$\frac{1}{\left[1 + (0.0335)\left(\frac{28}{360}\right)\right]\left[1 + (0.0365)\left(\frac{91}{360}\right)\right]} = 0.9883$$

This is the present value factor or discount factor to be applied to dollars received on 6/15/94. Reasoning in this fashion, the discount factor to be applied to cash flows to be received on 9/21/94 is

$$\frac{1}{\left[1 + (0.0335)\left(\frac{28}{360}\right)\right]\left[1 + (0.0365)\left(\frac{91}{360}\right)\right]\left[1 + (0.0398)\left(\frac{98}{360}\right)\right]} = 0.9777$$

This is how the discount factors listed in column 6 of Table 15.1 are obtained.[3]

Now to deal with the pricing question. At what level should the fixed rate be set in order for the swap to have zero value on the effective date? To answer this question, we need a methodology that attaches a market value to the swap. A swap can be viewed as a position that is long one type of loan, fixed or floating, and short another type of loan, floating or fixed. In our example, the dealer may be thought of as having purchased a fixed rate bond and issuing a floating rate bond, both bonds having a face value equal to the swap's notional principal, payable on the swap's maturity date. The two bonds begin accruing interest on 2/16/94 and mature on 3/20/96.

The floating leg's market value on the effective date should be par, in this case \$100 million. Here's why. Suppose there is one remaining

---

2. You would need to purchase $1 + (0.0335)(28/360)$ March futures to hedge the total amount to be invested on March 16. A tail might be added to nullify the effects of settlement variation.

3. One more point with regard to these discount factors: The implied futures rates for this particular swap example should be calculated using the futures bid prices, for the dealer would be hedging the receive fixed leg by selling futures. The bid prices will provide higher implied rates than the offer prices, leading to larger discount factors; and this, as we shall see, will result in a higher fixed rate coupon.

payment period prior to maturity. The payment rate set on the last reset date equals what the market requires. The market discounts cash flows at the required rate. Therefore, the after-payment value of the floater on the next-to-last payment date is par. Algebraically,

$$\text{\textit{floater's market value on next to last payment date}} = \frac{[\text{LIBOR}(\textit{fractional day count}) + 1]\ (\textit{notional principal})}{1 + \text{LIBOR}(\textit{fractional day count})}$$

$$= \textit{notional principal}$$

Stepping back to the second-to-last payment date, we find the corresponding after-payment value on that date by inserting the rate set two days prior to the payment date into the above formula. The notional principal is again obtained as the floater's value. As we continue to work our way back through time, we find, as expected, that the value on the trade date, which is the amount to be exchanged on the effective date, equals the notional principal. I say "as expected" because we know that any bond that pays a coupon equal to the market's discount rate sells at par. So on the trade date and on any reset date, the floating rate bond has a value equal to par—$100 million in our example.

The fixed rate bond is valued by discounting the quarterly payments and the $100 million face value at maturity. The quarterly payment will depend upon the fixed rate to be set and is the object of the swap pricing calculation. The fixed rate level we seek is that which sets the swap's value equal to zero on the effective date. Equivalently, given the manner in which we view this swap as long a fixed rate bond and short a floating rate bond, we need a fixed rate—label it R—that equates the fixed leg's value on the effective date to the floating leg's value, which we have determined to be the notional principal amount of $100 million. Applying the discount factors of Table 15.1 to the deannualized fixed rate payments plus the face value at maturity, and equating the sum of these discounted values to the floater's value on the effective date, we obtain the following equation:

$$10^8 R \left[\begin{array}{l} 0.9974 \left(\dfrac{28}{360}\right) + 0.9883 \left(\dfrac{91}{360}\right) + 0.9777 \left(\dfrac{98}{360}\right) \\[2mm] + 0.9671 \left(\dfrac{91}{360}\right) + 0.9566 \left(\dfrac{84}{360}\right) + 0.9440 \left(\dfrac{98}{360}\right) \\[2mm] + 0.9319 \left(\dfrac{91}{360}\right) + 0.9195 \left(\dfrac{91}{360}\right) + 0.9066 \left(\dfrac{91}{360}\right) \end{array} \right] + 0.9066 \cdot 10^8 = 10^8$$

The solution is $R = 4.63\%$ (normally quoted on a bond equivalent basis after multiplication by 365/360). At this fixed coupon rate, the swap has net present value of zero and is called a *par swap*. This rate is higher than the comparable maturity T-note rate, for it is manufactured using Eurodollar rates.

Recall that in arriving at this rate, the discount factors were obtained from the bid side of the Eurodollar futures prices—providing higher rates than the offer side of futures prices. The bid side was used because to hedge his long fixed position the dealer must fix his borrowing costs, the floating rate leg. The dealer does this by selling futures—usually at the bid. If everything works out, the 4.63% rate makes the dealer even. To make a profit that includes a risk premium, the dealer adds a spread to the calculated receive fixed rate. If the spread is 5 bps on the receive side, then the dealer's receive swap rate is 4.68%. This figure, 4.68%, represents more than a 5 bps spread over the comparable maturity T-note, because the 4.63% is, in effect, a long-term Eurodollar rate.

Where did the spread number come from? Besides the presence of dealers, brokers in the swap market serve to facilitate trades. They act as agents in the trades, unlike the dealers, who take on risk. If the broker can match two counterparties, a commission is charged each counterparty, say ½ bp per year on the notional principal. These brokers are always showing the swap spread for each maturity on electronic screens. In our example, the dealer would pick off the swap spread for the relevant maturity.

15.3 Hedging a Swap

The dealer has just entered into the par swap, in which he receives 4.63% (plus a spread) and pays three-month LIBOR on the IMM dates listed in Table 15.1. He does not have an offsetting swap customer and is concerned that rates will rise, causing the swap's value to deteriorate. He wishes to hedge this rate risk. The standard approach to hedging a swap is to list every input used to construct the discount function. For our example, these consist of the 28-day spot rate and the string of rates implied by the futures contracts. They are considered to be the parameters of the problem. Each parameter level is perturbed by one basis point, while all other parameter levels are held constant. The effect of this rate perturbation on the swap's value is noted, and a hedge position is taken in the appropriate financial instruments.

To keep the figures presented in the realm of four decimal places, consider a 10-basis-point change instead of a one-basis-point change. The dealer wishes to guard against a loss in value due to a ten-basis-point increase in any of the parameter levels. Focus on the first futures contract, the one that expires on 3/14/94. Suppose its rate immediately rises from 3.65% to 3.75%. How will the value of the swap be affected? Clearly, the floating leg's value remains at $100 million, since none of the parameters that affect its valuation have changed. So the change in the swap's value emanates from a change in the fixed leg's value. To calculate this change, the discount factors must be recomputed. Using the identical procedure employed to compute the discount factors presented in Table 15.1, we compute a new set of discount factors; the only change in the inputs is that the implied rate of the March 1994 futures is assumed to have increased from 3.65% to 3.75%. Table 15.2 lists the new discount factors.

Applying these discount factors to the fixed payments from a 4.63% rate gives a fixed leg value of $99,968,840. The swap's value, the difference between its fixed and floating legs, falls from zero to $-$31,160, or $99,968,840 − $100,000,000.

Knowing that a 10 bps rise in the futures rate results in settlement variation of $250 per contract, the dealer hedges this risk by selling 124.64 (31,160/250) March 1994 contracts. To complete the hedge, the dealer repeats the above steps for a 10 bps change in each futures rate and solves for the number of short futures contracts that would be needed to offset the decrease in the swap's value if any of these rates should rise. There is also the possibility that the 28-day rate

Table 15.2   Discount Factors after Increasing the March Futures Rate by 10 Basis Points

Payment Date	Day Count	Spot or Futures Rate	Discount Factor
3/16/94	28	3.35%	0.9974
6/15/94	91	3.75%	0.9880
9/21/94	98	3.98%	0.9774
12/21/94	91	4.32%	0.9669
3/15/95	84	4.72%	0.9564
6/21/95	98	4.90%	0.9438
9/20/95	91	5.14%	0.9317
12/20/95	91	5.35%	0.9192
3/20/96	91	5.61%	0.9064

immediately increases after the swap terms have been set. Such an event will also alter the value of the swap, although less significantly. To hedge against the event, the dealer might use one of the near-term Eurodollar futures or even the IMM's one month LIBOR futures contract—although the use of any of these contracts to hedge a change in the spot rate entails basis risk. In practice, dealers seem to be able to live with a change in the spot rate and do not, as a rule, hedge a change in it.

15.4 The Convexity Adjustment

The dealer who receives fixed, pays floating, and hedges this swap by shorting the appropriate number of Eurodollar futures holds a more favorable position than if he pays fixed, receives floating, and hedges the swap by buying Eurodollar futures. The edge to the former position (receiving fixed and shorting Euro futures) is due to the fact that the profit function of the fixed receive position is strictly convex while the profit function of any futures contract is linear, paying $25 per basis point irrespective of the current rate level. Analogously, the relative weakness of the latter hedged position (pay fixed, buy Euro futures) is the result of the concavity of the fixed position's profit function and the linearity of the futures payoff function.

A simple example can be used to illustrate these characteristics: The term of a new swap is six months, the fixed leg receives, quarterly, an annual rate of 11.9215686%, and the floating leg pays three-month LIBOR quarterly. The notional principal is $100 million. The current three-month Eurodollar rate is 8%. The three-month Eurodollar futures contract that expires in exactly three months is trading at 84.00. At present the floating leg and fixed leg have equal values—par. The fixed leg price, per dollar of principal, is calculated as

$$\frac{\dfrac{(0.119215686)}{4}}{1.02} + \frac{\dfrac{(0.119215686)}{4} + 1}{(1.02)(1.04)} = 1$$

The dealer is concerned that the yield curve may further steepen. He seeks to short hedge the specific event that the market will raise its expectation of the forthcoming LIBOR rate. The dealer calculates that a one-basis-point rise in that rate, from 16.00% to 16.01%, equivalently from 4.00% to 4.0025% (quarterly), decreases the fixed leg's value by $2,334 on the $100 million principal. The floating leg's value would be unaffected. He sets out to hedge against the risk of a decline in the fixed leg's value. Since a futures contract pays $25 in settlement variation for each basis point change, he must sell 93.36 (2,334/25) contracts.

Suppose the forward rate immediately rises from 16% to 17%; the futures price drops from 84.00 to 83.00. This generates settlement variation of $233,400 (93.36 × 100 × 25) to offset the $232,801 decrease in value of the fixed leg; the net gain is $599. Instead, assume that the forward rate drops to 15%; the futures moves up to 85.00. The loss on the futures is $233,400, but the gain on the fixed leg is $233,923; the net gain is $523. No matter which way interest rates change, the value of the hedged swap increases. And the greater the volatility in rates, the greater the gains to this hedged swap position. The converse is true for the swap in which the dealer pays fixed and long hedges the position in the futures market; variation in rates result in net losses, and the greater the rate volatility, the larger the losses to the hedged swap.

If the dealer enters a swap in which he is to receive fixed, then convexity works in his favor. Competition requires that the customer receive the benefit of the convexity edge held by the dealer. The dealer subtracts points from the rates observed in the Eurodollar futures market from which the discount factors are derived and used to calculate the coupon rate necessary to set the fixed leg's value equal to par. This results in the dealer's receiving a lower fixed coupon against his payment of LIBOR. But if the dealer pays fixed and receives floating, convexity works against his hedged position. In that case, the dealer must extract a concession from the customer on the fixed rate. The customer has the benefit of convexity, and the result is that the dealer will pay—and the customer will receive—a lower fixed rate than that implied by the set of futures prices.

15.5 Pricing a Swap with Payment Dates That Do Not Coincide with IMM Dates

A dealer enters into a two-year swap in which he pays six-month LIBOR and receives fixed semiannual payments on $100 million of notional principal. The trade date is 2/14/94 and the effective date is 2/16/94, the same dates as in the prior example. The payment dates are 8/16/94, 2/16/95, 8/16/95, and 2/16/96. The fixed rate and floating rate day counts are actual/360. The floating rate for the first six-month segment is set on the trade date at 3.70%. The problem is to determine the receive fixed swap rate that results in the swap having a zero value on trade date, which means that no funds are exchanged on the effective date. The key element in the solution is the determination of the discount factors to apply to the fixed leg's cash flows. The relevant data are presented in Table 15.3. The data in columns 1, 2, and 3 of Table 15.3 were obtained from Table 15.1.

A conventional way to arrive at the payment date discount factors is to first obtain the zero-coupon rates implied by the discount factors for an IMM swap's payment dates that surround each payment date of this non-IMM swap. Linear interpolation is then applied to these IMM implied zero-coupon rates to obtain the zero-coupon rate for this swap's payment date. The payment date discount factor is then derived from this rate. Given the IMM discount factor, the following equation is solved for the zero-coupon rate:

$$discount\ factor = \frac{1}{1 + (zero\text{-}coupon\ rate)\left(\dfrac{day\ count\ from\ effective\ date}{360}\right)} \tag{15.1}$$

Table 15.3 Discount Factors for the Non-IMM Fixed for Six-Month LIBOR Swap

(1)	(2)	(3)	(4)	(5)	(6)	(7)	(8)
Relevant IMM Payment Date	Day Count to IMM Payment Date	Discount Factor for Relevant IMM Payment Date	Implied Zero-Coupon Rate*	Payment Date for Non-IMM Swap	Interpolated Zero-Coupon Rate for Payment Date	Day Count to Non-IMM Date	Discount Factor for Payment Date
				8/16/94	3.70%	181	0.9817
12/21/94	308	0.9671	3.976%				
				2/16/95	4.106%	365	0.9600
3/15/95	392	0.9566	4.167%				
6/21/95	490	0.9440	4.358%				
				8/16/95	4.463%	546	0.9366
9/20/95	581	0.9319	4.528%				
12/20/95	672	0.9195	4.690%				
				2/16/96	4.799%	730	0.9113
3/20/96	763	0.9066	4.861%				

*Rates rounded to nearest one-tenth of a basis point.

These rates are listed in column 4. The zero-coupon rate for a payment date is then obtained by linearly interpolating between adjacent IMM zero-coupon rates.

$$\begin{array}{l} \textit{Zero-coupon rate} \\ \textit{on payment date} \end{array} = \begin{array}{l} \textit{zero-coupon rate} \\ \textit{on preceding IMM} \\ \textit{date} \end{array} \tag{15.2}$$

$$+ \cfrac{\begin{array}{c}\textit{days from prior IMM date} \\ \textit{to payment date}\end{array}}{\begin{array}{c}\textit{days between} \\ \textit{adjacent IMM dates}\end{array}} \left(\begin{array}{l}\textit{differences in adjacent} \\ \textit{IMM zero-coupon rates}\end{array} \right)$$

For example, to obtain the discount factor for the cash flow on 2/16/95, first use formula (15.1) to calculate the zero-coupon rates implied by the discount factors on 12/21/94 and 3/15/95. The numbers are 3.976% and 4.167%, respectively. Then apply formula (15.2) to these rates to obtain 4.106%.

$$3.976 + (4.167 - 3.976)\left(\frac{57}{84}\right) = 4.106$$

These numbers are presented in column 6. Finally, reapply (15.1) to obtain the discount factor of 0.9600 (see column 8).

From the reasoning presented in Section 15.2, we know that the floating rate leg's market value on trade date for the effective date that occurs two business days later is $100 million. Now we search for that fixed rate coupon that equates the present value of the fixed leg to $100 million. The following equation is solved:

$$10^8 R \left[\begin{array}{l} 0.9817 \left(\dfrac{181}{360}\right) + 0.9600 \left(\dfrac{184}{360}\right) \\ + 0.9366 \left(\dfrac{181}{360}\right) + 0.9113 \left(\dfrac{184}{360}\right) \end{array} \right] + 0.9113 \cdot 10^8 = 10^8$$

$R = 4.62\%$. To this figure a spread is added to arrive at the swap's receive rate.

15.6 Valuing an Off-Market Swap

There are instances in which a counterparty to a swap may wish to terminate the swap. Perhaps the reason for the financing was a construction project that has been completed early and sold, or a business venture that fared poorly and was prematurely terminated. The reason could be that a financial institution that is the counterparty to this swap wishes to assume a different degree of interest rate exposure and judges that the best way to do so is by terminating the swap.

There are three ways for a party to a swap to terminate the swap:

1. Buyout: The party pays to or receives from the counterparty a lump-sum payment equal to the swap's present value.

2. Assignment: The party assigns its swap, with the consent of the counterparty, to a third party. From that point forward, the third party receives from and delivers to the counterparty the payments remaining to the swap's maturity. The assigning party either receives or makes a payment to the third party equal to the swap's present value.

3. Offset: The party enters into a swap that has the same fixed and floating rate terms as the original swap, but the direction of this swap's cash flows are opposite to that of the original swap's flows. For example, if the original swap received fixed at 10% semiannually and paid six-month LIBOR, then the offsetting swap would pay fixed at 10% semiannually and receive six-month LIBOR on the same dates as the original swap. Since it is unlikely that the offsetting swap's fixed rate equals the par rate for swaps of that maturity, a lump-sum payment will be made between the two parties. If the party requires an offsetting swap in which he pays fixed to the dealer at a higher rate than the current pay-fixed rate on par swaps, then the party will receive a lump-sum payment from the dealer equal to the present value of the swap. For example, the original swap receives 10% fixed and pays LIBOR. To offset, the party enters into a swap with a dealer in which he pays 10% fixed to the dealer and receives LIBOR, when the receive rate on par swaps charged by the dealer is 6%. Clearly the dealer is receiving a swap with positive value and must make a settling payment to the party. In this case, the dealer pays the party the swap's present value.

It is important to understand why the party requires that the offsetting swap have the same fixed rate as the original swap. Assume it does not. Suppose the original swap receives 10% fixed and on the offsetting swap the party would pay 6% fixed. Then the future cash inflows due to the difference in fixed rates are subject to reinvestment rate risk. To defease this risk, one must borrow the present value of these flows at today's rates, and allow the future flows to pay off the loan. Conversely, if the original swap receives 10% and on the off-setting swap the party must pay 14% fixed, then funds must be found in the future at uncertain costs in order to meet the cash outflows caused by the fixed rate differential. To defease this risk, an amount of money must be lent today whose future cash flows will match the future outflows that emanate from this fixed rate difference.

In all three cases, the present value of an off-market swap, a swap with a fixed rate different from the current par swap fixed rate, must be computed. In previous sections we discussed how to arrive at the par swap rate, the fixed rate that sets the swap's present value equal to zero. The floating leg's present value is computed and then the coupon rate on a fixed rate bond is determined that equates the fixed leg's present value to the floating leg's present value. These same present value calculations are used to value an off-market swap; the only difference is that the fixed rate coupon is known and is not the object to be determined as in pricing the par swap.

For example, the swap to be terminated receives 8% fixed quarterly against three-month LIBOR on a notional principal of $100 million. The swap matures on 6/21/95. The swap is to be valued on 2/14/94 for value date 2/16/94. On the last reset date, 12/20/93, three-month LIBOR was set at 3.0%. This rate applies to the next payment date, which is 3/16/94. The data presented in Table 15.1 apply. The floating leg's value is calculated as the discounted value of the sum of the interest payment plus the after-payment value of the floating leg, which we have reasoned is par. Thus,

$$\textit{value of floating leg} = \left[0.03\left(\frac{28}{360}\right) + 1\right](0.9974)10^8 = 99{,}972{,}727$$

The value of the fixed leg is computed by discounting the quarterly fixed payments plus the face value at maturity by the appropriate discount factors listed in Table 15.1. This gives a fixed leg value of

$$\textit{fixed leg value} = (0.08)\left[\begin{array}{c} 0.9974\left(\frac{28}{360}\right) + 0.9883\left(\frac{91}{360}\right) + 0.9777\left(\frac{98}{360}\right) \\ + 0.9671\left(\frac{91}{360}\right) + 0.9566\left(\frac{84}{360}\right) + 0.9440\left(\frac{98}{360}\right) \end{array}\right]10^8 + 0.9440 \cdot 10^8$$

$$= 104{,}945{,}547$$

The current value of this off-market swap is $4,972,820 ($104,945,547 − $99,972,727).

15.7 Valuing a Long-Dated Swap

Consider the task of valuing, on 1/4/94 for value date 1/6/94, a swap maturing on 1/7/2002 in which the dealer receives a 6% fixed coupon semiannually and pays six-month LIBOR on $100 million principal. The date 1/6/94 is a payment date. We seek the after-payment value of the swap for that date. The fixed day count fraction is 30/360 and the floating day count fraction is actual/360. Eurodollar futures are listed out to ten years, but trading is liquid, depending on whom you speak with, out to six or seven years. So, using the procedure set out in the previous sections, we can determine zero-coupon rates and the corresponding discount factors for any payment dates within seven years of the swap's effective date. For this particular swap's payment dates, the day counts between dates, the discount rates, and the fixed rate for a par 7-year swap (the only one needed for our problem) are listed in Table 15.4.

Since the dealer's swap extends out to eight years, we must obtain the discount factors for the payment dates extending past the seventh year, namely for the dates 7/6/01 and 1/7/02. Dealers proceed by noting the yield of the on-the-run (latest) T-note issue whose maturity just exceeds the payment date for which a discount factor is needed. In this case, the dealer's spread is added to the yield on the 10-year T-note to obtain the 10-year par swap rate. Given the 7-year and 10-year swap rates, the next step is to obtain par swap rates for the value dates 7/6/01 and 1/7/02. A number of dealers say they do this by linear interpolation. Therefore, assuming a 10-year par swap rate (to receive fixed) of 5.8%, the par swap rates are, for 7/6/01,

$$5.50\% + \left(\frac{178}{1080}\right)[5.80\% - 5.50\%] = 5.5494\%$$

and for 1/7/02,

$$5.50\% + \left(\frac{359}{1080}\right)[5.80\% - 5.50\%] = 5.5997\%$$

The valuation date 1/4/94 is a reset date, so we know that on 1/6/94, a payment date, the after-payment value of a swap's floating leg is par—in this case $100 million. But, by definition, a par swap with a maturity date of 7/6/01—a 7.5-year swap, must have a fixed leg value on 1/4/94 for value date 1/6/94 of $100 million. By interpolation, we have designated a par coupon of 5.5494% for this 7.5-year swap. We

Table 15.4   Information Needed for the Valuation of the 8-Year Swap

Payment Date	Fixed Day Count (30/360)	Payment (in millions)	Discount Factors Derived from Euro-Futures	Receive Par Swap Rate
7/6/94	180	3.0000	0.9818	—
1/6/95	180	3.0000	0.9626	—
7/6/95	180	3.0000	0.9423	—
1/6/96	180	3.0000	0.9211	—
7/6/96	180	3.0000	0.8991	—
1/6/97	180	3.0000	0.8763	—
7/7/97*	181	3.0167	0.8533	—
1/6/98	179	2.9833	0.8300	—
7/6/98	180	3.0000	0.8066	—
1/6/99	180	3.0000	0.7835	—
7/6/99	180	3.0000	0.7603	—
1/6/00	180	3.0000	0.7375	—
7/6/00	180	3.0000	0.7150	—
1/8/01*	182	3.0333	0.6928	5.50%
7/6/01	178	2.9667	—	—
1/7/02*	181	3.0167	—	—

*Since 7/6/97, 1/6/2001, and 1/6/2002 are nonbanking days, the modified following business day rule is followed, and the next business day in the month becomes the payment date.

know the payment date discount factors for the next fourteen semian-nual payments. What we lack is the discount factor for this 7.5-year swap's last payment date, 7/6/01. Call it F. F must satisfy the following present value equation for a 7.5-year par swap:

$$
10^8(0.055494)
\begin{bmatrix}
0.9818\left(\dfrac{180}{360}\right) + 0.9626\left(\dfrac{180}{360}\right) + 0.9423\left(\dfrac{180}{360}\right) \\[2mm]
+ 0.9211\left(\dfrac{180}{360}\right) + 0.8991\left(\dfrac{180}{360}\right) + 0.8763\left(\dfrac{180}{360}\right) \\[2mm]
+ 0.8533\left(\dfrac{181}{360}\right) + 0.8300\left(\dfrac{179}{360}\right) + 0.8066\left(\dfrac{180}{360}\right) \\[2mm]
+ 0.7835\left(\dfrac{180}{360}\right) + 0.7603\left(\dfrac{180}{360}\right) + 0.7375\left(\dfrac{180}{360}\right) \\[2mm]
+ 0.7150\left(\dfrac{180}{360}\right) + 0.6928\left(\dfrac{182}{360}\right) + F\left(\dfrac{178}{360}\right)
\end{bmatrix}
+ F \cdot 10^8 = 10^8
$$

The solution is $F = 0.6553$. This method for obtaining the next sequential discount rate from the preceding discount rates and the information that the par coupon is being discounted is called *bootstrapping*.

The technique is reapplied to the fixed leg of the par swap that extends to the last payment date, 1/7/01—the maturity date of the 8-year swap that we wish to value. From the previous reasoning, the discount rate that we seek must satisfy

$$10^8(0.055997)\begin{bmatrix} 0.9818\left(\dfrac{180}{360}\right) + 0.9626\left(\dfrac{180}{360}\right) + 0.9423\left(\dfrac{180}{360}\right) + 0.9211\left(\dfrac{180}{360}\right) \\ + 0.8991\left(\dfrac{180}{360}\right) + 0.8763\left(\dfrac{180}{360}\right) + 0.8533\left(\dfrac{181}{360}\right) + 0.8300\left(\dfrac{179}{360}\right) \\ + 0.8066\left(\dfrac{180}{360}\right) + 0.7835\left(\dfrac{180}{360}\right) + 0.7603\left(\dfrac{180}{360}\right) + 0.7375\left(\dfrac{180}{360}\right) \\ + 0.7150\left(\dfrac{180}{360}\right) + 0.6928\left(\dfrac{182}{360}\right) + 0.6553\left(\dfrac{178}{360}\right) + F\cdot\left(\dfrac{181}{360}\right) \end{bmatrix} + F\cdot 10^8 = 10^8$$

The solution to this equation is $F = 0.6344$. This is the discount factor applied to the maturity date cash flow of the 8-year fixed leg.

We are now prepared to value the 8-year swap. Since the calculation is made on a reset date, 1/4/94, the floating leg's value is $100 million. The fixed leg's value is

$$10^8(0.06)\begin{bmatrix} 0.9818\left(\dfrac{180}{360}\right) + 0.9626\left(\dfrac{180}{360}\right) + 0.9423\left(\dfrac{180}{360}\right) + 0.9211\left(\dfrac{180}{360}\right) \\ + 0.8991\left(\dfrac{180}{360}\right) + 0.8763\left(\dfrac{180}{360}\right) + 0.8533\left(\dfrac{181}{360}\right) + 0.8300\left(\dfrac{179}{360}\right) \\ + 0.8066\left(\dfrac{180}{360}\right) + 0.7835\left(\dfrac{180}{360}\right) + 0.7603\left(\dfrac{180}{360}\right) + 0.7375\left(\dfrac{180}{360}\right) \\ + 0.7150\left(\dfrac{180}{360}\right) + 0.6928\left(\dfrac{182}{360}\right) + 0.6553\left(\dfrac{178}{360}\right) + 0.6344\left(\dfrac{181}{360}\right) \end{bmatrix} = 102{,}613{,}611$$
$$+ 0.6344 \cdot 10^8$$

The swap's value to the dealer receiving fixed is $2,613,611 ($102,613,611 − $100,000,000).

15.8 Extending the Hedging Methodology

Suppose the dealer chooses to hedge the long-dated swap that was valued in the previous section. We have already explored how to construct a hedge in which the swap's input parameters consist solely of Eurodollar rates. Each Eurodollar rate is perturbed while all other rates are held constant. The corresponding change in the swap's value is computed, and the appropriate number of Eurodollar futures are sold or bought in order to neutralize the value change. But one of the parameters used to compute the 8-year swap's value was the 10-year par swap rate. How is a change in that parameter hedged?

Suppose we consider a 10-basis-point increase in the 10-year par swap rate. Altering the ten-year swap rate will cause the interpolated par swap rates for 7/6/01 and 1/7/02 to change. What is the corresponding change in the 8-year swap's value? For 7/6/01, the new par swap rate becomes

$$5.50\% + \left(\frac{178}{1080}\right)(5.90\% - 5.50\%) = 5.5659\%$$

while the 2/7/02 par swap rate is calculated as

$$5.50\% + \left(\frac{359}{1080}\right)(5.90\% - 5.50\%) = 5.6330\%$$

Bootstrapping with the new 7/6/01 par swap rate of 5.5659% gives a discount factor for the 7/6/01 payment date of 0.6544. Bootstrapping with the new 2/7/01 par swap rate of 5.6330% gives a discount factor for this payment date of 0.6323. Substituting these new discount factors into the fixed leg's value equation yields a fixed leg value of $102,396,000. Since the floating leg's value on 1/4/94 for value on 1/6/94 is $100,000,000, the swap's value falls to $2,396,000. The net drop is $217,611. On 1/4/94, the ten-year T-note has a coupon of 5.30%, a yield to maturity of 5.32%, and a maturity date of 11/15/03. Its price is 99.84112%. A 10-basis-point rise in its yield results in a price of 99.08548%. The net change is 0.75563% per dollar of face value, or $7,556 per $1,000,000 in face value. Therefore, the face amount of ten-year T-notes to short is $28.8 (217,611/7,556) million.

15.9 Trading against a Swap Position: A Futures-Swap Arbitrage

The Idea

Paying fixed and receiving floating on a swap is a position that has a financing and profit profile similar to a short forward or short futures contract on a Treasury note. With regard to financing, par swaps, forwards, and futures have zero net cash flows at initiation. If Treasury rates rise, the pay fixed–receive floating swap will have a positive value, as will the short forward; the short futures will receive settlement variation. Conversely, if Treasury rates fall, all three positions will lose money. It follows that traders will naturally begin to examine the relative pricing of swaps and futures to see if there is mispricing that can be arbitraged. Since the swap market concentrates in maturities ranging up to ten years, a natural futures market to study is the ten-year Treasury note contract. Recall that the T-note and T-bond contracts are identical in all respects except in defining a deliverable issue. The T-note contract restricts delivery to original issue T-notes with at least 6.5 to 10 years remaining to maturity.

The Data and the Trade

The following describes a trade that some arbitragers showed to various money managers at the end of 1985. If the manager liked the trade, he would undertake the trade, agreeing to pay the arbitrager a percentage of profits, or he would place the required transactions through the arbitrager, permitting the latter to earn commissions. It is 12/19/85. A 10-year swap is available in which you pay 10.35% semiannually and receive six-month LIBOR, which is currently 8.50%. Accepting the position is similar to being short the ten-year T-note rate—actually, the ten-year T-note rate plus the swap spread. You examine a long position in the T-note futures. If you deem the futures to be underpriced, then the long futures position becomes an obvious counterweight to the pay fixed–receive floating 10-year swap.

A long T-note futures position is essentially long the cheapest-to-deliver (CTD) note financed at the repo rate. (Glance back at the futures pricing equation in Section 12.4, equation (12.3). Consider it from that point of view. On 12/19/85, the CTD note on the June 1986 futures contract is the 11.25% T-note of 11/15/95. It carries a yield to maturity of 10.1019%. Its clean price is 107.0625 (decimal) with accrued interest amounting to 1.06 and a conversion factor of 1.2093. The June futures price is 86.09375 (decimal). By 6/19/86, the last day of trading for the June contract, this T-note will have accrued interest of 1.07. The coupon to be received on 5/15/86 is to be lent out for 35 days, until 6/19/86, at the term reverse repo rate of 7.00%. These numbers imply a term repo rate for the 12/19/85–6/19/86 period, 183 days, of 4.98%. Just solve the following futures equation for *r*.

$$1.2093(86.09375) + 1.07 = (107.0625 + 1.06)$$
$$\times \left[1 + r\left(\frac{182}{360}\right)\right] - \left(\frac{11.25}{2}\right)\left[1 + 0.07\left(\frac{35}{360}\right)\right]$$

You see the situation as follows. Over the next six months, the swap involves borrowing at 10.35% and lending at 8.5%, entailing a loss of 1.85%. The long futures position involves lending at 10.1% and borrowing at 4.98% for a gain of 5.12%. You believe that these rate differentials are too far apart, that they will converge by the last delivery day of the June futures contract, and that convergence will result in a greater gain (or smaller loss) on the long futures than the loss (or gain) on the swap. Of course, the spreads between long- and short-term rates in these two markets should not be expected to converge to equality. They represent spreads on instruments that are similar but not identical. Furthermore, one should not expect to capture the entire amount of the expected convergence because of the problem in forming a completely riskless hedge. This is not practically possible: one would have to continuously adjust the number of contracts in the futures position in an attempt to neutralize value changes in the swap position induced by variations in the Treasury yield curve.

The Hedging Analysis

To complete the arbitrage position, the swap must be hedged. This involves determining the number of futures needed to match the swap's value volatility due to interest rate changes. For this trade, duration was used as the value sensitivity measure.

The duration of the fixed rate loan portion of the swap is calculated to be 6.542 years; the duration of the variable portion, 0.50 years. The swap's net duration is 6.042 years. The duration of the 11/15/95 CTD note is 6.253 years. If the CTD note is used to hedge the swap, then *x* number of notes must be purchased for each $100,000 notional principal of the pay-fixed swap. Employing the duration hedging formula of Chapter 12,

$$x = \frac{6.042(100,000)}{6.253(108,123)} = 0.89366$$

The $108,123 figure represents the gross price of the CTD note on 12/19/85. However, the choice is to use T-note futures to hedge the swap. Recalling the hedging methodology of Chapter 12, the number of long futures needed is

$$\frac{1.2093}{1 \, + \, 0.075\!\left(\dfrac{182}{360}\right)} \, = \, 1.16512$$

The 0.075 number in the denominator of the hedge ratio calculation represents the actual term repo rate for the trading period. Consequently, for each $100,000 notional principal of the swap, $89,366 face value of the CTD note is needed. But then 1.16512 × $89,366 = $104,122 in face value of futures is required. In summary, for a $10,000,000 par swap, approximately 104 long futures are required to complete the hedge.

Profit Analysis

The position's potential profits under various interest rate scenarios for 6/19/86 are reviewed here. The date 6/19/86 is selected as the day to unwind the position, since that is the last trading day for the June futures contract. The following is a sample scenario that was studied and presented to the arbitrager's clients. It assumes that the yield curve remains stationary. Other scenarios were presented—for example, a +100 bp change in the curve and a −100 bp change in the curve. Each showed a profit.

The Spot Curve Remains Unchanged The current 9.5-year par swap rate of 10.20% was used to discount the fixed leg's 10.35% semiannual coupon. The computed value of a 10.35%, 9.5-year pay-fixed swap as of 6/19/86, expiring on 12/19/95, is $10,000,000 − $10,089,906 = −$89,906. The $10,000,000 is the floating leg's value; the $10,089,906 is the fixed leg's value.

If the current yield curve remains unchanged, then the 11.25%, 11/15/95 T-note will have a yield to maturity on 6/19/86 of 10%. The yield diminishes by ten basis points as the maturity shortens. This yield corresponds to a net price of 107.48617 and accrued interest of 1.07. If this T-note remains CTD, then the futures price on that date is computed as[4]

$$\frac{1}{1.2093}\left\{\left[107.48617 + 1.07\right]\left[1 + 0.075\left(\frac{11}{360}\right)\right] - 1.40625\right\} = 88.8106$$

The profit on the 104 long futures amounts to 104 × (88.8106 − 86.09375) × $1,000 = $282,552. The net profit to the arbitrage would be $282,552 − $89,906 = $192,646.

A Caveat to the Buyer

There is risk to this arbitrage, apart from the basis risk due to the swap spread over Treasuries. Some reflection on futures pricing reveals why this is so. The implied repo rate is low because the futures contract is not at full carry. The futures is not at full carry because of the short's options. Consequently there might be some market environments in which the long will lose. To take an extreme case, the spot rates on 6/19/86 can be configured so that the swap makes money in a rising rate environment but the futures lose more because the CTD note has changed. An extreme inversion of the yield curve would give this result. The key to judging the attractiveness of the arbitrage is not to take the implied repo rate at face value but to take into account the value of the short future's options. At the time, arbitragers undertaking this position estimated that the options embedded in the T-note futures contract were worth no more than 150 basis points. If we take this into consideration, the spread comparison changes from −1.85% + 5.12% to −1.85% + 3.62%. The arbitrage is still considered to be attractive.

---

4. Since carry is positive, the note is expected to be delivered on the last day of the month, June 30, eleven days away. The 1.40625 figure is the note's accrued interest on June 30.

Chapter **16**

Nongeneric Swaps

A *NONGENERIC* swap is one whose terms deviate from those that define a generic swap. The class includes swaps whose notional principal changes over the swap's life, those whose floating rate maturity does not coincide with the length of the payment period, swaps with an effective date that is not two business days after the trade date, and so on. Because the pricing of a number of nongeneric swaps cannot be accomplished using the technique illustrated in Chapter 15, another, more general technique is introduced. Its application is illustrated. The chapter concludes with a listing and description of various nongeneric swaps.

16.1 A General Methodology for Swap Pricing

The previous pricing methodology, sometimes called the *floating rate note method* and hereafter referred to by that name, reasons that the swap's two legs can be viewed as bonds. The floating rate bond is worth its face value on the swap's effective date, and the swap's fixed rate is determined by finding the coupon rate that sets the fixed rate bond's present value equal to that of the floating rate bond. This methodology works fine for the type of swaps described earlier, fixed against a floating rate, where the floating rate set for the payment period is identical to the return required on the reset date for that period. In such cases, the floating rate leg can be viewed as a bond with a value on each reset date equal to its face value. However, when the floating rate set for a payment period differs from the required rate for that period, the floating rate leg bond's value on a reset date does not equal its face value.

A case in point would be one in which the floating rate set for the period corresponded to a longer term than the length of the payment period. For example, a dealer's customer wishes to pay, quarterly, a floating rate calculated as the average of the LIBOR three-month rate, reset daily; he receives fixed in return. Or suppose that an insurance company agrees to pay its annuity holders, semiannually, at a rate based on whatever the five-year T-note rate is on the selected reset date. The company might choose to invest the front-end customer payments in high-yielding corporate bonds and then enter into a swap with a dealer in which the insurance company receives the constant maturity five-year T-note rate, as published in the Fed's H.15 report, and pays the dealer the fixed swap rate semiannually. This swap's floating leg is now composed of semiannual payments based on a five-year rate. Yet another instance is where the floating rate follows a non-LIBOR index, such as the 30-day commercial paper index published in the Fed's H.15 report, and the required rate for the payment period is LIBOR.[1] In each of these instances the floating rate note technique either does not work or is an awkward methodology to apply. So dealers employ a different methodology, described here.

First, recall the meaning of a forward interest rate. Consider an investor with a two-period investment horizon who is deciding between two alternate strategies: (1) placing his money in a two-period security (day count fraction α_2) promising an annual return of r_2, or (2) placing his funds in a one-period security (day count fraction α_1) that will return r_1 annually and then reinvesting the accrued funds for the remaining period (day count fraction α^f) at the new one-period rate. What one-period rate must prevail one period from today to make the wealth received from either strategy equal? Symbolize the annual equivalent of that rate by r^f. Then the answer to the question is provided by the solution of

$$(1 + \alpha_1 r_1)(1 + \alpha^f r^f) = (1 + \alpha_2 r_2)$$

In this case, the rate r^f is called the one-period forward rate, one period from today.

Notice that the above equation implies that the present value of $1 to be received two periods from today is $1/(1 + \alpha_2 r_2)$, symbolized by F_2. This present value is also represented by $1/[(1 + \alpha_1 r_1)(1 + \alpha^f r^f)]$. Symbolizing $1/(1 + \alpha_1 r_1)$ by F_1, the following relation is implied.

---

1. The dealer will discount cash flows by the Eurodollar rates, because they are the rates at which he can borrow or lend. In essence, Eurodollar market rates represent the dealer's opportunity costs and thus his required rates of return.

$$F_2 = F_1\left(\frac{1}{1 + \alpha^f r^f}\right)$$

Consequently, given the F_1 and F_2 discount factors, the one-period forward rate one period from today is obtained as

$$r^f = \left(\frac{F_1}{F_2} - 1\right)\frac{1}{\alpha^f}$$

We conclude that forward rates can be inferred from the zero-coupon yield curve (the spot yield curve) or, studying the last equation, from the discount factors implied by the spot yield curve.

Once the forward rates are obtained from the discount factors, they are used to forecast the floating leg's cash flows. These forecasted flows are discounted back to obtain the present value of the floating leg. The next step is to find the fixed rate that equates the present value of the fixed leg's cash flows to the present value of the floating leg. In the discounting process, the fixed and floating legs are no longer treated as bonds paying their face value on maturity, but instead are viewed as a sequence of interest payments. Call this pricing methodology the *forward rate pricing approach* or the *forecast rate pricing method*.

If the forward rate pricing approach is to be of more general applicability than the floating rate note approach, then, at the very least, it must be able to price the swaps discussed in the previous chapter. The nature of these swaps is that the term of the floating rate corresponds to the length of the payment period and the floating rate paid equals the required rate. For such swaps, the forward rate approach should provide the same value as the floating rate note approach. It does. To gain an understanding of the validity of this statement, consider a two-period fixed-for-floating swap. The swap's two segments have fractional day counts of α_1 and α_2. The rate set for the floating leg's first segment is r_1, and the forward rate for the second segment is r_2^f. The forward rate pricing method determines the fixed rate, c, from the following equation.

$$\frac{\alpha_1 c}{(1 + \alpha_1 r_1)} + \frac{\alpha_2 c}{(1 + \alpha_1 r_1)(1 + \alpha_2 r_2^f)} = \tag{16.1}$$

$$\frac{\alpha_1 r_1}{(1 + \alpha_1 r_1)} + \frac{\alpha_2 r_2^f}{(1 + \alpha_1 r_1)(1 + \alpha_2 r_2^f)}$$

Add 1 to the numerator of the second term on each side of the equation to obtain

$$\frac{\alpha_1 c}{(1 + \alpha_1 r_1)} + \frac{\alpha_2 c + 1}{(1 + \alpha_1 r_1)(1 + \alpha_2 r_2^f)} = \qquad (16.2)$$

$$\frac{\alpha_1 r_1}{(1 + \alpha_1 r_1)} + \frac{\alpha_2 r_2^f + 1}{(1 + \alpha_1 r_1)(1 + \alpha_2 r_2^f)} = 1$$

Equation (16.2) is the determining equation for the fixed coupon by the floating rate note method. The fact that (16.2) can be obtained from (16.1) or (16.1) from (16.2) points to the equivalency of the two pricing methodologies in determining the fixed rate of the generic swap.

Illustration of the Forward Pricing Methodology

Amortizing swaps are usually related to real estate financing. For example, a real estate firm purchases a commercial property for $120 million. The financing is to be composed of $20 million of equity and $100 million of debt. The firm wishes to finance through fixed rate debt and concludes that its most attractive alternative along these lines is to borrow floating at six-month LIBOR and swap into fixed rate payments. The firm's management forecasts that the building's rents will be sufficient to amortize the debt in ten semiannual $10 million payments. The swap's notional principal should therefore be reduced by $10 million every six months, and the swap's payments must reflect this fact. Trade date and effective date are 3/7/94 and 3/9/94, respectively. The swap's maturity date is 3/9/99. On trade date, spot six-month LIBOR is 4.71%. The dealer must determine the fixed rate to be received against his LIBOR payments. The fixed rate day count is 30/360; the floating rate day count is actual/360. Table 16.1 contains the necessary input data.

The forward rates necessary to estimate the floating leg's cash payments are listed in the last column of Table 16.1. These forward rates are implied by the discount factors listed in the next-to-last column. For example, the implied six-month forward rate for the payment period beginning on 3/9/95, call it $r_{3/95}^f$, is found by solving

$$0.9521 = 0.9765 \left[\frac{1}{1 + r_{3/95}^f \left(\dfrac{181}{360}\right)} \right]$$

Table 16.1   Information for Pricing an Amortizing Swap

Payment Date	30/360 Day Count*	Actual/360 Day Count*	Discount Factor	Spot or Forward Rate**
9/9/94	180	184	0.9765	4.71%
3/9/95	180	181	0.9521	5.10%
9/11/95	182	186	0.9265	5.35%
3/11/96	180	182	0.9023	5.31%
9/9/96	178	182	0.8790	5.24%
3/10/97	181	182	0.8565	5.20%
9/9/97	179	183	0.8346	5.16%
3/9/98	180	181	0.8137	5.11%
9/9/98	180	184	0.7929	5.13%
3/9/99	180	181	0.7731	5.09%

*The day counts presented in each row are measured from the previous payment date.

**These forward rate estimates have been rounded to the nearest full basis point.

for $r^f_{3/95}$. In this case, $r^f_{3/95} = 5.10\%$. Employing these forward rates, forecasts of the swap's floating rate payments are generated. Table 16.2 contains these payments along with their present values and the present value of the entire floating leg.

Table 16.2   The Amortizing Swap's Forecasted Floating Rate Payments

Payment Date	Forecasted Floating Payment	Present Value of Payment
9/9/94	0.0471 × (184/360) × 100* = $2,407,333	$2,350,761
3/9/95	0.0510 × (181/360) × 90 = 2,307,750	2,197,209
9/11/95	0.0535 × (186/360) × 80 = 2,211,333	2,048,800
3/11/96	0.0531 × (182/360) × 70 = 1,879,150	1,695,557
9/9/96	0.0524 × (182/360) × 60 = 1,589,467	1,397,141
3/10/97	0.0520 × (182/360) × 50 = 1,314,444	1,125,822
9/9/97	0.0516 × (183/360) × 40 = 1,049,200	875,662
3/9/98	0.0511 × (181/360) × 30 = 770,758	627,166
9/9/98	0.0513 × (184/360) × 20 = 524,400	415,797
3/9/99	0.0509 × (181/360) × 10 = 255,914	197,847
		Total Present Value = $12,931,762

*Notional principal is given in millions.

To compute the fixed swap rate, solve the following equation.

$$R\sum_{j=1}^{10} (FDCF_j) \cdot F_j \cdot N_{j-1} = 12{,}931{,}762$$

where R, $FDCF_j$, F_j, and N_{j-1}, respectively, represent the fixed rate, the fixed day count fraction, the discount factor for the jth payment date, and the notional principal existing immediately after payment date $j - 1$. (For the first payment date, the $(j - 1)$ notional principal is that existing on the effective date.) Inserting numbers into the equation gives

$$R\begin{bmatrix} 0.9765 \left(\dfrac{180}{360}\right) 100 + 0.9521 \left(\dfrac{180}{360}\right) 90 + \\[2mm] 0.9265 \left(\dfrac{182}{360}\right) 80 + 0.9023 \left(\dfrac{180}{360}\right) 70 + \\[2mm] 0.8790 \left(\dfrac{178}{360}\right) 60 + 0.8565 \left(\dfrac{181}{360}\right) 50 + \\[2mm] 0.8346 \left(\dfrac{179}{360}\right) 40 + 0.8137 \left(\dfrac{180}{360}\right) 30 + \\[2mm] 0.7929 \left(\dfrac{180}{360}\right) 20 + 0.7731 \left(\dfrac{180}{360}\right) 10 \end{bmatrix} = 12.931762$$

The solution is $R = 5.19\%$. Adding a dealer profit margin to this figure gives the receive fixed swap rate for this amortizing swap.

A Comment on Pricing an Amortizing Swap

The amortizing swap could have been priced by the floating rate note method. To use the method, work backward from the last payment date to arrive at the conclusion that on the first payment date the floating bond's ex-interest payment value equals its face value. Notice that on the next-to-last payment date, the $10 million balance must have a present value equal to $10 million by virtue of the reset. Add to this amount the $10 million amortization payment, and the ex-interest payment value on the next-to-last payment date is $20 million. Now step back to the second-to-last payment date. By identical reasoning you can conclude that the ex-interest payment value is $30 million. Continuing backward to the first payment date demonstrates that the ex-interest payment value on that date is $100 million. By application of the floating rate note method to the first interest payment plus the $100 million principal value, the present value of the floating leg, valued for the effective date, must be $100 million. To complete the analysis, use the discount factors in Table 16.1 to express the present value of the fixed rate bond, with amortizing payments of $10 million and coupon rate R. Set that expression equal to $100 million, and solve for R.

An Example of a Swap for Which the Forward Rate Method Must Be Used

Suppose an insurance company offers an annuity that promises to pay, every six months, a rate based upon the five-year T-note rate, as published in the Federal Reserve's H.15 report. The firm has invested the front-end annuity payments in high-yielding corporate bonds. To hedge its risk, it considers entering into a fixed-for-floating swap, where it pays fixed and receives from the dealer semiannual payments based on whatever the five-year T-note rate is determined to be on the reset date. To price this swap, the dealer must first value the floating leg's payments. To do so, he obtains the forward rates implied by the U.S. Treasury spot yield curve and uses these forward rates to forecast the cash flows that will be paid to the swap counterparty. The present value of these forecasted cash flows is arrived at by applying the discount factors obtained from Eurodollar futures prices.[2] If the swap's maturity is greater than seven years, after which point the futures are illiquid, these discount rates must be blended with those implied by the par swap rate curve (see Chapter 15). Having obtained the present value of the forecasted floating rate payments, find the fixed rate that provides the same present value for the fixed rate leg. Add a dealer spread to obtain the swap rate.

To illustrate the problem, suppose the dealer agrees to pay, semiannually, the two-year fixed rate, determined on the reset date (this is the floating leg of the swap), in exchange for a fixed rate, to be received semiannually, on $100 million notional principal over a three-year period (this is the fixed leg of the swap). For the purpose of this example, consider the two-year rate that is to be paid semiannually to be measured as the rate offered for two-year Eurodollar deposits on the reset date. The payment dates are 9/9/94, 3/9/95, 9/11/95,

---

2. Remember, the dealer will discount cash flows based on Treasury rates by the Eurodollar rates, because the latter are the rates at which he can borrow or lend.

3/11/96, 9/9/96, and 3/10/97. On 3/7/94, the trade date, the two-year rate that applies to the first segment of the floating leg is set at 5.15%. The effective date is 3/9/94. Both floating and fixed rate day counts are actual/360.

To price the swap, we must compute the floating leg's present value. In order to do that, we generate forecasts of the floating leg's cash payments. This entails the computation of two-year forward rates. A two-year forward rate for any period is obtained by recalling that discount factors, separated by two years, imply a two-year forward rate. Using the data presented in Table 16.1, the forward rate for the two-year period commencing on 9/9/94, $r^f_{9/94}$, is obtained by comparing the discount factors of 9/9/94 and 9/9/96. In particular, solve the following equation for $r^f_{9/94}$:

$$.8790 = .9765 \left[\cfrac{1}{1 + r^f_{9/94}\left(\cfrac{731}{360}\right)} \right]$$

$$r^f_{9/94} = 5.463\%$$

This is the two-year rate expected to be observed on 9/7/94, the reset date. It applies to the floating payment to be made at the end of the six-month period that begins on 9/9/94 and ends on 3/9/95. So this rate applies to the 3/9/95 payment date. The remaining forward rates are obtained in an identical manner. They are listed in column 3 of Table 16.3. Each two-year forward rate is listed alongside the appropriate payment date, so $r^f_{9/94}$ is next to the 3/9/95 payment date.

The corresponding estimates of cash flows and present values are presented in columns 5 and 6. The present value of the floating leg is $15,004,946. Solving for the fixed rate that equates the present value of the fixed leg's payments to $15,004,946 gives 5.38%.

16.2 Other Swap Structures

To this point, three types of swaps have been used in our discussion of pricing, valuation, and hedging: the generic fixed-for-floating, an amortizing swap, and a fixed-for-floating, where the floating rate is pegged to a maturity different from the length of the payment period. As one would suspect, since swaps are an over-the-counter

Table 16.3 Fixed for Constant Maturity Floating Rate Swap

(1) Payment Date	(2) Discount Factor	(3) Forward Rate*	(4) Actual Day Count**	(5) Floating Payment	(6) Present Value
9/9/94	0.9765	5.150%	184	$2,632,222	$2,570,365
3/9/95	0.9521	5.463%	181	2,746,675	2,615,109
9/11/95	0.9265	5.489%	186	2,835,983	2,627,539
3/11/96	0.9023	5.438%	182	2,749,211	2,480,613
9/9/96	0.8790	5.384%	182	2,721,911	2,392,560
3/10/97	0.8565	5.355%	182	2,707,250	2,318,760
				Total Present Value =	$15,004,946

*The forward rates have been rounded to the neareat one-tenth of a basis point.

**The day count presented in each row is measured from the previous payment date.

instrument, there are many forms of swaps. This section describes some other structures that are frequently encountered.

Accreting Swap

Like amortizing swaps, accreting swaps are often tied to real estate finance. However, as the name implies, the notional principal of the accreting swap increases during the life of the swap (unlike that of the amortizing swap). A commercial developer might negotiate a floating rate bank loan against which he will draw funds as construction of the project progresses. The loan balance increases during the life of the loan. To hedge the interest rate exposure, the developer enters into a swap in which he agrees to pay fixed and receive floating on a notional principal that increases in step with the loan balance.

Rollercoaster Swap

To hedge a floating rate loan in which the balance first increases and then diminishes, one would swap fixed payments for floating rate payments based on a notional principal that initially accretes and subsequently amortizes. This type of swap is referred to as a rollercoaster swap.

Basis Swap

A financial institution raises funds by issuing 30-day commercial paper and lends these funds out at six-month LIBOR plus a spread.

The risk is that the difference between six-month LIBOR and the 30-day commercial paper rate will narrow—i.e., that the basis will close. To hedge this risk, the institution may enter into a basis swap, in which it pays six-month LIBOR and receives the 30-day commercial paper index as reported in the Federal Reserve H.15 report.

Zero-Coupon Swap

A zero-coupon swap is an extreme example of an off-market swap. The fixed swap rate is zero. If the firm is receiving fixed and paying three-month LIBOR on a zero-coupon swap, then the firm will receive a single payment at the termination or the inception of the swap. The amount to be received is calculated by applying the present value methodology previously described. If the lump-sum payment is to be deferred, then find the amount that has a discounted value equal to the present value of the floating leg's projected cash payments; these projections are obtained through use of the implied forward rates. The zero-coupon swap in which the fixed side pays at termination would be employed by a firm that is cash short until termination day.

Forward Swap

A forward swap is an interest rate swap that is scheduled to begin accruing interest at a future date. The forward swap is attractive to prospective debt issuers who find the current level of forward swap rates acceptable and expect a rate increase prior to issuance date. It enables the issuer to fix his debt cost without being forced to fund immediately. For example, a firm intending to borrow $100 million in two months for a period of five years wishes to lock in the cost of that debt. It enters into a forward swap in which it agrees to pay fixed semiannually and receive six-month LIBOR on $100 million of notional principal for a five-year period; the effective date will correspond to the date of debt issuance, two months from the trade date, and the floating rate will be set two days prior to the effective date. In two months, the firm may borrow $100 million floating rate debt at six-month LIBOR and simultaneously take down the swap on which it pays fixed semiannually and receives six-month LIBOR. The forward swap enables the firm to lock in today the fixed swap rate forecasted for the date of debt issuance.

Alternatively, the firm might simply unwind its forward swap commitment on the trade date and issue fixed rate debt. If rates have risen prior to the trade date, then the fixed pay–receive floating swap will have a positive present value. Termination of the forward swap captures this present value for the firm. The gain will serve to offset the higher rate that its new debt must carry. If, in the interim between the forward swap's trade date and issuance day, rates have fallen, then the pay fixed swap will have negative present value. The loss serves to reduce the gains the firm obtains by issuing its debt at the lower market rate. The choice between taking down the swap on the forward contract or simply terminating the forward swap and issuing fixed rate debt depends on the relative issuance costs.

Forward swaps, sometimes called *delayed start swaps,* are priced using the same methodology applied to the other types of swaps previously described. Taking into account the delayed payment period, find the fixed swap rate that equates the present value of the fixed leg's payments that begin at that future date to the present value of the floating leg's future payments. The objective of the pricing is to find a swap rate that gives the forward swap contract a zero dollar value when initiated.

The forward swap hedge of the future issuance of corporate debt is not a perfect hedge, for the change in the forward swap's value depends upon the change in the fixed swap rate. It is possible that the corporation's cost of debt increases while swap rates remain unchanged or even decline. In such cases, the forward swap hedge may be of no help in reducing the risk of higher financing costs, and may even be harmful.

A Digression on Spread Locks

The type of basis risk just mentioned, which may result in the forward swap turning out to be a less than perfect hedge, is common in hedging programs. After all, many prospective corporate issues are hedged with Treasury futures. However, there is an added dimension of risk in using the forward swap contract—not large in size, but nevertheless a risk. Specifically, the swap's spread over the corresponding T-note rate may change independently of the level of the T-note rate. This swap spread can be viewed as representative of the general level of the corporate credit spread for Eurodollar funding.

A *spread lock* is a forward transaction that permits the debt issuer to fix the spread independent of any hedge on the underlying Treasury rate. In a spread lock, the debt issuer agrees to consummate a swap at a future date at a fixed spread from the appropriate T-note rate.

The underlying T-note rate is not fixed at initiation of the spread lock contract, but must be set no later than the beginning of the date that the swap is to be taken down. When the underlying T-note rate is fixed, the fixed spread rate is added to it to obtain the swap's fixed rate.

A spread lock may be an attractive choice for an issuer who believes T-note rates may fall between today and issue date but is concerned about an increase in swap spreads. Note that the spread lock hedges the changes only on the general credit spread and not on the firm-specific credit spread. For example, the firm's LIBOR margin may increase while all other firms' margins remain constant.

Asset Swaps

Interest rate swaps are also used to alter an asset's cash flows to a desired pattern. For example, a firm has floating rate assets and fixed rate liabilities. It wishes to match up the maturity of its assets with that of its liabilities. We are now aware that an asset-liability match can be achieved through a liability swap; the firm would pay floating and receive fixed. However, an asset swap may also be executed to achieve an asset-liability maturity balance. The firm would pay the cash flow from its floating rate assets to the swap dealer and, in return, receive fixed rate payments.

Index Amortization Swaps (IAS)

An *index amortization swap* (IAS) is one that is designed to compete with various types of mortgage securities. It is a swap whose notional principal depends upon the path of an interest rate index, as does the principal of a mortgage.[3] Unlike a mortgage, the link between the amortization of the IAS's principal and the level of interest rates is precisely defined; it is not subject to the uncertain demographic factors that contribute to a mortgage's amortization rate.

We describe the salient features of an IAS by example. An investor, perhaps a bank, enters into a five-year IAS to receive a fixed rate of 6% and pay three-month LIBOR. Payments are quarterly. The swap's notional balance is not subject to amortization for the first two years; this period is known as the swap's *lockout period*. Subsequent to the

---

3. The most popular IAS indices are three-month LIBOR, six-month LIBOR, the seven-year Constant Maturity Treasury (CMT) rate, and the ten-year CMT rate. The latter two rates are published in the Federal Reserve's H.15 report.

lockout period, the principal declines according to an agreed-upon schedule. The quarterly amortization rate applied to the swap's remaining balance is determined on each reset date by the difference between the seven-year Constant Maturity Treasury (CMT) rate and a base rate. The base rate equals the level of the seven-year CMT rate on the swap's trade date. It is equal to 7%. To avoid uneconomical administrative costs, the fixed rate payer may call the swap's balance at par, if that balance falls below a minimum level. This is called a cleanup provision. In our example, the minimum balance is set at 15% of the original principal. An amortization schedule for this IAS is presented in Table 16.4.

If the interest rate differential on a reset date falls between the rates appearing in the schedule, then the amortization rate is determined by linearly interpolating between the adjacent amortization rates. If the interest rate differential is +1.75%, then the amortization rate is 8.84%.

The average life figures that appear in Table 16.4 are calculated under the assumption that the interest rate differential remains constant over the life of the swap. Each of these numbers is obtained by multiplying the time to payment by the fraction of the original principal that the payment represents, and summing over all such products. The average life does not represent the swap's expected life, because the interest rate differential is unlikely to remain constant. In fact, the informational content of such calculations is difficult to decipher. However, the industry has adopted this method to describe the swap's features vis-à-vis another swap.

The pricing methodologies described earlier in this chapter and in the previous chapter are inappropriate for IAS valuation. They would consistently overvalue the receive fixed IAS. The reason is that

Table 16.4　An IAS Amortization Schedule

Seven-Year CMT Rate Less the Base Rate	Quarterly Amortization Rate	Swap's Average Life (Implied by the Amortization Rate)
− 1.50%	100.00%	2.0 years
0.00%	17.65%	3.0 years
+ 1.50%	11.26%	3.5 years
+ 2.00%	6.42%	4.0 years
+ 2.50%	2.84%	4.5 years
+ 3.00%	0.00%	5.0 years

the IAS swap, like a mortgage, is short an option—actually, short two types of options. If the seven-year CMT rate falls, the amortization rate increases. This event resembles that of the homeowner prepaying—essentially exercising his call option to prepay. If the seven-year CMT rate increases, the amortization rate declines. It is as if the payer of fixed on the swap elects to exercise a put option that allows him to protect the principal amount, upon which he will continue to pay a fixed rate that is now below the market rate. A correct pricing method is that which is applied to interest rate securities with embedded options. It was illustrated in Chapter 7 for callable bonds and bonds with sinking fund provisions. Part IV, which deals with mortgage derivatives, further examines this pricing technique.

Chapter *17*

Options on Swaps

T*HE NATURAL* evolution of markets would dictate that once swaps became generally accepted as risk management devices, it was time to offer options on swaps. In this chapter, various types of options on swaps are described, and their applications in forming desired payment profiles are examined. We begin with some definitions and terminology regarding options on swaps, then turn to payment profiles when options on swaps are used in conjunction with swaps and/or other debt instruments. A pricing parity relation for swaptions is explained, and then the pricing of a swaption is illustrated.

17.1 Definitions and Terminology

Some options are embedded in swaps. For example, a *callable swap* contains an option that grants the fixed rate payer the right, but not the obligation, to terminate the swap. The payer of fixed will exercise the option if rates fall. This permits him to terminate the current swap and enter into a new swap in which he pays a lower fixed rate. A *putable swap* contains an option granting the fixed rate receiver the right to cancel the swap. If rates rise, the receiver of fixed will exercise his right to terminate the swap and enter into a new swap in which he receives a higher fixed rate.

A *swaption* is a stand-alone option granting the owner the right to enter into a swap. Though both American and European swaptions are traded, most are European. A call swaption gives the holder the right to receive fixed at a predetermined rate, the strike rate. If the swaption gives the holder the right to receive fixed, then it will be exercised only if the fixed rate on new swaps is below the strike rate. If rates fall, the swaption holder has the opportunity to exercise and enter into a swap to receive fixed at the strike rate—which is higher than the fixed rate on new swaps. In contrast, a put swaption grants the owner the right to enter into a swap in which he will pay fixed at the strike rate and receive floating. Exercise will occur only if the pay fixed rate on new swaps is above the strike rate. In that event, the put swaption owner will exercise to enter into a swap, paying fixed at the strike rate, which is below the current market rate.

One cautionary note: It is somewhat dangerous to discuss swaptions using put-call terminology. The reason is that, while many in the trade appear to accept the above put-call swaption definitions, some do not. (See Brown and Smith 1990; Miron and Swannell 1991.) There are traders and academics who will refer to a swaption that grants the right to pay fixed as a call and one that grants the right to receive fixed as a put. They reason that because "buying a swap" means paying fixed, then an option that gives the holder the right to buy a swap should be termed a call—that would be consistent with the way calls are thought of in other financial markets. Analogously, since "selling a swap" means receiving fixed, then a swaption that grants the owner the right to sell the swap should be referred to as a put, for consistency. Clearly, a conservative approach in trading swaptions is to state whether you are interested in purchasing or selling a swaption that gives the owner (buyer) the right to receive fixed (receiver swaption) or pay fixed (payer swaption). This is the prevailing custom.

17.2 Forming Payment Distributions with Swaptions and with Options Embedded in Swaps

Callable Debt into Noncallable Debt

A firm has a bond outstanding that pays a k percent annual coupon, has eight years to maturity, and can be called at par in three years. To transform the bond's future payment stream into one that matches that of a noncallable bond paying k percent per year, it sells a European swaption granting the buyer the right to receive fixed at an annual rate of k percent and to pay floating on a five-year swap. The swaption's expiration date coincides with the date that the bond becomes callable—in three years. If at the end of three years the fixed swap rate is lower than k, the swaption will be exercised. The bond issuer then assumes the obligation to pay fixed at k and receive floating. (The swaption holder receives fixed and pays floating.) In response to the swaption exercise, the issuer calls the outstanding debt, paying the par value with funds raised through borrowing at the floating rate.[1] The issuer pays the floating rate on its external debt and receives the floating rate on the swap through the eighth year. The net result is debt with a fixed rate of k for eight years. Table 17.1 summarizes the positions and actions taken in response to different interest rate scenarios.

Why might the corporation choose to synthesize the fixed rate debt in this manner rather than simply issuing eight-year noncallable debt at the start? Because it sees an arbitrage opportunity. The bond buyers may be selling the embedded option in the callable bond at a lower premium than the swaption premium. However, in today's markets, the more frequently cited reason for selling the receiver swaption is to monetize the value of the embedded call option. Specifically, if the corporation has decided to call the debt because rates are

Table 17.1 Callable Debt into Noncallable Debt

Rates on Swaption's Exercise Date	Rates Lower	Rates Higher
Position of Firm		
Callable Debt	Issuer calls debt, paying its par value to bondholders with funds raised by borrowing at six-month LIBOR.	No call of debt. Issuer continues to pay k fixed on outstanding debt.
Short a Receiver Swaption	Swaption is exercised by holder. Issuer is required to enter a five-year swap, paying k fixed and receiving six-month LIBOR.	Swaption unexercised.
Issuer's Net Payments	k	k

1. Selling a European swaption against the callable debt is theoretically nonoptimal. After all, the issuer purchased an embedded American call on that debt but is selling only a European swaption. To sell an American swaption for exercise beginning at the end of the third year, the issuer would have to fix the maturity date of the swap, making the swap's length (tenor) variable. This means that if the swaption buyer exercises at the end of year three, he receives fixed on a five-year swap, but should he exercise at the end of year six, he receives fixed on a two-year swap. While this solution to the debt transformation problem may be aesthetically appealing, it is not economical. The reason is that this type of American swaption would be far from the norm in terms of design and desirability and thus difficult to trade. If it is difficult to trade, it is difficult to sell in the first place.

below k, then it sells a European swaption with a strike rate of k and an expiration date that coincides with the corporation's planned call date. The premium obtained for the swaption represents the present value of the savings that could be obtained from refinancing the debt at a fixed rate lower than k. By selling the swaption and continuing to pay k, because of the actions outlined in Table 17.1, the corporation has decided to take its refinancing gains now.

Putable Debt into Nonputable Debt

A putable bond gives its owner the right, but not the obligation, to sell the bond back to the issuer at a predetermined price, usually par. If rates rise, driving the bond's price below par, the put option is likely to be exercised. Suppose the corporation has a bond outstanding that pays an annual rate of k, matures in eight years, and is putable at par in three years. The firm has essentially issued nonputable debt and sold a put on that debt. To transform this debt into nonputable bonds, the firm buys a swaption, exercisable in three years, in which the underlying swap pays fixed at an annual rate of k for five years and receives floating.[2] The actions taken by the involved parties in reaction to the different interest rate levels result in the firm paying a fixed rate k for eight years. The positions and actions are delineated in Table 17.2.

Callable Debt into Floating Rate Debt

To transform the firm's debt, maturing in ten years, callable in five, and paying k percent annually, into floating rate debt, the firm enters into a ten-year swap to receive k and pay floating. The swap agreement grants the counterparty to the corporation the option to terminate after five years. The positions and actions appropriate to each position in a particular interest rate environment are listed in Table 17.3.

Since the counterparty has the option to terminate the swap, the firm must await that party's exercise before calling the debt issue.

Putable Debt into Floating Rate Debt

To transform a firm's fixed rate debt that pays k annually, matures in ten years, and is putable in five years, the firm enters into a ten-year swap to receive fixed at k and pay floating. The swap agreement

---

2. Theoretically, to achieve complete protection against the short put position embedded in the bond, the corporation must purchase an American swaption. The swaption could be exercised on any day between the end of the third and eighth years on a swap with a fixed maturity date, which means a variable swap tenor.

Table 17.2   Putable Debt into Nonputable Debt

Rates on Swaption's Exercise Date	Rates Lower	Rates Higher
Position of Firm		
Putable Debt	Not exercised. Issuer continues to pay *k*.	Exercised. Firm borrows at six-month LIBOR to pay par value on the debt put to it.
Long a Payer Swaption	Swaption is not exercised.	Swaption is exercised into a swap to pay *k* and receive six-month LIBOR.
Issuer's Net Payments	*k*	*k*

Table 17.3   Callable Debt into Floating Rate Debt

Rates on Exercise Date	Rates Lower	Rates Higher
Position of Firm		
Callable Debt	Issuer calls debt, paying its par value to bond holders with funds raised by borrowing six-month LIBOR.	No call of debt. Issuer continues to pay *k* fixed on outstanding debt.
Swap that pays fixed and receives floating and grants the counterparty the right to terminate after five years.	Swap is terminated by counterparty.	Option remains unexercised by counterparty. Corporation continues to receive *k* fixed and pay six-month LIBOR.
Issuer's Net Payments	Six-month LIBOR	Six-month LIBOR

grants the firm the option to terminate the swap after five years. The entries in Table 17.4 demonstrate that these transactions create synthetic floating rate debt.

17.3 Pricing Swaptions

A Pricing Parity Formula for Swaptions

Just as there is a parity relation for European options on stocks and forwards, there is a parity relation for European swaptions. In

Table 17.4   Putable Debt into Floating Rate Debt

Rates on Exercise Date	Rates Lower	Rates Higher
Position of Firm		
Putable Debt	Put option not exercised by bond holders. Firm continues to pay *k*.	Exercise of put option by bond holders. Firm borrows at six-month LIBOR to pay off bond holders.
Swap to receive fixed and pay floating. The firm holds an option to terminate the swap.	Firm does not exercise its option. It continues to receive *k* and pay six-month LIBOR.	Firm exercises its option to terminate the swap.
Issuer's Net Payments	Six-month LIBOR	Six-month LIBOR

particular, the following relation holds with regard to swaptions:

$$\begin{array}{c} premium\ on\ a \\ receiver\ swaption \end{array} - \begin{array}{c} premium\ on\ a \\ payer\ swaption \end{array} = \begin{array}{c} value\ of\ a\ forward\ swap \\ that\ receives\ fixed \\ and\ pays\ floating \end{array} \quad (17.1)$$

where the fixed rates on the forward swap and on both swaptions are identical and equal to k, and both swaptions expire on the same date. In addition, the swap on which the forward contract is written has the same effective date, and is identical in all other respects, to those deliverable on the swaptions.

PROOF.   Denote the premiums on the receiver and payer swaptions by C and P, respectively. Symbolize by V_F the value of the swap. Form a portfolio by purchasing a swaption to receive fixed, selling a swaption to pay fixed, and selling forward the receive fixed swap that is deliverable on both swaptions. *Selling* the receive fixed swap commits you to pay fixed. The current cash flows from these transactions amount to

$$-C + P + V_F = current\ portfolio\ value \quad (17.2)$$

Table 17.5 summarizes the future cash flows to this portfolio. The symbol k^* represents the fixed rate on a par swap having the same tenor as the swap underlying both swaptions and that deliverable on the for-

Table 17.5 Future Cash Flows of the Parity Portfolio

Position	$k^* \le k$	$k^* > k$
Long a swaption to receive k and pay floating.	Exercise. You receive k and pay floating.	No exercise.
Short a swaption in which long pays k and receives floating.	No exercise.	Exercised by long. You receive k and pay floating.
Forward swap that commits you to pay k and receive floating.	You pay k and receive floating.	You pay k and receive floating.
Net cash flows	0	0

ward swap contract. This rate, k^*, is observed on the swaptions' expiration date, which is the same as the forward's delivery date.

Since the portfolio's value generates zero cash flows in each future state, the no-riskless-arbitrage condition requires that its current value must be zero, i.e., $-C + P + V_F = 0$. This implies that (17.1) holds.[3]

Exactly Pricing a Swaption: An Example

A swaption can be valued in the same way as any other interest rate option. At each node of an arbitrage-free tree of one-period interest rates consistent with the existing swap spot rate curve, place the underlying swap's net cash payment. Calculate the discounted value of expected future payments for each of the swaption's expiration dates. Start at the expiration date nodes, and place the exercise values of the swaption at the appropriate nodes. The swaption's exercise value is the maximum of zero and the underlying swap's value at that node. Discount back these values, weighted by the risk neutral probabilities of occurrence, to arrive at the swaption's current value. A three-period interest rate tree is depicted in Figure 17.1. The risk neutral probability of an up move or a down move is 0.5.

In this interest rate environment, we wish to price a one-period swaption on a two-period swap to receive fixed at 15% and pay the floating one-period rate on $100 of notional principal. The underlying swap's effective date is $t = 1$; it matures at $t = 3$. The swap's cash flows are calculated at the $t = 2$ and $t = 3$ nodes by computing the

---

3. The parity relation just proved abstracts from all transactions costs, including the spread between the dealer's fixed receive rate and fixed pay rate.

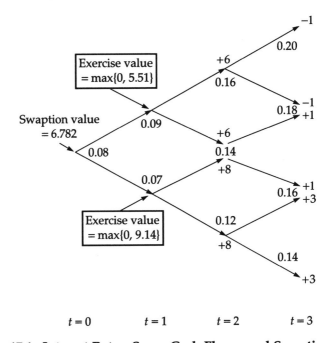

Figure 17.1 Interest Rates, Swap Cash Flows, and Swaption Value

difference between the fixed rate of 15% and the one-period rate at the previous node. For example, the swap's cash flow at $t = 3$, given a one-period rate at the previous node of 0.16, amounts to $(0.15 - 0.16) \times 100$. The swap's discounted values at $t = 1$ are shown inside the max operators. They are used to determine the swaption's value on exercise date. The present value of 5.51 is arrived at by computing:

$$0.5\left[\frac{+6}{1.09} + \frac{-1}{(1.09)(1.16)}\right] + 0.5\left[\frac{+6}{1.09} + \frac{+1}{(1.09)(1.14)}\right] = 5.51$$

The swaption's value at $t = 0$ is obtained by discounting its expected value at $t = 1$:

$$\frac{1}{1.08}[0.5(5.51) + 0.5(9.14)] = 6.782$$

This is quoted as a percentage of notional principal, i.e., 678 basis points.

PART IV

Mortgage Derivatives

Chapter **18**

The Underlying Instruments and Market Characteristics

AS IS TRUE of other derivative instruments, an understanding of mortgage derivatives requires some familiarity with the market for the underlying instrument, in this case mortgages and mortgage pass-throughs.[1] We begin this chapter by delineating the mortgage types that are eligible for the collateralization of mortgage pass-throughs guaranteed by federal agencies. Next, the entities that are responsible for the generation (origination) of most mortgages are identified and some mortgage market terminology is explained. The reasons for the development of the mortgage pass-through and the steps involved in its issuance are outlined. Distinctions are drawn between the pass-through programs of the various federal agencies. Market conventions relating to the trading and settlement of pass-throughs are detailed. The chapter concludes with a description of the clearing and settlement functions performed by the MBS Clearing Corporation, the Participants Trust Company, and the Depository Trust Company.

18.1 Mortgage Types

The Fixed Rate Mortgage (FRM)

A mortgage is a legal document representing a pledge of property to secure the payment of a debt. Prior to the closing, the time when

---

1. Strictly speaking, the mortgage pass-through is a derivative, for its return is derived from the return of the mortgage pool. However, when traders refer to the class of securities known as mortgage derivatives, the mortgage pass-through is generally not included. One reason is that its investors receive a pro rata share of the pool's cash flows, net of servicing, and guarantee fees.

the loan is legally formalized, several conditions are imposed to protect the lender's (mortgagee's) position. (1) If the ratio of the loan principal to the appraised value of the property (the loan-to-value ratio, or LTV) is considered high, the lender will require the borrower to purchase mortgage insurance. Hazard insurance must be purchased by the borrower to ensure the structure's value is protected. (2) In most cases, insurance premiums and property taxes must be remitted to the lender with the mortgage payments and are kept in an escrow account until disbursed to the appropriate parties. (3) Title insurance must be purchased to protect against an encumbrance or other defect that was not revealed in the title search. The mortgage loan or note is the actual payment schedule that the borrower (mortgagor) agrees to meet. The borrower is normally granted the right, without penalty, to prepay the balance of the loan prior to maturity.

The traditional mortgage loan has been a fixed rate, specified maturity, level payment loan. This remains the most widely used mortgage form and is usually referred to as a fixed rate mortgage (FRM). The level monthly payment per dollar of loan balance—the amount that is sufficient to pay interest on the outstanding balance and yet fully pay off the mortgage loan by the specified maturity date—is found by equating the present value of the monthly payments to the initial $1 loan balance. That is,

$$1 = \frac{X}{\left(1 + \dfrac{i}{12}\right)} + \frac{X}{\left(1 + \dfrac{i}{12}\right)^2} + \ldots + \frac{X}{\left(1 + \dfrac{i}{12}\right)^{12n}} \tag{18.1}$$

where X, i, and n, respectively, represent the level payment, the stipulated annual mortgage interest rate or mortgage coupon, and the years to maturity. Notice that in discounting, the annual mortgage rate is divided by 12 to arrive at a rate appropriate for discounting monthly flows, of which there are $12n$, the number of months to the maturity date. The right-hand side of (18.1) represents the present value of an X-dollar annuity and can be algebraically compressed.

$$1 = X \left[\frac{1 - \dfrac{1}{\left(1 + \dfrac{i}{12}\right)^{12n}}}{\left(\dfrac{i}{12}\right)} \right] \tag{18.2}$$

Solving for X gives

$$X = \frac{\left(\frac{i}{12}\right)1}{1 - \dfrac{1}{\left(1 + \dfrac{i}{12}\right)^{12n}}}$$

(18.3)

Since X represents the monthly payment per dollar of original principal, simply multiply X by the amount borrowed to arrive at the monthly mortgage payment. The difference between the monthly payment per dollar of original principal, X, and the interest due on the outstanding balance, $(i/12)B$, where B denotes the balance per dollar of original principal, represents that month's amortization (decrease) in the balance. On some future date, when there remain only m months to maturity, with $m < 12n$, the fraction of the original \$1 balance that remains is given by the present value of the remaining monthly payments, discounted at the mortgage coupon rate.[2] The remaining balance with m months to maturity is

---

2. To derive this result, simply start one payment prior to maturity. Let B_0 and B_1, respectively, represent the balances at maturity and one month prior to maturity. Starting with a balance of B_1, the amount owed one month later would be

$$B_0 = \left(1 + \frac{i}{12}\right)B_1 - X$$

The right-hand side represents the balance at one month prior to maturity plus the interest on that balance less the monthly payment at maturity. Since the loan must be paid off by maturity, $B_0 = 0$. Thus

$$B_1 = X / \left(1 + \frac{i}{12}\right)$$

Now step back another month to $m = 2$. Then

$$B_1 = \left(1 + \frac{i}{12}\right)B_2 - X$$

or

$$B_2 = \left[1 / \left(1 + \frac{i}{12}\right)\right]\left[X + B_1\right]$$

Substituting for B_1 gives

$$B_2 = X / \left(1 + \frac{i}{12}\right) + X / \left(1 + \frac{i}{12}\right)^2$$

Continuing in this manner, equation (18.4) is obtained.

$$B = \frac{X}{\left(1 + \dfrac{i}{12}\right)} + \frac{X}{\left(1 + \dfrac{i}{12}\right)^2} + \ldots + \frac{X}{\left(1 + \dfrac{i}{12}\right)^m} \qquad (18.4)$$

Some Alternative Mortgage Forms

Besides the traditional fixed rate, level payment mortgage, other mortgage forms are packaged together ("pooled"), securitized, and sold in the secondary market. A listing and brief descriptions of the types that make up the set securitized with the guarantees of the Government National Mortgage Association (GNMA, "Ginnie Mae"), the Federal Home Loan Mortgage Corporation (FHLMC, "Freddie Mac"), and the Federal National Mortgage Association (FNMA, "Fannie Mae")—perhaps the three most important players in the secondary market—are provided below.

Adjustable Rate Mortgage (ARM) The adjustable rate mortgage is designed to allow the mortgage rate to move, at predetermined intervals, in response to changes in an agreed-upon interest rate index. The impetus for the introduction of this loan form was to provide thrift and commercial banking institutions with assets whose interest rate sensitivity matched that of their deposits. Since a lower return would be required on an instrument with such risk-reducing properties, the interest rate costs to the borrower would be expected to be lower than those incurred under a fixed rate mortgage of similar maturity. The share of ARM originations (new mortgages) has ranged from 20% to 70% of total mortgage originations in recent years and is currently more than 40%. However, when mortgage rates are relatively low, ARM originations fall in favor of fixed rate originations.

Graduated Payment Mortgage (GPM) The monthly payment on a graduated payment mortgage is arranged to begin at a level that is relatively low in comparison with the payments on a fixed rate, level payment mortgage, and then increases in steps, annually, on dates corresponding to the anniversary of the first monthly payment date. After a stipulated period, often five or ten years from the mortgage's origination, the payment increases stop, and the remaining mortgage payments are set. The rate on the loan remains constant over the GPM's life; only the payments change. If the interest rate on a GPM is the same as that on an FRM with identical maturity, the initial payments on the GPM will be less than on the FRM, but the later payments will be higher. The major cause of the higher payments in later years of the GPM in comparison to those of the FRM is the policy of setting the initial payments on the GPM below the amounts necessary to cover the interest owed on the principal balance. The difference between the interest owed and the payments made in these early years adds to the mortgage balance—an occurrence referred to as *negative amortization*. An increasing balance results in increasing interest and amortization payments. This is necessary in order to pay off the loan in the scheduled time. The intent of the GPM is to make home owning affordable to young families in their early career years.

Growing Equity Mortgage (GEM)   A growing equity mortgage is one whose first monthly payment equals that of a level payment FRM with the same maturity and interest rate but then increases annually, at a stated percentage, over a predetermined number of years. Because of the increasing payments, the amortization schedule of a GEM provides for the borrowed principal to be repaid sooner than under an FRM with identical interest rate and maturity.

Buydown Mortgage   In a buydown mortgage, a third party, typically the builder of a home, provides funds to the lender that are used to reduce the borrower's monthly payments during the early years of the mortgage. The builder's goal is to assist the potential buyer to obtain financing, and in so doing, sell the house. The builder will often recapture part or all of the sum used to "buy down" the mortgage interest rate through a higher sale price than otherwise would have been obtained.

Balloon Mortgage   More popular than GPMs, GEMs, and buydown mortgages are five- and seven-year balloon mortgages. A five-year balloon mortgage is a level payment mortgage in which the monthly payments are based upon a 30-year amortization schedule. At the end of the five-year period, the borrower is required to repay the entire remaining principal balance—the balloon payment. When faced with a steep, rising yield curve, a homeowner who expects to move in a few years and wants fixed rate financing often opts for a balloon mortgage. The borrower can realize a significant reduction in interest payments in comparison to those that would be incurred under a long-term, fixed rate mortgage because the balloon is priced off of the short-term end of the yield curve. Balloon mortgages are inadmissible for GNMA securitization programs but are significant in the FNMA and FHLMC programs. For a balloon mortgage that is scheduled for inclusion in a FNMA or FHLMC pool, the agency guarantees that upon maturity the mortgagor will obtain financing at the then-existing market rate for a fixed rate, level payment mortgage. Depending on whether the balloon mortgage was written for five or seven years, the latter mortgage will have a life of 25 or 23 years.[3]

18.2 Mortgage Originators

In effect, there are three major groups of entities that generate (originate) mortgage loans: commercial banks, thrifts, and mortgage bankers. The thrift class is largely made up of savings and loans (S&Ls) along with a smattering of mutual saving banks. S&Ls are federally chartered and assume the legal structure of a corporation with ownership divided among common stock holders. Mutual savings banks are state chartered and are structured as cooperatives. Commercial banks and thrifts use their depositors' money, to varying degrees, to lend money in the mortgage origination process.

Like these other financial institutions, mortgage bankers (MBs) originate loans. However, the main source of an MB's financing is the commercial banking sector (although some of the larger MBs issue commercial paper to finance their activities). Whereas commercial banks, and especially thrifts, will retain a portion of the mortgages originated for their investment portfolios, MBs sell all the loans they originate. High turnover is their road to high profits, for they earn profits on mortgage origination fees, loan commitment fees, and servicing fees.

The period that begins with the borrower's loan application and extends to the time when the loans are sold is referred to as the *mortgage pipeline*. The activity of holding and financing the loans until their sale is called *warehousing the loans*. Obviously, while the loans are in the pipeline the holder of the loans is at risk. If the loans have been closed but not yet sold, there is interest rate risk. If the loans

---

3. Furthermore, borrowers often choose balloon mortgages because this form of financing allows them to qualify for a larger loan. To qualify for a mortgage that is to be securitized by FNMA or FHLMC, the borrower must satisfy, among other things, two payments-to-income criteria: 1) The sum of the monthly mortgage payment, property tax payment, and home insurance premium must not exceed 28% of the borrower's gross monthly income; and 2) The sum of the aforementioned items plus the monthly payments on any other debt, e.g., a car loan, cannot exceed 36% of the borrower's gross monthly income. The interest payments are generally lower on the balloon mortgage than on a 30-year fixed rate-level payment mortgage, as a consequence of the lower mortgage rate on the balloon. Thus for a given income level, the prospective homeowner can borrow a larger amount under a balloon mortgage and still meet the criteria.

have not been closed but have already been sold, then there is the risk that the potential borrower may walk away from the loan should interest rates fall prior to the closing. This latter type of risk is termed *fall-out risk*. Both types of risks should be hedged. As we know, there are a variety of ways to hedge the interest rate risk: forwards, futures, options, short sales in the spot U.S. Treasury market, etc. Hedging the fall-out risk is usually accomplished through the purchase of puts on interest rate instruments.

Subsequent to origination and sale, the mortgage must be serviced over the life of the loan. The servicing function entails the collection of principal, interest, and funds to be escrowed for the payment of taxes and insurance premiums on the property. The scheduled principal payments, interest, and unscheduled principal payments—i.e., mortgage prepayments—must be delivered in a timely fashion to the mortgage investors. This means that the servicer is responsible for advancing uncollected principal and interest payments. The servicing function also includes supervising the foreclosure on a property in the event of a default by the mortgagor and, in addition, periodically apprising borrowers and investors of the pertinent financial status of the mortgage, such as the current balance. For performing these activities on behalf of the investor, the servicer retains a small portion of the mortgage interest payment, called the servicing fee. The originator may choose to retain the servicing function or sell it to obtain the present value of the servicing function's future net income.

18.3 The Mortgage Pass-Through Certificate (MPT)

Broadening the secondary mortgage market is a way of expanding the source of capital to originators. By enhancing the transferability of mortgages, the pass-through security advanced this cause. The MPT security came into existence in 1968 when GNMA agreed to guarantee, for a fee, the *timely* payment of both the interest and principal of mortgages insured by the Federal Housing Authority (FHA) or guaranteed either by the Veterans Administration (VA) or the Farmers Home Administration (FmHA).[4] The GNMA guarantee is

---

4. FHA operates as a traditional insurer, collecting premiums from borrowers and paying losses to lenders. Its intent is to make housing affordable to low-income families. Because the lender is insured against losses, a lower down payment is required from the home buyer. VA and FmHA have the same affordability goal, but their clientele are veterans and farmers, respectively. In addition, VA and FmHA do not operate as insurance companies in the sense of collecting premiums. The funds that are needed to cover lender losses on the guaranteed loans are paid from U.S. government subsidies.

evidenced by the issuance of a security collateralized by the mortgage pool.

The procedures involved in the issuance of the GNMA mortgage pass-through, on an acceptable mortgage pool, can be generally described as follows:

1. An originator collects a group of FHA or VA or FmHA mortgages. The group, commonly referred to as the *pool*, must be fairly homogeneous in the characteristics that have the strongest effects on the probability that the mortgage will prepay and on when that event might occur. Though it is never easy, the greater the similarity of the component mortgages, the less difficult it is to obtain a sense of the future cash flow pattern that might be produced by a pool. The more predictable the cash flow stream, the higher the price of the security. Consequently, pools contain mortgages that have identical or very similar coupons, maturities, and collateral.

2. The mortgages are placed with a custodian, and GNMA assigns a pool number that uniquely identifies the type and term of the loans underlying the MPT to be issued.

3. For each dollar of mortgage principal in the pool, one dollar of MPT security principal is issued by GNMA. The security is issued in certificate form. Because the MPT is collateralized by the pool of mortgages, it is frequently referred to as a *mortgage-backed security* (MBS).

4. The MPT security is then sold by the originator or his agent to investors. The scheduled principal, interest, and any unscheduled payments (prepayments) are collected by the servicer from the mortgagor, and are "passed through" to the investors, i.e., the owners of the MPTs. The amount of interest received by the purchasers of the MPT is reduced by the servicing fee and the guarantee premium. The MPT coupon rate will be lower than the lowest mortgage coupon rate in the pool. If the stated coupon rate on the MPT was greater than that of the minimum mortgage rate in the pool, and if all mortgages except the one with the minimum rate prepaid, the servicer would be unable to meet the interest obligation on the MPT.

Under its original securitization program, GNMA I, GNMA extends its guarantee to MPTs issued on residential loans, manufactured home loans (often called mobile home loans), project loans, and the loans made to finance the construction plan of a project; all must be FHA-VA mortgages. Project loans comprise mortgages on multifamily rental apartments for low- to moderate-income families, hospitals, nursing homes, and retirement centers. Only fixed rate, level payment construction and project loans are acceptable for securitization by GNMA. For one- to four-family residences and mobile homes, FRMs, GPMs, GEMs, and buydowns are acceptable. In these pools, all mortgage coupons must be identical, 80% of the mortgages must have maturities within 30 months of the longest loan maturity, and 90% of the mortgages must have maturities of twenty years or more.

A more recent program, GNMA II, was designed to foster the formation of large, reasonably homogenous mortgage pools by combining the production of several originators of small mortgage pools into one multi-issuer pool, the theory being that larger security issues are more liquid than smaller ones and thus more attractive to potential investors. Under GNMA II, a central agent is given responsibility for combining the payments received on the several issues in a pool and writing a single check to the investor. In cases where the investor owns shares in more than one multi-issuer pool, the payments from all such pools would be combined into one payment to the investor. Only one- to four-family residence and mobile home mortgages, either FRMs, GPMs, GEMs, or ARMs, are acceptable for securitization under the GNMA II program. A 1% dispersion is permitted among the mortgage coupon rates that make up the pool. The dispersion among mortgage maturities is greater than that permitted under the GNMA I program.

While GNMA restricts its guarantee to MPTs issued on government-insured or -guaranteed mortgages—for the most part FHA-VA mortgages—FHLMC and FNMA provide guarantees for MPTs issued on pools of *conventional mortgages,* i.e., mortgages that are not insured or guaranteed by the government. FHLMC, originally a government agency and now a private corporation sponsored by the U.S. government, guarantees the timely payment of interest to the pass-through owner and the eventual payment of principal. FNMA, structured like FHLMC, guarantees the timely payment of both interest and principal to the pass-through owner. Both entities are overseen by the Department of Housing and Urban Development (HUD), and each has a $2.25 billion line of credit with the U.S. Treasury.

The process by which the originator of conventional mortgages obtains a FHLMC or FNMA pass-through is similar to that described for GNMA. The essential difference is that GNMA has agreed in advance to insure pass-throughs on FHA-VA mortgages, whereas FHLMC and FNMA examine the characteristics of the mortgage collateral to see if it meets the agency's criteria. Among the collateral characteristics for which guidelines are imposed is a maximum mortgage size (anything higher is kicked out of the pool), a maximum LTV ratio (80%) if there is no accompanying mortgage insurance, and a limit on the maximum maturity in the pool. In addition, there are limits on the dispersion of the component mortgages' coupon rates and maturities. If the mortgages do fit within the guidelines, then the mortgages are said to *conform* and are eligible for the agency's pass-through program.

The MPTs issued by FHLMC are named *participation certificates* (PCs). PCs issued on behalf of an originator are described as having been "swapped" by FHLMC for the mortgage pool, and the PCs are said to be issued under Freddie's Guarantor Program. On the other hand, if Freddie purchases mortgages from originators, pools them, and issues PCs on that pool, then the PCs are said to be issued under Freddie's Cash Program. The MPTs issued by FNMA are named *mortgage-backed securities* (MBSs). If they are issued on behalf of an originator, then those MBSs are described as being issued under Fannie's Swap Program. Fannie Mae also issues MBSs on pools of mortgages that it purchased for its own portfolio. In both Freddie's Guarantor Program and Fannie's Swap Program, a fee is charged for the agency's guarantee with respect to principal and interest payments. FRMs, GPMs, and ARMs on one- to four-family residences and multifamily rental properties are acceptable for securitization by both FHLMC and FNMA.

Nonconforming mortgages are often pooled by a large financial institution, pool insurance is normally purchased, and private label MPTs are issued and distributed.[5] Mortgages that are not used to back MPTs but are either sold in their pristine form or simply retained in portfolios are termed *whole loans*.

The monthly payments of scheduled principal and interest (P&I) and prepayments from borrower to servicer are not immediately transferred to the MPT holder. There is a delay in the pass-through of these cash flows. The time line diagrams of Figure 18.1 depict the sequence of cash receipts and payments and key dates for the MPTs of GNMA, FNMA, and FHLMC. Payment delays for GNMA I and

---

5. Two of the larger pool insurers are the General Electric Mortgage Insurance Company (GEMICO) and the Mortgage Guaranty Insurance Company (MGIC).

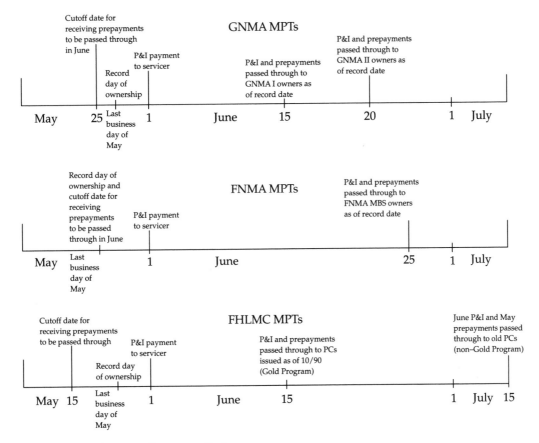

Figure 18.1 Agency Payment Delays

II, FNMA, and the FHLMC Gold and Non-Gold programs are 14, 19, 24, 14, and 44 days, respectively.

18.4 Trading and Settlement of Mortgage Pass-Throughs

Given that the trade is to be done at a stipulated price, there are three ways to execute the order: specified with respect to pool number, specified with respect to origination year, and to-be-announced (TBA). In all three types, the following information must be included:

1. guarantor of the MPT, i.e., GNMA, FNMA, etc.;

2. collateral type, e.g., single-family, GPM;

3. coupon rate;

4. pool maturity, e.g., 30-year or 15-year, labeled by the longest original term mortgage in the pool;

5. principal balance to be bought or sold;

6. price, stated as a percentage of the principal balance, with a minimum increment of $\frac{1}{32}$; e.g., a price of 102-16 means $102^{16}\!/_{32}\%$ of the principal balance.

If a pool number or an origination year is placed on the order form, then the order is specified. If either the pool number or the origination year is omitted, then the order is TBA and the seller has the option to deliver whatever pool possesses the characteristics that satisfy the criteria 1 through 5. Most trades are TBA. Obviously, in a TBA trade, the seller will deliver the least valuable pool that satisfies the order's stated criteria.

In a trade that is specified with respect to pool number, the exact amount of the stated *original* principal balance (the face amount of the securities) must be delivered. Trades specified with respect to pool number usually involve mortgages in the seller's possession—often mortgages that are not recently originated. They normally settle in three business days after the trade date, referred to as corporate settlement. It is not an active market. In contrast, the market for trades specified by origination year is fairly active. Such a trade grants the seller the same latitude as a TBA trade with regard to the principal permitted to be delivered, as discussed in the next paragraph.

A round lot for a TBA trade is $1,000,000 in *current* principal balance, often referred to as *current face*. But, given the odd sizes of mortgages, the seller may not be able to deliver exactly $1,000,000 in current principal balance. Therefore, on a TBA trade the seller may deliver an amount that varies from this principal amount by 2%. Consequently, on a $1 million TBA trade, the seller may deliver a balance ranging from $980,000 to $1,020,000. Clearly if interest rates have risen during the period between trade date and settlement date, then the seller will try to deliver $1,020,000. This follows because the extra $20,000 has a lower value than that provided by the trade date price. Conversely, a decline in rates between trade date and settlement date favors the delivery of $980,000 in principal. The aforementioned trade rules and criteria and those yet to be mentioned are set by the Public Securities Association (PSA), a national trade association that deals with trading and operation procedures. With regard to a TBA trade, the PSA limits the number of different pools (all having in common the data listed above as 1 through 4) that may be delivered in satisfaction of the $1 million principal, plus or minus the 2% variance.[6]

The dollar amount that the buyer pays is contingent upon the pool balance measured on settlement day. Information relevant to the calculation of this amount is provided by the *pool factor,* which is the ratio of the pool's current mortgage principal balance to the pool's original principal balance. This current principal balance, to which the trade price is applied, is computed by multiplying the pool's original balance by the pool factor figure applicable to the settlement date.[7] The corresponding dollar amount paid for the current principal is computed as the product of the trade price and this principal amount. Adding the accrued interest due the seller, where the day count follows the 30/360 convention, gives the invoice price to be paid by the buyer.[8]

To illustrate the calculation, assume a trade of $1,000,000 in principal of GNMA 8s to be settled on August 21, 1994, at a price of 102-16. The pool factor is 0.8500.

$$value\ of\ current\ balance\ =\ 1.025 \times \$1,000,000 \times .8500$$

$$=\ \$871,250.00$$

$$accrued\ interest\ =\ .08 \times \left(\frac{20}{360}\right) \times \$1,000,000 \times .8500$$

$$=\ \$3,777.78$$

$$invoice\ price\ =\ \$871,250.00 + \$3,777.78 = \$875,027.78$$

On TBA trades, settlement dates are set by the PSA. To settle a trade, the pool factor is required. Since some pool factors are not available until mid-month, settlement dates for the various classes of mortgage pass-throughs (GNMAs, FNMAs, etc.) and other mortgage derivatives are settled at predetermined dates grouped around the third Wednesday of the month. Commitments made through a TBA

---

6. On a $1 million principal TBA trade, the rule is this: For coupons <11%, seller may deliver a maximum of three different pool numbers; for coupons ≥11%, seller may deliver up to five different pool numbers.

7. The applicable pool factor is that published in the same month as the settlement date.

8. The 30/360 rule means that every month has 30 days. Count each day from the first of the month (the P&I date) up to, but not including, the settlement date.

trade can be erased by executing the exact opposite trade. However, to offset, both initial and offsetting trades would have to be cleared (trade-matched) on the same system.

18.5 Clearing and Settlement Facilities

The MBS Clearing Corporation (MBSCC)

The MBSCC, a clearing agency that is owned by its members and registered with the Securities Exchange Commission, is the largest clearing system for mortgage-backed securities. It clears TBA trades in GNMA, FNMA, and FHLMC mortgage pass-throughs. To begin the clearance process, the opposite parties to a trade submit the following information: (1) buy/sell, (2) principal amount traded, (3) trade price, (4) security description, e.g., single-family, 30-year fixed rate, (5) trade date, (6) settlement date, (7) submitting party, and (8) counterparty. Complete correspondence of the information sets submitted by the parties to the trade results in the trade becoming a legal contract between buyer and seller. At this point, the trade is referred to as a *compared* trade. If the submitted sets of information do not match in all categories, the trade is classified as an *uncompared* trade. The parties to the trade are notified of the discrepancies and advised to resubmit after they have resolved them. Upon successful comparison, both parties are required to have sufficient collateral on deposit with MBSCC (called *margin*) to ensure that financial obligations will be met. The clearance process comprises this comparison of information sets, the acceptance or nonacceptance of the trade should the data not match, the posting of margin on a compared trade, the eventual netting of all buys and sells of each member vis-à-vis all other members in order to reduce the number of deliveries on settlement day, and the notification to each member of the net amount of securities and cash to be delivered and received. The term *settlement* is reserved for that part of the trade in which the security is delivered against payment.[9]

Every day, until the arrival of the settlement day, each party's margin requirement varies with the price of the security traded. If the security price moves above the trade price, the seller is required

---

9. Dealers may choose not to clear a trade through a clearing entity. The trade between two dealers may be compared directly between their back office staffs. If the trade details match, the trade is accepted and margin requirements, if any, are negotiated. Information on where and how to deliver the securities and money is then exchanged.

to post collateral (margin) equal to 130% of this difference in prices. Remember, the seller would be subject to the temptation to walk away from his commitment to deliver at the trade price and instead sell the security at the now higher market price. The prospect of losing his collateral deposit inhibits him from walking. If the security price falls below the trade price in the days following the trade, then the buyer must post collateral equal to 130% of this difference in prices.[10] This margin deposit serves to deter the buyer from walking away from the trade and instead purchasing the security at the now lower market price. At the initiation of the trade, before the market price changes and the 130% margin requirement on price differentials takes effect, each member's general security deposit with MBSCC serves as the good faith collateral for the trade. It is this deposit that provides assurance that the seller (buyer) will honor the trade in the event the first price change after the trade results in a higher (lower) price.

Besides providing economies in processing and implementing credit controls to enhance financial performance by the parties to a trade, MBSCC provides another service that lowers the cost of settlement (delivery against payment). It is referred to as the *netting process.* The aim of the netting process is to minimize deliveries. Four to five days prior to a settlement date, the buys and sells of each member of a particular security are paired off, and a net amount to be delivered or received is obtained. The recipients or deliverers of the security and the commensurate money transfers are also identified by the netting procedure. The salient features of the netting process are illustrated by the following example.

Consider three dealers, A, B, and C; all are members of MBSCC. The following two trades occurred for settlement on the same day. Dealer B bought $1 million in current principal balance, or *current face,* of a security from A at 94 and sold $1 million of the identical security to C at 98. These were the only trades recorded for the settlement date of interest. Since B has essentially contracted to take delivery from A and redeliver to C identical amounts of the same security, MBSCC takes B out of the delivery process and tells A that it must deliver $1 million in principal of the security to C on settlement day; MBSCC coincidentally informs C to expect the security delivery from A. Instead of two deliveries occurring, A

---

10. In practice, from a member's trades that show unrealized losses (long/short position has a lower/higher current price than the trade price), the unrealized gains on the member's other trades are subtracted. The 130% factor is then applied to the difference— but only if that difference represents an unrealized loss.

to B and then B to C, only one occurs, A to C. This is the benefit of the netting process.

Dealer A is instructed by MBSCC to deliver $1 million in principal of the specific security to C. Note that this means that if the pool factor for that security is 0.5, then $2 million of original principal must be delivered to C. Of course, A will use the 2% variance rule to deliver more than $1 million in principal if rates have risen since trade day or deliver less than the $1 million principal if rates are lower by settlement day. Dealer C is instructed to pay a price of 96, the average of the trade prices of 94 and 98 for that day, upon delivery by A. This average price is referred to as the *class average price* (CAP) by MBSCC. Now A originally sold to B at 94. So A is receiving $20,000 too much. To square things, MBSCC debits A's account $20,000. In general, the seller must pay MBSCC an amount equal to the CAP less the trade price. On the other side, C pays 96, the CAP, to A on receipt of the security. But C originally contracted to buy from B at 98. Dealer C is paying $20,000 less than he should. To right matters, MBSCC debits C's account $20,000. In general, the buyer must pay MBSCC an amount equal to the trade price less the CAP. Dealer B bought at 94 and sold at 98, so he is entitled to a cash credit of $40,000. This is what he gets. As a buyer, B must pay MBSCC the trade price of 94 less the CAP of 96, or −2. This means B collects 2 from MBSCC. As a seller, B must pay MBSCC the CAP, 96, less the trade price of 98, or −2. So B collects another 2 from MBSCC. In total, dealer B collects 4, or $40,000.[11]

The day before settlement day, MBSCC collects the debits. On settlement day, MBSCC pays the credits. The credits are paid before MBSCC has knowledge that a good delivery was made. Remember

---

11. In practice, it is a bit more complicated. Each member will have made a number of trades with various other members in a security class for a particular settlement date. Two average trade prices are calculated for each firm against each counterfirm: one represents the average of all buys of a security class from a specific counterfirm, and the other represents the average of all sales to that same counterfirm of that same security class. The former is called the *buy* firm class average price (FCAP) and the latter the *sell* FCAP. A firm's payments to MBSCC amount to the difference between the CAP and its sell FCAP times the units of that security class sold, plus the difference between the buy FCAP and the CAP times the number of units of that security class bought.

To see how it works, add another trade to the example in the text. In addition to B buying from A at 94 and selling to C at 98, B buys from A at 95 and sells to C at 97. The average of all trade prices, the CAP, is 96. A's sell FCAP is 94.5. It has no buy FCAP. C's buy FCAP is 97.5. It has no sell FCAP. B's buy FCAP is 94.5, and its sell FCAP is 97.5. A's payment to MBSCC is $(96 - 94.5) \times 2 = 3$. C's payment to MBSCC is $(97.5 - 96) \times 2 = 3$. B's payments to MBSCC are $(96 - 97.5) \times 2 = -3$ on the sell side and $(94.5 - 96) \times 2 = -3$ on the buy side. So B collects 6 from MBSCC.

that it still holds the original deposit and the collateral received from mark-to-market pricing. After both parties, in this case A and C, have notified MBSCC that a good delivery was made and of the complete details describing the delivery, the mark-to-market margins are released. At this point A received and C paid amounts commensurate with the original trade prices on $1 million of principal, 94 and 98, respectively.

There is still the 2% variance in principal that requires an adjustment to the monies the two parties paid and received on settlement day. MBSCC makes an adjustment between the two parties to reflect this factor. If A decided to deliver $980,000 in principal to C rather than $1,000,000, then MBSCC must credit A's account $400. Recall that one day prior to settlement day, A was debited $20,000 on the assumption that $1,000,000 in principal would be delivered. The $20,000 debit came about because A was paid 96 by C when A's actual sale price was 94. If MBSCC had known that A intended to deliver only $980,000 in principal on settlement day, then A's debit would have amounted to $19,600 [$(0.96 - 0.94) \times \$980,000$]. Consequently, when MBSCC is made aware of the full trade details, A receives a $400 credit. Following the same line of reasoning, one sees that C also receives a $400 credit. Dealer B is debited the sum of these two credits, $800.

Notice that MBSCC matches trades, collects margin, nets trades, and oversees deliveries. These are essentially the same functions performed by the clearing entities in futures and options markets. For example, the clearing house of a futures exchange matches trades, pairs off and offsets the buys and sells of a clearing firm (the equivalent netting process, serving to reduce deliveries), and collects margin to ensure performance—although it makes daily cash payments and collections to clearing members instead of altering the amount of collateral that a clearing member must have on deposit with the clearing house. A futures contract delivery is overseen by the exchange clearing house. Delivery on a futures contract takes place at that day's settlement price, the average of trade prices at day's end, while prior settlement variation flows ensure that the original contract price is obtained. Delivery is overseen by MBSCC. Delivery takes place at the average trade price and cash payments are made to or received from the member to make the effective delivery price equal to the original trade price. In these respects, the two clearing organizations appear similar. However, there is a difference: MBSCC does not guarantee trades. This means that if a member cannot meet its contracted obligations because of insolvency, MBSCC will not assess other members the necessary amounts to make the counterparties to the trade whole. The rules of the futures and options exchanges require them to do so.

One last point on delivery. If FNMA or FHLMC securities are involved, then delivery and payment occur over the Fed wire. If GNMAs are the securities traded, then delivery may be effected by the selling firm's physically delivering the certificate to the buying firm or through a securities depository. The physical delivery of the certificate by the seller to the buyer requires the selling firm to present the endorsed certificate to the buyer's back office, accept a receipt, and await payment later that day. Delivery through a depository, the predominant form, is described in the next two subsections.

Participants Trust Company (PTC)

The Participants Trust Company (PTC) immobilizes all GNMA certificates and then provides for the transfer of ownership through book entry recordings. Participants submit their certificates to Chemical Bank (soon to be called Chase Manhattan, after completion of the Chemical-Chase merger), the transfer agent for GNMA securities. Chemical combines these certificates into one jumbo certificate that is registered to PTC. In response, PTC's records are updated to reflect each participant's share in this new jumbo certificate. Once ownership is registered in PTC's name, then the servicers' principal and interest payments flow to PTC and are credited to the accounts of the participants. On a settlement date, transfers and pledges of securities are recorded on PTC's books as they occur throughout the day, and credits and debits are applied to corresponding cash balances. The cash balances are settled between participants, in Fed funds, by day's end.

To ensure performance by participants, PTC has instituted the following risk management procedures.

1. Participants must meet minimum capital standards.

2. A participant's transactions must be fully collateralized with cash, U.S. Treasury securities, GNMAs, FNMAs, or FHLMC mortgage pass-throughs. This means that if a firm has agreed to pay $100 million for the delivery of securities, then the value of the collateral held for its account by PTC must total at least $100 million. With the understanding that this collateral might have to be quickly converted into cash to fulfill a defaulting participant's obligations, the value of

the collateral in a participant's account is discounted to reflect the liquidity of each class. For example, the market value of U.S. Treasury securities is not discounted, whereas that of an agency MPT is reduced by 5% prior to including it in the collateral value calculation. These discounts from market value are called *haircuts*. The collateral value net of haircuts is referred to as the participant's *net free equity*. It should be pointed out that the securities being received count in the calculation of the account's net free equity. Therefore, if the account currently has on deposit $10 million of GNMAs and is receiving $100 million in GNMAs, then the account's net free equity is $104.5 million (0.95 × $110). The amount is sufficient to cover the $100 million debit to the cash account generated by the completion of delivery. The security transfer is made. The recipient of the securities must still wire $100 million cash to PTC by close of the business day to offset the cash account debit.

3. A participant's net cash debit, the amount needed to pay for the day's deliveries, is capped at the lesser of PTC's lines of credit or a multiple of the participant's capital. This restriction is intended to assure that PTC can obtain the necessary cash in a timely manner to enable it to meet a defaulting member's settlement obligation. If a participant defaults, PTC pledges the participant's collateral to its banks for the cash necessary to meet that day's settlement obligation. The PTC credit line is currently $2 billion. A participant with $1 billion in collateral and taking delivery of $3 billion in GNMAs is calculated to have net free equity of $3.8 billion (0.95 × $4 billion). His net debit will amount to $3 billion. There is sufficient net free equity to cover the debit, but the delivery will be disallowed by PTC because the debit exceeds the cap.

4. If the default is deemed to be due to operational problems and not to the insolvency of the participant, PTC may use a limited portion of its nondefaulting members' collateral, in addition to the collateral of the defaulting member that is subject to PTC's lien, to obtain the cash necessary to make good that day's settlement. Should the defaulting party fail to meet its obligations by the following day, its collateral would be liquidated. Any resulting losses would be allocated to the defaulting party's counterparties in the trades. This tends to encourage a prudent evaluation of the creditworthiness of the counterparty to a trade before the trade is consummated. Notice that, unlike the options and commodity clearing entities but like MBSCC, Participants Trust Company does not guarantee the financial obligations of the counterparties to a trade.

Depository Trust Company (DTC)

Other types of mortgage-backed securities, such as REMICs and STRIPs—to be encountered in Chapter 20—are not cleared (i.e., compared, etc.) at a central facility like MBSCC. Rather they are compared by the counterparties' back offices. These types of mortgage-backed securities can be settled, delivery versus payment, between back offices, but more frequently will be settled at Depository Trust Company (DTC). Founded prior to PTC to provide book entry settlement of stocks, corporate and municipal bonds, DTC has a structure similar to PTC's. With respect to mortgage-backed securities, DTC now settles trades for its members in FHLMCs, FNMAs, and private-label REMICs and STRIPs. PTC handles the settlement of REMICs and STRIPs on GNMA pass-throughs and VA-guaranteed mortgages.

Chapter **19**

Valuation and Hedging of Mortgage Pass-Throughs

*I*F ONE knows how to price the mortgage pass-through (MPT), the valuation of mortgage derivatives is relatively straightforward. Similarly, the concepts necessary to arrive at the correct hedge ratio of an MPT portfolio are the same as those used in hedging mortgage derivatives. Consequently, though this chapter often discusses pricing and hedging techniques in terms of the MPT, its lessons apply to both MPTs and mortgage derivatives—hereafter both subsumed under the title *mortgage-backed securities* (MBSs).

One cannot hope to value an MPT without some knowledge of the prepayment option held by the mortgagor. We begin with a discussion of prepayment rates, their measurement, and the economic and demographic factors that affect them. We then turn to the valuation of the MPT. The methodology employed is essentially that used in Chapter 7 to value interest rate instruments with embedded options. An explanation follows of the option-adjusted spread concept as a measure of an MPT's relative value. Its calculation is demonstrated with a simple example. We close with the consideration of two quantitative measures of the MPT's price behavior with respect to interest rate changes: its price sensitivity and its convexity. Both quantities are essential in determining the instruments and amounts to be utilized in hedging an MPT.

19.1 Prepayment Rates and Models

A high-coupon mortgage with a $90 balance is purchased for $100. Immediate prepayment of the full balance results in an instantaneous loss of 10%. On the other hand, if a mortgage with a $110 balance, purchased for $100, is immediately prepaid, an instantaneous

10% return is earned. Obviously, in order to value an MBS, one must attempt to make a reasonably accurate forecast of the size and timing of the underlying pool's prepayments.[1]

Measuring the Pool's Prepayment Rate

The *single monthly mortality* (SMM) is a traditional way to measure the pool's past prepayment rate, also known as the pool's *prepayment speed*. The SMM measures the percentage difference between the scheduled pool balance one month from today, i.e., the balance that would have existed if only the scheduled amortization payments were made during the month, and the actual pool balance one month from today.

$$SMM = \frac{\left(\begin{array}{c} \text{month-end scheduled pool balance } - \\ \text{month-end actual pool balance} \end{array}\right)}{\text{month-end scheduled pool balance}}$$

The average SMM over a one-year period would be calculated to satisfy

$$\begin{array}{c} \text{actual pool balance} \\ \text{at year end} \end{array} = (\text{scheduled pool balance at year end}) \times (1 - SMM)^{12}$$

An equivalent annual prepayment rate known as the *conditional prepayment rate* (CPR) is defined by

$$\begin{array}{c} \text{actual pool balance} \\ \text{at year end} \end{array} = \left(\begin{array}{c} \text{scheduled pool balance} \\ \text{at year end} \end{array}\right)(1 - CPR)$$

The preceding equations imply that

$$1 - CPR = (1 - SMM)^{12}$$

or

$$CPR = 1 - (1 - SMM)^{12}$$

and

$$SMM = 1 - (1 - CPR)^{1/12}$$

---

1. Although defaults on the underlying mortgages are not strictly considered to be prepayments, their effect is identical to that of prepayments. They compose only a small fraction of the pool's unscheduled payments, and few attempts are made to forecast them.

Factors Affecting the Prepayment Rate

Prepayments arise from moving to a new home, referred to as *turnover*; defaulting on the mortgage payment; prepaying a portion of the mortgage balance, called *curtailment*; and refinancing the mortgage on the existing property. The factors considered of prime importance in determining prepayment rates are discussed in this section. The first three, the size of the mortgage coupon rate relative to the market rate, homeowner equity, and *burnout* (soon to be defined), relate to the refinancing decision. The last three, the pool's age, seasonality, and economic activity, relate to the total of prepayments that arise from turnover, default, and curtailment.

Mortgage Coupon Rate versus Current Market Rate   The lower the current market rate relative to the mortgage's coupon rate, the greater the incentive to refinance. Implicitly, the borrower calculates the present value of his future mortgage payments discounted at the market rate, recognizing that this calculation amounts to the current value of his liability in meeting the future mortgage payments. It is this dollar amount that would have to be invested at the market rate to generate the cash flows necessary to meet those future mortgage payments. The borrower compares this figure, less any costs of refinancing, with the outstanding mortgage balance. If the balance is less than the present value of his future payments, he prepays. The lower the market rate, the higher the liability's value relative to the mortgage balance. Thus, as interest rates fall, prepayments increase; as rates rise, prepayments decrease.

Refinancing does not immediately occur when the market rate drops below the mortgage coupon rate. However, at some rate differential, sufficient to compensate the mortgagor for his financing costs and trouble, a prepayment environment exists. This critical differential between the market rate and the mortgage's coupon rate is referred to as the *refinancing threshold*.

Another way to view the relative interest rate factor in the refinancing decision is to note that the lender is granting a prepayment option to the borrower. Effectively, the latter holds a call on the mortgage. The mortgage will be called at an exercise price equal to the mortgage balance if the mortgage's discounted value, computed at the market rate, exceeds the exercise price—the mortgage balance—by a sufficient amount to represent a net savings from refinancing.

Relying on this call paradigm, we can make a statement about the price behavior of the mortgage—or MBS—as the market rate changes. One can think of an investment in a mortgage as the purchase of a noncallable bond accompanied by the sale of a call on that bond. Consequently, one may write

$$mortgage\ value\ =\ noncallable\ bond\ value\ -\ call\ value$$

As rates fall, the bond's value rises, but so does the call's. In the process, the call's gain attenuates the increase in the mortgage's value.

If the market rate is high relative to the mortgage coupon, the call's value is relatively insensitive to a change in the market rate. Over this region, the mortgage price stays close to but somewhat below the bond price. If the market rate is below the mortgage coupon rate, the call's value is quite sensitive to a change in the market rate, and an increase in the mortgage value in response to a fall in the market rate can be substantially less than the noncallable bond's corresponding increase in value. This price behavior is depicted in Figure 19.1.

Notice that whereas the noncallable bond price versus interest rate relationship is convex over the entire range of rates, the mortgage price–interest rate relationship is convex in the high rate region and then turns concave—or, in the parlance of the trade, "negative convex"—in the lower market rate region.

The quantitative representation of the relative coupon rate factor as the difference between the market rate and the mortgage coupon rate poses a problem when the pool's mortgage rates exhibit some

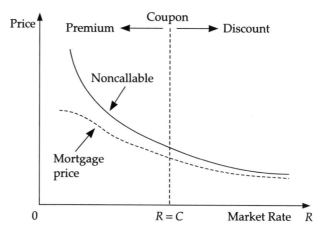

Figure 19.1 Mortgage Price and Noncallable Bond Price versus Yield Relations

dispersion—as they can in all but the GNMA I program. To obtain a measure of this prepayment factor, one must devise a measure of the pool's representative coupon rate. The measure used is the weighted average of the individual mortgage rates in the pool, where the weights are the individual mortgage balances divided by the total pool balance. This measure is termed the *weighted average coupon* (WAC).[2]

Homeowner Equity   The lower the level of homeowner equity, the less likely the homeowner can qualify for refinancing.

Burnout   Consideration of the *burnout* factor is predicated on the notion that some of the pool's mortgagors are more attuned to a refinancing opportunity than others. Consequently, when the market rate reaches the threshold, the more alert mortgagors in the pool refinance. The next time the threshold is reached, the next most attentive group of mortgagors prepay, and so on. With each return to the threshold, there are fewer mortgagors alert to a prepayment opportunity.

Apart from this asymmetric information argument, other explanations for burnout are offered. Given fixed costs of refinancing, mortgagors with smaller loan balances have less incentive to prepay. When the threshold is first breached, those with larger mortgage balances prepay. The next time the threshold is crossed, there are fewer individuals with mortgage balances large enough to economically justify refinancing.

Another reason offered for the attenuation of prepayments with each subsequent return to the threshold is related to the economic activity of a geographic area. Consider a pool composed of mortgages from California and Illinois. When the threshold was first crossed, there was no significant difference between the prepayment rates of the two regions. Subsequent to that time, housing prices in California declined while those in Illinois increased. Soon after, the threshold was again crossed. Prepayments from mortgagors in Illinois emulated those that had occurred at the prior threshold crossing. However, because of the decrease in home values, the mortgagors in California saw their loan-to-value ratios (LTVs) rise to a level that prevented

---

2. For the most part, original balances are used in calculating the weights, for those are the data normally available. Recently, FNMA and FHLMC have begun to report WACs based on current mortgage balances.

refinancing. Therefore, the prepayments from mortgagors in California decreased, and the pool's overall prepayment rate declined from the previous level.

Mortgage researchers attempt to quantify this factor. Some use the pool factor as a degree-of-burnout indicator; others count the number of times the threshold has been hit during the pool's life. Still others calculate the amount that the market rate is below the threshold—the in-the-money amount—and the length of time that it stays there. Each time the threshold is breached, the product of this in-the-money amount and the length of time that it was in-the-money is calculated. The running total of these products is used as a measure of the pool's burnout.

Influence of the Pool's Age   Once originated, a mortgage begins to age. Evidence indicates that few mortgages prepay in the first two to three years subsequent to their origination. This makes sense, for the demographic factors that tend to cause a family to move are inactive during this stage. It is unlikely soon after the purchase and financing of a home that a family will suffer a divorce, trade up to a more expensive home, or have one of its members change jobs. Additionally, the owner who just closed on a mortgage is less able to refinance after having incurred the costs of the recent closing.

However, as time passes, the demographic factors become more active and the incidence of prepayments increases. The property owner becomes more sensitive to refinancing opportunities and is better able to deal with them. So as a mortgage ages, the prepayment rate tends to increase. Technically, the time over which the prepayment rate increases is called the pool's *seasoning period.* When the pool's prepayment rate levels off, the pool is said to contain seasoned mortgages.[3]

The aging factor of a pool is often quantified as either (1) the average loan age, which equals the mortgage's age, measured in months from origination, weighted by the corresponding mortgage balance as a fraction of the pool balance, and summed over all such products, or (2) the weighted average maturity (WAM), sometimes called the weighted average remaining maturity (WARM), which is

---

3. Pools originated at the same time, containing different collateral, may exhibit significantly different aging properties. Because FHA-VA mortgages are assumable, can be passed from the seller of the home to the buyer, while conventional mortgages contain a due-on-sale clause, cannot be passed from seller to buyer, conventional pools tend to prepay at a higher rate than GNMA pools.

calculated as the product of each mortgage's remaining maturity and the ratio of that mortgage's balance to the pool balance, summed over all products.

Seasonality Prepayment rates are usually higher during the summer months, because families wait to move when their children have completed the school year, vacations normally occur during summer, and the weather makes moving a more amenable activity. Conversely, prepayments are slower in the winter months.

Economic Activity Increasing economic activity in a region normally leads to increased prepayments, as new jobs become available that are worth the effort involved in relocating.

Econometric Prepayment Models

The larger financial firms have developed econometric models to forecast the CPR of a pool. A regression is run across pools and time with the CPR as the dependent variable and a set of independent variables representing (1) the pool's market rate–mortgage coupon differential, (2) homeowner equity, (3) burnout, (4) aging, (5) seasonality, and (6) the economic environment. After the regression's coefficients have been estimated, forecasts of values for the independent variables are inserted into the regression equation to obtain an estimate of the pool's CPR.

The PSA Model

The Public Securities Association (PSA) proposed a prepayment model that is based on the aging experience of FHA mortgages. The pool's CPR, an annualized rate, is assumed to rise at 0.2% each month for a period of 30 months. At the end of this aging period, the pool's CPR has reached 6%. It remains there during the rest of the pool's life. For example, in the twelfth month of the pool's life, the CPR is estimated at 2.4%. Translating this into an equivalent SMM, the proportion of the pool balance expected to prepay during the month would be

$$1 - [1 - 0.024]^{1/12}$$

Obviously, the model has some weaknesses. Among other things, it ignores the effect of the market interest rate level on the prepayment rate, and the FHA experience is not entirely applicable to the aging process of conventional pools. However, the model does provide an industry standard for pool prepayment speeds. A financial firm may project a pool prepayment rate from its own model and then translate it into the equivalent PSA rate. For example, suppose the financial firm's model predicts a CPR of 15% for the pool's 31st month: the pool would be described as having a speed of 250% PSA for that month. The equivalent single monthly mortality for that month is $1 - (1 - 0.15)^{1/12}$. Additionally, the firm may publish a PSA "lifetime equivalent" for the pool by finding the PSA rate that provides the same average life as that estimated from the econometric prepayment model. The average pool life is defined as the average number of years that each dollar of pool principal remains outstanding. The formula for its calculation is

$$average\ life\ = \frac{\sum_{t=1}^{12n} t P_t}{12(principal\ balance)}$$

where $12n$, t, and P_t, respectively, denote the pool's remaining months to maturity, the number of months to the tth principal payment, and the principal payment on that date. The principal balance is the remaining principal on the date that the calculation is performed. The division by 12 converts the measure into equivalent years.

19.2 Valuation: A Review of Methodology

We have previously discussed the valuation of interest rate instruments with embedded options. Initially, develop an arbitrage-free tree of one-period U.S. Treasury rates with properties consistent with the current term structure. Then, placing the instrument's cash flows at the appropriate nodes, iteratively discount the expected flows back to the current date. This produces the instrument's current value. If the above method is not used but instead a traditional type of approach is employed, such as discounting the expected cash flows by the expected interest rate over the instrument's life, an incorrect valuation might be obtained.

To illustrate the point, consider the following problem. Value $1 of a 10% coupon, two-year, level payment pass-through pool, assuming that the entire pool will prepay after one year if the market rate,

C_m, on new one-year pools is less than or equal to 9%. The mortgages that compose the pool pay $0.5762 each year. The servicing fee is zero. The tree of one-period rates, containing the C_m value for each date, levels of the one-period Treasury rate, i_g, and the pool's cash flows, CF, are presented in Figure 19.2. The transition probabilities are all equal to 0.5.

Applying the methodology developed for the valuation of interest rate instruments with embedded options, the pool's value at $t = 0$ equals

$$0.5 \left[\frac{.5762}{1.09} + \frac{.5762}{(1.09)(1.10)} \right] + 0.5 \left(\frac{1.1}{1.09} \right) = 1.0092$$

Now consider a standard type of methodology. A glance at the tree in Figure 19.2 indicates that the expected one-period Treasury rate is 9%. The expected payments at $t = 1$ equal

$$(.5 \times .5762) + (.5 \times 1.1) = .8381$$

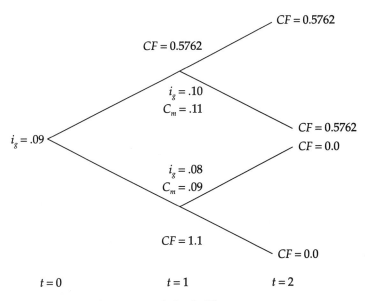

Figure 19.2   Tree of Rates and Cash Flows

The expected cash flow at $t = 2$ is

$$(.5 \times .5762) + (.5 \times 0) = .2881$$

The present value of these expected flows, using 9% as the discount rate, is

$$\frac{.8381}{1.09} + \frac{.2881}{(1.09)^2} = 1.0114$$

The value obtained by application of the tree analysis is less than that given by the expected rate–expected cash flow methodology. This is not a particularly surprising result. The mortgagor will exercise the prepayment option only when it is optimal to do so. The latter methodology implicitly assumes that the option has an equal chance of being exercised when $C_m = 0.11$ and when $C_m = 0.09$. This is false, and its assumption reduces the value of the prepayment option and correspondingly increases the value of the pool. (The arithmetic is that some payments on the 10% mortgages are assumed to continue to be received at $t = 2$ and discounted back at a rate lower than the coupon rate.)

19.3 The Option-Adjusted Spread (OAS): A Relative Valuation Method

In applying the binomial tree method to the valuation of mortgage-backed securities, securities firms generally find that the computed theoretical value almost always exceeds the actual market value of the MBS. Part of the explanation for this phenomenon may be that, unlike that from U.S. Treasury securities, the interest income from mortgage-backed securities is not exempt from state taxes. This implies that the appropriate discount rate to be applied to the MBS's cash flows might be somewhat higher than the rates obtained from the U.S. Treasury term structure. In addition, greater transactions costs associated with MBSs in contrast to U.S. Treasuries would contribute to the observation of a gap between observed and theoretical MBS prices. Again this would lead one to argue that one-period U.S. Treasury rates do not provide quite high enough discount rates. Finally, the uncertainty about the behavior of prepayments would dictate that a mortgage rate should be higher than the rate for a Treasury of similar maturity. Nevertheless, securities firms see the differences between theoretical and observed prices as being too large to be explained by these tax and cost factors. Mispricing, it is surmised, is the reason for the gap.

A popular measure used to quantify the underpricing is to add a positive constant to each one-period rate on the tree. Raising these discount rates lowers the theoretical price. An iterative search is undertaken to find the value of the constant that equates the calculated theoretical price to the market price. This equilibrating constant value is called the *option-adjusted spread* (OAS) for the MBS. An OAS is calculated for each MBS. The MBS with the highest OAS is deemed the most underpriced. Why? Because for this security, the largest positive constant had to be added to the Treasury rates to obtain discount rates high enough to bring the theoretical price down to the actual market price. Why is it called an option-adjusted spread? Because the framework into which the OAS is introduced attempts to take optimal exercise (prepayment by the mortgagor) into account by using empirical prepayment models.

Calculating the Option-Adjusted Spread: An Example

Compute the OAS for an MPT issued on an underlying mortgage pool of 10%, two-year fixed rate, level payment mortgages with a $100 balance. The mortgages pay annually, and the pool's servicing fee is 0.5%. Therefore, the pass-through's coupon is 9.5%. The pool completely prepays if the mortgage rate on new pools maturing at $t = 2$, C_m, is less than 0.08. The relevant interest rate tree and the MPT's cash flows are presented in Figure 19.3. The transition probabilities are equal to 0.5.

The $57.12 figure attached to the node at $t = 1$, $i_g = 0.09$, is obtained as follows. The mortgage pool's annual payment is calculated to be $57.62. Of this amount, $10.00 is the interest on the original balance and $47.62 is the scheduled amortization payment. The servicer receives 0.5% of the beginning-of-period $100.00 balance, or $0.50. This amount is deducted from the $10.00 mortgage interest payment. The total passed through to the pass-through holder is $57.12.

To obtain a theoretical value for the mortgage pass-through (TVMPT), calculate the present value of the cash flows along each interest rate path, weight each by the path's probability, and sum across all paths.

$$TVMPT = +.25\left[\frac{57.12}{1.08} + \frac{57.36}{(1.08)(1.09)}\right]$$

$$+.25\left[\frac{57.12}{1.08} + \frac{57.36}{(1.08)(1.09)}\right]$$

$$+.50\left(\frac{109.50}{1.08}\right) = 101.5$$

You observe that this MPT is trading at $99\frac{25}{32}$. You attribute the difference between the theoretical and market prices to underpricing. To obtain a relative measure of this underpricing, you search for the OAS. After several trials, you find that the constant that must be added to all one-period rates in order to bring the theoretical price down to $99\frac{25}{32}$ is 1.5%. Consequently, this MPT has an OAS of 1.5%. In comparison to another MPT that has an OAS of 1.0%, the MPT with a 1.5% OAS is considered a better buy.

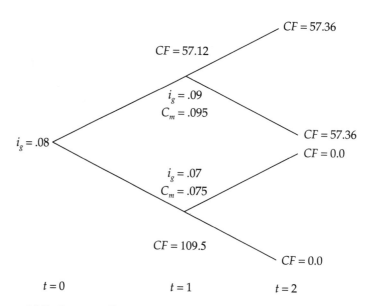

Figure 19.3 Interest Rates and Cash Flows for a 9.5%, Two-Year, $100 Balance MPT, 0.5% Servicing Fee

19.4 Calculating a Mortgage-Backed Security's Price Sensitivity to a Shift in the Yield Curve

To hedge any mortgage-backed security, one must first calculate the price sensitivity of that security to a change in interest rates. Given the current market value (MV_0) and having already calculated the security's OAS, here are the steps to compute market sensitivity.

1. Perturb the yield curve. Usually, the size of the perturbation is a basis point, say, $+0.01\%$. In our illustration, the perturbation's size will be 1%. Generate a new set of rates for the tree.

2. In response to this change, adjust the current mortgage rate, C_m, accordingly. The level of C_m plays an important role, for it is a determining factor in prepayments. Consequently, if Treasury rates change—of course, one would then expect mortgage rates to respond—one must calculate the new C_m value.[4]

3. Recalculate the cash flows at each node. Effectively, this means using a prepayment function to provide a new prepayment estimate at each node.

4. Add the security's OAS to each new one-period rate on the tree to obtain a new set of discount rates.

5. Discount along each path, weight by the probability of each path's occurring, and sum to obtain a new market value for the security. Label it $MV_{+.01\%}$.

6. Calculate the absolute change in value, $|MV_{+.01\%} - MV_0|$.

7. Repeat steps 1–6 for a -0.01% change in the yield curve, obtaining an absolute security price change of $|MV_{-.01\%} - MV_0|$.

8. Average the calculated changes obtained in steps 1–7.

An Illustration of a Price Sensitivity Calculation

Assume the mortgage pool characteristics, interest rate tree, and corresponding OAS of the previous example. For purposes of this example, C_m is equal to $i_g + 0.5\%$, and instead of perturbing the yield curve and obtaining new one-period rates, we simply perturb the

---

4. This calculation is often done by a regression that relates the coupon rate on new mortgages to, say, the five-year Treasury rate. The latter is obtained at each node of the tree through the process described in Part I of this book.

original one-period rates by $\pm 1\%$. In Figure 19.4, the new rates and appropriate cash flows at the appropriate nodes are presented, given a 1% rise in rates.

Note that no prepayments occur in this tree, since C_m is never less than 8%. Recalling that the OAS is 1.5%, we calculate the new market value as

$$MV_{+1\%} = +.5\left[\frac{57.12}{1.105} + \frac{57.36}{(1.105)(1.115)}\right] + .5\left[\frac{57.12}{1.105} + \frac{57.36}{(1.105)(1.095)}\right]$$
$$= 98.67$$

Calculating the absolute change gives $|98.67 - 99.78| = 1.11$. Remember that 99.78, or $99\frac{25}{32}$, is the observed market price.

For a 1% drop in rates, the cash flows and new one-period rates are presented in Figure 19.5. We calculate market value, again using an OAS of 1.5%.

$$MV_{-1\%} = .5\left[\frac{57.12}{1.085} + \frac{57.36}{(1.085)(1.095)}\right] + .5\left(\frac{109.5}{1.085}\right) = 100.92$$

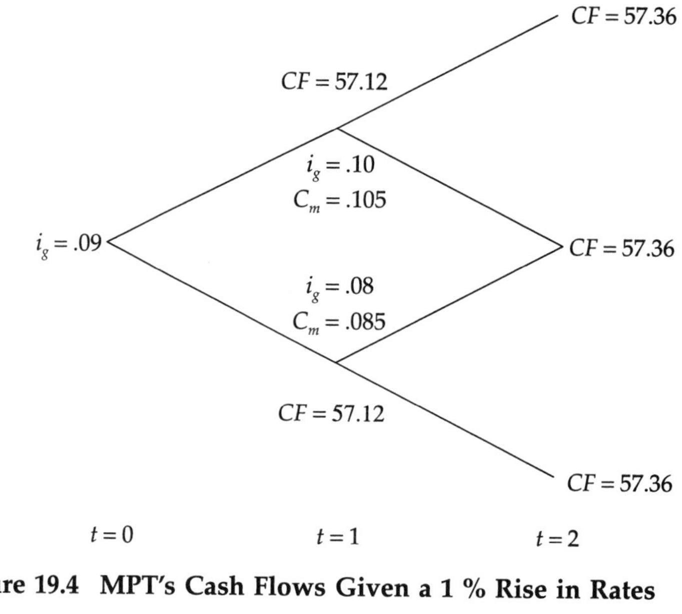

Figure 19.4   MPT's Cash Flows Given a 1 % Rise in Rates

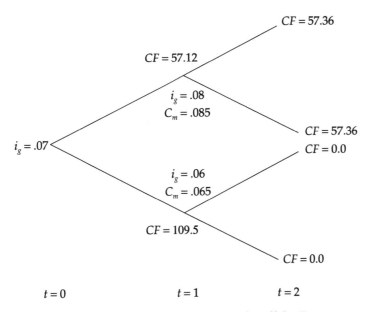

Figure 19.5 MPT's Cash Flows Given a 1% Fall in Rates

The absolute change equals $|100.92 - 99.78| = 1.14$. Averaging the absolute changes gives 1.125. This is a measure of this MPT's interest rate sensitivity.

Why do you need to know this? Suppose you bought an MPT because it was underpriced. You would want to hedge it. Someone tells you that a 1% change in rates would result in a 4.50 change in the five-year T-note futures contract. Therefore, for every $1 invested in the MPT, you short 0.25 futures contracts.

19.5 The Convexity of the Mortgage-Backed Security

Convexity is a positive attribute for a security. We have discussed this in earlier sections for swaps. Perhaps it is worth explaining in a different manner. Figure 19.6 gives the price-yield relationship for two fixed-income securities, A and B.

Clearly, bond B dominates bond A. If rates rise, B loses less than A; if rates fall, B gains more than A. Consequently, convexity is worth something. This is one reason to measure the convexity of a security. Another reason is to ascertain the degree of price sensitivity. After all, choosing a hedge ratio for a price change in response to a basis point

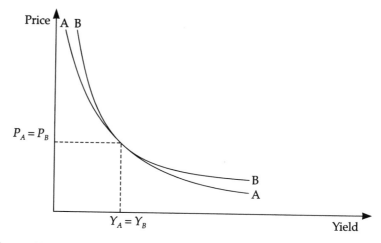

Figure 19.6 Price (*P*) versus Yield (*Y*) Relations for Bonds A and B Where Both Currently Have the Same Price and the Same Yield

perturbation does not result in a terribly comfortable situation. An immediate, larger move in rates makes that hedge ratio obsolete and may result in significant losses.[5] In 1986, long MPT positions had been hedged with short Treasury bond futures. As rates dropped precipitously, the losses on the short futures positions far outweighed the gains on the long MPT portfolios. The reason for this was that the convexity of the MPT was far different from the convexity of the bond futures.

Measuring Convexity: A Calculation

A security's convexity is measured by the change in the security's price sensitivity. Using the $\pm 1\%$ perturbations of our previous example, we calculate the convexity of this MPT.

$$convexity = \frac{\dfrac{(MV_{+1\%} - MV_0)}{1.00} - \dfrac{(MV_0 - MV_{-1\%})}{1.00}}{1.00}$$

$$= \frac{\dfrac{(98.67 - 99.78)}{1.00} - \dfrac{(99.78 - 100.92)}{1.00}}{1.00}$$

$$= 0.03$$

5. A nonparallel shift of the Treasury yield curve may also result in significant losses on a position hedged in this manner.

So in the current interest rate region of our example, the MPT exhibits positive convexity. If the result of the computation had been negative, then the MPT would exhibit negative convexity. Note that the numerator of the calculation represents the difference in price changes per 1% change in the rate level. Effectively, the numerator represents the change in the slopes of the MPT price curve as we move in the direction of higher rates along the horizontal axis. So the convexity calculation is obtained by computing the change in the slope per change in the interest rate—that is why the 1.00 (%) appears in the denominator. Also notice that we did not use absolute values.

Chapter **20**

CMOs, STRIPs, and Other Mortgage Derivative Instruments

$W_{E\ BEGIN}$ this chapter with an introduction to the composition and valuation of collateralized mortgage obligations (CMOs). The structuring and characteristics of CMO classes such as the planned amortization class, targeted amortization class, and the inverse floating class are then discussed, and the alternative approaches taken to the credit enhancement of a mortgage security are contrasted. The chapter closes with an examination of the structure, valuation, and price behavior of stripped mortgage-backed securities.

20.1 Collateralized Mortgage Obligations (CMOs): Basic Structure

Because of the mortgagor's option to prepay, the cash flow from a mortgage pass-through is uncertain with respect to timing. CMOs redistribute that risk. Unlike an MPT, in which there is a single securitized ownership class receiving whatever cash the collateral pool generates less a servicing charge, the CMO is structured to have several classes of sequentially maturing bondlike securities to which the collateral pool's cash flow is distributed. The result is a set of securities with risk-return characteristics that are significantly different from those of the collateral pool and of other debt instruments.

Basic Structure

The number of bond classes that a CMO contains may run into double digits. However, for the purpose of elucidating the CMO's essential characteristics, the CMO structure described here has four bond classes, labeled A, B, C, and Z. Each bond class is assigned a coupon rate and a principal amount. In addition, there is a residual equity class that captures any net flows that emanate from a spread between the collateral's coupon rate and the coupon rates of the bond classes; the residual class is also entitled to any pool collateral that is in excess of the amount needed to pay the bonds' principal amounts.

The collateral pool's monthly interest payments are distributed in the following manner:

1. The coupon payments to the A, B, and C classes (tranches) are made.

2. The part of the pool's interest income that is due to the Z bond holders is not distributed to the Z class as long as a principal balance remains in any one of the A, B, or C classes. Instead, an amount equal to the Z bond interest is credited to Z's principal balance, and the cash flow is used first to pay down A's principal balance. Once the A bonds have been retired, the Z coupon payment is then applied toward the retirement of B's principal, and after that to C's principal retirement. Only after the A, B, and C classes have been retired is interest on Z's then-outstanding principal paid to Z bond owners.

3. The difference between the monthly interest payment received from the pool and that due to A, B, C, and Z holders is distributed to the residual class, less any expenses related to running the CMO.

The pool's monthly principal payments, both scheduled and unscheduled, are distributed as follows:

1. All of the pool's scheduled principal flows and prepayments are first distributed to the A class. Once A's outstanding principal has been paid off, the pool's principal payments flow to B, and after that to C.

2. Any principal payments in excess of the amount needed to retire all of the bond classes, including Z, flows to the residual class. This excess principal would be the result of overcollateralizing the bond classes. For example, if the A, B, C, and Z issues have original principal amounts of $25 million each and the pool's collateral is $102 million, then the residual class

should expect a $2 million cash flow attributable to the overcollateralization.

Economic Benefits Conferred by a Collateralized Mortgage Obligation

By prioritizing cash flows to the various bond classes, the CMO structure confers a distinct expected maturity to each bond class. Because to a large extent, investment is undertaken with the objective of matching the nature and life of asset income to forecasted liability flows, particular groups of fixed-income investors are drawn to specific CMO classes. Thrifts and commercial banks gravitate toward the A class. Intermediate-term investors, such as insurance companies that offer guaranteed investments contracts (GICs), find the next group of bond classes attractive—the B and C tranches of our example. Pension funds choose the Z class. The residual class draws other investor interests because of its unique characteristics.[1]

Because the creation of these bond classes with unique characteristics seems to satisfy investor needs that could not be effectively satisfied with existing fixed income securities, a CMO creates value. This value is evidenced by the CMO issuer's ability to sell the CMO bond classes plus the residual at a higher price than what was paid for the mortgage pool collateral.

Selecting a Tax Classification for the CMO

As has been discussed, the issuer's intent in securitizing a mortgage pool is to insulate the investor from the credit risk of the originator, i.e., the consequences of the mortgagor defaulting. In securitizing the pool, a tax classification must be selected for the business entity that is formed to issue the CMO's securities.

Mortgage pass-throughs are normally issued through creation of a grantor trust. The trust form requires the originator to pool and deposit the mortgages with a trustee, usually a bank, and to issue

---

1. The residual security exhibits low or even negative price sensitivity. As rates decline, prepayments accelerate. Since the residual owner's income comes from the spread between the pool's interest income and the CMO bonds' weighted average coupon, the lower the pool's principal, the smaller the income flow to the residual security class. Consequently, as the market rate falls and prepayments increase, the residual class market value is likely to drop.

This negative price sensitivity is somewhat offset by any overcollateralization of the pool. The excess collateral flows to the residual class when the Z class is retired. As the market rate falls, the present value of this excess collateral cash flow increases.

securities granting the holder the benefits of the trust: all principal and interest payments. The trustee represents the security holders in the event of default by the servicer of the pool. As a business form, the trust is a passive entity. For example, unlike a business organized under a corporate charter, the trust may not sell and replace its assets.

With regard to taxes, the grantor trust is ignored by the Internal Revenue Service; that is, the income received by the trust from the pool is not taxed at the trust level. The security owners pay the tax on their share of the trust's total income. Thus double taxation is avoided. However, the grantor trust is not an effective tax form for CMO issuances; with two exceptions, it may issue only one class of securities against the collateral pool.[2] If more than one class were issued, the pool's income would be taxed at the trust level and then taxed again at the investor level.

Since CMOs have multiple security classes, structuring them as grantor trusts would result in double taxation. So, prior to 1987, CMOs were structured as corporations, and the bond tranches constituted the corporation's debt. As such, the coupon payments to those tranches would be tax deductible from the corporation's income, i.e., the pool's income. To assure that the various tranche securities would be viewed as corporate debt by the IRS, the issuing structure had to resemble a corporation in that an equity class had to exist. This was achieved by the overcollateralization of the tranche securities. In addition, it was required that the timing of payments to the bond classes be different from the schedule of payments to the collateral pool. To accomplish this, the monthly pool of interest payments was usually reinvested for three or six months and then paid out as quarterly or semiannual bond coupons.

While avoiding double taxation, this organizational form had some unattractive features. The contribution of equity capital was expensive. The income to equity holders, the residual class, was taxed at the corporate level, in addition to being taxed at the personal level. The requirement that the receipt and pass-through of interest income be nonsynchronous provided a potential reinvestment problem.

To do away with these disadvantages in forming a CMO, Congress created a new tax classification, the Real Estate Mortgage Investment

---

2. The exceptions are mortgage pools that are stripped into interest only and principal only classes or where one class of securities is subordinate to the other class should the servicer default. In the latter type of structure, choosing a grantor trust as the vehicle for issuing senior and subordinate classes, restricts the issuer from selling the subordinated class.

Conduit (REMIC). Electing to organize the CMO under the REMIC classification meant that several classes of securities backed by mortgage collateral could be issued with no taxes paid on the pool income received at the REMIC level.[3] Selecting the REMIC tax classification frees the issuer from overcollateralizing the pool, allows the receipt of pool income and payment to security classes to be synchronous, and avoids taxation of the residual income at the REMIC level.[4]

Illustration of a CMO's Cash Flows

Suppose that mortgages with a balance of $102 million, a coupon of 10%, ten years to maturity, and a zero service fee are pooled to collateralize a CMO with three bond classes, A, B, and Z. There is also a residual class. The A, B, and Z bonds, respectively, carry coupons of 9%, 9.5%, and 10%; the face amounts are $30 million each for the A and Z classes and $40 million for the B class. The pool has excess collateral of $2 million, which will flow to the residual class.[5] The pool's conditional prepayment rates are 6% the first year, 12% the second year, and 18% thereafter.

The cash flows of the mortgage pool and to the A, B, and C tranches and the residual class are shown in Tables 20.1–20.4. To understand the rules followed in the allocation of cash flows, begin with Table 20.1. The second row starts with the 102 initial pool balance. The scheduled annual payment on a 10%, 10-year, 102 million balance mortgage pool is 16.60. This amount, entered in the second-row, third-column cell of Table 20.1, is paid out at the end of the first year. Of this amount, 6.40 represents the scheduled amortization payment—i.e., the scheduled principal payment—and 10.20 the interest payment. The balance after scheduled amortization is 95.60, to which the 6% first-year prepayment rate is applied to obtain prepayments of 5.74. The total interest owed to the A, B, and Z classes in that first year is 9.5 $[(0.09 \times 30) + (0.095 \times 40) + (0.10 \times 30)]$. At the end of the first year, the pool balance has been reduced to 89.86 (102.00 − 6.40 − 5.74). Since 6% of the mortgages have prepaid by the end of the first

---

3. The REMIC tax classification may be used with any form of legal organization. Thus the CMO business entity may be structured as a corporation or trust and still obtain the REMIC tax benefits.

4. Election of the REMIC classification also permits the sale of a subordinated class by the originator.

5. Since the establishment of the REMIC classification, the need to establish a distinguishable equity class has disappeared. Thus, CMOs issued since 1987 are rarely overcollateralized. However, for generality, we do so in our example.

Table 20.1 Example of CMO Cash Flows
10% Coupon, Ten-Year Mortgages, $102 Million Principal

Year	Beginning-of-Year Mortgage Balance	Annual Mortgage Payment	Interest Part	Amortization Part	Year-End Balance after Amortization but before Prepayment
1	102.00	16.60	10.20	6.40	95.60
2	89.86	15.60	8.99	6.61 (15.6 − 8.99)	83.25 (89.86 − 6.61)
3	73.26	13.73	7.33	6.40	66.86 (73.26 − 6.40)
4	54.83	11.26	5.48	5.78	49.05 (54.83 − 5.78)
5	40.22	9.23	4.02	5.21	35.01 (40.22 − 5.21)
6	28.71	7.57	2.87	4.70	24.01 (28.71 − 4.70)
7	19.69	6.21	1.97	4.24	15.45 (19.69 − 4.24)
8	12.67	5.09	1.27	3.82	8.85 (12.67 − 3.82)
9	7.26	4.17	0.73	3.44	3.82 (7.26 − 3.44)
10	3.13	3.44	0.31	3.13	0.0
11	0.0				

year, the second year's annual payment is reduced to 15.60 (0.94 × 16.60).

At the end of the first year, class A receives the promised interest of 2.70 (0.09 × 30) and principal payments of 15.14, reducing A's outstanding balance to 14.86. The funds used to pay down A's principal balance are composed of the 6.40 scheduled pool amortization, the 5.74 of pool prepayments, and the 3.0 interest payment due to the Z class. The B class receives its 3.8 promised coupon payment, but no paydown of its balance, since all pool principal payments plus the Z class coupon interest are directed toward the A holders until the A bonds are retired. The interest of 3.0, due but not paid to the

Prepayment on After-Amortized Balance	Interest Owed to A, B, & Z Classes	Residual to Equity Holders	Explanatory Notes
5.74 (.06 × 95.60)	9.50 (.09 × 30 + .095 × 40 + .10 × 30)	0.70 (10.20 − 9.50)	Year-End Balance = 102.00 − 6.40 − 5.74 = 89.86
9.99 (.12 × 83.25)	8.44 (1.34 + 3.8 + 3.3)	0.55 (8.99 − 8.44)	Annual Mortgage Payment = 15.60 Calculated as (1 − .06) × 16.60
12.03 (.18 × 66.86)	6.95 (3.32 + 3.63)	0.38 (7.33 − 6.95)	
8.83 (.18 × 49.05)	5.22 (1.23 + 3.99)	0.26 (5.48 − 5.22)	
6.30 (.18 × 35.01)	3.82 (All to Z)	0.20 (4.02 − 3.82)	
4.32 (.18 × 24.01)	2.67	0.20 (2.87 − 2.67)	
2.78 (.18 × 15.45)	1.77	0.20 (1.97 − 1.77)	
1.59 (.18 × 8.85)	1.07	0.20 (1.27 − 1.07)	
0.69 (.18 × 3.82)	0.53	0.20 (.73 − .53)	
0.0	0.11	2.20 (.31 − .11 + 2.00)	← Amortization That Does Not Go to Z (3.13 − 1.13) = 2.0

Z bond holders, is added to the original balance of 30.0 to arrive at Z's new balance of 33.0 at the end of the first year. This balance will continue to earn interest at the Z coupon rate of 10%.

20.2 Valuation of a Two-Period CMO: An Example

The collateral pool consists of $102 million of two-year mortgages paying 10% annually. Assume no service fee. If the market coupon rate, C_m, falls below the mortgage coupon rate of 10%, half of the pool's mortgages prepay. The probability that interest rates will rise

Table 20.2 Example of Cash Flows of "A" Tranche 9% Bond, $30 Million Principal

Year	Beginning-of-Year Balance	Principal Allocation from Mortgage Pool (Amortization + Prepayment) + Z Class Interest	A's Coupon Interest	Total Payments to A	Explanatory Notes
1	30	15.14 (Amortization = 6.40, Prepayment = 5.74, Z Interest = 3.0)	2.70 (.09 × 30)	17.84	
2	14.86	14.86 (14.86 of 6.61 + 9.99 + 3.3)	1.34 (.09 × 14.86)	16.20	Amount of Principal Payments + Z Tranche Interest to Go to B Is (6.61 + 9.99 + 3.3) − 14.86 = 5.04
3	0.0				
4					
5					
6					
7					
8					
9					
10					

Table 20.3 Example of Cash Flows of "B" Tranche 9.5% Bond, $40 Million Principal

Year	Beginning-of-Year Balance	Principal Allocation from Mortgage Pool (Amortization + Prepayment) + Z Class Interest	B's Coupon Interest	Total Payments	Explanatory Notes
1	40.00	0.0 All Allocated to "A" Tranche	3.80	3.80	
2	40.00	5.04 (6.61 + 9.99 + 3.30) − 14.86 = 5.04	3.80	8.84	14.86 in Column 2 Is Paid to the A Class.
3	34.96	22.06 (6.40 + 12.03 + 3.63)	3.32	25.38	
4	12.90	12.90 (12.90 of 5.78 + 8.83)	1.23	14.13	14.61 − 12.90 = 1.71 Goes to Retirement of the "Z" Debt
5	0.0				
6					
7					
8					
9					
10					

Table 20.4   Example of Cash Flows of "Z" Tranche 10% Bond, $30 Million Principal

Year	Beginning-of-Year Balance	Principal Allocation from Mortgage Pool (Amortization + Prepayment)	Z's Coupon Interest	Z's Total Payments	Explanatory Notes
1	30	0.0 All Allocated to "A" Tranche	0.0	0.0	
2	33	0.0	0.0	0.0	
3	36.3	0.0	0.0	0.0	
4	39.93	1.71	3.99*	5.70 (3.99 + 1.71)	All Other Classes Have Been Paid Off. Annual Interest Is Now Paid on Z.
5	38.22 (39.93 − 1.71)	11.51	3.82	15.33	
6	26.71	9.02	2.67	11.69	
7	17.69	7.02	1.77	8.79	
8	10.67	5.41	1.07	6.48	
9	5.26	4.13	0.53	4.66	
10	1.13	1.13	0.11	1.24	
11	0.0				

*If part of the 3.99 had to be used to retire B's tranche, then that part would have been accrued; the remaining part of the 3.99 would be paid to Z holders in year 4.

equals that of interest rates falling, 0.5. Against this collateral pool, an A tranche, a Z tranche, and a residual class are issued. The A and Z classes are each assigned a principal value of $50 million and coupons of 9% and 10%, respectively. The $t = 0$ portion of Figure 20.1 depicts the interest rate tree extending to the first period and the cash flows to the pool, the bond classes, and the residual class. End-of-period balances for the pool, the bond classes, and the residual are also shown. The $t = 1$ portion of Figure 20.1 shows the corresponding data at maturity, $t = 2$.

The theoretical value of the pool is

$$103.16 = .5\left[\frac{58.77}{1.09} + \frac{58.77}{(1.09)(1.10)}\right] + .5\left[\frac{85.49}{1.09} + \frac{29.38}{(1.09)(1.08)}\right]$$

The theoretical values for the A, Z, and residual classes are

$$A: \quad 50.00 = \left(\frac{54.5}{1.09}\right)$$

$$Z: \quad 50.67 = .5\left[\frac{3.57}{1.09} + \frac{56.57}{(1.09)(1.10)}\right] + .5\left[\frac{30.29}{1.09} + \frac{27.18}{(1.09)(1.08)}\right]$$

$$residual: \ 2.49 = .5\left[\frac{0.7}{1.09} + \frac{2.20}{(1.09)(1.10)}\right] + .5\left[\frac{0.7}{1.09} + \frac{2.20}{(1.09)(1.08)}\right]$$

Notice that the sum of the theoretical values of the CMO's classes equals the theoretical value of the collateral pool. This is what one would expect. It is a Modigliani-Miller (1958) result for derivative assets. But, in reality, since CMO bonds tend to meet special needs, the average option-adjusted spread for the CMO bonds is lower than that of the collateral pool.

To continue the numerical illustration, suppose the following OASs have been placed by the market on the pool and the CMO's classes: collateral pool, 2%; A class, 1/2%; Z class, 1%; and residual, 0%. The corresponding value of the pool is

$$pool: 100.65 = .5\left[\frac{58.77}{1.11} + \frac{58.77}{(1.11)(1.12)}\right] + .5\left[\frac{85.49}{1.11} + \frac{29.38}{(1.11)(1.10)}\right]$$

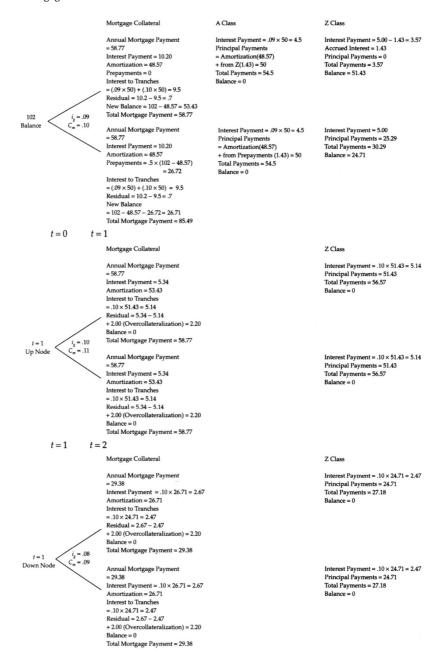

Figure 20.1 CMO Cash Flows

and those for the CMO classes are

$$A: \quad 49.77 = \left(\frac{54.5}{1.095}\right)$$

$$Z: \quad 49.89 = .5\left[\frac{3.57}{1.10} + \frac{56.57}{(1.10)(1.11)}\right] + .5\left[\frac{30.29}{1.10} + \frac{27.18}{(1.10)(1.09)}\right]$$

$$residual: \quad 2.49 = .5\left[\frac{0.7}{1.09} + \frac{2.20}{(1.09)(1.10)}\right] + .5\left[\frac{0.7}{1.09} + \frac{2.20}{(1.09)(1.08)}\right]$$

The pool's market value, 100.65, is less than the sum of the parts that it can be sold for through the CMO structure, 102.15. Construction of and sale of the CMO bonds and residual takes advantage of an arbitrage opportunity.

20.3 Planned Amortization Class (PAC)

CMOs were created to redistribute uncertainty of MPT cash flows. Planned amortization classes (PACs) were developed in response to investor demand for securities with even lower principal payment uncertainty. A PAC constitutes a class of a CMO and is structured to provide its investors with prepayment protection should the pool's speed unexpectedly rise, yet protect the investor from ending up with a security having a longer than expected average life, called *extension,* should the pool's prepayment speed precipitously fall. At inception, the PAC has its *principal* payment schedule specified for its entire life.

The PAC Structure

A PAC's future principal flows are specified by first calculating the principal cash flows available from the pool at two different prepayment speeds—one quite high, the other quite low. These two prepayment speeds are said to constitute the PAC's collar. Two principal payment schedules are thus obtained. The PAC principal cash flow at any future date is defined as the minimum principal cash flow of the high- and low-speed principal payment schedules. If the pool prepays at a single speed within the collar for the life of the pool, then the specified PAC schedule will be met. However, if the pool's speed demonstrates marked variability, although never straying outside the collar, then there are scenarios in which the pool's collateral will be insufficient to meet the PAC's prespecified payment path.

Adherence to the PAC schedule is achieved through use of the other CMO class (or classes) as support. If prepayments exceed the amount necessary to meet the PAC schedule, the excess principal flow is absorbed by the support class. On the other hand, in a slow-speed environment, scheduled principal amortization and prepayments that would normally flow to the support class are redirected to the PAC to meet its schedule. If the redirected principal payments from the support class to the PAC prove insufficient to make good the PAC schedule, then any shortfall is paid in future years, before the support class receives further principal payments. One can see that the relative predictability of the PAC's cash flows is obtained through an increase in the volatility of the support class's cash flows.

Determining a PAC Schedule: An Illustration

Consider a 10%, five-year mortgage pool with a $100 million principal balance. Assume that interest and scheduled principal payments are made at year end. There is no servicing charge. A CMO is to be created with a PAC and a support class; both are to carry coupons of 10%. There is no residual class. The upper and lower prepayment speed bounds that form the PAC collar are CPRs of 20% and 5%. Table 20.5 lists the principal payment schedules produced by these two CPRs. The schedules are plotted in Figure 20.2. The minimum of these two schedules' principal payments in each year specifies the PAC payment schedule.

In this simple example, the PAC and support classes are respectively assigned collateral amounts of 82.78 and 17.22. If the CMO

Table 20.5   Total Principal Payment Schedules of $100 Million, 10%, Five-Year Mortgage Pool at CPRs of 20% and 5%

	CPR	
Year	5%	20%
1	20.56	33.10
2	20.23	24.91
3	19.95	18.54
4	19.72	13.62
5	19.54	9.83

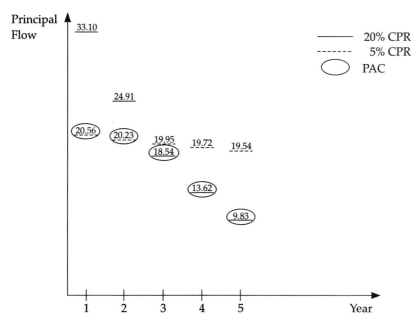

Figure 20.2 Determining a PAC's Cash Flows

issuer wishes to assign different collateral amounts to the PAC and support classes, say 75 and 25, then the PAC schedule generated in Table 20.5 must be scaled. In particular, multiply each of the PAC's scheduled principal payments by the ratio of the desired total principal amount, 75, to the total principal amount generated, 82.78. Multiplying the PAC flows by 0.9060 alters the PAC's annual flows to 18.63, 18.33, 16.80, 12.34, and 8.90. These numbers sum to 75.

Deviations from the PAC Schedule

A single prepayment speed over the life of the PAC within the 5%–20% collar will result in the schedule being met. Consider the PAC with 82.78 of collateral, the unscaled version. Suppose the pool experiences a 10% CPR for five years. The principal amounts available for distribution to the PAC in years one through five are 24.74, 22.12, 19.76, 17.64, and 15.74—sufficient to cover the PAC's schedule payments.

However, if the pool's CPR remains within the PAC collar but moves between the extreme prepayment speed bounds, the PAC schedule may not be met. For example, suppose the pool's CPR is

20% for the first two years and then equals 5% during the pool's last three years. Then the total principal payments available from the pool in years one and two are 33.1 and 24.91, respectively. The scheduled PAC payments are met (20.56 and 20.23), and the support class is retired: $(33.1 - 20.56) + (24.91 - 20.23) = 17.22$. With 41.99 of remaining collateral, a CPR of 5% results in principal payments in years three, four, and five, of 14.15, 13.99, and 13.85. The pool's actual principal payments cannot ensure the PAC's originally scheduled payments. In particular, the scheduled third-year payment of 18.54 cannot be met; 4.39 of it is pushed into the fourth and fifth years. In this case, the PAC bonds are described as undergoing an extension as their average life increases.

20.4 Targeted Amortization Class (TAC)

PACs are designed to offer prepayment protection over a wide spectrum of speeds. To obtain this protection the investor gives up some yield. There was evident demand for a bond class that provides protection against unexpectedly high prepayment speeds without the PAC's protection against slower speeds. This is what a TAC is designed to do. The TAC investor gives up the low-speed protection offered by a PAC for a higher yield.

Structuring a TAC: An Illustration

The TAC's expected principal flow schedule is generated using a single prepayment speed. Assume the CMO's collateral pool has a 10% coupon, five years to maturity, and a $100 million balance and pays interest and principal annually. A CPR of 10% is attached to the pool. A CMO is formed with a TAC and a single support class. The TAC is assigned 75% of the pool's collateral; the support class receives the remaining 25%. The scheduled principal flows to the pool and to the TAC are listed in Table 20.6.

The support class contains sufficient collateral to protect the TAC's scheduled payments as long as the pool's speed does not exceed 16.25%. At speeds above this figure, the TAC must accept higher principal in the middle years and less in the later years. At a CPR of 20%, the TAC receives 16.40 in principal instead of the scheduled 14.82 in year three; the average life of the TAC bond shortens.[6]

---

6. If the CPR is 20%, then the support class's principal is reduced to 2.14 after two years: $25 - (33.10 - 18.56) - (24.91 - 16.59)$. In the third year the 18.54 of the pool's principal payment exceeds the 14.82 scheduled TAC payment plus the 2.14 of collateral remaining in the support class. This results in a 16.40 payment to the TAC class.

Table 20.6   Principal Flows to the Pool and to the TAC

Year	Pool CPR					TAC*
	0%	3%	10%	16.25%	20%	10%
1	16.38	18.89	24.74	29.97	33.10	18.56
2	18.02	19.39	22.12	24.02	24.91	16.59
3	19.82	19.94	19.76	19.11	18.54	14.82
4	21.80	20.55	17.64	15.10	13.62	13.23
5	23.98	21.23	15.74	11.80	9.83	11.80

*Payments are calculated as 75% of the pool's principal payments assuming a 10% CPR.

Unlike the PAC, where the principal payment schedule is set after taking into account what the available collateral can support at a range of rates below the expected speed, the TAC takes no such precaution. Thus, at lower than expected speeds, the TAC extends; that is, its average life lengthens as principal payments are deferred. Although in the above example, the pool happens to have sufficient collateral to meet the TAC schedule at a wide range of rates below 10%, it is worthwhile to consider an extreme rate that forces extension, simply to illustrate the allocation rule of a CMO containing a TAC.

At a zero CPR, the TAC's scheduled principal payment of 18.56 in year one cannot be met. There is a shortfall of 2.18 (see Table 20.6). This amount accrues to the TAC. In later years, when the pool principal payments are more than sufficient to meet the TAC schedule, the prior shortfalls are paid before the support class receives any principal payments. In the zero CPR case, 1.43 of the shortfall is made up in the second year (of course, interest is paid to the TAC class on the higher-than-scheduled balance), and the remaining 0.75 shortfall is paid in the third year.

Notice that the TAC may not extend if the actual speed is consistently less than the targeted (expected) speed. At a CPR of 3%, the pool's principal payments are sufficient to meet the TAC schedule. In more complicated structures than that presented in the above illustration, where the TAC's scheduled initial payment begins sometime after the pool's and ends before the pool matures, a realized speed above the target speed but below the upper bound may result in an extension of the TAC, because there is insufficient collateral to generate the principal flows necessary to meet the TAC schedule in its middle to later years.

20.5 Floater and Inverse Floater Classes

Some CMOs are structured to have a floating class and an inverse floating class. The floater's coupon will be tied to an index but will usually exceed it by some margin.[7] The inverse floater has a coupon that varies inversely with the same index. At times, a CMO floating class can be constructed to provide a higher yield and at least as strong a credit rating as competing floating securities. Formation of an inverse floater class during a time when long-term rates are sharply higher than short-term rates, provides, as we shall see, a short-term, high-yield security. If the sum of the market values of these two classes exceeds the cost of the mortgage collateral used to support them, then the CMO will include a floating class and an inverse floating class.

An inverse floater bond is created by apportioning the fixed rate collateral between the floating and inverse floating classes. The floating class interest income is equal to the product of the floating rate and the floating class principal. The interest income to the inverse floater amounts to the difference between the collateral pool's interest income and the interest income paid to the floating rate class. As an example, let the collateral pool have a $200 million principal and an 8% fixed coupon. This principal amount is divided equally between a floating class and an inverse floating class. The interest income owed each class is given by

$$\begin{matrix} \textit{floating class} \\ \textit{interest income} \end{matrix} = \begin{matrix} \textit{floating rate} \times \\ \textit{floating class principal} \end{matrix} \qquad (20.1)$$

and

$$\begin{matrix} \textit{inverse class} \\ \textit{interest income} \end{matrix} = (.08 \times 200) - \begin{matrix} \textit{floating class} \\ \textit{interest income} \end{matrix} \qquad (20.2)$$

One immediately sees that the most that could be paid to the floating class is all of the collateral's income. So, in this case, the floater's coupon rate would have to be capped at 16% (8% × 200 / 100). If the floating rate reaches 16%, then there is no residual income to the inverse class, and one would say that the inverse class has a

---

7. The most commonly used indices are one-month LIBOR, the COFI (book cost of funds for thrift institutions) of the 11th district (California, Arizona, and Nevada), and the one-year and ten-year Constant Maturity Treasury (CMT) indices.

zero floor, i.e., a minimum coupon of zero percent. If the inverse coupon is also capped at 16%, then this sets a zero floor for the floating coupon. Given the principal allocation, the selection of two of the four cap-floor parameters determines the other two. The choice of a floater cap of 12% and a floor of 2% establishes an inverse floor of 4% [(0.08 × 200 − 0.12 × 100)/100], and an inverse cap of 14% [(0.08 × 200 − 0.02 × 100)/100].

The Leverage Inherent in the Inverse Floater

Look at equation (20.2). One can view the ownership of an inverse floater as the purchase of the fixed coupon collateral with 50% financing at a floating rate. If the yield curve is positively sloped, then the inverse floater class gains the differential between the higher, long-term fixed rate and the lower, shorter-term floating rate—at least initially.[8] Conversely, if the yield curve is negatively sloped, the inverse floater loses the difference between the floating and fixed rates. Thus, the inverse floater's creation can be viewed as a levered transaction, with the floating class principal representing the amount borrowed.

The higher the yield curve's slope, the greater the incentive to increase leverage, i.e., to allocate more of the collateral to the floating class. However, as is the rule with leverage, it increases the volatility of the asset's income. If we allocate $180 million of the collateral to the floating class, then the inverse floater's income is expressed by formula (20.3).

$$\begin{matrix} \textit{inverse class} \\ \textit{interest income} \end{matrix} = (.08 \times 200) - (\textit{floating rate} \times 180) \quad (20.3)$$

If the floating rate happens to equal 8%, then the coupon rate of the inverse floater will be 8% [(0.08 × 200 − 0.08 × 180)/20]. However, should the floating rate fall to 7%, the inverse floater's income will rise to 3.4 million, implying a coupon rate of 17% (3.4/20.0). A 1% change in the floating rate is magnified nine times in the inverse rate. A 0.5% rise in the floating rate decreases the inverse rate by 4.5%—again a ninefold magnification. Now divide both sides of (20.3) by the principal of the inverse floater's class, 20, to obtain

$$\textit{inverse class coupon} = (.08 \times 10) - (9 \times \textit{floating rate}) \quad (20.4)$$

---

8. An upward-sloping yield curve may indicate that short-term rates are expected to climb. If this event occurred, then the leverage advantage would disappear.

The coefficient that multiplies the floating rate, 9 in this case, is called the *coupon leverage* of the inverse floater.[9]

Valuation Considerations

The arbitrage-free tree approach is generally applied to the valuation of the inverse floater class. Again, to each node, an interest rate–time state, a cash flow must be assigned. Application of the no-arbitrage pricing principle leads to a theoretical price. An iterative search is then undertaken to find the inverse floater's OAS. But, apart from this direct valuation methodology, some comments are warranted about how the inverse floater's value should react to yield curve shifts.

A change in the market rate required on the collateral securities will normally be accompanied by a change in the floater's rate. If the floating rate movement does not run into a cap or floor constraint, then the floating rate adjustment will preserve the value of the floating bonds. But since the rate required on the collateral has changed and the sum of the changes in value of the floating and inverse floating classes should approximate the change in collateral value, then the change in collateral value should be completely transmitted to the inverse class.[10]

If rates fall and prepayments increase, the inverse's coupon rate will increase, yet its market value may decline. The explanation is that higher prepayments will decrease the security's average life, so although the rate will be somewhat higher than before, the horizon over which it is expected to be earned may be significantly shorter.

20.6 Credit Enhancement of a Mortgage Security

For mortgage collateral that does not conform to agency standards, the problem of credit enhancement arises. There are two paths toward upgrading the credit rating of the mortgage collateral: (1) external enhancement, which includes pool insurance purchased from

---

9. With a floor and a cap on an inverse floater, the effective leverage is lower than that implied by the coupon leverage coefficient.

10. This is somewhat of an abstraction. First, the value of the floater is unlikely to retain its full value as it approaches its cap, for the market recognizes that the next rate adjustment necessary to match a higher market rate might not be feasible. Second, we know that the purpose of the CMO was to create value in excess of the collateral value. Since the original class values did not sum to that of the original collateral amount, it cannot be asserted that the changes in values in response to the new rates will be exactly equal.

a private insurance company, a bank letter of credit, or the guarantee of the parent corporation; or (2) creation of a subordinated or junior security class to absorb the losses that would normally be borne by the senior class.

External Enhancement

Pool insurance policies are designed to cover principal losses up to a stated percentage of the pool's balance. However, such policies must often be supplemented with special hazard insurance policies, to cover earthquake and flood damage, and with the purchase of a cash performance bond, to ensure that cash shortfalls arising from mortgage payment delinquencies do not interrupt the promised timing of cash flows to the bond investor. Additionally, insurance must be purchased for losses in the event of fraud or misrepresentation by the issuer. The drawback of this form of credit enhancement is that, should the insurer's credit rating fall, so will the credit rating of the CMO bonds.

Two external alternatives to insurance policies are a performance guarantee by the parent corporation of the CMO issuer and a bank letter of credit that covers a portion of the collateral balance. The corporate guarantee has the same weakness as the private insurance policy: if the corporation's credit rating falls, so will the CMO's. A letter of credit is open to the same criticism, and in addition usually has a shorter life than the expected maturity of the CMO class. So the letter of credit is subject to the risks that accompany renewal. These forms of credit enhancement have become less popular as the credit ratings of parent corporations and banks have been downgraded in recent years.

Subordination of a CMO Class

The subordination of the cash flows of one CMO bond class to another class is a means of self-insurance. The cash flows of the subordinated class provide the insurance to the senior class in the event of mortgage collateral delinquencies and defaults, irrespective of the cause. The subordinated class is usually allocated sufficient principal to absorb the senior class's losses in worst-case scenarios. As expected, the probability of default and the projected maximum loss should default occur are the key factors determining the size of the subordinated class.

As a means of further enhancing the credit protection provided by the subordinated class to the senior class, the principal payments that would normally flow to the subordinated class owners are redirected to a reserve fund that is maintained to make up any shortfalls in the cash flows due the senior class. Formation of this type of reserve fund grants the issuer the choice of providing the same level of protection with a diminished collateral allocation to the subordinated class or using the reserve fund to raise the credit quality of the senior class.

Still another means of providing extra protection to the senior class is to shift prepayments from the subordinated class to the senior class until the senior class is retired. With no shortfall in cash flows on a payment date, the senior class is likely to receive excess payments. Of course, under this credit enhancement mechanism, termed a *shifting interest structure*, the senior class will have a shorter average life.

20.7 Stripped Mortgage-Backed Securities (STRIPs)

In general, derivative mortgage securities, such as CMOs, are created when the collateral's cash flow is divided into at least two pieces, creating at least one security that has performance characteristics substantially different from those of the underlying mortgage collateral. Mortgage strips are created by altering the pro rata distribution of collateral interest and principal to an unequal allocation. In the extreme case, the entire interest from the collateral pool is paid to one security class, the *interest only* (IO) class, while all of the pool's principal payments are paid to another security class, the *principal only* (PO) class.

For the IO class, the amount of interest received varies directly with the principal balance outstanding, which in turn depends upon the prepayment rate of the underlying mortgage pool. The greater the prepayment rate, the faster the principal balance pays down, resulting in diminished future interest payments. Conversely, the lower the prepayment rate, the more slowly the outstanding balance diminishes, with the result that interest payments remain relatively high. Because lower interest rates lead to greater prepayments, which in turn reduces the income stream to the IO security holder, the IO's market value will drop when interest rates fall. Analogous reasoning leads to the conclusion that as interest rates rise, the IO's price will rise. Of course, for this *negative duration* characteristic to be present, the value change associated with the change in the magnitude of the IO's cash flow must dominate the value change associated with the altered discount rate.[11] Over the greater part of the interest rate range, the former effect does dominate the latter, with the result that the IO strip is generally characterized as having negative duration. The qualification of this negative duration characteristic arises from the phenomenon that at very high interest rates relative to the underlying mortgage rate, the prepayment speed of the pool declines only marginally. Before such a point is reached, the IO strip will begin to fall in value, as investors discount the relatively constant cash flows at higher rates.

The PO strip is also sensitive to prepayments, but its price response is opposite to that of the IO strip. Because a PO strip is a discount instrument, its value increases when interest rates fall and prepayments accelerate. Of course, when interest rates rise, causing a deceleration in prepayments, the PO's value declines. So POs have *positive duration.*

Convexity of Interest-Only and Principal-Only STRIPs

We have discussed the *slope* of stripped security prices with respect to interest rate changes—positive for IOs and negative for POs. Now we look at the second derivative of the IO and PO prices with respect to the interest rate. Figure 20.3a depicts a typical prepayment rate–interest rate relationship for a wide range of collateral types. The zero point on the horizontal axis represents the situation where the current coupon rate equals the mortgage pool's coupon rate. Figure 20.3b depicts the stripped securities' values versus relative coupon.

For a sizable region around the pool's coupon rate, the PO exhibits positive convexity whereas the IO exhibits negative convexity (concavity). That is, the PO's value increases more rapidly when interest rates fall than it declines when interest rates rise. The negative convexity of the IO means that its value increases less rapidly when interest rates rise than it falls when interest rates decline.

---

11. Recall that an instrument's duration is a measure of the percentage change in its price in response to a 1% change in its yield to maturity. (For a mathematical definition and more information, see Chapter 12.) An interest rate instrument is said to have *positive duration* if its price declines when interest rates increase—the usual case, exemplified by a price versus yield to maturity curve that is negatively sloped. If the price of an interest rate instrument increases as interest rates rise, i.e., its price versus yield to maturity curve is positively sloped, then it is said to have *negative duration.*

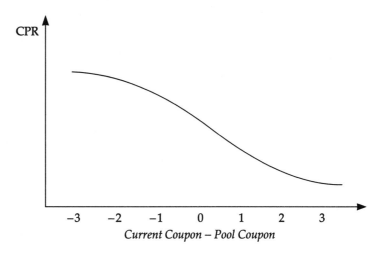

Figure 20.3a The Prepayment Function

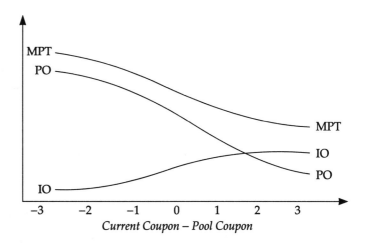

Figure 20.3b Value as a Function of Relative Coupon

These properties can be explained in terms of the response of prepayments to interest rate movements. Notice that the prepayment function's shape projects that the pool's prepayment speed will rise substantially when interest rates fall but will suffer only a moderate drop should interest rates rise. It follows that since POs benefit from high prepayments, the value gain in a falling interest rate environment will be large. The PO's value drop will be small when interest rates rise, since the prepayment speed is not projected to decline significantly. In contrast, the value loss to the IO when interest rates fall is large, because prepayments are projected to rise substantially, while the value gain of an IO is small should interest rates rise, because the prepayment function projects only a relatively small drop in prepayments.

As one moves to lower coupon differentials, the PO function turns negative convex while the IO function exhibits positive convexity. This follows from the shape of the prepayment function. In this region the prepayment function predicts a dampening of the response of the prepayment speed to a further fall in the market rate. The smaller the increase in prepayments, the less the increase in the PO's price and the smaller the decrease in the IO's price.

Hedging with IO and PO STRIPs

The purchase of an IO strip can be used to hedge against a rise in interest rates that would lower the value of a bond portfolio; or a long IO position could be used to hedge a discount mortgage inventory against a rise in interest rates, which would cause a drop in pool prepayments. A long PO position could be used to hedge a short bond position against an interest rate decline; or the long PO could be a hedge for a mortgage security portfolio that is vulnerable to a rise in prepayment speed, such as one composed of premium pass-throughs.

Valuation of IO and PO STRIPs: An Illustration

Consider a pool of pass-throughs collateralized by mortgages with a $100 million balance, two years to maturity, and a 10% mortgage coupon rate. The servicing fee is 0.5% of the outstanding mortgage balance. Therefore, the MPT coupon is 9.5%. The mortgage pool balance is completely prepaid if the coupon rate on new mortgages falls below 8%, that is, if $C_m < 0.08$. This rate, C_m, is assumed to exceed the one-period Treasury rate, i_g, by 0.5%. The probability of a rate increase is 0.5, as is the probability of a rate decrease.

The MPT's cash flows, *CF*, are presented against the interest rate lattice (Figure 20.4). Discounting the cash flows by the one-period rates gives a theoretical pool value of 101.50. A market value of 99.79 implies an OAS of 1.5%.

In Figure 20.5, the IO's and PO's cash flows are presented at the nodes of the interest rate tree.

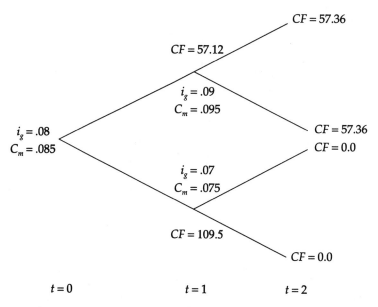

Figure 20.4   The Pool's Cash Flows

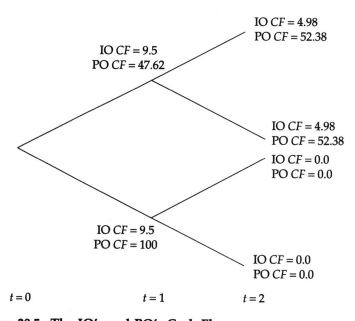

Figure 20.5   The IO's and PO's Cash Flows

The theoretical values of the IO and PO are 10.91 and 90.59. Notice, as expected, the theoretical values of the IO and PO sum to that of the collateral.

Because the strips serve investor needs that could not be satisfied prior to their creation, investors underprice them by less than the securities that compose the collateral pool. If the OASs attached to the IO and PO are 0.5% and 0%, respectively, then the corresponding market prices are 10.85 and 90.59.[12]

Price Characteristics of IO and PO STRIPs

We illustrate the price behavior of this example's IO and PO in both a higher and a lower interest rate environment.

Higher Rates   Suppose all rates rise by 100 basis points. The revised cash flows are presented against the new interest rate tree. See Figure 20.6.

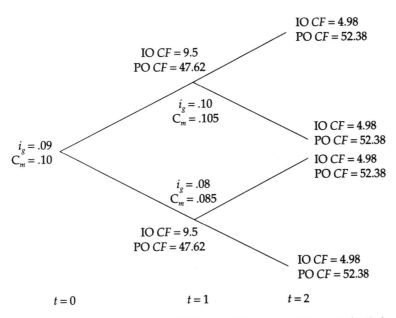

Figure 20.6   IO's and PO's Cash Flows with Interest Rates 1% Higher

---

12. Most dealer pricing models show that the IO's OAS tends to exceed the OAS of the underlying collateral. Since the market value of the IO plus the PO exceeds that of the underlying collateral, it then follows that the PO's OAS is sufficiently low to more than offset the negative impact of the IO's OAS on the value of the total STRIP package.

To calculate the IO's and PO's new market values, add their OASs (0.5% and 0%, respectively) to the one-period Treasury rates prior to discounting. The IO's new market value is 12.83. A rise in rates has increased the IO's market value by 1.98. The reason is that because higher rates have curtailed prepayments, the IO holder will now receive that much more interest in the event that either of the two lower nodes is reached in the second period. This cash flow increase outweighs the negative effects of the higher discount rates. So we have a vivid example of why IOs are described as having negative duration. Of course, if rates were to jump another 100 bps, the IO's market value would fall, since there would be no prepayments left to curtail. With no commensurate increase in cash flows, the higher interest rates result in higher discount rates being applied to stable cash flows.

The 100 bps rise in rates results in a new PO market value of 87.78. The combination of lower prepayments and higher discount rates serves to make the PO less attractive. The PO's price behavior is consistent with that of any other zero coupon; it exhibits positive duration.

Lower Rates   Suppose all rates drop by 200 bps. Figure 20.7 contains the new cash flows and interest rates.

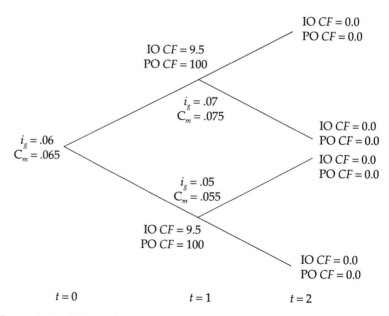

Figure 20.7   **IO's and PO's Cash Flows with Interest Rates 2% Lower**

The IO's market value falls from 10.91 to 8.92. True, we are discounting by lower rates, but prepayments have drastically reduced cash flows to IO holders. The PO's market value has significantly increased, from 90.59 to 94.34, as lower interest rates have increased prepayments to this zero-coupon instrument and reduced the discount rates applied to all cash flows.

References and Suggested Reading

Arak, M., A. Estrella, L. Goodman, and A. Silver. 1988. "Interest Rate Swaps: An Alternative Explanation." *Financial Management* 17 (Summer): 12–18.

Arditti, F.D., S. Ayaydin, R. Mattu, and S. Rigsbee. 1986. "A Passive Futures Strategy That Outperforms Active Management." *Financial Analysts Journal* 42 (July/August): 63–66.

Asquith, J.P., and D.P. Cunningham. 1992. "Swaps and Termination Events: Legal and Business Considerations." Presentation at the International Swap Dealers Association Annual Meeting, Paris, 13 March.

Bank for International Settlements. 1992. "Delivery versus Payment in Securities Settlement Systems." Report prepared by the Committee in Payment and Settlement Systems of the central banks of the Group of Ten countries, Basle.

Bansal, V.K., J.L. Bicksler, A.H. Chen, and J.F. Marshall, 1993. "Gains from Synthetic Financings with Interest Rate Swaps: Fact or Fancy?" *Journal of Applied Corporate Finance* 6 (Fall): 91–94.

Bansal, V.K., M.E. Ellis, and J.F. Marshall. 1993. "The Spot Swaps Yield Curve: Derivation and Use." *Advances in Futures and Options Research* 6: 279–290.

Banz, R.W., and M.H. Miller. 1978. "Prices for State-Contingent Claims: Some Estimates and Applications." *Journal of Business* 51 (October): 653–672.

Bartholomew, L., J. Berk, and R. Roll. 1986. "Adjustable Rate Mortgages: An Introduction." New York: Goldman Sachs Mortgage Securities Research, November.

Bartholomew, L., J. Berk, and R. Roll. 1987. "Adjustable Rate Mortgages: Prepayment Behavior." New York: Goldman Sachs Mortgage Securities Research, February.

Bartlett, W.W. 1989. *Mortgage-Backed Securities: Products, Analysis, and Trading.* New York: New York Institute of Finance.

Basle Committee on Banking Supervision. 1994. "The Capital Adequacy Treatment of the Credit Risk Associated with Certain Off-Balance Sheet Items." Basle, Switzerland, July.

Belonsky, G.M. 1988. "CMO Residuals." In *The Handbook of Mortgage-Backed Securities,* ed. F.J. Fabozzi. Chicago: Probus, 433–453.

Belton, T. 1988/89. "The New Breed: Option Adjusted Spreads." *Secondary Mortgage Markets* 5 (Winter): 6–11.

Benson, R., and N. Daniel. 1992. "Up, Over and Out." In *From Black-Scholes to Black Holes.* London: RISK Magazine Ltd., 179–182.

Berk, J., and R. Roll. 1987. "Adjustable Rate Mortgages: Valuation." New York: Goldman Sachs Mortgage Securities Research, August.

Bhattacharya, A.K. 1992. "Self-Insuring Non-Conforming Mortgages Using Senior-Subordinated Structures." In *The Handbook of Mortgage-Backed Securities*, ed. F.J. Fabozzi. Chicago: Probus, 131–154.

Bicksler, J., and A. Chen. 1986. "An Economic Analysis of Interest Rate Swaps." *Journal of Finance* 41 (July): 645–656.

Bierwag, G.O., and G.G. Kaufman. 1992. "Duration Gaps with Futures and Swaps for Managing Interest Rate Risk at Depository Institutions." *Journal of Financial Services Research* 5 (February): 217–234.

Black, F. 1976. "The Pricing of Commodity Contracts." *Journal of Financial Economics* 3 (March): 167–179.

Black, F., E. Derman, and W. Toy. 1990. "A One-Factor Model of Interest Rates and its Application to Treasury Bond Options." *Financial Analysts Journal* 46 (January/February), 33–39.

Black, F., and M. Scholes. 1973. "The Pricing of Options and Corporate Liabilities." *Journal of Political Economy* 81 (May/June): 637–659.

Bookstaber, R.M. 1991. *Option Pricing and Investment Strategies*. Chicago: Probus.

Bookstaber, R.M., and J.A. Langsam. 1988. "Portfolio Insurance Trading Rules." *Journal of Futures Markets* 8 (February): 15–31.

Borg, B., B. Lancaster, and J. Tang. 1992. "Inverse Floating-Rate CMOs." In *The Handbook of Mortgage-Backed Securities*, ed. F.J. Fabozzi. Chicago: Probus, 483–518.

Breeden, D.T., and R.H. Litzenberger. 1978. "Prices of State-Contingent Claims Implicit in Option Prices." *Journal of Business* 51 (October): 621–651.

Brown, K.C., and D.J. Smith. 1990. "Forward Swaps, Swap Options, and the Management of Callable Debt." *Journal of Applied Corporate Finance* 2 (Winter): 59–71.

Brueggeman, W.B., J.D. Fisher, and L.D. Stone. 1989. *Real Estate Finance*. Homewood, Ill.: Irwin.

Burghardt, G.D., and T.M. Belton. 1994. *The Treasury Bond Basis*. Chicago: Probus.

Burghardt, G., T. Belton, M. Lane, G. Luce, R. McVey. 1991. *Eurodollar Futures and Options*. Chicago: Probus.

Cameron, S., K. Holme, and A. Rapoport. 1990. "Managing Interest Rate Risk in Real Estate Development." *Journal of Applied Corporate Finance* 3 (Spring): 56–64.

Capozza, D., and B. Cornell. 1979. "Treasury Bill Pricing in the Spot and Futures Markets." *Review of Economics and Statistics* 61 (November): 513–520.

Carlson, S.J., and T.D. Sears. 1988. "Stripped Mortgage Pass-Throughs: New Tools for Investors. In *The Handbook of Mortgage-Backed Securities*, ed. F.J. Fabozzi. Chicago: Probus, 553–584.

Carron, A.S. 1988. "Mortgage Strips." In *The Handbook of Mortgage-Backed Securities*, ed. F.J. Fabozzi. Chicago: Probus, 501–520.

Chicago Board of Trade of the City of Chicago Rules and Regulations. 1994. Chicago: Chicago Board of Trade.

Clauretie, T.M., and J.R. Webb. 1993. *The Theory and Practice of Real Estate Finance*. Fort Worth: Dryden Press.

Clearing House Manual of Operations. 1994. Chicago: Chicago Mercantile Exchange.

Cochran, T. 1993. "FLEX Grows Stronger." *Barron's*, 14 June, 55–56.

Constantinides, G.M., and R.W. Rosenthal. 1984. "Strategic Analysis of the Competitive Exercise of Certain Financial Options." *Journal of Economic Theory* 32 (February): 128–138.

Cooper, I.A., and A.S. Mello. 1991. "The Default Risk of Swaps." *Journal of Finance* 46 (June): 597–620.

Cornell, B., and M. Reinganum. 1981. "Forward and Futures Prices: Evidence from the Foreign Exchange Markets." *Journal of Finance* 36 (December): 1035–1045.

Cox, J.C., J.E. Ingersoll, and S.A. Ross. 1981. "The Relation between Forward and Futures Prices." *Journal of Financial Economics* 9 (December): 321–346.

Cox, J.C., and S.A. Ross. 1976. "The Valuation of Options for Alternative Stochastic Processes." *Journal of Financial Economics* 3 (January/March): 145–166.

Cox, J.C., S.A. Ross, and M. Rubinstein. 1979. "Option Pricing: A Simplified Approach." *Journal of Financial Economics*, 7 (September): 229–263.

Cox, J.C., and M. Rubinstein. 1985. *Options Markets*. Englewood Cliffs, N.J.: Prentice Hall.

Cunningham, D.P., W.P. Rogers Jr., G.W. Bilicic Jr., R.Y. Casper, and C.T. Abruzzo. 1994. "An Introduction to OTC Derivatives." New York: Cravath, Swaine, and Moore, 8 April.

Curtin, W.J., and P.T. Van Valkenburg. 1992a. "Introduction to CMO PAC Bonds." In *The Handbook of Mortgage-Backed Securities*, ed. F.J. Fabozzi. Chicago: Probus, 351–369.

Curtin, W.J., and P.T. Van Valkenburg. 1992b. "Introduction to CMO TAC Bonds." In *The Handbook of Mortgage-Backed Securities*, ed. F.J. Fabozzi. Chicago: Probus, 371–376.

Das, S., and J. Martin. 1991. "Protective Strategies." *RISK* 4 (September): 93–97.

Dattatreya, R.E., R.E.S. Venkatesh, and V.E. Venkatesh. 1994. *Interest Rate and Currency Swaps*. Chicago: Probus.

Davidson, A.S., and M.D. Herskovitz. 1994. *Mortgage-Backed Securities: Investment Analysis and Advanced Valuation Techniques*. Chicago: Probus.

Depository Trust Company. 1992. "Operational Arrangements Necessary for an Issue to Become Eligible for DTC Services." Memorandum to Participants, Underwriters, Agents, Trustees, Bond Counsel, and Others Affected. New York, 27 February.

Depository Trust Company. 1994a. "Mandatory Use of the Collateralized Mortgage Obligation (CMO) Trade Adjustment System (CTAS)." Memorandum to all Participants of the Depository Trust Company. New York, 30 October.

Depository Trust Company. 1994b. *Rules, By-Laws and Organization Certificate of The Depository Trust Company Index*. New York: Depository Trust Company.

Derivatives: Practices and Principles. 1993. Washington, D.C.: Group of Thirty, July.

Derman, E., and I. Kani. 1993. "The Ins and Outs of Barrier Options." New York: Goldman Sachs Quantitative Strategies Research Notes, June.

Derman, E., and I. Kani. 1994. "Riding on a Smile." *RISK* 7 (February): 32–39.

Duffie, D. 1989. *Futures Markets*. Englewood Cliffs, N.J.: Prentice Hall.

Dupire, B. 1994. "Pricing with a Smile." *RISK* 7 (January): 18–20.

Ederington, L.H. 1979. "The Hedging Performance of the New Futures Markets." *Journal of Finance* 34 (March): 157–169.

Einzig, R., and B. Lange. 1990. "Swaps at Transamerica: Analysis and Applications." *Journal of Applied Corporate Finance* 2 (Winter): 48–58.

Fabozzi, F.J., ed. 1992. *The Handbook of Mortgage-Backed Securities*. Chicago: Probus.

Federal Deposit Insurance Corporation. 1994a. "Examination Guidance for Financial Derivatives." Washington, D.C.: FDIC, 18 May.

Federal Deposit Insurance Corporation. 1994b. "Interim Revision to Supervisory Policy Statement on Accounting and Reporting for Securities Activities." Washington, D.C.: FDIC, 21 April.

Federal Financial Institutions Examination Council. 1994. "Request for Comment on Disclosures for Certain Off-Balance Sheet Activities." Washington, D.C.: FFIEC, 23 March.

Federal Home Loan Mortgage Corporation. 1988. "How to Service for FreddieMac." Washington, D.C.: FHLMC, 28 December.

Federal Home Loan Mortgage Corporation. 1989. "How to Swap Mortgages for PCs." Washington, D.C.: FHLMC, 13 April.

Federal Home Loan Mortgage Corporation. 1990. "Guidelines for Underwriting Home Mortgages." Washington, D.C.: FHLMC, 19 May.

Federal National Mortgage Association. 1992. "Basics of Sound Underwriting." Washington, D.C.: FNMA.

Figlewski, S. 1986. *Hedging with Financial Futures for Institutional Investors.* Cambridge, Mass.: Ballinger.

"Financial Derivatives: Actions Needed to Protect the Financial System." 1994. Washington, D.C.: United States General Accounting Office, May.

"Forward Rate Agreements (FRABBA terms)." 1985. London: British Bankers' Association (in association with the Foreign and Currency Deposit Brokers' Association), August.

French, K. 1983. "A Comparison of Futures and Forward Prices." *Journal of Financial Economics* 12 (November): 311–342.

Fung, H., and W. Leung. 1993. "The Pricing Relationship of Eurodollar Futures and Eurodollar Deposit Rates." *Journal of Futures Markets* 13 (April): 115–126.

Gallop, S.C. 1992. "Not all TACs are Created Equal: Generic TACs Versus TAC POs." In *The Handbook of Mortgage-Backed Securities*, ed. F.J. Fabozzi. Chicago: Probus, 377–386.

Garman, M. 1992. "Recollection in Tranquillity." In *From Black-Scholes to Black Holes.* London: RISK Magazine Ltd., 171–175.

Geske, R. 1979. "The Valuation of Compound Options." *Journal of Financial Economics* 7 (March): 63–81.

Goldman, B., H. Sosin, and M.A. Gatto. 1979. "Path Dependent Options: Buy at the Low, Sell at the High." *Journal of Finance* 34 (December): 1111–1127.

Goodman, L.S. 1990. "The Use of Interest Rate Swaps in Managing Corporate Liabilities." *Journal of Applied Corporate Finance* 2 (Winter): 35–47.

Government National Mortgage Association GNMA I Mortgage-Backed Securities Guide. 1984. Handbook GNMA 5500.1. Washington, D.C.: U.S. Department of Housing and Urban Development, April.

Government National Mortgage Association GNMA II Mortgage-Backed Securities Guide. 1994. Handbook GNMA 5500.2. Washington, D.C.: U.S. Department of Housing and Urban Development, March.

Grupe, M.R., J.F. Tierney, and C. Willis. 1988. "Option Valuation Analysis of Mortgage-Backed Securities." New York: Kidder, Peabody, and Co. Fixed Income Group Mortgage-Backed Securities Research, July.

Hadley, G. 1964. *Nonlinear and Dynamic Programming.* Reading, Mass.: Addison-Wesley.

Harrison, J.M., and D.M. Kreps. 1979. "Martingales and Arbitrage in Multiperiod Securities Markets." *Journal of Economic Theory* 20 (July): 381–408.

Harty, E. 1992. "Pains and Gains of PERCS and LEAPS." *RISK* 5 (July / August): 36–39.

Hayre, L.S., D. Foulds, and L.A. Pendergast. 1988. "Introduction to Collateralized Mortgage Obligations." *The Handbook of Mortgage-Backed Securities*, ed. F.J. Fabozzi. Chicago: Probus, 337–380.

Heath, D., R. Jarrow, and A. Morton. 1990. "Bond Pricing and the Term Structure of Interest Rates: A Discrete Time Approximation." *Journal of Financial and Quantitative Analysis* 25 (December): 419–440.

Ho, T., and S. Lee. 1986. "Term Structure Movements and Pricing Interest Rate Contingent Claims." *Journal of Finance* 41 (December): 1011–1029.

Hudson, M. 1992. "The Value in Going Out." In *From Black-Scholes to Black Holes*. London: RISK Magazine Ltd., 183–186.

Hull J.C. 1993. *Options, Futures, and other Derivative Instruments*. Englewood Cliffs, N.J.: Prentice Hall.

Hull, J.C., and A. White. 1990. "Pricing Interest-Rate-Derivative Securities." *Review of Financial Studies* 3:573–592.

Hull, J.C., and A. White. 1992a. "Coming to Terms." In *From Black-Scholes to Black Holes*. London: RISK Magazine Ltd., 111–114.

Hull, J.C., and A. White. 1992b. "Modern Greek." In *From Black-Scholes to Black Holes*. London: RISK Magazine Ltd., 71–74.

Hull, J.C., and A. White. 1992c. "New Ways with the Yield Curve." In *From Black-Scholes to Black Holes*. London: RISK Magazine Ltd., 107–110.

Hull, J.C., and A. White. 1992d. "Root and Branch." In *From Black-Scholes to Black Holes*. London: RISK Magazine Ltd., 101–105.

International Swap Dealers Association, Inc. 1986. *Code of Standard Wording, Assumptions and Provisions for Swaps*. New York: ISDA.

International Swap Dealers Association, Inc. 1987a. *ISDA Interest Rate Swap Agreement*. New York: ISDA.

International Swap Dealers Association, Inc. 1987b. *User's Guide to the Standard Form Agreements*. New York: ISDA.

International Swap Dealers Association, Inc. 1991. *1991 ISDA Definitions*. New York: ISDA.

International Swap Dealers Association, Inc. 1992a. *ISDA Master Agreement*. New York: ISDA.

International Swap Dealers Association, Inc. 1992b. *User's Guide to the 1992 ISDA Master Agreements*. New York: ISDA.

International Swap Dealers Association, Inc., Board of Directors. 1993. "Statement on Termination Payments." Memo, New York, 5 March.

Jamshidian, F., and R.A. Russell. 1990. "Evaluation of Complex Sinking-Fund Options by Backward-Induction Methods." In *Advances in Futures and Options Research.* Greenwich, Conn.: JAI Press, 83–106.

Jarrow, R., and M. O'Hara. 1989. "Primes and Scores: An Essay on Market Imperfections." *Journal of Finance* 44 (December): 1263–1287.

Johnson, H. 1987. "Options on the Maximum or the Minimum of Several Assets." *Journal of Financial and Quantitative Analysis* 22 (September): 277–283.

Karcher, L.J. 1989. *Processing Mortgage-Backed Securities.* New York: New York Institute of Finance.

Kawaller, I. 1986. "Hedging with Futures Contracts: Going the Extra Mile." *Journal of Cash Management* 6 (July/August): 34–36.

Kawaller, I. 1989. "Interest Rate Swaps versus Eurodollar Strips." *Financial Analysts Journal* 45 (September/October): 55–61.

Kazarian, Dick. 1992. *The Introduction of Adjustable Rate Mortgages.* Ph.D. thesis, University of Chicago.

Kemna A., and A. Vorst. 1990. "A Pricing Method for Options Based on Average Asset Values." *Journal of Banking and Finance* 14 (March): 113–129.

Kolb, R. 1991. *Understanding Futures Markets.* Miami, Fla.: Kolb.

Kraus, A. 1983. "An Analysis of Call Provisions and the Corporate Refunding Decision." *Midland Corporate Finance Journal* 1 (Spring): 46–60.

Krzyzak, K. 1989a. "Asian Elegance." *RISK* 3 (December/January): 30–34, 49.

Krzyzak, K. 1989b. "Insurance against the Unknown." *RISK* 2 (October): 17–23.

Krzyzak, K. 1989c. "Swaptions Deciphered." *RISK* 2 (February): 9–17.

Kulason, R.A., and K.J. Person. 1989. "CMO Structures—An Update." New York: Salomon Brothers Mortgage Research, 18 January.

Kulason, R.A., and M. Waldman. 1988. "Understanding TAC and PAC CMO Structures." New York: Salomon Brothers Mortgage Research, September.

Lereah, D. 1986. "The Growth of Interest Rate Swaps." *Bankers Magazine* 169 (May/June 1986): 36–41.

Levy, E., and S. Turnbull. 1992. "Average Intelligence." In *From Black-Scholes to Black Holes.* London: RISK Magazine Ltd., 157–164.

Litzenberger, R.H. 1992. "Swaps: Plain and Fanciful." *Journal of Finance* 47 (July): 831-850.

Livingston, M. 1993. *Money and Capital Markets.* New York: New York Institute of Finance.

Madura, J., A.L. Tucker, and J.F. Marshall. 1994. "Pricing Currency Futures Options with Lognormally Distributed Jumps." *Journal of Business Finance and Accounting* 21 (September): 857–874.

Margin Manual. 1991. Chicago: Chicago Board Options Exchange.

Margrabe, W. 1978. "The Value of an Option to Exchange One Asset for Another." *Journal of Finance* 33 (March): 177–186.

Marshall, J.F. 1995. "Derivatives and Risk Management." *Journal of Financial Engineering* 4 (September): 307–313.

Marshall, J.F., and A.F. Herbst. 1992. "A Multiperiod Model for the Selection of a Futures Portfolio." *Journal of Futures Markets* 12 (August): 411–428.

Marshall, J.F., and K.R. Kapner. 1993. *Understanding Swaps.* New York: Wiley.

Marshall, J.F., and J.G. Whittaker. 1994. "Pricing Nonamortizing Constant Maturity Swaps." *Journal of Financial Engineering* 3 (March): 43–64.

McDermott, K. 1988. "Analysis of PAC CMOs." In *The Handbook of Mortgage-Backed Securities,* ed. F.J. Fabozzi. Chicago: Probus, 417–431.

McDermott, S., and M. Huie. 1994. "Index Amortization Swaps and Notes." In *Advanced Interest Rate and Currency Swaps,* ed. R.E. Dattatreya and K. Hotta. Chicago: Probus, 69–79.

Merton, R.C. 1973. "Theory of Rational Option Pricing." *Bell Journal of Economics and Management Science* 4 (Spring): 141–183.

Miron, P., and P. Swannell. 1991. *Pricing and Hedging Swaps.* London: Euromoney Publications.

Modigliani, F., and M.H. Miller. 1958. "The Cost of Capital, Corporate Finance, and the Theory of Investment." *American Economic Review* 48 (June): 261–297.

Moore, P., and J.F. Tierney. 1992. "Trading, Settlement, and Clearing Procedures for Agency MBS." New York: Lehman Brothers Fixed Income Research Mortgage Strategies, October.

NASD Manual. 1994. Chicago: Commerce Clearing House.

Overview of the Government Securities Clearing Corporation. 1994. New York: Government Securities Clearing Corporation, September.

Parkinson, P., J. Stehm, A. Gilbert, E. Gollob, L. Hargraves, R. Mead and M.A. Taylor. 1992. "Clearance and Settlement in U.S. Securities Markets." Washington, D.C.: Board of Governors of the Federal Reserve System, March.

Person, K.J. 1989. "Introduction to Mortgages and Mortgage-Backed Securities: 1989 Update." New York: Salomon Brothers Mortgage Research, September.

Pettersen, B., and Raghavan, V. 1994. "Indexed Amortizing Swaps." In *Advanced Interest Rate and Currency Swaps,* ed. R.E. Dattatreya and K. Hotta. Chicago: Probus, 53–67.

"Public Securities Association Uniform Practices: Settlement Dates for April 1994–June 1994." New York: Public Securities Association.

Ramaswamy, K., and S. Sundaresan. 1985. "The Valuation of Options on Futures Contracts." *Journal of Finance* 40 (December): 1319–1340.

Rassnick, L.S. 1991. Statement of Participants Trust Company for the Permanent Subcommittee on Investigations, Committee on Governmental Affairs, United States Senate, 14 October.

Ravindran, K. 1994. "Exotic Options." In *Advanced Interest Rate and Currency Swaps,* ed. R.E. Dattatreya and K. Hotta. Chicago: Probus, 81–169.

Rendleman, R., Jr. 1993a. "How Risks are Shared in Interest Rate Swaps." *Journal of Financial Services Research* 7 (January): 5–34.

Rendleman, R., Jr. 1993b. "Share and Share Unlike." *RISK* 6 (February): 50–54.

Rendleman, R., Jr., and C. Carabini. 1979. "The Efficiency of the Treasury Bill Futures Markets." *Journal of Finance* 34 (September): 895–914.

Roberts, R.B. 1988. "The Relative Valuation of IO/PO Stripped Mortgage-Backed Securities." In *The Handbook of Mortgage-Backed Securities,* ed. F.J. Fabozzi. Chicago: Probus, 521–552.

Roll, R. 1986a. "Adjustable Rate Mortgages: The Indexes." New York: Goldman Sachs Mortgage Securities Research, December.

Roll, R. 1986b. "Collateralized Mortgage Obligations: Characteristics, History, Analysis." New York: Goldman Sachs Mortgage Securities Research, April.

Roll, R. 1988. "Stripped Mortgage-Backed Securities." In *The Handbook of Mortgage-Backed Securities,* ed. F.J. Fabozzi. Chicago: Probus, 455–500.

Rosen, K.T., and J. Spratlin. 1986. "The Impact of Tax Reform on the Mortgage Market." New York: Salomon Brothers Mortgage Research, December.

Rosenthal, J.A., and J.M. Ocampo. 1988. *Securitization of Credit: Inside the New Technology of Finance.* New York: Wiley.

Rouhani, R. 1994. "Applications of Index Amortization Swaps." In *Advanced Interest Rate and Currency Swaps,* ed. R.E. Dattatreya and K. Hotta. Chicago: Probus, 381–396.

Rubinstein, M. 1985. "Alternative Paths to Portfolio Insurance." *Financial Analysts Journal* 41 (July/August): 42–52.

Rubinstein, M. 1992a. "Guiding Force." In *From Black-Scholes to Black Holes.* London: RISK Magazine Ltd., 39–48.

Rubinstein, M. 1992b. "One for Another." In *From Black-Scholes to Black Holes.* London: RISK Magazine Ltd., 191–194.

Rubinstein, M. 1994. "Implied Binomial Trees." *Journal of Finance* 49 (July): 771–818.

Rubinstein, M., and H.E. Leland. 1981. "Replicating Options with Positions in Stock and Cash." *Financial Analysts Journal* 37 (July/August): 63–72.

Rubinstein, M., and E. Reiner. 1991. "Breaking Down the Barriers." *RISK* 4 (September): 28–35.

Schwartz, R.J., and C.W. Smith Jr. 1990. *The Handbook of Currency and Interest Rate Risk Management.* New York: New York Institute of Finance.

Securities and Exchange Commission. 1992. "Self-Regulatory Organizations; The Depository Trust Company; Order Approving DTC's Proposed Trade Adjustment System for Participants Trading Collateralized Mortgage Obligations." Release No. 34-30277; File No. SR-DTC-91-19, 22 January.

Senft, D. 1983. "Pass-Through Securities." In *The Handbook of Fixed Income Securities,* ed. F.J. Fabozzi and I.M. Pollack. Homewood, Ill.: Dow Jones-Irwin, 469–532.

Senft, D. 1988. "Mortgages." *The Handbook of Mortgage-Backed Securities,* ed. F.J. Fabozzi. Chicago: Probus, 5–33.

Sharpe, W. 1978. *Investments.* Englewood Cliffs, N.J.: Prentice Hall.

Shimko, D. 1993. "Bounds of Probability." *RISK* 6 (April): 33–37.

Shirreff, D. 1989. "Unwise Councils." *RISK* 2 (April): 13–16.

Shirreff, D. 1991. "Dealing with Default." *RISK* 4 (March): 19–27.

Siegel, D., and D. Siegel. 1990. *Futures Markets.* Fort Worth, Tex.: Dryden Press.

Silber, W. 1981. "Innovation, Competition, and New Contract Design in Futures Markets." *Journal of Futures Markets* 1 (Summer): 123–155.

Silber, W. 1984. "Marketmaker Behavior in an Auction Market: An Analysis of Scalpers in Futures Markets." *Journal of Finance* 39 (September): 937–953.

Smith, D. 1990. "By the Bootstraps." *RISK* 3 (June): 40–42.

Smith, D. 1991. "A Simple Method for Pricing Interest Rate Swaptions." *Financial Analysts Journal* 47 (May/June): 72–76.

Smith, C.W., Jr., C.W. Smithson, and L.M. Wakeman. 1988. "The Market for Interest Rate Swaps." *Financial Management* 17 (Winter): 34–44.

Smith, C.W. Jr., C.W. Smithson, and L.M. Wakeman. 1990. "The Evolving Market for Swaps." In *The Handbook of Currency and Interest Rate Risk Management,* ed. R.J. Schwartz and C.W. Smith Jr. New York: New York Institute of Finance, chap. 6.

Smith, C.W., Jr., C.W. Smithson, and D.S. Wilford. 1990. "The Growth of the Swap Market." In *Managing Financial Risk.* New York: HarperBusiness, 213–228.

Spratlin, J. 1986. "An Investor's Guide to CMOs." New York: Salomon Brothers Mortgage Research, May.

Spratlin, J., and P. Vianna. 1986. "An Investor's Guide to CMO's." New York: Salomon Brothers Mortgage Research, May.

Stehm, J. 1992. "Clearance and Settlement of Mortgage-Backed Securities through the Participants Trust Company." Washington, D.C.: Federal Reserve Board, November.

Stigum, M. 1990. *The Money Market.* Homewood, Ill.: Dow Jones-Irwin.

Stovall, R. 1991. "PERCing Up Equities." *Financial World* 160 (15 October): 68, 71.

Stulz, R.M. 1982. "Options on the Minimum or the Maximum of Two Risky Assets: Analysis and Applications." *Journal of Financial Economics* 10 (July): 161–185.

SuperTrust Trust for Capital Market Fund, Inc., Shares. "Prospectus." 1994. SSC Distribution Services, Inc., 1 March.

Titman, S. 1992. "Interest Rate Swaps and Corporate Financing Choices." *Journal of Finance* 47 (September): 1503–1516.

Tompkins, R. 1992. "The A to Z of Caps." In *From Black-Scholes to Black Holes.* London: RISK Magazine Ltd., 115–120.

Turnbull, S.M. 1987. "Swaps: A Zero Sum Game?" *Financial Management* 16 (Spring): 15–21.

Waldman, M., and M. Gordon. 1986. "Evaluating the Option Features of Mortgage Securities: The Salomon Brothers Mortgage Pricing Model." New York: Salomon Brothers Mortgage Research, September.

Waldman, M., M. Gordon, and S. Guterman. 1985. "The Salomon Brothers Prepayment Model: Impact of the Market Rally on Mortgage Prepayments and Yields." New York: Salomon Brothers Mortgage Research, 4 September.

Waldman, M., M. Gordon, T.A. Zimmerman, and K.J. Person. 1987. "Interest Only and Principal Only STRIPs." New York: Salomon Brothers Mortgage Research, May.

Weigel, E. 1994. "SuperUnits and SuperShares." *Interfaces* 24 (May/June): 62–79.

Winchell, M.L., and M. Levine. 1992. "Understanding Inverse Floater Pricing." In *The Handbook of Mortgage-Backed Securities,* ed. F.J. Fabozzi. Chicago: Probus, 519–532.

Index

A

Accreting swap, 291
Accrued interest, 210
Actual/actual, 257
Actual/360, 257
Actual/365 (fixed), 256–257
Adjustable rate mortgage (ARM), 310, 315, 316
American call, 3
American Express Shares, 99
American put, 7
American Stock Exchange (ASE), 99, 103
Amortizing swap, 286–288, 291
  comment on pricing, 288–289
Appreciation SuperShare, 103
Arak, M., 254
Arbitrage
  and Eurodollars, 199–200
  strategies, pure, using T-bill futures, 189–191
  strategies, quasi, using T-bill futures, 191–193
Arbitrage-free tree requirement, 119–131
Asian option, 105, 113–115
As of trades, 20
Asset swap, 294
At-the-money, 4, 8
Auction, 173–174, 207–209
Autoquote, 22

B

Back stub period, 255
Balloon mortgage, 311–312
Barrier option, 105, 110–113
Basis, 156, 231
Basis point, 175
Basis swap, 291–292
Benefits, real vs. illusory, to swap parties, 251–254
Bicksler, J., 252
Bid rate, 196
Binomial model, *see* Multiplicative binomial option pricing model
Black, F., 44, 127, 131, 171
Black-Scholes model, 44, 59, 60–61, 65, 75, 88, 89
  and calculation of parameter sensitivities, 91–92
  as limiting case of binomial model, 56–58
Bond equivalent yield
  converting, 259

on T-bills, 175–176
Bootstrapping, 277, 278
Bought the swap, 254
Box
  buying, 36–37
  selling, 36, 37
Breeden, D.T., 17
British Bankers Association (BBA), 196
Brown, K.C., 298
Burnout, 329, 331–332
Butterfly, 17–18
Buydown mortgage, 311, 315
Buying a swap, 298
Buying the box, 36–37
Buy stop, 25

C

Call, 3–7
  See also Put-call parity
Callable bonds, 138–140
  real benefit of overpriced, to swap parties, 254
Callable debt
  into floating rate debt, 300
  into noncallable debt, 298–300
Callable swap, 297
Call premium, 3
Call price, 138–139
Cap, 133–134, 135
  pricing interest rate, 136–137
Cap premium, 134
Cap rate, 133
Carry, 222
Cash flows emanating from trade, 153–155
Cheapest-to-deliver (CTD) bond, 222, 227
  and CTD option, 228–230
  delivery period approximation for implied futures price, 224–225
  implied futures price as means of determining, 223–224
  implied repo rate on, 222–223
  and switch option, 233–234
  and wild card option, 230–232
Chen, A., 252
Chicago Board of Trade (CBT), 150, 224, 231
  Clearing Corporation, 216
Chicago Board Options Exchange (CBOE), 3, 19, 60–61, 151
  and collateralization of trade obligations, 26

Designated Primary Market Maker (DPM) of, 24, 25
founding of, 150
long-term option products offered by, 100–101, 103
and market maker, 22
Chicago Mercantile Exchange (CME), 177, 197–198, 202, 236
Class, options identified by, 19
Class average price (CAP), 322
Clean price, 209–210
Cleared trade, 20, 151
Clearing and settlement facilities, 320–326
Clearing firm, 20–22
and collateralization of trade obligations, 26, 27, 29
Closed book, 197
Collar, 135
Collateralization of trade obligations, 26–29
Collateralized mortgage obligation(s) (CMOs), 345, 366
basic structure of, 345–347
class, subordination of, 365–366
economic benefits conferred by, 347
and floater and inverse floater classes, 362
illustration of cash flows of, 349–351
and planned amortization class, 357–359
selecting tax classification for, 347–349
and targeted amortization class, 360–361
valuation of two-period, 351–357
Commercial banks, 312
Comparative advantage, illusory benefit of, to swap parties, 251–252
Compared trade, 320
Competitive auction, 208–209
Competitive bid, 174
Compound option, 105, 117–118
Conditional prepayment rate (CPR), 328, 333, 334, 358–360
Conforming mortgages, 316
Constant Maturity Treasury (CMT) rate, 295, 296
Conventional mortgages, 315
Conversion, 35, 36
Convexity
adjustment, 269–270
of interest-only and principal-only STRIPs, 367–369
of mortgage-backed security, 341–343
Cornell, B., 165
Corridor, 136
Coupon leverage, 364
Cover, 174, 208
Covered call, 12–14
Cox, J.C., 43, 48, 70, 71, 161–164
Credit enhancement of mortgage security, 364–366

Credit spread, 17
Cross hedge, 157
CTD option, 228–230
See also Cheapest to deliver (CTD) bond
Current face, 318, 321
Current market rate, mortgage coupon rate vs., 329–331
Current principal balance, 318
Curtailment, 329
CUSIP (Committee for Uniform Securities Identification Procedures), 211

D

Debit spread, 17
Deep-in-the-money, 5, 8
Deep-out-of-the-money, 5, 8
Delayed start swap, 293
Delta, 75, 81
Delta neutral hedge, 75, 76, 82, 83–88, 90
Depository Trust Company (DTC), 307, 326
Derivatives, defined, xiii
Derman, E., 69, 70, 71, 73, 127, 131
Derman-Kani model, 69–74
Designated Primary Market Maker (DPM), 24, 25
Disallowance factor, 214
Discriminatory auction, 209
Distribution-free restrictions on option prices, 37
other, 37–42
Doubling up option, 141, 142–143
Down-and-in options, 110
Down-and-out options, 110
Dual trading, outlawing, 25–26

E

Econometric prepayment models, 333
Economic activity, prepayment and, 333
Effective date, 133, 254–255
Eligible payment date conventions, 258
Eurodollar(s), 195
and forward rate agreements (FRAs), 200–202
futures, hedging subtlety in using, 203–206
futures, relationship between swaps and, 261–263
futures contract, defining features of, 197–198
hedging example, 198–199
pure arbitrage example, 199–200
spot market for, 195–197
strip, replicating zero-coupon instrument with, 202–203
Eurodollar Certificates of Deposit, 195
European call, 3
European put, 7

Exchange option, 105, 106–110
Exercise price, 3, 7
Exercise process, 21–22
Exotic options, xvi–xvii, 105
    See also Asian option; Barrier option;
    Compound option; Exchange option;
    Lookback option
Exploding tree, dealing with, 115
Extension, 357

F

Fall-out risk, 313
"Fannie Mae," *see* Federal National Mort-
    gage Association
Farmers Home Administration (FmHA),
    313, 314
Federal Deposit Insurance Corporation
    (FDIC), 196
Federal Home Loan Mortgage Corpora-
    tion (FHLMC, "Freddie Mac"), 211, 310,
    312, 315–317
    Cash Program of, 316
    and Depository Trust Company, 326
    Guarantor Program of, 316
    and MBS Clearing Corporation, 320, 324
    and Participants Trust Company, 324
Federal Housing Authority (FHA), 313,
    314, 315–316, 333–334
Federal National Mortgage Association
    (FNMA, "Fannie Mae"), 211, 310, 312,
    315–317, 319
    and Depository Trust Company, 326
    and MBS Clearing Corporation, 320, 324
    and Participants Trust Company, 324
    Swap Program of, 316
Federal Reserve Board ("the Fed"), 26–27,
    187–188, 209, 289, 292
FHLMC, *see* Federal Home Loan Mort-
    gage Corporation
Fixed-for-floating swap, 285, 289
Fixed leg, 255
Fixed rate day count fraction (FIDCF), 256
Fixed rate loan
    converting variable rate loan into, at
    favorable rate, 179–182
    and generic swap, 246–249
Fixed rate mortgage (FRM), 307–309, 315,
    316
FLEX options (FLEXible exchange traded
    options), 101
Floater class, 362–364
Floating leg, 255
Floating rate day count fraction (FLDCF),
    256
Floating rate debt
    callable debt into, 300
    putable debt into, 300–301
Floating rate financing, and generic swap,
    246–249

Floating rate note method, 283
Floor, 134–135
Floor premium, 134
Floor rate, 134
FNMA, *see* Federal National Mortgage
    Association
Forecast rate pricing method, 285
Forward contracts
    futures vs. 149–150
    pricing, 166–169
Forward prices vs. futures prices, 161–166,
    203–206
Forward rate agreements (FRAs), 200–202
Forward rate pricing approach, 285
    example of swap using, 289–290
    illustration of, 286–288
Forward swap, 292–293
Forward trades, 209
"Freddie Mac," *see* Federal Home Loan
    Mortgage Corporation
Front stub period, 255
Full carry, 222
Full Two-Way Payment (FTP), 250–251
Futures contract(s)
    design, issues in, 155–159
    forward vs., 149–150
    need for, 183
    options on, 169–172
Futures exchange, 150–155
Futures prices, 156–157
    vs. forward prices, 161–166, 203–206
    necessity of obtaining high positive cor-
    relation between spot and, 158–159
Futures-swap-arbitrage, 278–282

G

Gamma, 75, 81
Gamma neutral portfolio, 82, 85, 90
Gatto, M.A., 105
Generic interest rate swap, 245–246
    illustration of, 246–249
Geske, R., 105
"Ginnie Mae," *see* Government National
    Mortgage Association
Global hedging technique, 76, 90, 98
GNMA, *see* Government National Mort-
    gage Association
Goldman, B., 105
Government National Mortgage Associa-
    tion (GNMA, "Ginnie Mae"), 310, 311,
    313–317, 319
    GNMA I, 314, 331
    GNMA II, 315
    and MBS Clearing Corporation, 320, 324
    and Participants Trust Company, 324,
    325, 326
Government Securities Clearing Corpora-
    tion (GSCC), 207, 210–214

Graduated payment mortgage (GPM),
310–311, 315, 316, 317
Gross price, 210
Growing equity mortgage (GEM), 311, 315
Guaranteed investments contracts (GICs),
347

H

Hadley, G., 61
Haircut equity, 28
Haircuts, 28, 325
Hedging, hedges, 24
alternative, using spot instruments,
183–189
and Eurodollars, 198–199, 203–206
instrument, swap as low-cost, 253–254
with IO and PO STRIPs, 369
methodology, extending, 277–278
non-CTD bond, 225–227
with S&P futures contract, 241–242
subtlety in using Eurodollar futures,
203–206
swap, 267–269, 280–281
technique, general, 88–90
with three-month Treasury bill futures,
178–183
U.S. T-bond, 218–221
Homeowner equity, 331
Housing and Urban Development (HUD),
Department of, 315
Hunter-gatherers, 24

I

IMM dates, pricing swap with payment
dates not coinciding with, 270–272
IMM swap, 263–267
Implied futures price (IFP), 227–228
delivery period approximation for,
224–225
as means of determining CTD, 223–224
Implied repo rate (IRR), 222–223
Implied volatility, 61
In-barriers, 110
Income and Residual SuperShare, 103
Index amortization swap (IAS), 294–296
Index arbitrage, 236–240
Index Trust SuperUnit, 102–103
Inferred prices, 70
Information asymmetries, real benefit of,
to swap parties, 254
Ingersoll, J.E., 161–164
Initial margin, 27, 151–153
Insurance put, 10–12
Intention day, 216
Interest only (IO) class, 366
Interest-only (IO) STRIPs
convexity of, 367–369
hedging with, 369
price characteristics of, 371–373
valuation of, 369–371

Interest rate option(s)
instruments with embedded, 138–145
methodology for pricing, 119–131
pricing, 131–133
Intermarket arbitrage opportunities, illu-
sory benefit of, to swap parties, 252–253
Internal Revenue Service (IRS), 348
International Monetary Market (IMM)
Index, 177–178, 182, 197, 199
International Swap Dealers Association
(ISDA), 251
International Swaps and Derivatives
Association (ISDA), 250, 256
In-the-money, 4, 8
Intrinsic value, 5, 8
Inverse floater class, 362–363
leverage inherent in, 363–364
valuation of, 364

J

Jamshidian, F., 141, 142

K

Kani, I., 69, 70, 71, 73
See also Derman-Kani model
Kappa, 75, 81
Kappa neutral portfolio, 82, 85
Knock-in options, 110
Knock-out boundary, 111
Knock-out options, 110, 111–113

L

Leaning on a customer order, 25
LEAPs (Long-Term Equity Participation
Product), 100–101
Leftover substitution, 141
LIBOR (London Interbank Offer Rate),
196, 200–201, 254, 255, 256, 259
and generic swap, 246–249, 250
Limited Two-Way Payment (LTP), 250–251
Limit order, 24
Litzenberger, R.H., 17, 251
Loan-to-value ratio (LTV), 308, 331–332
Lockout period, swap's, 294–295
Long, 3, 7
Long-dated swap, valuing, 275–277
Long hedge, 156
with three-month Treasury bill futures,
178–179, 183
Long stock position, 9–10
Long straddle, 14–15
Lookback option, 105, 115–116
Lower bound, 218

M

Maintenance margin, 27, 151–153
Managing the gap, 245
Margin, 29, 320
floating rate equal to LIBOR plus, 254

settlement variation and, 151–153
Margin factor, 213
Margrabe, W., 105
Market maker, 22–24
  positions, collateral required for, 27–28
Market order, 24
Market risk, defined, xiii
Marking, 27
Marking-to-market, 27
Martingales, 123
Matched book, 197
Matched sales, 188
Matched trade, 20, 151
MBS Clearing Corporation (MBSCC), 307, 320–324, 325, 326
Mean reverting, 131
Merton, R.C., 38, 58
Merton model, 75, 77, 88, 89, 91
  for European call on stock paying dividends continuously. . ., 58–60
Miller, M.H., 355
Miron, P., 298
Modigliani, F., 355
Money Market Trust SuperUnit, 102–103
Mortgage-backed securities (MBSs), 314, 316, 327
  calculating price sensitivity of, to shift in yield curve, 339–341
  convexity of, 341–343
  option-adjusted spread valuation method for, 336–338
  See also Mortgage pass-through(s); STRIPs
Mortgage bankers (MBs), 312
Mortgage coupon rate vs. current market rate, 329–331
Mortgage pass-through(s) (MPTs), 307, 327, 341
  certificate, 313–317
  and collateralized mortgage obligations, 345, 357
  and prepayment rates and models, 327–334
  trading and settlement of, 317–320
  valuation of, 334–336
  See also Mortgage-backed securities
Mortgage pipeline, 312
Mortgages, 307
  originators of, 312–313
  types of, 307–312
Mortgage security, credit enhancement of, 364–366
Multiplicative binomial option pricing model, 42–44
  Black-Scholes model as limiting case of, 56–58
  estimating u, d, and r, 54–56
  numerical valuation of two-period American call and puts by iteration, 52–54

pricing call on dividend-paying stock, 48–49
pricing formula for two-period call on non-dividend-paying stock, 50–52
pricing one-period call on non-dividend-paying stock, 44, 48
pricing one-period put, 50
Multiprice auction, 209
Mutual savings banks, 312

N

Naked call position, margin required on, 27
Naked put, 13
Negative amortization, 311
Negative carry, 222
Negative convex, 140, 330
Negative duration, 366–367
Negative margin, 254
Net free equity, 325
Netting, 211–212, 321–322
Newton-Raphson procedure, 61
New York Stock Exchange, 24, 236
No-arbitrage pricing, 216–218
Nodes, 43
No dual trading, 25–26
No exercise, 40, 42
Noncallable debt, callable debt into, 298–300
Noncompetitive bid, 174
Nongeneric swap, 283
Nonputable debt, putable debt into, 300
Notional amount, 134

O

Offer rate, 196
Off-market swap, valuing, 272–274
Offsets, 213
Open book, 197
Optimal time to deliver, 221–222
Option-adjusted spread (OAS), 336–338
Options Clearing Corporation (OCC), 20, 22, 26, 29, 101, 151
Order types, 24–25
Original principal balance, 318
Out-barriers, 110
Out-of-the-money, 4, 8
Out-of-the-money strangle, 15–16
Out-trades, 20, 21
  dealing with, 21
Overnight repo rate, 186
Overnight reverse repo rate, 187
Over-the-counter (OTC)
  market, 19, 101, 105
  option trades, clearing, 29–30

P

Par swap, 267
Par swap rate, 256

Participants Trust Company (PTC), 307, 324–325, 326
Participation certificates (PCs), 316
Par value, 212
Performance Equity Redemption Cumulative Stock (PERCS), 101–102
Placement, 196
Plain vanilla swap, *see* Generic interest rate swap
Planned amortization class (PAC), 357, 360, 361
　schedule, determining, 358–359
　schedule, deviations from, 359–360
　structure of, 357–358
Pool, 314
Pool factor, 319
Pool's age, influence of, on prepayment, 332–333
Portfolio insurance, 93–98
Position day, 216
Position trader, 22–23
Positive carry, 222
Positive duration, 367
Positive margin, 254
Prepayment rates and models, 327–334
Prepayment speed, 328
Price sensitivity calculation, illustration of, 339–341
Pricing methodology, revisions to, 60–61
　Derman-Kani model, 69–74
　generating binomial tree consistent with risk neutral terminal probabilities, 65–68
　generating tree's parameters by recursively working backward, 68–69
　implied volatility, 61
　inferring risk neutral probability density function, 63–65
　pricing with smile, 62–63
Pricing results from minimum information, 31, 32–37
PRIME (Prescribed Fix Right to Income and Maximum Equity), 99, 100
Principal only (PO) class, 366
Principal-only (PO) STRIPs
　convexity of, 367–369
　hedging with, 369
　price characteristics of, 371–373
　valuation of, 369–371
Principal payment schedule, 357
Priority SuperShare, 103
Protection SuperShare, 103
Pseudoprobabilities, 47
Public customer position, collateral required for, 26–27
Public Securities Association (PSA), 318–319
　prepayment model of, 333–334
Purchase substitution, 141, 144–145

Pure arbitrage strategies using T-bill futures, 189–191
Put, 7–10
Putable debt
　into floating rate debt, 300–301
　into nonputable debt, 300
Putable swap, 297
Put-call parity, 32–34, 37
　relation, 33, 36, 42, 172
　trader's view of, 34–36
Put premium, 7

Q

Quality option, 228–230
Quality spreads, 248
Quasi arbitrage strategies using T-bill futures, 191–193

R

Refinancing threshold, 329
Reg T margin requirements, 27
Reinganum, M., 165
REMICs (Real Estate Mortgage Investment Conduit), 326, 348–349
Repurchase agreements ("repos"), 186
　features of, 187–188
　using, 188–189
Reset date, 133, 255
Retail Automatic Execution System (RAES), 22
Reuters, 255
Reverse conversion, 35–36
Reverse repurchase agreements ("reverse repos"), 186, 187
　features of, 187–188
Rho, 75, 82
Rho neutral portfolio, 82, 85
Riskless arbitrage, 31
Risk management
　of option position, 82–88
　swaps and, 245, 246
Risk neutral probability density function, inferring, 63–65
Risk neutral terminal probabilities, generating binomial tree consistent with, 65–68
Rollercoaster swap, 291
Ross, S.A., 43, 48, 70, 71, 161–164
Rubinstein, M., 43, 63–65, 67, 70, 71, 92, 106
Running the Eurodollar book, 197
Russell, R.A., 141, 142
Russell 2000 Index, 101

S

Savings and loans (S&Ls), 312
Scalping, 23–24
Scholes, M., 44

See also Black-Scholes model
SCORE (Special Claim on the Residual Equity), 93, 98–100, 101
Scratched part of the trade, 23
Seasonality, prepayment and, 333
Seasoned mortgages, 332
Securities Exchange Act (1934), 28
Securities Exchange Commission (SEC), 14, 29, 30, 320
Selling a swap, 298
Selling the box, 36, 37
Sell stop, 24–25
Series, options identified by, 19
Servicing fee, 313
Settlement, 320
Settlement price, 153–155, 158–159
Settlement variation, 150, 159
  and margin, 151–153
Sharpe, W., 43
Shifting interest structure, 366
Short, 3, 7
Short hedge, 156
  with Treasury bill futures, 179–182, 183
Short put, 14
Short stock position, 10
Single monthly mortality (SMM), 328
Single-price auction, 209
Sinking funds, 140–145
Slope, 367
Sloppy smile, 61
Smile, 61
  pricing with, xvii, 62–63
Smith, C.W., Jr., 251, 253
Smith, D.J., 298
Smithson, C. W., 251, 253
Sold the swap, 254
Sosin, H., 105
Spot date, 196, 255
Spot instruments, alternative hedges using, 183–189
Spot market
  for Eurodollars, 195–197
  for U.S. Treasury bills, 173–176
  for U.S. Treasury bonds and notes, 207–210
Spot prices, 150, 156
  necessity of obtaining high positive correlation between futures and, 158–159
  and yield conventions, 174–175
Spot transaction, 150
Spreader, 22
Spread lock, digression on, 293–294
Spreads, 17, 248–249, 256
Standard & Poor's 500 Stock Price Index (S&P Index), 27, 61, 65, 101, 102, 158, 235–236
Standard & Poor's 500 Stock Price Index futures, 235

defining characteristics of, 236
hedging with, 241–242
pricing implications of, 236–240
Standard calls and puts, 3
  See also Call; Put
Stochastic process, 42–44
Stop loss order, 24–25
Stop-out yield, 174, 208
Strike price, 3, 7, 138
Strike rate, 133
Strip, replicating zero-coupon instrument with Eurodollar, 202–203
Strip of three calls, 134
Strip of three futures, 180
STRIPs (stripped mortgage-backed securities), 326, 366–367
  convexity of interest-only and principal-only, 367–369
  hedging with IO and PO, 369
  price characteristics of IO and PO, 371–373
  valuation of IO and PO, 369–371
Stub rate, 264
Student Loan Marketing Association, 211
SuperShares, 93, 102–103
Swannell, P., 298
Swap(s)
  hedging, 267–269
  options on, 297–301
  parties, real vs. illusory benefits to, 251–254
  position, trading against, 278–282
  pricing, general methodology for, 283–290
  pricing, with payment dates not coinciding with IMM dates, 270–272
  pricing simple, 263–267
  relationship between Eurodollar futures and, 261–263
  and risk management, 245–246
  structures, other, 290–296
  valuing long-dated, 275–277
  valuing off-market, 272–274
Swap spread, 248–249, 256
Swaptions, 297–298
  forming payment distributions with, 298–301
  pricing, 301–304
Switch option, 233
Synthetic long call, 12
System price, 212
System value, 212

T

Tail, 174, 208
Tailing the hedge, 205
Tail of the hedge, 221
Taking Euros, 196

Targeted amortization class (TAC), 360
  structuring, 360–361
Telerate, 196, 255
Tendering, 118
Tenor, swap's, 255
Ten up, 22
Termination Claim, 99
Termination Date, 99
Term repos, 186
Term reverse, 187
Theoretical value for mortgage pass-
  through (TVMPT), 337–338
Theta, 75, 82
Theta neutral portfolio, 82, 85
30/360, 257–258
30E/360 (Eurobond Basis), 258
Thrifts, 312
Time premium, 5, 8
TIMS (Theoretical Intermarket Margin
  System), 29
To-be-announced (TBA) trade, 317,
  318–320
Toy, W., 127, 131
Trade date, 254
Trade initiating price, 153
Trade process on exchange, 19–22
Transaction adjustment payment (TAP),
  212–213
Transition probabilities, estimating,
  137–138
Treasury bill futures, *see* U.S. Treasury bill
  (T-bill) futures
Treasury bond and note futures, *see* U.S.
  Treasury bond (T-bond) and note
  (T-note) futures
Turnbull, S. M., 251
Turnover, 329

U

Uncompared trade, 320
Underlying security, 3, 7
  or commodity, supply of, 155–159
Underpriced credit risk, illusory benefit
  of, to swap parties, 253
Unit investment trust, 98–99
Up-and-in option, 110
Up-and-out option, 105, 110, 111–113
Upper bound, 217, 218
U.S. Treasury, 102, 174, 187, 188, 207–209,
  315
  and Government Securities Clearing
    Corporation, 211
U.S. Treasury bill (T-bill) futures, 173
  and alternative hedges using spot instru-
    ments, 183–189
  defining features of three-month,
    177–178

hedging with three-month, 178–183
  pure arbitrage strategies using, 189–191
  quasi arbitrage strategies using, 191–193
  spot market for, 173–176
U.S. Treasury bond (T-bond) and note
  (T-note) futures, 106, 207
  defining features of, 214–216
  and Government Securities Clearing
    Corporation, 210–214
  hedging bond, 218–221
  hedging non-CTD bond, 225–227
  identifying cheapest to deliver (CTD),
    222–225
  no-arbitrage pricing, 216–218
  optimal time to deliver, 221–222
  options implicit in, 227–234
  spot market for, 207–210

V

Value, option's
  determinants of, 76–77
  effects of parameter changes on, 77–82
Value date, 196, 254–255
Variable rate loan, converting, into fixed
  rate loan at favorable rate, 179–182
Vega, 75
Veterans Administration (VA), 313, 314,
  315–316, 326
Volatility plays, 15, 17
Volatility skew, 61
Voluntary redemption, 141, 142–143

W

Wakeman, L.M., 251, 253
Warehousing the loans, 312
Weighted average coupon (WAC), 331
Weighted average maturity (WAM),
  332–333
Weighted average remaining maturity
  (WARM), 332–333
When issued (WI) trade, 209
Whole loans, 316
Wild card option, 230–233
World Bank, 211

Y

Yield conventions, spot pricing and,
  174–175
Yield curve, calculating mortgage-backed
  security's price sensitivity to shift in,
  339–341

Z

Zero-coupon instrument, replicating, with
  Eurodollar strip, 202–203
Zero-coupon swap, 292
Zero margin, 254